Thomas Nugent

The Grand Tour

Vol. IV, Third Edition

Thomas Nugent

The Grand Tour
Vol. IV, Third Edition

ISBN/EAN: 9783337128111

Printed in Europe, USA, Canada, Australia, Japan

Cover: Foto ©Andreas Hilbeck / pixelio.de

More available books at **www.hansebooks.com**

THE
GRAND TOUR;
Or, A JOURNEY through the
NETHERLANDS, GERMANY, ITALY and *FRANCE.*

CONTAINING

I. A Description of the principal Cities and Towns, their Situation, Origin, and ancient Monuments.

II. The public Edifices, the Seats and Palaces of the Princes and Nobility, their Libraries, Cabinets, Paintings, and Statues.

III. The Produce of the Country, the Customs and Manners of the People, the different Coins, their Commerce, Manufactures, Learning, and present Government.

IV. An exact List of the Post-routes, and of the different Carriages by Water and Land, with their settled Prices.

By MR. *NUGENT.*

THE THIRD EDITION,
Corrected and considerably Improved.

To which is now added,
The EUROPEAN ITINERARY.

VOLUME THE FOURTH.

LONDON,
Printed for J. RIVINGTON and Sons, B. LAW, T. CASLON, G. ROBINSON, T. CADELL, W. GOLDSMITH, J. BEW, S. HAYES, W. FOX,
AND
T. EVANS in the STRAND.

MDCCLXXVIII.

THE CONTENTS.

                                      Page

CHAP. I. *General description of* France.   1
SECT. I. *Of the situation, extent, climate, soil, seasons, rivers, mountains, and forests of* France.   ibid
SECT. II. *Division of* France.   4
SECT. III. *Of the* French *government*.   5
SECT. IV. *Of the* French *clergy*.   10
SECT. V. *Of the persons, manners, customs, learning, language, trade, coins, and manner of travelling of the* French.   12
CHAP. II. *Journey from* Dover *to* Paris.   19
CHAP. III. *Description of* Paris.   39
CHAP. IV. *The environs of* Paris.   112
CHAP. V. *Journey from* Paris *to* Italy   144
CHAP. VI. *Journey from* Paris *to* Strasburg.   200
CHAP. VII. *Journey from* Paris *to* Basil.   209
CHAP. VIII. *Journey from* Paris *to* Bourdeaux *and* Bayonne.   219
CHAP. IX. *Journey from* Paris *to* Narbonne *and* Perpignan   233
CHAP. X. *Journey from* Paris *to* Bourges.   254
CHAP. XI. *Journey from* Paris *to* Rochelle *and* Rochfort.   256
CHAP. XII. *Journey from* Paris *to* Brest, *thro'* Tours *and* Nants.   260

CONTENTS.

CHAP. XIII. *Journey from* Paris *to* Rennes *and* S. Malo. 273
CHAP. XIV. *Journey from* Paris *to* Rouen, Caen, *and* Cherburg. 278
CHAP. XV. *Journey from* Paris *to* Havre de Grace *and* Dieppe. 291
CHAP. XVI. *Journey from* Paris *to* Rheims *and* Sedan, *in the way to* Luxemburg. 295
CHAP. XVII. *Journey from* Paris *to* Lille *and* Valenciennes. 300
The European *Itinerary.* 305

THE

THE
GRAND TOUR.
FRANCE.

CHAP. I.
General Description of France.

I. *Of the situation, extent, climate, soil, seas, rivers, mountains, and forests of* France.

FRANCE is a large kingdom of Europe, situated between five degrees west, and seven degrees east longitude; and between 42 and 51 degrees of north latitude. It is bounded by the English channel and the Austrian Netherlands on the north; by Germany, Switzerland, Savoy, and Piedmont, on the east; by the Mediterranean sea and the

Situation of France.

Py-

The GRAND TOUR.

Pyrenean mountains, by which it is separated fro *Spain* on the south, and by the bay of *Biscay* on the west; being almost a square of about 550 miles on each side, except that *Britany* makes it somewhat irregular, by stretching further than any other province to the westward. It was formerly called *Gallia*, from its ancient inhabitants the *Gauls*; but its present name is derived from the *Franks*, a *German* nation inhabiting that part of *Germany* still called *Franconia*, who, upon the decline of the *Roman* empire, made a conquest of this country.

Extent.

Name.

Air.   The air of *France* is very temperate, pleasant, and healthful, being exempt from the excess of heat and cold, which generally prevails in more southern or northern latitudes. The soil is exceeding fruitful, particularly in corn, wine, oil, silk, flax, hemp, and fruits. The fields are large and open, generally intermingled with vines and corn, and bordered and interlined with variety of fruits. They have a great many large forests, well stored with all sorts of game, and several mountains, most of which are covered over with numerous flocks, and some of them lined with rich and valuable mines.

Soil.

Rivers.   *France* is watered by a great many large and navigable rivers: the principal of these are the *Seine*, the *Loire*, the *Garonne*, and the *Rhone*, to which we may now add the *Rhine*, which for some hundred miles separates the *French* territories from *Germany*.

The Seine.   1. The *Seine* has its rise near *Dijon* in *Burgundy*, and running north-west through *Champagne* and the isle of *France*, visits *Troyes* and *Paris*; continuing its course north-west, it crosses *Normandy*, where it passes by the city of *Roan*, and falls into the *British* channel, between *Havre de Grace* and *Honfleur*. The *Youne*, the *Marne*,

the

FRANCE.

the *Oyse*, and the *Eure*, are the principal rivers it receives in its course. 2. The *Loire* is reckoned the finest river in *France*; it rises in the *Vivarez*, near the *Cevennes*, and running north and north-west, through the *Lionois* and *Orleanois*, visits the cities of *Nevers* and *Orleans*; after which it directs its course due west by *Tours*, *Angers*, and *Nants*, in *Britany*, 40 miles below which city it falls into the *Bay of Biscay*. Its whole course, in which it receives the *Allier*, the *Cher*, the *Vienne*, the *Mayenne*, and several other rivers, is computed to be about 500 miles. 3. The *Garonne* rises in the *Pyrenean* mountains, and running north-west, visits the city of *Toulouse*; continuing its course north-west, it divides the provinces of *Guienne* and *Gascony*, passing by the city of *Bourdeaux*, and empties itself into the *Bay of Biscay*, about 60 miles below that city, having received the river *Dordonne*, and several others, during its course. It has also a communication with the *Mediterranean*, by the royal canal made by *Lewis* XIV. 4. The *Rhone* rises in the mountain *la Fourche* in *Switzerland*, and running west through the country called the *Valais*, divides it into two parts, then passing through the lake of *Geneva*, visits that city, from whence it runs south-west to *Lyons* in *France*, where receiving the river *Soane*, it continues its course due south, and passing by *Orange*, *Avignon*, and *Arles*, falls into the *Mediterranean*, to the westward of *Marseilles*. There are several cataracts in the upper part of the river, so that it is not navigable till 12 or 15 miles below *Geneva*, and it runs afterwards with such rapidity, that it is very difficult to get vessels up the stream.

The most remarkable mountains in *France* are those called the *Cevennes*, which are very high, and extend from *Lower Languedoc* to *Auvergne*. Forests and woods are not so large, so nume-

The Loire.

The Garonne.

The Rhone.

Mountains and forests.

numerous, nor so thick in *France* as in *Germany*. The principal forests are those of *Orleans*, *Fontainbleau*, *Montargis*, &c.

II. *Division of* France.

Division of antient Gaul.

Antient *Gaul* was divided by *Augustus Cæsar* into four parts, namely *Gallia Narbonnensis*, *Aquitania*, *Lugdunensis*, and *Belgica*. I. *Gallia Narbonnensis* comprehended all that district which is now divided into *Languedoc*, the county of *Foix*, *Gevaudan*, *Velay*, *Vivarais*, *Provence*, *Dauphiné* and *Savoy*. II. *Aquitania* was bounded by the *Pyrenees*, the ocean, and the river *Loire*. III. *Gallia Lugdunensis*, the largest of all, was bounded by the ocean, the *Loire*, the *Seine*, the *Marne*, and the mountains of *Vosges*. IV. *Gallia Belgica*, was bounded by the ocean, the county of *Caux*, the *Seine*, the *Marne*, the mountains of *Fosges*, and the *Rhine*.

Modern Division.

Of the modern divisions of *France*, the most received is that into twelve general governments, subdivided afterwards into lesser provinces, to which are added the new acquisitions. These governments are, 1. *Picardy*, chief town, *Amiens*. 2. *Normandy*, chief town, *Roan*. 3. The *Isle of France*, chief town, and capital of the kingdom, *Paris*. 4 *Champagne*, chief town, *Rheims*. 5. *Britany*, chief town, *Rennes*. 6. The *Orleanois*, chief town, *Orleans*. 7. *Burgundy*, chief town, *Dijon*. 8. The *Lyonois*, chief town, *Lyons*. 9. *Dauphiné*, chief town, *Grenoble*. 10. *Provence*, chief town, *Aix*. 11. *Languedoc*, chief town, *Toulouse*. 12. *Guienne*, chief town, *Bourdeaux*. In regard to situation, it may be observed of these twelve general governments, or great provinces, that four of them are towards the north, and near the banks of the *Seine*, viz. *Picardy*, *Normandy*,

FRANCE.

Normandy, the *Isle of France*, and *Champagne*; four are in the middle of the kingdom, and near the banks of the *Loire*, viz. *Britany*, *Orleanois*, *Burgundy*, and *Lyonnois*; and four towards the south, near the banks of the *Rhone* and the *Garonne*, viz. *Provence*, *Dauphiné*, *Languedoc*, and *Guienne*. The new acquisitions which *France* has made the last hundred years, are those of *Alsace* and *Lorrain*, on the side of *Germany*; of *Franche Comté* on the side of *Switzerland*; of *Artois*, the *Cambresis*, part of *Flanders*, *Hainault*, and *Luxemburg*, on the side of the *Netherlands*; and of *Roussillon*, on the side of *Spain*. The capital of *Alsace* is *Strasburg*; of *Lorrain*, *Nancy*; of *Franche Comté*, *Besançon*; of *Artois*, *Arras*; of *Cambresis*, *Cambray*; of *French Flanders*, *Lisle*; of *French Hainault*, *Valenciennes*; of *French Luxemburg*, *Thionville*; of *Roussillon*, *Perpignan*.

III. *Of the* French *government*.

Since the first establishment of the *French* monarchy, there have been three different races of princes viz. the *Merovingian*, *Carolovingian*, and *Capetine*; from the last of which the present king is descended. The crown is hereditary in the heirs male of the king, all females being excluded by the *Salique Law*. The regal power was formerly very much limited, either by the nobility of the kingdom, who generally claimed a great authority in their respective provinces: or by the assembly of the three states, consisting of the clergy, nobility, and commons, whose consent was requisite in making laws, or raising money; or by the parliaments of the several governments, particularly that of *Paris*, which often assumed a right to oppose the royal autho-

The GRAND TOUR.

authority, in defence of the liberty and privileges of the people. But the cardinals *Richlieu* and *Mazarine* made their masters absolute sovereigns, by reducing the power and jurisdiction of the nobility; by suppressing the assembly of the three estates, which has not been convened since the year 1614; and by depriving the parliaments of their share in the government.

Parliaments of France. The legislative, as well as the executive power, is vested solely in the king; the parliaments are assembled at present, only to register the king's edicts; but in civil causes, when the court does not interpose, they are still the last resort. They consist of a certain number of presidents and inferior judges, who purchase their places openly, which brings a considerable revenue to the crown. They are 15 in number, viz. that of *Paris*, *Toulouse*, *Roan*, *Grenoble*, *Bourdeaux*, *Dijon*, *Aix*, *Rennes*, *Pau*, *Besançon*, *Mets*, *Doway*, *Perpignan*, *Arras*, and that of *Alsace*, held at *Colmar* or *Strasburg*. Of these, the parliament of *Paris* is the most considerable, for hither the king frequently comes in person, and sees his royal edicts recorded.

Other courts. Besides the parliaments of *France*, there are several other supreme courts for particular branches of business, as the chambers of accounts, and the courts of aids, established in several parts of the kingdom. The chambers of accounts examine the accounts of the treasury, receive the homage of the vassals of the crown, record treaties of peace, and other contracts and grants of the crown. The courts of *aids* are for determining all causes relating to the king's revenue, without any appeal to a higher judicatory. Under these supreme courts, there are others for smaller matters, established in all the considerable towns of the kingdom, and distinguished by the name of *presidials*.

FRANCE.

prefidials. Each prefidial is divided under two chiefs; the firſt judges without appeal, to the capital ſum of 250 livres; the ſecond to the capital ſum of 500 livres. There are alſo officers and magiſtrates in every conſiderable town, who are commonly lawyers appointed by the king, for adminiſtering juſtice, and puniſhing criminals; they have different titles, being in ſome places called *Bailiffs,* in others *Provoſts,* in others *Seneſchals,* but their power and duty is much the ſame.

The taxes uſually levied in *France,* are the *taille,* or land-tax, the *taillon,* the ſubſiſtance-money, the *aids,* and the *gabelles.* The *taille* is only paid by thoſe who hold by baſe tenures, and tradeſmen; the nobility, clergy, and gentry, as alſo the burgeſſes of *Paris,* and ſome other free cities, being exempted from this duty. The *taillon* was eſtabliſhed by king *Henry* II. for augmenting the ſoldiers pay, and is payable by the ſame perſons as the *taille,* amounting to about a third of that tax. The *ſubſiſtance* is a tax which was firſt levied by *Lewis* XIV. for the ſubſiſtance of his armies in their winter-quarters, and is paid in the ſame manner as the *taille.* The *aids* are all duties and cuſtoms on goods and merchandizes, except ſalt. The *gabelles* are the taxes ariſing by ſalt. The other extraordinary taxes are the *capitation,* or poll tax; the tenths of all eſtates, offices, and employments; the fiftieth penny, from which neither the nobility nor clergy are exempted; the tenths of all the eſtates of the kingdom; and the tenths and free-gifts of the clergy, who are allowed to tax themſelves, but 'tis expected they ſhould pay at leaſt as much as the laity; and laſtly, the revenue ariſing from the crown-lands, rents, fines, and forfeitures, all which are computed to amount to upwards of 15 millions *ſterling, per annum;* beſides which, vaſt ſums are levied by raiſ-

Taxes.

The GRAND TOUR.

ing and lowering the coin at pleafure, by compounding debentures and government-bills, and by other oppreffive methods.

Manner of collecting the taxes. For the better collecting of thefe taxes, *France* is divided into twenty-five generalities, or provinces, over each of which there is an officer, called an intendant, appointed by the king, who takes cognizance both of civil and criminal caufes, as well as of the finances, and other matters concerning the public good, and the king's interefts. Subordinate to the *generality*, there is another court called the *Election*, compofed of feveral perfons, who compute the proportion which every parifh in their divifion muft raife of the fum demanded by the *generality*, and fend out their orders for collecting it. This court judges fmall caufes relating to the impofts and taxes. The number of parifhes contained in all the *generalities*, amount to 38,502; which comprehends 1,585,112 families liable to pay the land tax: and the whole number of the inhabitants of *France* is reckoned at about twenty millions.

Crown officers. The great officers of the crown, are the chancellor, who prefides in all courts and councils of ftate in the king's abfence, the keeper of the feals, four fecretaries of ftate, the marfhals of *France*, the colonel-general of the horfe, the great mafter of the artillery, the admiral of *France*, two viceadmirals, the general of the galleys, the four great officers of the order of the Holy Ghoft, *viz.* the chancellor, the mafter of the ceremonies, the great treafurer, and the fecretary; the chief prefidents of the feveral parliaments, the governors and lieutenant-generals of the provinces.

Military power. The military power of *France* furpaffes that of any other kingdom in *Europe*. In time of peace they have generally 200,000 men in pay, and in time

FRANCE.

time of war sometimes 400,000; a great many of whom are foreigners, viz. *Swifs, Germans, Scotch, Irish, Italians*, and *Swedes*. With so formidable an army, their king is not only able to support his arbitrary power among his own subjects, but likewise to keep all his neighbours in continual alarm. Their naval power was very considerable under the reign of *Lewis* XIV. till the famous battle of *La Hogue*, when it was almost totally demolished. From that time it did not recover itself, till under the administration of Cardinal *Fleury*, when this great minister, by putting the *Finances* into good order, and promoting trade and navigation, raised a very considerable fleet. The last war it was thought, would have effectually broke their power at sea, by the two complete victories gained over the *French* in 1747, the first by the admirals *Anson* and *Warren*, and the second by Sir *Edward Hawk*; yet to the amazement of all *Europe*, they have, since the peace of *Aix la Chapelle*, created as it were another navy, which, from the present disputes about our *American* colonies, appears to be far too considerable for the tranquility of *Great Britain*.

The arms of *France* are three flower-de-luces Or, in a field Azure, supported by two angels in the habit of *Levites*, having each of them a banner in his hands with the same arms. The crest is an open crown, the whole under a grand Azure pavillion, strewed with flower-de-luces Or, and ermins, and over it a close crown with a double flower-de-luce Or; on the sides of it are flying streamers, on which are written the words used in battle, *Montjoye, S. Dennis*, and above them, on the royal banner or oriflame, *Lilia non laborant neque nent.*

Arms of France.

The GRAND TOUR.

The prefent king. The prefent French king is *Lewis* XV. great-grandfon of *Lewis* XIV. and fon of the late duke of *Burgundy*, and *Mary Adelaide*, daughter of *Victor Amadeus*, duke of *Savoy*. He was born *Feb.* 15, 1710, fucceeded to the crown, *Sept.* 1, 1715, and married on *Sept.* 5, 1725, Princefs *Mary Lecſinſky*, daughter of *Staniſlaus*, the depofed king of *Poland*, by whom he has iffue feveral daughters, and a dauphin, named *Lewis*, born *Auguſt* 24, 1729. The *Dauphin* married in 1744 an *Infanta* of *Spain*, who died in child-bed, and left no living iffue. He was married again, *June* the 13th, to the princefs *Anna Maria* of *Poland*, by whom he has iffue a duke of *Burgundy*. The king has fix great councils to affift him in the government of the kingdom, *viz.* the council of ftate, the council of finances, the council of difpatches, or that of the fecretaries of ftate, the privy council, the council of confcience, and the council of commerce.

IV. *Of the* French *clergy.*

The eſta-blifhed religion. The eftablifhed worfhip in *France* is the Roman *Catholic*, but with feveral reftrictions and privileges in point of difcipline peculiar to the *Gallican* church. The proteftant religion was received by a great number of the inhabitants foon after the Reformation, and after a long feries of civil wars was eftablifhed by a royal edict, called *the edict of Nants*, under the reign of *Henry* IV.
Perfecutions of the Proteſtants. But this edict having been repealed by *Lewis* XIV. in 1685, a perfecution enfued, which obliged immenfe numbers of the proteftant inhabitants to fly for fhelter to foreign countries. Yet, in matters of religion, the *French* are ftill divided into two great parties, one of them zealous in defending the rights of the *Gallican* church againft the encroachments

FRANCE.

ments of the fee of *Rome*, and the other no lefs zealous in fupporting the pope's authority. The former are called *Janfenifts*, from their adhering to fome fpeculative notions of *Janfenius*, bifhop of *Ipres*, concerning grace and free-will; and the others *Molinifts*, from following the oppofite fentiments of *Molina*, a *Spanifh Jefuit*. The opinions of the former were condemned by feveral popes, and laft of all by *Clement* XI. in the famous Bull beginning with thefe words, *Unigenitus Dei Filius*. This bull, by being regiftered in parliament, was for fome time confidered as an act of ftate, and *Janfenifm* was thought in great meafure fuppreffed; but the prefent difputes between the parliament and the clergy, have revived the drooping fpirits of the *Janfeniftical* party, and feem to have kindled a new flame, which is likely to throw the kingdom into a general combuftion.

All mere fpiritual caufes are cognizable in the ecclefiaftic courts, of which there are nine fuperior ones in different parts of the kingdom. The king nominates to all bifhoprics and abbeys, by virtue of the concordat at *Bologna* between *Francis* I. and *Leo* X. the pope afterwards grants his bulls of confecration, and receives the annates or firft fruits. The crown feizes the temporalities of all vacant archbifhoprics and bifhoprics, and this in *France* is called the Regale. The liberties of the *Gallican* church are two; firft that the pope cannot intermeddle in things relating to temporal affairs in any of the king's dominions; and fecondly, that though he be acknowledged head of the church in fpirituals, yet his power is neverthelefs bounded by canons, and the decrees of general councils.

The clergy of *France* have their affemblies, which cannot be held without leave from the king.

king. The business of their ordinary assemblies is to grant a further supply to the crown, which supply passes under the name of a free gift, and is levied on all the clergy of *France*, according to the necessities of the state.

Archbishoprics. The whole kingdom contains eighteen archbishoprics, and an hundred and thirteen bishoprics. The archbishoprics are *Paris*, *Lyons*. *Roan*, *Tours*, *Sens*, *Rheims*, *Cambray*, *Besançon*, *Vienne*, *Arles*, *Bourges*, *Alby*, *Bourdeaux*, *Auche*, *Narbonne*, *Toulouse*, *Aix*, and *Embrun*. The revenues of the clergy, and of the religious houses of all kinds, are said to amount to twenty-six millions *sterling per annum*.

V. *Of the persons, manners, customs, learning, language, trade, coins, and manner of travelling of the* French.

Persons and virtues of the French. The *French* are generally of a middling stature, more robust, and better made than the *Spaniards* and *Italians*, but inferior in this respect to the *English* and *Germans*. The women in general are not handsome, but sprightly and agreeable. They are a people of quick understanding and nice taste, of an active and enterprizing disposition. They are ready at imitating foreign inventions, and quick themselves at inventing, especially with regard to modes, dresses, and manner of living. They are brave and valiant, particularly the better sort, extremely fond of their prince, polite and affable to strangers, so as to be looked upon as masters of complaisance and good breeding.

Their vices. But these virtues are balanced by several vices; for they are generally reckoned fiery, impatient, inconstant, and of a restless disposition, which

which involves them either in continual lawfuits, and civil broils at home, or obliges their princes to engage them in foreign wars. They are much addicted to gaming, which is the very foul of all their affemblies, and the only means for a foreigner to ingratiate himfelf in their company. The young people are debauched and irreligious; but we muft own that this is compenfated by the folidity, and judicious behaviour of thofe who are more advanced in life. They are charged likewife with infincerity in their complaifance, and with being little better than genteel hypocrites in their cringes and impertinent ceremonies.

The *French* nation are divided into three claffes or eftates, the clergy, the nobility, and the third eftate. Of the clergy we have fpoken in the preceding fection. The nobility confifts of four degrees, *viz.* the princes of the blood, the higher nobility, the ordinary nobility, and the nobility lately made. The dukes and counts, peers of *France*, have the precedence among the higher nobility, next to the princes of the blood. There are three orders of knight-hood in *France*, that of *S. Michael*, inftituted in 1469 by *Lewis* XI. and confifting of about 100 knights, but at prefent in no great efteem. That of the Holy Ghoft, inftituted 1578, by *Henry* III. compofed of 100 perfons, and conferred only on people of the firft quality; and that of *S. Lewis*, inftituted in 1693, by *Lewis* XIV. and defigned purely for the encouragement of the generals and officers of the army. The *French* include all their gentry under the general title of nobility or nobleffe. The third are the *Roturiers*, and comprehends their tradefmen, yeomen, and hufbandmen, or peafants.

Difference of ranks and conditions.

The

Diet.

French diet is not near so gross as ours, for it consists chiefly of bread and herbs. Their bread is exceeding good, and so is their beef and mutton, but their veal is inferior to ours. They boil and roast their meat much longer than we do, which exempts them from gross humours. They are fond of soups, ragoos, and made dishes, which they dress the best of any people in *Europe*. The wines about *Paris* are small, but good in their kind: those of *Champagne* and *Burgundy* are deservedly the most esteemed. They have likewise several other good wines; such as *Vin de Turenne* in *Anjou*, *Vins de Camp de Perdrix* and *Cote Brulée* in *Dauphiné*, *de L'Hermitage* upon the *Rhône*, the red and white *S. Laurence* from *Provence*, the white wines of *Orleans*, *Bourdeaux* claret, those excellent wines from *Cahors*, and the red and white *Cabreton*, from about *Boyonne*. They are great drinkers of coffee, tea, and chocolate, which are used not only in private houses, but likewise in publick coffee-houses, as with us.

Diversions.

The usual diversions of the *French* are either plays, gaming, walking, or taking the air in coaches. They have two kinds of theatres, one for operas, and another for comedies. Their operas at *Paris* are extremely fine, the music and singing excellent, the stage large and magnificent, and supplied with good actors; the scenes well suited, and changed almost imperceptibly; the dancing exquisite; the cloathing rich and proper, and with great variety; they are frequented by a vast concourse of the nobility, who usually join in chorus with the actors. The disposition of their theatres for comedies is much the same, and they have generally some farce or entertainment after the play, a custom which

FRANCE.

which we have borrowed of them. They avoid all obscenity and immorality upon the stage as much as possible, and in general it may be said, that they have carried their theatrical entertainments to the highest degree of perfection.

Since the recovery of letters the *French* have distinguished themselves in the arts and sciences, so as to rival most nations in *Europe*. The encouragement given by the late king to men of letters, and the several useful establishments for promoting the arts and sciences, contributed not a little to the progress this nation made in the last century, in all branches of learning. The reputation they have acquired in this respect, has been raised by the spreading of their language, which is now become almost universal, and commonly used in most courts in *Europe*. This language is chiefly composed of the *Latin*, with a mixture of several *German* and *Gothic* words, but has been lately refined by the *French* academy at *Paris*, so as to be admired for its sweetness, perspicuity, and elegance; though for strength and copiousness it is inferior to the *English*. Besides the several academies at *Paris*, for promoting the sciences and the polite arts, of which we shall take farther notice in the description of that metropolis, the *French* have nineteen universities, which, according to their alphabetical order, are those of *Aix*, *Angers*, *Avignon*, *Besançon*, *Bourdeaux*, *Bourges*, *Caen*, *Cahors*, *Doway*, *Montpellier*, *Nantes*, *Orleans*, *Paris*, (the principal university of the whole kingdom) *Poitiers*, *Pont-à-Mouffon*, *Perpignan*, *Rheims*, *Toulouse*, and *Valence*.

<small>Learning and language.</small>

<small>Universities.</small>

The situation of *France* is very advantageous for trade, as it lies on the ocean, the *English* channel, and the *Mediterranean* sea, and is watered by so many large and navigable rivers.

<small>Trade.</small>

Their

Their manufactures of linen, woolen, silk, and lace, are vastly considerable; and their foreign trade to *Spain*, *Italy*, *Turkey*, and the *East* and *West Indies* prodigiously improved of late, especially during the administration of cardinal *Fleury*, whose chief intent was to increase the wealth and commerce of his country. Their trade to *Great Britain* is very beneficial in times of peace, the return of their wines, silks, linen, and lace being mostly in treasure. The chief commodities of this country, besides the manufactures above-mentioned, are salt, fish, corn, wine, oil, silk, flax, fruits of all sorts, coral, canvass, woods, skins, verdigrease, cremor tartari, &c.

Coins. The current coins of *France* are as follows: 1. Their lowest coin is called a *liard*, four of which make about one half-penny *English*. 2. Their next piece is two *liards*, or one farthing *English*. 3. Their third piece is one *sol* or *sou*, containing four *liards*, or one half-penny *English*; of which there are two pieces at the same value, the one is of copper, which is somewhat bigger than an *English* half-penny; the other is a small piece of mixt metal. 4. The fourth is of a *sol* and a half, of which there are various sorts, but they are all of one value, viz. three farthings *English*. 5. The fifth is a piece of two *sols*, and is of the same kind of mixt metal as the one *sol* piece. 6. The sixth, is a six *sols* piece, and is the lowest silver coin, the same as our three-pence. 7. The seventh is a twelve *sols* piece, the same as our six-pence. 8. The eighth is a twenty-four *sol*, piece, about the same as a shilling *English*. 9. The ninth is a three *livre* piece, like our half crown, and of the same value. *N. B.* A livre is an imaginary coin, containing twenty *sols*, or ten-pence *English*. 10. The tenth is a six *livres* piece, like our crown, and of the same value,

and

FRANCE.

and is the largest *French* silver coin. 11. The eleventh is the half *Louis d'Or*, a gold piece, worth 12 *livres*, and equal to about half a guinea. 12. The twefth is the *Louis d'Or*, which is a piece of gold worth 24 *livres*, and equal to about a guinea *English* money. You are to observe, that no coin of a former reign will pass in this king's time; for they call in all their coins upon the demise of their kings. Their accounts are kept in livres, sols and deniers; twelve deniers make a sol.

Travelling is no where more convenient than in *France*, with respect as well to carriages as accomodations on the road. Where there is conveniency of rivers, they have water carriages, which are large boats drawn by horses. Their land carriages are of four sorts, *viz.* post chaises, the *caroffe* or stage coach, the *coche*, and the *diligence* or flying coach. Their post-chaises are made much in the same manner as ours, and are to be had, at a minute's warning, all over the kingdom. For every post you travel, which is two leagues, or six *English* miles, you are to pay for two horses three livres two sols, that is, fifty sols for the two horses, and twelve sols the postillion. But if you are two in company, you must have three horses, and then you are to pay five livres two sols, that is, two livres more for the additional person. All those posts that lead from *Paris* or *Lyons*, or from any place where the king actually resides, are called royal posts, and the charge of riding them is double the others, with regard to the horses, but not to the postillion. The post-stages are seldom above one post and a half, or two posts long, and then you change both horses and postillion.

— sidenotes: Manner of travelling. Post chaises and horses.

The

Stage-coaches.

The *caroſſe* is not unlike our ſtage-coach, containing room for ſix paſſengers, but does not move ſo quick, and is more embarraſſed with goods and baggage. The *coche* is a large heavy machine, which ſerves the uſe both of waggon and coach; it is long-ſhaped, and provided with windows at the ſides, containing generally ſixteen paſſengers, *viz.* twelve in the body of the coach, ſitting two a-breaſt, and two each ſide, at the door of the entrance, a ſeat being provided there for that purpoſe. It is furniſhed with two large conveniences, one before and another behind, which are made of baſket wicker, and are therefore called baſkets. Into theſe baſkets they put large quantities of goods, which makes it very heavy in drawing. Sometimes both the baſkets are filled with goods, and ſometimes the fore one is left empty for paſſengers, in which the fare is leſs than in the coach, and they have a covering over-head to preſerve them from the injury of the weather. Its motion is but ſlow, ſeldom exceeding that of a briſk walk, and as the roads are generally paved with large ſtone, this kind of vehicle is generally very jumbling and diſagreeable. The expence of travelling with the *caroſſe* or ſtage-coach is leſs than half the ſum of riding poſt, but then you are to make an allowance for being longer upon the road. As for the particular fares of ſtage-coaches, we ſhall mention them in each journey; only we are to obſerve here, that the expence of baggage is paid apart, and is generally three ſols for every pound above fourteen or fifteen pound weight, which is free. With regard to proviſions on the road, your ſafeſt way, if you travel poſt, is to know the price of every thing before you order it; but with the ſtage-coach, your meals are generally regulated at fixed prices, as with us; your entertainment is exceeding good,

good, and the whole expence seldom exceeds five or six livres a day. The *Diligence* is a kind of stage-coach so called from its expedition, and differs from the *caroſſe*, or ordinary stage-coach, in little else but in moving with greater velocity. It is used chiefly in travelling from *Paris* to *Lyons*, and from *Paris* to *Bruſſels*, and has its fixed prices.

CHAP. II.

Journey from Dover *to* Paris.

TRAVELLERS setting out from *Dover* agree for their paſſage in the packet-boat to *Calais*, which is half a guinea for a gentleman, and five shillings for each servant or attendant; the mate and cabin-boy, who wait upon you on board, expect one shilling each as their perquisite. If you are several in company, and you would hire a packet or veſſel to yourselves the price is five guineas. Before you embark, you carry your baggage to the custom-house, where it is searched, for which you pay sixpence, and sixpence more, called head-money. The distance from *Dover* to *Calais* is twenty-one miles. Upon approaching the town, you see several batteries of cannon planted on the shore, to keep the coast clear in war-time. Coming ashore, you'll meet with men-waiters, who speak *English*, and make it their business to ply there, on *English* veſſels coming in, and who will conduct you and attend you in *Calais*, till you have got into your post-chaise for *Paris*. Having pitched upon one of these, you are conducted by a soldier upon the guard, which is always mounted

Directions for travellers from Dover to Paris.

ed upon the quay, to a searching office just by, where you must give in your name and quality, the purpose of your coming over, and intended tour; thence you are shewn into a small inner room, and very civilly searched by the proper officer, who only just presses upon your coat-pockets or outer garments; afterwards the soldier conducts you to the governor's house, where you are shewn to the governor. When this farce is over, you are at liberty to proceed to your inn, whither you are attended by the person or servant, whom you pitched upon at the water side. There are several good inns at *Calais*, as the *Golden Arm*, the *Golden Head*, the *French Horn*, the *Table Royal*, and the *Silver Lyon*, the last of which is reckoned the best. When you have refreshed yourself, you had best go yourself to the custom-house, where you will find your baggage has been carried by porters from the vessel, and will be there searched, to prevent your bringing in any thing new of a foreign manufacture. They allow only one watch to each person, and if they find any new cloaths, they will stop them. After your baggage has been searched, you had better have your trunk plumbed with a leaden stamp for *Paris*; for this will prevent the trouble of any further search of your baggage upon the road, or its being carried to the custom-house when you come to *Paris*; but you must take care not to open the custom-house cordage and plumbing till you get to that metropolis; for on going out of *Calais*, and at the several other garrison towns, both your *Calais* custom-house pass (which they give you in writing, and which you must take care of) and also the plumbing of your trunk, are examined. Therefore your best way is to take out at the custom-house at *Calais*, what necessaries
you

FRANCE.

you may want on the road. The fees at the custom-house for the pass, for your cloaths, and necessaries, and for the plumbing your trunks, are very trifling; but if they are civil, and do not tumble your cloaths, it is customary to give the officer half a crown. The porters who carry your goods from the ship to the custom-house, and from the custom-house to the inn, are like our watermen, never satisfied; about a livre for carrying each trunk will pay them; and three livres when you get into your post-chaise, will be sufficient for your attendant, who keeps close to you till you are gone, and shews you any thing the town affords, which is but indifferent. We gave a description of this town in the first volume of this work, p. 288. Here we shall only observe, that the principal things worth notice, are the great church, the ramparts, the citadel, the *English* convent of nuns, the market-place, and the canal. You must take care not to be too free with their small wines in *Calais*; for, like the water in *Paris*, they will certainly flux you, if you drink too plentifully of them. At the post-house, which is the *Silver Lion*, you bargain for a chaise to go to *Paris*; if there be only one person, he will let you have a pretty good one for two guineas and a half; and if two, he will have three guineas. You have the privilege of carrying a great weight of portmanteaus and trunks behind your post-chaise; but their horses are very indifferent, so that it is not advisable to encumber yourself with too much baggage, but rather to send it by the stage-coach, which sets out twice a week from *Calais* to *Paris*, and is seven days upon the road; the fare is thirty livres for each passenger, and three sols *per* pound for his baggage. The coach from *Paris* to *Calais* and *Dunkirk*, sets up at the *Grand Cerf*,

Rue

The GRAND TOUR.

Rue S. Dennis. The roads from *Calais* to *Paris* are pretty good; and you go with any of their post-horses very near a post an hour. After you have passed *Boulogne,* you will not find the beds like ours in *England*; for they raise them very high with several thick mattresses: their linen is ill washed, and worse dried, so that you must take particular care to see the sheets aired. From *Calais* to *Paris* are thirty-two posts; the last post from *S. Dennis* to *Paris* is a post royal, for which they take of you as for two posts, but the post-boy is to drive you to any part of the city or suburbs of *Paris,* which you please to go to; and in your return they also take a double post for carrying you from your lodgings back to *S. Dennis.* Upon the whole, for the thirty-two posts you pay, if you are two in company, 164 livres, 2 sols, which is about 6*l.* 16*s.* 6*d.* But if you are single, the whole cost will be, horses and boys, only 99 livres, 2 sols, which is about 4*l.* 6*s.* 9½*d. English.* As the post-road very often differs from the road used by the stage-coach; when this happens, we shall give both routes marking the distance in the post rout by posts, each of which is six miles; and the distance in the coach route by *English* miles, according to our usual method, with this addition, that we shall distinguish the stages where the coach stops to dine, by the letter D; and where it stops to sup, by the letter S; which letters must be understood in the same manner, wherever we give the coach route, throughout this volume.

FRANCE.

Route from *Calais* to *Paris*, 32 Posts.

	Posts		
CALAIS		AMIENS	1½
Hautbuisson	1	*Hebecourt*	1
Marquise	1	*Flers*	1
BOULOGNE	1½	*Breteuil*	1¾
Samers	1½	*Wavigny*	1½
Cormont	1	*S. Just*	1
MONTREUIL	1½	*Clermont*	1¼
Nampont	1½	*Lingueville*	1
Bernay	1	CHANTILLY	1
Nouvion	1	*Luzarche*	1
ABBEVILLE	1½	*Ecouen*	1½
Ailly le haut Clocher	1½	*S. Denis*	1
Flixcourt	1½	PARIS	Post Royal
Pequigny	1		

The Coach Route from *Calais* to *Paris*.

	Eng. miles		Eng. miles
CALAIS		S. BEAUVAIS	12
D. *Marquise*	12	D. *Tillard*	15
S. BOULOGNE	15	S. *Beaumont*	9
D. *Franc*	18	D. *Moisette*	12
S. MONTREUIL	12	S. PARIS	12
D. *Bernay*	12		—
S. ABBEVILLE	12		183
D. *Airennes*	12		
S. *Poix*	12		
D. *Oudeuil*	18		

Remarkable places in the post-route.

Hautbuisson, your first stage, is only a single house on the top of a hill, from whence you have a fine prospect of *Calais*, the flat country,

and

The GRAND TOUR.

and the fea. *Marquife* your next ſtage, is a little market-town.

I. BOULOGNE.

Boulogne. *Boulogne* is a ſea-port of *France*, in the province of *Picardy*, and capital of the diſtrict of *Boulonnois*, in eaſt longitude 1, 30. latitude 50, 40. ten leagues from the neareſt coaſt of *England*. This is a very ancient town, ſuppoſed by ſome to be the *Itius Portus* of *Cæſar*, and by others the *Geſoriacum* of *Pliny*. It ſtands at the mouth of the little river *Liane*, which forms its harbour; and is divided into the upper and lower town. The former is well fortified with good walls and a ſtrong citadel, adorned with a handſome ſquare, where they have a town-houſe remarkable for its clock, a cathedral dedicated to the virgin *Mary*, ſome monaſteries, a ſeminary for the education of eccleſiaſtics, a very good hoſpital, and a college of the fathers of the oratory. The lower town is inhabited chiefly by merchants, and lies along the harbour, which was formerly very conſiderable, but is now incapable of receiving veſſels of burthen, becauſe of a bank which the emperor *Maximilian* is ſaid to have raiſed before it. The road before *Boulogne* is extremely bad, no veſſels being able to keep there, unleſs the wind blows from ſome point between the north and the ſouth-eaſt. This harbour is defended towards the river by a mole which ſhelters it from the winds, and is frequented chiefly by the *Engliſh* ſmugglers. Near the harbour are ſome antient ruins, and among the reſt, an octagon tower, ſaid to be built by *Julius Cæſar*. *Boulogne* is now the ſee of a biſhop, ſuffragan of *Rheims*, whoſe yearly income is 12,000 livres; and likewiſe a feneſchal's juriſdiction, the ſeat of a bailiwic, and court of admiralty. King *Henry* VIII. of *England* took it in 1544,

and

FRANCE.

and fortified the lower town, but finding it would cost him more to keep it than it was worth, quitted it by treaty in 1546 for 800,000 crowns.

In this town they have a very good inn, called the *Red Lion*.

From *Boulogne* you proceed to *Samers*, a market-town, where they have a pretty good church, and a moſt beautiful chapel belonging to a monaſtery of *Benedictins*, with a very good garden. *Cormont*, the next poſt, is only a ſingle houſe.

But proceeding nine miles, you come to *Mn-treuil*, a town of *France* in the province of *Picardy*, and county of *Ponthieu*, in eaſt long. 1. 45. lat. 50. 50. It is ſituate on a hill, the foot of which is watered by the river *Canche*, about nine miles from the ſea, from whence pretty large boats come up with the tide. They divide it into the upper and lower town; the lower lies along the river *Canche*, and is ſeparated from the upper by a ſingle wall. The town in general is pretty well fortified, and defended by a good citadel. 'Tis the ſeat of a bailiwic, and has two ancient abbeys of *Benedictins*, one of monks, the other of nuns, from whence its *Latin* name, *Monaſterielum*, is moſt probably derived. It has eight pariſhes, a ſeminary, an hoſpital, and a convent of *Carmelites*, with another of *Capuchins*. The royal bailiwic belongs to the juriſdiction of *Amiens*.

Montreuil.

At the ſign of the *Court of France*, you meet with very good entertainment.

II. ABBEVILLE.

Abbeville is a city of *France* in the province of *Picardy*, and capital of the county of *Ponthieu*, in eaſt long. 2. lat. 50. 7. A caſtle was built here in 936, by *Hugh Capet*, and the town itſelf was built by *S. Riquier* the abbot, from whom it took its name of *Abbatis Villa*, or *Abbevilla*. It is a large

Abbeville.

large city, situated in a marshy dirty country, on the river *Somme*, which divides it into two parts. The place is strong by situation, and moreover the walls are flanked with bastions, and surrounded with large ditches; it is called *The maiden town*, because it was never taken by an enemy. There is a very considerable woollen manufacture in this city, said to be equal to that of any town in *England*. They also make here sail and other coarse cloth, and linens, which being died, serve for linings. They have besides a considerable manufacture of black and green sope; and they have armourers, who make muskets and pistols that are very much esteemed. The town has likewise a pretty good trade in wool and corn, being but 14 miles distant from the *English* channel; with which it has a communication by the river *Somme*, which brings vessels up to the middle of the town. It enjoys many privileges, has a bailiwic and presidial court, and contains 12 parishes, with several monasteries, and a college. About 27 miles from *Abbeville* is the borough of *Cressy*, on the river *Authie*, near the borders of *Artois*, in the province of *Picardy*, made memorable by the victory obtained by *Edward* III. king of *England* over the *French* in 1346.

Pequigny. Fifteen miles further is *Pequigny*, a small town of *France*, in the province of *Picardy*, and county of *Ponthieu* in east long. 2. 15. lat. 49. 55. It is situated on the river *Somme*, and has the title of a barony. The earth of the adjacent country is of a combustible nature, and furnishes the inhabitants with turf for fuel. About three miles from hence stands the famous *Abbey du Gard* of the *Cistercian* order.

III. AMIENS.

Amiens. *Amiens* is the capital of the province of *Picardy* in *France*, in east long. 2. 30. lat. 49. 50.
It

It is a large pleasant city, agreeably situated on the river *Somme*, and said to have received its *Latin* name, *Ambianum*, from being every where encompassed with water. 'Tis a place of great antiquity, being mentioned by *Cæsar* as a town that had made a vigorous resistance against the *Romans*, and where he convened a general assembly of the *Gauls*, after having made himself master of it. The emperors *Antoninus*, and *Marcus Aurelius* enlarged it; and *Constantine*, *Constans*, *Julian*, and several others, resided here a considerable time. The town is encompassed with a wall, and other fortifications; and the ramparts are planted with trees, which form a delightful walk. The citadel was built by *Henry* IV. The river *Somme* enters *Amiens* by three different channels, under as many bridges; and these channels, after washing the town in several places, where they are of use in its different manufactures, unite at the other end by the bridge of *S. Michael*. Here is a quay for the boats that come from *Abbeville* with goods brought by sea. At the gate of *Noyon* there is a suburb, remarkable for the abbey of *S. Achen*. Next to this gate you come to that of *Paris*, where they have a long mall between two rows of trees. The houses are well built, the streets spacious, embellished with handsome squares and good buildings. The cathedral, dedicated to our *Lady*, is one of the largest and most magnificent churches in *France*, adorned with handsome paintings, fine pillars, chapels, and tombs; particularly the nave is greatly admired. The other places worth seeing are the palace of the bailiwic, the town-house, the square *des Fleurs*, and the great market-place. This town is the seat of a bishop, suffragan of *Rheims*, as also of a presidial, bailiwic, *Vidam*, a chamber of accounts, and a generality. The bishop's revenue is thirty thou-

thousand livres. They have some linen and woolen manufactures, and they also make a great quantity of black and green sope.

Clermont. The country from hence to *Clermont* is a fine open plain. *Clermont* is a small town in the isle of *France*, and county of *Beauvais*, in east long. 2. 30. lat. 49. 24. It is situated on a hill near the river *Erecle*, 15 miles from *Beauvais*, and as many from *Senlis*.

IV. CHANTILLY.

Chantilly. From *Clermont*, the next place worth notice you come to, is *Chantilly*, a village, remarkable for being the seat of the prince of *Condé* or duke of *Bourbon*; for this family in a peculiar manner, take these two different titles alternately in succession. The palace belonging to the prince is, next to *Versailles*, the most magnificent in all *France*, as well for the beauty of the structure, as for the richness of its furniture. The chapel is extremely beautiful, where you see an excellent piece of the *Ascension*. The stables are more magnificent than can be conceived. *Chantilly* formerly belonged to the house of *Montmorency*; the equestrian statue of brass before the palace was made for the last constable of that name. The gardens are laid out in a most elegant taste, extending six miles in length, and of a very considerable breadth. The great variety of canals and water-works, the woods cut in avenues, with fountains playing, cascades murmuring; the number of fowls, as partridges, pheasants, flying about: the delightful walks, and little groves with aviaries, all together, render this one of the most charming places upon earth. Within one hundred yards of the palace, and almost adjoining to the stables, is the post-house, where you are very well entertained, but extravagantly dear, so that you must be upon your guard in ordering dainties, if you consult œconomy. The present prince of *Condé* is *Lewis Joseph de Bourbon*, born at *Paris August* 9, 1736.

From *Chantilly* you come to *Luzarche*, a small **Luzarche.** market town in the isle of *France*, six miles from *Senlis*. From thence you proceed to *Ecouen*, **Ecouen.** another market town in the isle of *France*, where you may stop to see an exceeding fine house and gardens; the house was built by the constable *de Montmorenci* in 1542, and now belongs to prince *Condé*. From *Ecouen* you come to

V. S. DENIS.

S. Denis is a small town of *France*, situated in **S. Denis.** a fine plain, near the *Seine*, about six miles to the northward of *Paris*. It received its name from a magnificent abbey of *Benedictins*, founded here by *Dagobert* I. in 630, on the tomb of *S. Denis* the *Areopagite*, the apostle of *France*; though it is questioned by several learned writers, whether that *S. Denis* was ever in this kingdom. The ab- **Monuments** bey is remarkable for the sepulchres of the *French* **of the French kings.** kings, princes, and princesses of the blood; the chief of which is that of *Lewis* XII. one of the finest pieces of architecture in *Europe*, all of white marble, and adorned with the victories of this prince in *basso-relievo*, the whole by the famous architect *Paolo Poncio* of *Florence*. Here is also a tomb erected to the memory of the celebrated *Marshal de Turenne* by *Lewis* XIV. It stands in a marble chapel, built on purpose, where his effigies lies at full length, surrounded with laurels and trophies in *relievo*. It was made by *Tuby*, from the designs of *Le Brun*, and there are few such monuments in *France*. The abbey **The abbey-** church is 390 feet long, 100 wide, and 90 high; **church.** supported by 60 pillars, and adorned with copper gates.

gates. The church being fallen to decay, was rebuilt several times; but the present portal is by *Charlemaigne*, and the rest of the church by the abbot *Suger*, in 1140. The beauty of the architecture, tho' in the *Gothic* taste, and the delicacy and lightness of its structure, are much admired. On the middle gate they have drawn our Saviour in his glory, and on the other two you see figures of kings and queens. The windows are of a very thick glass, finely painted, which darkens the church. The organ is esteemed the best in *France*; and the rails of the choir and gallery, which were made by a monk of that house, are reckoned an incomparable piece of workmanship. Over the door of these rails there is a large cross of massy gold, set with diamonds and rich pearls, and said to have been made by *S. Eloi*. The great altar is in the antique taste, with four columns of copper, and a table adorned with five *basso-relievo's*, three of which are of gold; the whole enriched with a prodigious number of diamonds. Over the abovementioned table there is a large cross six feet high, adorned with precious stones. On the right of this great altar, there is another of a lesser size, called the communion altar; and opposite to that stands always the funeral altar of their last king, which at present is that of *Lewis* XIV.

The treasure.

The treasure belonging to this church is inestimably rich, containing a great number of relics, and an immense quantity of ancient medals and jewels, in six presses or cabinets. The monks are very civil in shewing the treasure; explaining every thing most distinctly, and pointing out the time and manner in which all the valuable curiosities were brought to this place. In the fourth

The regalia press they preserve the Regalia of *France*; these are *Charlemagne*'s golden crown set with diamonds,

FRANCE.

monds, which is worn by the *French* kings the day of their coronation; the scepter of *Charlemagne*, as also his sword and spurs, all enriched with diamonds; the pontifical for the king's coronation; and a book of the *Epistles* and *Gospels*, covered with gold and precious stones. In the sixth press they preserve the royal robes in which *Lewis* XV. was crowned at *Rheims*, *October* the 24th, 1722; likewise a set of ivory chessmen belonging to *Charlemagne*, every one as big as a man's fist; a hunter's horn belonging to *Rowland*, nephew to *Charlemagne*; and the sword of the maid of *Orleans*. On the top of this press there is a great chair of gilt copper, which is said to have been the throne of king *Dagobert*. They shew you also a vase of oriental agate, representing a *Bacchanal*, which is said to be worth more than a great many intire treasures. Upon the whole, this is thought to be the richest treasure in *Europe*, next to those of *Loretto* and *S. Mark* at *Venice*.

The inside of this abbey is a large antient structure; but they have lately begun to erect a new building, which when finished will be one of the finest in *Europe*. It is divided into several halls of a surprizing greatness and beauty, designed to receive the princes, parliament, and other superior courts upon such ceremonies as the king thinks proper to invite them. The top of this majestic edifice is a fine dormitory for the monks, where they have each a neat commodious cell. The abbot had formerly very great privileges, which are now much lessened; however, he is still a counsellor of the Parliament of *Paris*, and has the privilege of keeping the Regalia, which he sends to the place where the kings are consecrated, *viz*. the city of *Rheims*. There are several other churches and parishes in the town, a

The abbey.

good hospital, and some convents of nuns and friars.

<small>Road from S. Dennis to Paris.</small> On the road from hence to *Paris* there are six colonades (the seventh is at *S. Chaumont* in the street of *S. Denis* at *Paris*) which were erected in those places where *Philip the Bold*, and his brothers, the sons of *S. Lewis*, stopped to rest themselves in carrying the body of their deceased father to the abbey of *S. Denis*, which happened *May* 22, 1271. These are now so many stations of rest at the funerals of the *French* kings.

VI. *Remarkable places in the coach-route from* Calais *to* Paris.

The coach from *Calais* to *Paris* goes the same road as the post, as far as *Abbeville*, where it turns off, and the next night it goes to *Poix*, a small town of *Picardy*, situate on the river *Somme*, about five miles N. W. from *Conti*.

<small>Beauvais.</small> Travelling 30 miles further, the next night you come to *Beauvais*, a city of the isle of *France*, and capital of the *Beauvaisis* which is in E. long. 2. 20. lat. 49. 30. It is situated on the river *Therin*, and is a place of great antiquity, being the *Bellovacum* and *Cæsaromagus* of the *Romans*. It is now a handsome large town, surrounded with walls, and deep broad ditches. 'Tis the seat of a bishop, suffragan of *Rheims*, who is the first count and ecclesiastical peer of *France*, and has a yearly revenue of 55000 livres. The cathedral church of *S. Peter* is a very good structure, remarkable for its beautiful choir; besides which there are four collegiate churches, several parishes, a great number of religious houses, an hospital for the sick, and an hospital-general. The treasure of the cathedral, and the public library deserve a traveller's notice. The market-place is reckoned one of the finest in the kingdom. The inhabitants have a pretty good trade for cloth, stuffs, and fine potters ware. The adjacent

jacent country abounds with good wine, corn, and fruits of all sorts, and produces the best mutton in *France*.

The coach goes on the next day to a pretty good town, called *Beaumont*, a name derived from its beautiful situation on the declivity of a hill, at the foot of which runs the river *Oise*. On the top of the hill there is a ruinous castle, which commands the city, and over the river there is a handsome bridge. The next day, by noon, the coach comes into the post-road again, about three miles on this side of *S. Denis*.

Beaumont.

VII. *Directions for strangers upon their first coming to* Paris.

As soon as you enter *Paris*, you will be stopt in your chaise, and your pass and plumbings, and every corner of the whole chaise will be examined. When they have done, you order the postilion to drive to the hôtel you intend to lodge at; otherwise he will endeavour to carry you to his own favourite house, which has him in fee. You will probably be followed from the place of search, or from your entrance into *Paris*, to your hôtel, by men-servants out of place, many of whom can speak a little broken *English*, and have generally written characters in their pockets from some *English* gentlemen whom they have served. You may venture upon one whose character you most approve of, and let him immediately begin and stay with you, and assist in taking off your trunks, &c. but do not hire him till the next day, when your banker or correspondent is along with you, and you are thoroughly satisfied as to his character. Thirty *sols*, or fifteen pence *English* a day, is the usual wages, out of which he finds himself in every thing, unless you give him a livery. There are a great many very good inns at *Paris*, where you are sure of being extremely well accommodated,

Inns. dated, according to the figure and expence you intend to make. The principal of these are, the *Hôtel Imperial*, in the *rue Dauphin* and *Faubourg de S. Germain*; the *Hôtel d'Anjou*, the *Hôtel d'Hambourg*, the *Hôtel d'Orleans*, and the *Hôtel de Picardie*, in the *rue Mazarin*; the *Hôtel d'Espagne*, in the *rue de Seine*; the *Hôtel Imperial*, in the *rue de Tour*; the *Doge of Venice*, in the *rue de Boucherie*; the *Grand Hôtel de Luine*, and the *Little Hôtel de Luine*, on the quay *des Augustins*; the *Croix de Fer*, the *Croix Blanche*, and the *Croix Dorée*, in the *rue S. Denis*; besides several others too tedious to enumerate.

Lodgings. Those who intend to stay some time at *Paris*, and do not choose to be at the expence of living in those hôtels, may hire a furnished lodging. An apartment two pair of stairs, for a single frugal gentleman, will be as well as the first floor: and indeed the first floor is generally let all together at a considerable price, perhaps one hundred livres a week; and you will hardly get an apartment to please you up two pair of stairs for less than 15 or 20 livres a week. For lodging is the dearest article, especially to those who make but a short stay, and take them only by the week. The people of the house find you nothing but you bed and bed-linen, water-bottle, bason, and towels. Your servant, for about fifteen shillings *English*, will immediately set you up for a housekeeper, by buying you a tin tea-kettle, some charcoal and a dish, a tea-pot, some tea-cups, saucers, milk-pot, a decanter, and about half a dozen glasses; he will also buy you *French* rolls and sugar, and good hyson tea for about 17 livres a

Eating and Drinking. pound; and so much for breakfast. With regard to your dinners and suppers, if you choose to live in a family way, you had best have them drest and sent in by a cook, or from a tavern, to your lodgings,

lodgings, at your own hour, and he will find you linen and knives. For eight livres a day, you may have for dinner two good dishes and a soop, which will serve four in company, and servants. Their mutton is much better than their beef or veal, and their hare, patridges, and wild-fowl are excellent. Their soops, especially those on meagre or fast days, are not very agreeable to *Englishmen*; the best is the plain gravy, with a roll and vermicelli in it. If you have any odd thing for supper, as partridge, pigeon, chicken, or a bit of fish, you have no occasion to bargain for them as for your dinners, but the cook will make you a bill; and if you go out of town, you have only to give notice to the cook. But for a single person, or if not more than two in company, the public ordinaries seem more eligible, and you may easily get a recommendation to the best sort of them; there you will meet with company from almost all nations, and have variety of dishes; besides their prices are very reasonable, from twenty sous to forty-five a dinner. Another way is to board in a private family, where you may be furnished with a neat room, a hot dinner and supper (breakfast you find yourself) with a pint of wine at each meal, for the sum of sixty livres. As to your drink, it is proper to observe, that it is dangerous to drink much water, or too plentifully of their small wines, for this will assuredly throw you into a looseness; therefore you had better mix your water always with the common wines of about thirty sous a bottle, and drink no wine under that price. The wines most commonly drank at *Paris*, are these, 1. *Bon vin vieux de Beaune*, and *De Volne l'Année passée*, these are the best thirty sols red wines to drink at meals, and mix with water. 2. *Preignac*, a tolerable common white-wine, for the same purpose, and the same price. 3. *Frontignun,* excellent for a glass or two, especially with walnuts, two livres ten sols a bottle. 4. *Champagne,* you'll get good at *Paris,* at four livres a bottle. 5. *Cote Rotie,* is a light, pleasant, drinking wine, and more used to sit over than any other, at two livres ten sols a bottle. 6. *Hermitage,* for those who can bear a strong wine, at three livres a bottle. There are many other wines, but these seem to be the best. As to claret they have none at *Paris;* and good *Burgundy* is very dear, and hard to be got.

Coach-hire. Having settled now the article of eating and drinking, you are to equip yourself for your excursions about the town; for which purpose we need not mention, that a *French* taylor and barber are absolutely requisite. The next thing is, to get you a conveniency to carry you abroad, that you may with elegance and ease go and see every thing that is curious in and about *Paris.* Your best way is to have a recommendation to some of those people who let coaches out to hire; and if you are only two in company, a chariot is most advisable. You may have a gay and easy gilt coach or chariot, and a coachman, with a good pair of horses, for twelve livres, which is about ten shillings a day, to attend you from seven in the morning till midnight, and to carry you to *Versailles,* &c. This is certainly the best way, because their hackney-coaches are dirty and mean, and few people of any fashion, especially strangers, either use them, or walk much in the streets. It is to be observed, that you must sign a contract for your coach or chariot, to have it a month as your own; the lawyer or notary draws the contract by the coach-lender's orders, and you pay five shillings for his fee, and one shilling for

his

his clerk, who attends you to get it signed. This contract the coachman carries in his pocket, to entitle him to drive you out of town to *Verſailles*, &c. for without it the coach is not privileged to carry you out of the gates of *Paris*. But tho' you contract for a month for the ſake of this privilege, yet you may give up your coach at the end of ten days, or a fortnight, paying for the days you have had it; and a fortnight will be long enough to carry you to moſt of the diſtant places you want to ſee in and about *Paris*. While your cloaths are making, which will be three or four days, you may walk a little about, and go up to the top of *Notre Dame*, &c. to familiarize yourſelf with the town. Before we proceed to give you a deſcription of *Paris*, and to point out to you the remarkable curioſities of this great metropolis, with the moſt valuable pieces of architecture, painting, &c. and the names of the ſeveral artiſts; we ſhall firſt lay down the method or order you may follow in making your progreſs; this will be a kind of guide, and help you to huſband your time, which is always precious, but eſpecially in travelling.

VIII. *Order to be obſerved in ſeeing the curioſities of* Paris.

You may begin then, and ſpend three whole days in ſeeing the *Palace Royal*, which is not too long a time for examining the fineſt collection of paintings in *Europe*. The next day you may viſit the *Hotel d' Antin*, and that of Count *Toulouſe*. Then you may ſee the palace of the *Tuilleries*, and the *Louvre*, the ſquare called *Place Vendome*, and the *Place des Victoires*, all which are not far diſtant from one another.

Next day you may ſee the pumps, and other water-works of the *Samaritaine* on the *Pont Neuf*; and after having ſeen the churches of *S. Euſtache*

Euſtache and *S. Roch*, you may go to the library of the little fathers in the *Place de Victoires*.

Another day you may ſee the *Hotel de Maine*, and the new palace lately built for the dutcheſs of *Bourbon*, both which are near the royal hoſpital of the *Invalids*.

In the ſame quarter are alſo the abbey of *S. Germain des Prez*, where they have a very fine library; the pariſh church of *S. Sulpice* not yet finiſhed; the Noviciate belonging to the *Jeſuits*; the *Hôtels de Verrue*, *de Villars*, *de Roquelaure*, and ſeveral others; the hoſpital for mad people, called *les petites maiſons*; that of the incurables; the church of the barefooted *Carmelites*; the palace of *Luxemburg*; the *Carthuſian* monaſtery near *Luxemburg*; and the anatomies in waxwork.

Another day you may go to the *Faubourg S. Jacques*, where you ſhould ſee the church of the *Carmelite* nuns, the church of the *Feuillantines*, and that of *Val de Grace*, and without that barrier is the Obſervatory.

In the *Faubourg S. Marcel*, not far diſtant from the other, you may ſee the *Gobelins*, the hoſpital called *Biceſtre*, and the hoſpital general, both which are in the fields without the barriers.

Another day you may go to the quarter called the *Univerſity*, where you ſhould ſee the church of *S. Genevieve*, and the fine library belonging to the abbey; the church of *S. Etienne du Mont*; the church of *S. Nicholas du Chardonrets*, and the antient abbey and library of *S. Victor*. In the ſame quarter may be ſeen alſo the *Sorbonne*, and ſeveral colleges, not forgetting that built by Cardinal *Mazarin*, tho' at a little diſtance from the others.

In the part called the city, are to be ſeen the cathedral of *Notre Dame*, the hoſpital called
Hotel

FRANCE.

Hôtel Dieu, the *enfans trouvés*, or foundling hospital, the *Palais* where the courts of judicature sit, and the *Sainte Chapelle*.

In the quarter of *S. Antony* are the *Hotel de Ville*, the churches of *S. Gervais*, and of the great *Jesuits*, the *place Royale*, the *Arsenal*, and the *Bastille*, and without the gate of *S. Antony* is the manufactory of looking-glasses.

In the quarter called the *Marais*, stands the antient building called the *Temple*, which now belongs to the knights of *Malta*; the grand Prior's palace is worth seeing, as also the *Hotel de Soubize*, and the gates of *S. Martin* and *S. Denis*.

As to the royal palaces, you may see one in a day, except *Versailles*, where you may spend several days; near to it is *Clagny*, and not far distant are *Marli*, *S. Cyr*, *S. Germains*, and *Maisons*. Returning from *Versailles* to *Paris*, you may see *S. Cloud*, *Meudon*, and *Seaux*; but when you have time, each of these deserves a day. Another day may be agreeably spent in seeing *Conflans*, *Choisy*, *Bagnolet*, *Vincennes*, and *S. Maur*. So much for a general view of *Paris*, now we come to a particular description.

CHAP. III.

Description of PARIS.

PARIS is the metropolis of the kingdom of *France*, and of the government of the isle of *France*, situate on the river *Seine*, in E. long 2. 25. lat. 48. 50. The origin of this great city is very uncertain, no mention being made of it in history before the time of *Julius Cæsar*, by whom it is called

Its name.

Antiquity.

called *Lutetia*, which some derive from the word *lutum*, because of the marshy ground in the neighbourhood. It was then the capital of the people called *Parisians*, confined within the isle formed by the river *Seine*, and surrounded with woods and marshes. The *Romans*, having subdued it under *Julius Cæsar*, enlarged and improved its buildings, and were the first that surrounded it with walls. Its agreeable situation soon made it increase under succeeding emperors, and at last rendered it the metropolis of the country under *Clovis* their first christian king, who removed the seat of government hither from the city of *Tours*. *Philip Augustus* was the first that walled in the several suburbs with which the town was enlarged in process of time; and by the encouragement given by succeeding princes, especially *Francis* I. *Henry* II. and *Henry* IV. it became at length one of the largest, most populous and flourishing cities in the universe.

Situation. Its situation is most delightful, having a mountain on the south which abounds with wholesome springs, and the adjacent country is full of stone quarries. On the north there are pits from whence they dig their plaister; and on the banks of the *Seine* and *Marne*, there are very pleasant woods. The plain on the north abounds with corn, and the hills from *Mount le Hery*, as far as *Poissy*, produce excellent wine. The neighbouring country is watered with innumerable streams which fall into the *Seine* and the *Marne*, and facilitate the transportation of commodities to this city.

Division of Paris. *Paris* is generally divided into three parts, the town, the university, and the city. The town, which is the largest, contains all that part towards the north, bounded by the *Seine*, the gates of *la Conference*, of *S. Honoré*, Montmartre,

FRANCE.

martre, S. *Denis*, S. *Martin*, and S. *Antony*. The city, which is much the least but the most antient lies betwixt the town and the university upon three little islands in the middle of the *Seine*, and joined to the other parts by bridges, extending from the little *Chatelet* to *Pont Notre Dame*. The university, so called from the colleges it includes for promoting learning, lies on the south side of the river, on a rising ground, and contains that part which is bounded by the *Seine*, and the gates of S. *Bernard*, S. *Victor*, S. *Marcel*, S. *James*, S. *Michael*, and the suburb of S. *Germain*. There is another division of *Paris*, for the better regulation of the civil government, into twenty quarters or wards. The whole town, taking in the suburbs, is of a circular form, about six leagues in circumference, and two in diameter, containing, according to the *French* calculation, near 1000 streets, 20000 houses, fifty-two parishes, one hundred and thirty-four religious houses, sixty for men, and seventy-eight for women, upwards of two hundred conventual and parochial churches and chapels, more than fourteen thousand coaches, and about nine hundred thousand inhabitants. The annual revenue which *Paris* brings in to the king is twenty-five millions of livres, and fifteen millions for the capitation. The streets are generally straight and uniform, but somewhat narrow. The houses look handsome without, being built with free-stone; most of them have sash-windows, and are generally six or seven stories high. The curiosities of this great city would require a whole volume to describe; we shall therefore be content with a short view of such as are most worthy of a traveller's notice, which, for the sake of order, we shall reduce under the following heads. 1. Churches. 2. Palaces. 3. Hôtels. 4. The *Hôtel de Ville*, the Arsenal, and the Bastile. 5. Hos-

Circumference.

Inhabitants.

Streets.
Houses.

5. Hospitals. 6. Public squares. 7. Gates. 8. Bridges and fountains. 9. Colleges. 10. Academies, physic garden, and observatory. 11. Libraries. 12. Paintings. 13. Theatres. 14. Trade and manufactures. 15. Cabinets of medals. 16. Antiquities. 17. Public walks. 18. Government.

I. CHURCHES.

The church of Notre Dame. The cathedral of *Notre Dame* is situated on a little island of the *Seine*, to which it communicates its name. It is a majestic old *Gothic* structure, founded in 522 by King *Childebert*, and dedicated to the blessed *Virgin*; but begun to be rebuilt under *Robert the Devout*, son of *Hugh Capet*, towards the year 1000, and finished under *Philip Augustus* towards 1150. It is built in the form of a cross, sixty-five toises long, four and twenty broad, and seventeen high. The roof is supported by an hundred and twenty large pillars: the front is admired for its sculpture, on which are the statutes of eight and twenty of their kings; the last is *Philip Augustus*. In the middle there is a small spire, and at the west end are two large square towers, thirty-four toises high, which you ascend by three hundred and eighty-nine steps; they are flat at top, with balusters round them, which makes the front look spacious and noble. From these towers you have a fine prospect of the city of *Paris*. The great bell is the biggest in the kingdom next to that of *Roan*. The choir has been lately rebuilt in a most magnificent manner; it was begun in 1688, after the design of *Manfart*, but executed after the design of *Decotte* the father, and finished in 1714 by *Decotte* the son. Cardinal *Noailles* laid out in the repairs of the whole church above 500,000 livres. The organ is reckoned the best in the kingdom.

The

The high altar, begun by *Lewis* XIII. and finished by *Lewis* XIV. is all encrusted with marble. The two angels on the side, are of brass gilt, and the pedestals of white marble. These two angels are cast from the models of *Cayot*. The oval *basso-relievo* adorning the steps betwixt the two angels, is by *Vasse*. The figure of the Virgin, in the middle of the niches, holding Our Saviour on her knees, is an excellent piece, by *Coutoux* the elder. The statue of *Lewis* XIII. in white marble, on the left, is by *Coutoux* the younger; and that of *Lewis* XIV. on the right hand, is by *Coisevox*. Behind the high altar there is another, called *L'Autel de Feries*, which is also of marble, with several ornaments in sculpture, by *Coutoux* the elder; here are six angels of brass gilt, as large as the life, holding the several instruments of Our Saviour's passion. At the bottom of the steps of the sanctuary, you see a piece of white marble, under which there is a vault where the entrails of *Lewis* XIII. and of *Lewis* XIV. are preserved. The decoration of the chapel of the Virgin, without the choir, is extremely rich in marble and gilding; and the chapel of the martyrs on the other side, is in the same taste. The wainscot of the choir deserves to be taken notice of, as also the treasury, and the great silver lamp before the high altar, which was given to the church by *Anne* of *Austria*, upon the birth of *Lewis* XIV.

The Jesuits church in the quarter of S. *Anthony* is a modern structure, founded by *Lewis* XIII. but the front was built by Cardinal *Richlieu*. The design is by father *Francis de Derrand Lorrain*, a jesuit. The front is about 24 toises high, bearing three orders of architecture one over the other, two *Corinthian*, and one *Composite*; but the whole is in a bad taste, and over-loaded with ornaments.

The Jesuits church.

ments. The pulpit, made of iron, is a very curious piece of workmanship. On the side of the great altar, on the left hand, is the heart of *Lewis* XIII. supported by two silver angels, almost as big as the life. On the right hand they have placed the heart of *Lewis* XIV. in the very same taste. The chapel of *Bourbon* is one of the most magnificent things in *France*; the monument erected here to the great *Condé*, by *John Perrault*, president of the chamber of accounts, is said to have cost him 200,000 livres. It is adorned with four figures of brass, almost as big as the life, representing the cardinal virtues, designed by *Sarazin*, and cast by *Perlan*. The Jesuits have likewise another church called the *Noviciate*, in the quarter of *Luxemburg*, of excellent architecture, after the design of *Martel Ange*, one of their Society. The great altar was made in 1709, after the design of *Mansard*, and conducted by *Decotte*. It is encrusted with marble of different colours, which have a very pretty effect. The design of the figures of S. *Ignatius* and S. *Francis Xaverius*, is extremely correct.

S. Genevieve.

The church of S. *Genevieve* belongs to the regular canons of S. *Austin*, and is said to have been founded by king *Clovis*. The architecture is *Gothic*, and very bad of the kind; but withinside there is something worth observing. The shrine where the relics of S. *Genevieve*, the patroness of *Paris*, are kept, is said to have cost 193 marks of silver and eight of gold: it was made by *Robert de la Ferté-Milon*, abbot of this house, in 1442, and is supported by a detached building in the *Ionic* order, formed by four marble columns, the work of the famous architect *Jaques le Mercier*. The tabernacle is extremely fine, being composed precious of stones, and supported by columns of antient *Greek* Brocatelle,

which

FRANCE.

which are now very rare. In the middle of the choir there is a brass eagle, with three little geniuses, which is looked upon as a finished piece. In this church there are three tombs very remarkable, that of King *Clovis* for its antiquity; that of Cardinal *Richlieu* for its magnificence; and that of *Des Cartes*, for the esteem paid to learning. The sacristy is full of rich vestments, and other ornaments; but it is difficult to get a sight of them. The monks of *S. Genevieve* have a good apothecary's shop, and a handsome library, with a curious collection of coins, medals, antiquities, and other rarities.

The new church of the *Invalids* was designed by the famous *John Harduin Mansart*, and is justly allowed to be one of the finest buildings in *France*. The front is eight and twenty toises broad, and fifty high, reckoning from the floor to the dome. Its is composed of the *Doric* and *Corinthian* order, and the *Attic* on the top, the whole adorned with columns, pilasters, and statues, by the most eminent masters. The two angels over the door are by *Vancleve*. The four virtues reclining, as also the figure of *Charlemagne*, are by *Coisevox*. Saint *Lewis* is by *Coutoux*, but modelled by *Girardon*, and reckoned a very curious piece. All these statues are of marble. The dome has nothing to compare to it in all *France*; being, as we mentioned above, 50 toises from the level of the ground to the cross; it is covered with lead, and decorated with sculptures and gildings. The platform which surrounds the dome, on the outside, is paved with stones artfully cut, and put together without cement or mastic. The first vault is elegantly painted by different masters. The high altar is placed in such a manner, that it may be seen equally from the old and new church. It has two faces,

Church of the Invalids.

so that two masses may be said on it at the same time. This altar, with all its appurtenances, is only of wood; tho' it was at first designed to be made of brass, gilt with leaf gold. There are six chapels, in each of which is a statue of white marble, instead of a picture. The figure of the Virgin, and the *bas-relief* in the chapel at the extremity of the cross-isle, are by *Vancleve*. The figure of *S. Teresa* in the opposite chapel, is by *Philip Maniere*. The other four chapels are dedicated to the four doctors of the *Latin* church. The whole pavement of the church is of marble of different colours; and the steps of the great and small altars are also of marble of different colours, wrought in *Mosaic*. In short, such is the magnificence of this building, that it would require a large work to give a proper description of it; the reader may consult that which was published in 1706, by *J. F. Felibien*, a *French* writer.

Church of S. Germain. The church and abbey of *S. Germain* are very antient: it is called *S. Germain des Prés*, from having been built originally in the midst of meadows, and from its being the place where *S. Germain*, bishop of *Paris*, lies buried. Here also the *French* kings used formerly to be interred; many of their tombs are still to be seen, among the rest that of king *Chilperic*. The church is a plain Gothic building; but the high altar was magnificently rebuilt in 1704, after the design of *Gille Marie Oppenard*. *S. Germain*'s shrine is vastly rich, and very well finished, tho' in the *Gothic* taste: it was made in 1408, by the sixtieth abbot of this place. On the two sides of the choir there are two chapels built by *Bulet*, a famous architect; the lesser is that of *S. Margaret*, where you may see the tomb of the *Catelans*, by *Girardon*; and the tomb of the count *de la Mark*, by *Colsevox*.

In

FRANCE.

In the other chapel, dedicated to *S. Casimir*, is the tomb of *John Casimir*, king of *Poland*, by *Marsc.* In the sacristy there are a great many costly curiosities, especially a cross inriched with precious stones.—Of the famous library belonging to this abbey, we shall take proper notice under the article of libraries.

The church and nunnery of *Val de Grace* were founded by *Anne* of *Austria*, mother to *Lewis* XIV. on the unexpected birth of that Prince, after she had been married 22 years. The church is without dispute one of the handsomest buildings in *Europe*. The first stone was laid in *April* 1645, by *Lewis* XIV. who was then only seven years old; the whole was finished in 1669. The first design was by *Mansart*, who carried it even with the ground; he was afterwards set aside, and *Muet* was appointed architect, and under him *Gabriel le Duc* for the inside, and *Duval* for the outside. The area before the church is 25 toises in breadth, and 22 in depth, separated from the street by iron rails eighteen feet high. The portal is raised upon sixteen steps, adorned with a peristile or portico, supported by eight fluted *Corinthian* columns. Here you see the statues of *S. Benedict*, and *S. Scholastica*, done in marble. Over this there is a second order of architecture; and upon the frize of the portico are to be seen the following words in golden letters.

Val de Grace.

Jesu nascenti Virginique matri.
To the infant Jesus and his virgin mother.

The dome is covered with lead, with large gilded bands; it is surmounted by a lanthern, surrounded with an iron ballustrade, and supporting a large ball of gilt brass with a cross, which terminates
the

the whole. The infide is adorned with a *Corinthian* order of pilafters, with fluted columns. The pavement is divided into four large compartments of different colours. The dome is eleven toifes in diameter, and fupported by four great double arches. The great altar was contrived by *Gabriel le Duc*; it is adorned with fix large wreathed columns two feet broad, of the *Compofite* order, made of black *Barbançon* marble, veined with white. Thefe columns are charged with palms, and other gilt ornaments; above there is a fpherical compartment, and they fupport a canopy formed by fix grand curves, which in the middle finifh in a fmall ceiling. Two angels, feven feet high, fupport cenfors; and other fmall ones fufpended, hold labels, on which are written the verfes of the *Gloria in excelfis Deo*. Between the columns, the infant *Jefus* in the manger, with the holy virgin and *S. Jofeph*, are carved in white marble; this is a mafter-peice of *Anguier* the younger. Of the two great iron rails to the right and left of the high altar, one feparates the church from the choir of the nuns, and the other fhuts up a chapel hung in mourning, which no body is permitted to enter; in the middle of this chapel is raifed a bed of black velvet, with variety of ornaments, where the heart of *Anne* of *Auftria* is repofited. Underneath is made a fmall vault, incrufted with marble, and containing feveral niches where the hearts of the princes and princeffes of the royal family are preferved. Round the dome, in the frize, the following infcription is put in letters of brafs, gilt.

Anna Auftria, D. G. Francorum regina, regnique reftrix, cui fubjecit Deus omnes hoftes, ut conderet domum in nomine fuo.

Anne of *Auftria*, by the grace of God, queen of the *French*, regent of the kingdom, to whom
God

God subjected all enemies, that she might build a house in his name. A. M. D. CL.

In the sacristy a great many rich ornaments, and other valuable things are preserved; and among the rest a golden sun, in which they expose the sacrament, adorned with diamonds, which the workman was seven years about; the fashion alone cost 15,000 livres.

The church of the *Carmelite* nuns, *rue St. Ja-* ques, tho' very antient, and without any delicacy as to the outside, is one of the best adorned within-inside, of any in *Paris*, especially in paintings. The enclosure betwixt the nave and the choir is shut by four columns of sea-green marble, which are very remarkable. The brazen crucifix, over the opening of the door, is an excellent work, by *Sarazin*. The great altar is very much raised; and the disposition of its steps is in a grand taste, as well as the columns, which are of marble of *Dinan*; and the capitals, bases, and modillons, which are of brass, gilt with leaf-gold. The tabernacle is one of the most remarkable things to be seen in this church; it is in the form of the ark of the covenant. All the goldsmiths work is well wrought, especially the front *bass-reliefs*. In one of the chapels there is an excellent marble statute of cardinal *Berulle*, who introduced these nuns into *France*, by *Sarazin*. In the sacristy they have a very rich golden sun for the exposing of the sacrament, which was made them a present by *Madame de la Valiere*.

<small>Carmelite nuns.</small>

The church of the *Sorbonne* is one of the most beautiful in *Paris*. The portal on the side of the square is adorned with two orders, the first of *Corinthian* columns, and the second of *Composite* pilasters. There are two niches in the intercolumniations of the first order, and two in the spaces

<small>The church of the Sorbonne.</small>

The GRAND TOUR.

spaces betwixt the pilasters of the second, adorned with marble statues of *Guillan*. On the top of the door is read this inscription,

Armandus Cardinalis de Richlieu.

Between the door and the sun-dial, you see a small picture, which shews all the phases of the moon. About the dome are four turrets, with bands of gilt lead; and it is terminated by a lantern, with an iron balluftrade, in the same taste as *Val de Grace*. The door on the side of the square is never opened but twice a year on two different festivals, and upon the death of any member of the house of *Sorbonne*. The ordinary entrance is on the side of the court, by another door under a magnificent portico, which projects ten feet, is raised upon fifteen steps, and formed by ten *Corinthian* columns, with this inscription,

Armandus-Johannes Card. Dux de Richlieu, Sorbonnæ provisor, ædificavit domum, & exaltavit templum Sanctum Domino. M.DC.XLII.

Armand John Cardinal, duke of Richlieu, *provisor of the* Sorbonne, *built this house, and elevated the holy temple to the Lord*, M.DC.XLII.

The inside of the church is adorned all round with *Corinthian* pilasters; between which are niches filled with statues of thunder stone, representing either apostles or angels, the work of *Bertelot* and *Guillain*. The pavement is in compartments of marble of different colours. The high altar is adorned with six *Corinthian* columns of marble of *Rance*. Instead of a picture, there is a crucifix of white marble, standing upon a support of black marble. This was *Anguier*'s last piece, but one of the most perfect that came from his hands. The body of the

virgin's

FRANCE.

virgin's chapel is of white marble, and the columns of marble of *Rance*. The bottom of the niche is filled with plates of gilt brass; the marble statue of the virgin, holding the infant *Jesus*, is by *Desjardins*. In the midst of the choir, is the tomb of Cardinal *Richlieu*, one of the most beautiful and most magnificent monuments in *Europe*; it was cut by *Girardon*, in white marble, and erected in 1694. The Cardinal is represented reclining, supported by Religion, with Science afflicted at his feet. Two angels in tears support his arms, adorned with the cardinal's hat, and the ribband of the order of the Holy Ghost.

The church of *Mazarin* college was built by the famous Cardinal *Mazarin*, at the same time as the college: it is round without and oval within, of the *Corinthian* order, paved with black, white, and jasper-coloured marble, in compartments with stars. The portal of the church is formed by four *Corinthian* columns, and two pilasters, that support a fronton, in which is a sun-dial. Above are figures representing the four evangelists, and the fathers of the *Greek* and *Latin* church, with this inscription:

The church of Mazarin college.

Jul. Mazarin. S. R. E. Cardinalis Basilicam et Gymnasium fieri curavit, Anno M.DC.LXI.

Julius Mazarin, cardinal of the holy Roman *church, caused this temple and college to be erected in the year* 1661.

The dome is covered with slate, and adorned with bands of gilt lead; on the top there is a lantern surrounded with an iron ballustrade, crowned by a globe, and a cross with a double traverse. The architect was *d'Orbai*. The eight beatitudes in *basso-relievo*, placed in the angles above the arcades, are by *Desjardins*. Cardinal *Mazarin's rin*'s monument is an exceeding fine piece, by *Coifevox*. The Cardinal is reprefented in white marble, kneeling upon a tomb of black marble; the brazen ftatues that accompany it, were defigned to reprefent the Virtues.

The church of the barefooted Carmelites. The church of the bare-footed *Carmelites* is a handfome ftructure, notwithftanding fome defects in the architecture. The firft foundation was laid in 1610. In the chapel of the Virgin there is an excellent ftatue of Our Lady, with the infant *Jefus*, in white marble, by *Antonio Raggi*, otherwife called the *Lombard*: it is reckoned one of the fineft pieces in *France*; the defign was by Cavalier *Bernini*.

The church of the Celeftins. In the church of the *Celeftin* monks, there are feveral monuments not inferior to the fineft pieces of antient *Rome*; efpecially the chapel of *Orleans* is capable of entertaining the curiofity of connoiffeurs. The tomb of the Duke of *Longueville*, loaded with trophies in white marble, incrufted in the borders with black marble, is by *Anguier*. To adorn it there are four Virtues in white marble, almoft as big as the life.---It is impoffible to help admiring the three Graces which fupport an urn, wherein the hearts of *Henry* II. and *Catherine* of *Medicis* are preferved. They are of marble, or rather of tranfparent alabafter, and were done by the fkilful hand of *Germain Pilon*.---The column of white marble feen there, was erected by *Charles* IX. to the memory of *Francis* II. and here the hearts of the two kings repofe.----The wreathed column of white marble is an ineftimable piece; it fupports a brazen urn, in which is preferved the heart of the Conftable *Anne de Montmorency*, who died in 1567, of the wounds he received at the battle of *S. Denis*. This column is fuppofed to be done by one *Bartholomew* a *French* proteftant, and the brazen Virtues that accompany it, are attributed

tributed to *Germain Pilon*.----The tomb of *Philip Chabot*, admiral of *France*, was done by *John Cousin*, who was an able painter as well as sculptor; though some attribute it to *Paul Ponce*. The other tomb of *Henry Chabot Rohan*, is by *Anguier* the elder. These are two valuable monuments. ----The tomb of the dukes of *Coffe Brisac* is adorned with a column of white marble, accompanied with two genii in white marble. In the chapel of *Tremes* there are some handsome monuments, erected to the dukes of *Gevres*.

The church of S. *Gervaise* is worth seeing, for the sake of its great portal, which is undoubtedly one of the finest pieces of architecture in *Europe*: but it is a pity it does not stand in a better light. It is composed of three orders, one over the other, which altogether form a frontispiece 26 toises in height. It was begun in 1609, under the direction of *Jacques de Brosse*, a famous architect, the same who drew the designs of the palace of *Luxemburg*. The church itself is a great deal older, very large, dark, and in a *Gothic* taste. One should not forget to see the beautiful tapestries that have been made after the pictures of the martyrdom of S. *Gervasius* and *Protasius*, which are preserved, together with the pictures, in this church.

The church of S. Gervaise.

In the church of S. *Nicholas du Chardonnet*, there is a chapel extremely worthy of the curiosity of a traveller, which is that of *Le Brun*. The tomb of this famous painter's mother is a master-piece: she is represented in white marble, as rising out of the tomb, with this inscription, taken from scripture.

Church of S. Nicholas du Chardonnet.

    Satiabor cum apparuerit gloria tua.

    I shall be satisfied when thy glory appears.

This admirable piece was executed by *Colignon*.

On the other face of the chapel, *Le Brun* is reprefented in a marble buft, at the bottom of a pyramid; this is the work of *Coifevox*. In a word, every thing in this chapel is either done or directed by that great artift *Le Brun*, who has done so much honour to *France*.

The church of S. Etienne du Mont.

The pulpit in the church of *S. Etienne du Mont* may be looked upon as one of the moft curious pieces of joiner's work any where extant. Befides the carvings and *bas-reliefs*, which are inimitably fine, the whole is fupported, or feems to be fupported by a large handfome ftatute of *Sampfon* in wood. This admirable work was done by *L'Eftocart*, after the defign of *La Hyre*, a famous *French* painter. In the fame church, on the little altar of the holy facrament, there is a *bas-relief* in marble, which reprefents our Saviour in the garden of olives; it is admirably well done: the fame may be faid of *Chrift* in the tomb, and of the *Maries* that attended him; all by the fame mafter, *Germain Pilon*. The crucifix and the other figures over the door of the choir, are fome of the beft pieces of *John Gougeon*, a *French* fculptor.

The church of S. Euftachius.

The church of *S. Euftachius* is remarkable for the tomb of *M. Colbert*, minifter of ftate to *Lewis* XIV. He is reprefented kneeling on a farcophagus of black marble; and this figure is by *Antony Coifevox*. The angel holding a book open to him, is by *Baptift Tuby*. There are two ftatues fitting, and as big as the life, to fill up the group; one is Plenty, by *Coifevox*, and the other is Religion, by *Tuby*. Upon one of the pillars of the nave of this church is a large *bas-relief* cut by *Tuby*, after a defign of *Le Brun*. It is the epitaph of *Marin Curcau de la Chambre*, who died in 1669.

The church of the Capuchine nuns.

The front of the church of the *Capuchine* nuns in the *Place de Vendome*, is greatly admired.

FRANCE.

The infide, tho' very pretty, contains nothing remarkable but the two following monuments. The chapel on the right hand belongs to the family of *Louvois*, and is one of the handfomeft in Paris. Here is the monument of the marquis *de Louvois*, minifter of ftate to *Lewis* XIV. in white marble. He is reprefented by *Girardon*, in the habit of an officer of the order of the Holy Ghoft, upon a large farcophagus of antient green *Egyptian* marble. The marchionefs *de Louvois*, his confort, is weeping at his feet. The grand bafe is fupported by two virtues in brafs, as big as the life. Prudence under the figure of *Minerva*, is alfo by *Girardon*, and Vigilance by *Desjardins*. The figure of the marchionefs was modelled by *Desjardins*, but finifhed by *Vancleve*. The *bas-relief* in gilt bronze upon the altar, reprefents our Saviour carried to the tomb.---Oppofite to this chapel is that of the family of *Crequi*, which is as beautiful as the former. Here the duke of that name, marfhal of *France*, is interred. He is reprefented in white marble upon a farcophagus. His head is fupported by Hope, and a genius weeps at his feet: two Virtues likewife of marble, are on the fides of the bafe, or patten. This fine monument was conducted by *Mazeline* and *Hurtelle*.

The church called the *Sainte Chapelle*, or *Holy Chapel*, was built by *S. Lewis* in 1145, the architect *Pierre de Montereau*. The boldnefs of it is much admired, though it is of *Gothic* architecture. Among the moft remarkable things, you are to look upon the ftatue of our Lady of *Piety*, which is in the nave, by *Germain Pilon*. The treafure of the holy chapel would be deferving of your curiofity; but as the King's *lettre de cachet* is requifite for that purpofe, very few ftrangers

The Holy Chapel.

can have admission. They may however see the curiosities that are kept in the sacristy, among others the head of *S. Lewis*, supported by two angels; the head and crown are of gold, and the angels of silver gilt: the chanter's staff, at the top of which there is a very considerable agate, representing a half length of *S. Lewis*: the antique onyx, which represents the apotheosis of *Augustus*, is inestimable; it is an oval 15 inches long.

Church of S. Sulpice. The church of *S. Sulpice*, in the suburb of *S. Germain*, will be one of the handsomest, largest, and richest in *France*, when it comes to be finished. The same may be said of the church of *S. Roch*. Travellers should not neglect going to see the famous monument of *Girardon*, made by himself in the church of *S. Landry*. In the church of *S. Sauveur*, they have lately built a chapel, which is worthy the attention of a stranger. We shall conclude this account of the churches of *Paris*, with a common saying among the *French*, viz. that in order to make a fine church, we should join the choir of *Beauvais*, the nave of *Amiens*, the portal of *Rheims*, the bells of *Chartres*, and the steeple of *Notre Dame* at *Paris*.

II. ROYAL PALACES.

The Louvre. Next to the sacred structures come the royal palaces, the chief of which is the *Louvre*, situate in that quarter of the town which goes by its name, on the banks of the river *Seine*. Its very name bespeaks its grandeur, signifying a finished work, by way of excellence. The *Louvre* is distinguished into the old and the new: the old
is

is that which is finished, and the other is that which we may say is only begun. The old Old Louvre. Louvre took several reigns to complete it. It was begun by *Francis* I. after the designs of the abbot of *Clagny*, which were preferred to those of *Sebastian Serlio* an *Italian*. It was continued by *Henry* II. and after him by *Lewis* XIII. Among other things the carved ornaments, by *John Gougeon*, a celebated artist, are much admired. The new *Louvre* was undertaken and carried New Louvre. on by *Lewis* XIV. only for three years, from 1667 to 1670, after the designs and under the direction of *Lewis le Vau*, a native of *Paris*, and after his decease, under the care of *Francis d'Orbai*, his pupil. Some attribute the designs of the *Louvre* to *Charles Perrault*, the translator of *Vitruvius*. The king did not think proper to follow the design of cavalier *Bernini*, whom he had sent for from *Rome*: but the models made by this famous artist are preserved in the academy of architecture. The grand front is 27 toises and a half in length, consisting of three advanced structures, and two peristyles. The principal entrance is into the middle structure, which is adorned with eight coupled columns. The pediment which terminates it is remarkable, consisting only of two stones, taken out of the quarries of *Meudon*, each of them 54 feet in length, eight feet broad, and eighteen inches thick; each of the peristyles, betwixt these advanced structures, is 27 toises long, and twelve broad. Their columns are *Corinthian* fluted and coupled, three feet seven inches in diameter. Instead of a pediment, there is a ballustrade all round, supported upon pedestals. The old *Louvre* has three stories; and the advanced structures are adorned with columns. The windows of the second order are very much esteemed

esteemed by the curious. In the hall of the hundred *Swifs* there are four gigantic figures, which support a kind of gallery; they are the work of *John Gougeon*; and *Sarazin* has copied them upon the Attic of the grand pavilion in the middle. The principal entrance of the *Louvre* on the side of the *Thuilleries*, is a porch, adorned with two ranks of double columns, in the *Ionic* order: this great pavilion *James Mercier* had the direction of under *Lewis* XIII. The inside of the *Louvre* corresponds to the external magnificence. As to the paintings we shall take notice of them in their proper place. The *French* academies of the belles lettres, the sciences, architecture, and painting, are held in the *Louvre*. In the halls which are occupied by the academy of painting, you see the capital performances done by the painters and sculptors to obtain the rank of academicians. The statues preserved in one of these halls are very remarkable, being excellent copies after the antiques. Most of the antiquities, *Roman* statues, and fine paintings, formerly preserved in this palace, have been since removed to *Versailles*. The gallery which joins the *Louvre* to the palace of the *Thuilleries* is 227 toises long: it was built under different reigns, and by different architects: the connoisseurs admire inimitable beauties in it. Here it is that the plans in *relief* of the principal fortresses in *Europe* are preserved. The number of these plans are about 170, which cost *Lewis* XIV. near five millions: the greatest part of them were made by *John Berthier*; but foreigners are not easily permitted to see them.

Inside of the Louvre.

The

The palace of the *Thuilleries*, is so called, from its having been built on a spot where tiles were formerly made. It was begun in 1554, by *Catherine* of *Medicis*, the architect *Philip de L'Orme*. *Henry* IV. finished it in 1700; but *Lewis* XIV. after the designs of *Le Vau*, and under the direction of *Francis d'Orbay*, gave it its present perfection. This palace is composed of five pavilions, and four sides, in which the architecture is admired, though differently treated. The sculpture is by the principal masters; and the whole is built upon a right line about 170 toises long. The large pavilion in the middle, is adorned with columns of marble on the side of the *Carousel*; those on the side of the garden, are of stone only. There is one among the rest, which is greatly admired. After ascending the stair-caise, which is ingeniously contrived, you enter the king's great apartment. As for the paintings here we shall mention them in their proper place. The figures of sculpture, which support the stucco chimney, in the king's great chamber, are by *Girardon*; and the others by *Lewis Lerambert*. The place where balls and plays were formerly exhibited before the court, is called the hall of machines. It is able to contain eight thousand persons commodiously placed, and is perhaps the finest theatre in *Europe*, that of *Parma* excepted.

The garden of the *Thuilleries* is the pleasantest and most frequented walk in *Paris*. It was begun by *Henry* IV. in 1600, and finished by *Lewis* XIV. in 1660. The famous *Andrew Le Notre* made the designs, and had the direction of the whole garden. The length of it is 360 toises, and the breadth 68, containing in all

67 * arpents of land. Mechanics and livery servants are forbid to enter this garden at the time of walking. The three principal alleys are 165 toises long; and that in the middle is 15 toises in breadth. The great terrass on the side of the river, which forms the principal ornament of the garden, is 280 toises in length, and 14 in breadth. There are four fountains in the garden, two of which have basons of pretty large circumference. On the side of the palace are six statues, and two vases of white marble. The hunter and the two huntresses next the river, are by *Coutou*. The fawn, the Hamadriad, and the goddess *Flora*, are by *Coijevox*. Of the four groups of marble figures, round the great bason of the parterre, the first is by *Flamand*; it represents the rape of *Orithia*, or rather Time carrying off Beauty. The second is the rape of *Ceres* by *Saturn*, under the figure of Time by *Renaudin*. The third is *Lucretia* stabbing herself before *Collatinus*: it was begun at *Rome* by *Theodon*, but finished at *Paris* by *Le Pautre*, who likewise carved the fourth, which represents *Æneas* carrying off his father *Anchises*, with his houshold gods, and his son *Ascanius*. In the semicircle, which forms the horseshoe, there are four marble rivers, upon pedestals of the same. The *Seine* is by *Coutou*; the *Loire* by *Vancleve*, the *Nile* and the *Tiber* were copied at *Rome* from antiques preserved in the capitol. At the further end of the garden, between the openings of the horseshoe, you see two figures on horse-back of very large size, raised upon rustic jambs; they are *Mercury* and *Fame* by *Coisevox*.

* An *arpent* is a *French* measure of land, containing 100 perches square, of 18 feet.

The palace of *Luxemburg* is reckoned the most regular building in *France*, and admired also for its magnificence: it was built under the direction of *Jaeques de Broſſe*, a *French* architect, by *Mary* of *Medicis*, who laid the foundation of it in 1615. This queen bought of *Henry* of *Luxemburg*, duke of *Pinei*, an old hôtel, upon the ruins of which ſhe erected a new palace, which ſtill preſerves the name of *Luxemburg*. She left it by her will to *John Gaſton* duke of *Orleans*, brother of *Lewis* XIII. which is the reaſon of *Palais d'Orleans* being written over the gate, though now it belongs to the king. The ground upon which this palace is built, is one of the higheſt ſpots in *Paris*. The architect is ſaid to have imitated in many parts the palace of the grand duke at *Florence*. The face of this palace, towards the ſtreet, is an open gallery, with a pavilion in the middle, enriched with two rows of columns, and crowned in the circumference with a round dome. Beneath this pavilion is the principal entrance, adorned with four *Doric* columns with niches betwixt them. Four large arcades form as many openings for the upper ſtory. Theſe arcades are each of them accompanied with four columns, and adorned within by marble columns. Two large ſquare pavilions, which project farther than the other parts of the face, form the extremities of the terraſſes, where you ſee the marble ſtatues of *Henry* IV. and of *Mary* of *Medicis*, tolerably well executed. The court is very large: on the two ſides are two galleries lower than the reſt of the building, ſupported each by nine arcades, which form covered paſſages. At the bottom of this

The Luxemburg.

this court is the principal body of apartments, which has four pavilions at the extremities and an advanced body in the middle. Under this pavilion are the stair-case, and the passage to the garden. This architecture is regularly composed of the *Tuscan, Doric,* and *Ionic* orders. They are accompanied with double pilasters, which have ballustrades and pediments on the roof, with statues reclining. But there is nothing more admired in this palace, than the great gallery on the right, containing the history of *Mary* of *Medicis,* in twenty large pieces, each ten feet high, and painted by the famous *Rubens.* The gardens have lost a great deal of their beauty, yet still are pleasant, and may be reckoned the finest walk in *Paris,* next to the *Thuilleries.* The remains of the ballustrades in white marble, upon the front of the terrasses, deserve particular notice, being so regular and well proportioned, as to be proposed for a model, by *Francis Blondel,* in his course of architecture.

Palace Royal. The Palace Royal was begun by cardinal *Richlieu* 1629, under the direction of *Jacques Le Mercier.* It was at first called the *hotel de Richlieu*; and afterwards *Palais Cardinal.* The cardinal having made a present of this palace i his life-time to *Lewis* XIII. *Anne* of *Austria* made it her residence in 1642, being then regent; and since it has been always called *Palace Royal. Lewis* XIV. afterwards settled it upon the duke of *Orleans,* in consideration for the duke's marrying *Mary* of *Bourbon,* the king's natural daughter. It consists of several piles of building, separated by spacious courts, the two largest of which are in the middle. The antient edifice, though of great extent,

extent, has nothing in it very remarkable, either in the apartments or the outward fronts. The invention of the whole is very simple. The Cardinal is said to have made it so plain on purpose, lest it should create the envy of the nobility. But the new apartments, which are large and commodious, are greatly esteemed; and the outward decoration has some beauty and regularity. The great gallery was designed by *Julius Hardouin Mansart*; and the apartment occupied by the Duke of *Orleans*, was designed by *Oppenord*, first architect to his highness. The new gallery is one of the finest that can be seen. The chimney, which is all of green marble, with large groups of gilt bronze, and many other rich ornaments, is esteemed one of the most magnificent that ever was executed. The bronzes alone cost ten thousand crowns. The design of the gallery is *Mansart's*; but the chimney is by *Oppenord*. But the greatest curiosity in this place, is the rich collection of pictures made by the Duke of *Orleans*, regent of *France*. The gardens belonging to this palace are small, but extremely well designed, by *Andrew Le Notre*, the same who laid out the garden of the *Thuilleries*: they are free for the inhabitants to walk in, and have been rendered more commodious by some late improvements.

Palace of Bourbon.

The palace of *Bourbon* is in *rue de Bourbon*, and belongs to the family of *Bourbon Condé*. It is, beyond all doubt, the most elegant, and at the same time one of the most magnificent buildings in *France*. It was begun in 1722, under the direction of *M. Hubert*; but the designs were drawn by *M. Gabriel*; and the whole

whole is finished in the utmost beauty. The carving in the pediments by *M. Coutoux*, deserve particular attention. The furniture of the whole palace is extremely magnificent. The gardens are in as fine a taste as the palace: the view of them on the side of the river, over against the *Thuilleries*, is charming.

III. HOTELS.

Next to the royal palaces, and those belonging to the blood royal, come the *Hotels*, or palaces of the nobility, most of which are magnificent buildings, with large courts and gardens. As there are a great number of these hotels in *Paris*, we should exceed the limits of our plan, if we entered into a detail of each; we shall therefore only give an account of some of the most curious, and to which there is the easiest access.

Hotel d'Antin. The hotel *d'Antin* is one of the first that is recommended to the curiosity of strangers. The architecture has nothing remarkable, but the furniture is some of the richest in *Europe*. The late duke *d'Antin*, director general of the king's buildings, adorned it not only with a great deal of magnificent furniture of his own, but also with many pieces of tapestry, and pictures of great value, belonging to the king. Among other pictures, the following are remarkable; a *Venus*, by *Titian*; a *S. Michael*, by *Raphael*; a *David* and a *S. John*, by *Domenichino*; the little *Cupids*, by *Albani*; *Æneas*, by *Caracci*; a *S. Stephen*, by the same, *&c*. In a gallery of this hotel, you see the history of *Don Quixote*, in twenty-two peices of tapestry, which the duke *d'Antin* had ordered to be made at the *Gobelins*.

The

FRANCE.

Hotel de Toulouse. The hotel *de Toulouse* was built towards the year 1620, after the designs of *Francis Mansart*, and was called the *Hotel de Vrilliere*, from its owner, till it came into the possession of the count *de Toulouse* in 1713. The two statues, *Mars* and *Pallas*, over the gate, were carved by *M. Perrier*. In the apartment on the ground floor, there is a hall with the portraits of all the admirals of *France*, to the number of sixty-six. In this hotel there are a great many pictures by the most eminent masters; the gallery is extremely magnificent, being 120 feet high, and twenty broad. The ornaments of sculpture are by *Vasse*. The ceiling was painted by *Francis Perrier*, in 1645; he has represented *Apollo* and the four Seasons. The pictures are all by eminent masters. *Furius Camillus*, by *Poussin*; *Coriolanus*, by *Guercino*; *Romulus* and *Remus*, by *Pietro di Cortona*; *Helena*, by *Guido*; *Cæsar* repudiating his wife *Pompeia*, by *Pietro di Cortona*; the battle of the *Romans* and the *Sabines*, by *Guercino*; *Cæsar* shutting the temple of *Janus*, by *Carlo Maratti*; a nobleman in his night-gown, by *Valentini*; a *Sibyl*, by *Pietro di Cortona*; the death of *Mark Antony*, by *Alexander Veronese*.

Hotel d'Evreux. The hotel *d'Evreux* is remarkable, not only for its furniture, like a great many others, but likewise for its architecture, being one of the most regular and handsomest buildings in *France*. The front on the side of the garden is the most remarkable. This hotel was erected in 1718, after the designs of *Molet*, by the count *d'Evreux*, a nobleman of the family of *Bouillon*. The furniture is suitable to the building; especially the lustres are of the most exquisite beauty. You may ask to see a moving picture, which is in a closet belonging to the count.

Hotel de Maine.

The hotel *de Maine*, in the *rue de Bourbon*, was begun in 1716, after the designs of *Decotte*, first architect to the king. The duchess of *Maine* bought it of the princess of *Conti*, second dowager. It is a very large building, greatly deserving the curiosity of a stranger, especially on the account of its furniture, which is extremely rich, and in the most elegant taste. The *Chinese* saloon is really magnificent, and has cost very near a hundred thousand livres. The little oratory is full of pictures in miniature, with light green frames. The portraits of the whole family of the duke of *Maine*, were painted by *M. de Troye*, the father; the same who painted that of the duchess, studying the sphere, with a mathematical teacher.

Hotel de Richlieu.

The hotel *de Richlieu* in the *place Royale*, is not only remarkable for its costly furniture, and the number of its fine pictures, but likewise boasts of a *Chinese* cabinet, the richest and the most elegant that can be imagined; it was made by the duke of *Richlieu* after his return from his embassy at *Vienna*.—The famous picture, called the *Quos Ego* of *Rubens*, formerly belonging to the duchess of *Richlieu*, came from *M. de la Faye*, who purchased it of an *English* nobleman for ten thousand livres.

Maison du president Lambert.

The house belonging to the president *Lambert*, *rue St. Louis dans l'Isle*, is very beautiful and regular. The architect was *Louis le Vau*. Its prospects are extremely fine, being the best situated in *Paris*, next to the house of *M. de Bretonvilliers*. But it is still more remarkable for the beauty and number of its paintings. Among other valuable peices in the great hall, is the rape of the *Sabines*, one of *Bassano*'s best pieces. In the great closet behind the hall, the fine large pictures representing the history of *Æneas*, are by *Romanelli*. The ceiling, which represents the birth of *Love*, was done

done by *Le Sueur*: the picture over the chimney is by the same hand. The apartment above is still more magnificent. The ceiling of that gallery is by *Le Brun*, who has exerted his whole skill, not to be outdone by *Le Sueur*, who worked at the same time in the same house. All the pictures in the closet are by *Le Sueur*, and some pretend that these are his best performances. On the ceiling he has represented *Phaeton* guiding the chariot of the Sun. The nine Muses, in different pictures, adorn the alcove in the same closet.

The hotel *de Bretonvilliers*, though at present only the general office *des Aides & Gabelles*, is worthy of particular notice. The extent of this building is very large, and the situation the most advantageous that can be imagined. The pictures in the lower hall are by *Mignard*, from the beautiful originals of *Raphael*; and the gallery of the first apartment was all painted by *Bourdon*. <small>Hotel de Bretonvilliers.</small>

The house of *M. Croizat, rue de Richlieu*, was formerly noted for one of the finest collections of pictures in *France*. But it was sold at the death of *M. Croizat:* and at present the curious have nothing to admire but the house itself, which is large, elegant, and adorned with handsome gardens. The lovers of painting may take notice of a master-piece of *La Fosse*, which is still to be seen, namely the ceiling of the gallery. <small>House of M. Croizat.</small>

The hotel *de Soubize* formerly belonged to the dukes of *Guise*, the court is one of the largest and most magnificent in *France*: it is surrounded by a colonade, the roof of which is bordered with balustrades; and the portal, which is also in an elegant taste, is adorned with columns and trophies, and with the arms of the *Soubize* family, to whom it now belongs. The stair-case is not only <small>Hotel de Soubize.</small>

only large and regular, but has been enriched with very fine paintings in *fresco*, which are suitable to the new apartments.

Hotel de Rohan.
The hotel occupied by the cardinal *de Rohan*, bishop of *Strasburg*, is remarkable for its library, and for the beautiful front on the side next the garden. The fine portal of the church of the *Fathers of Mercy*, just finished, is an additional ornament to the prospect of this court.

Hotel de Lassay.
The hotel *de Lassay*, belonging to the marquis of that name, is very near the palace of *Bourbon*, and is built with the same exactness. The furniture is almost as excellent; but there is moreover a very fine collection of pictures, by the most eminent *Italian* masters.

IV. *The Hotel* de Ville, *the* Bastille, *and the* Arsenal.

Hotel de Ville.
The hotel *de Ville* is the town-house or guildhall of *Paris*; it stands upon the square called the *Greve*, by the river side, and makes but an indiffernt appearance. It was founded by *Frances* I. in 1553, and finished by *Henry* IV. after the designs of *Dominic* of *Cortona*. It has a handsome front of stone, but in the *Gothic* taste, with a spire over the gate, two pavilions at the ends, a spacious hall, and some commodious apartments. The equestrian statue of *Henry* IV. over the door, is by *Peter Biard*, a disciple of *Michael Angelo*. The pedestrian statue of *Lewis* XIV. in brass, at the lower end of the court, is by *Coisevox*. In the apartments there are several portraits, by *Porbus Bobrun*, and *l'Argillicre*. Underneath are vaults of great and very curious construction, where the wines are kept that belong to the public
maga-

magazine. In this hotel they daily pay above 100,000 livres, for the annuities upon the Aids and Gabelles. In the square before this building public rejoicings are solemnized, and here likewise criminals are executed.

The *Bastille* is a large mass of building, somewhat like the tower of *London*, composed of eight large towers, and other fortifications. It is said to have been built in 1371, under the reign of *Charles* V. to defend the city of *Paris* against the incursions of the *English*. The ditches and ramparts that surround it, were made in 1534. This castle is now made use of only to confine state-prisoners. It is open for all who have a mind to see it one day in the year, the octave of the feast of *Corpus Christi*. Those who are not so strictly confined, may walk in a large garden, which is within the inclosure of the building. The arms are kept in the *Bastille*, in a very curious magazine. The government of this place is an important post, and usually entrusted to men of merit and probity.

The *Arsenal* is a spacious pile, consisting of three great courts, with a garden; the portal is supported by cannon instead of pillars. Here the artillery of the kingdom is cast, and the powder preserved. *Charles* V. built it at the same time as the *Bastille*. The grand saloon is remarkable for the paintings of *Mignard*. Here are a great many artificers employed by the king, in casting of statues, and other works of metal. Mr. *Titon* lives in one of the courts of the *Arsenal*: his cabinet is very curious, particularly the representation of *Parnassus* in bronze. The garden of the *Arsenal* is open for the public.

V. Ho-

V. Hospitals.

The hospitals of *Paris* are about thirty in number, some founded for poor and infirm persons, others for orphans, mad people, vagrants, and incurables. Of these the principal are the *Hotel Dieu*, or the house of God; the hospital of *Charity*; the hospital *General*; the hospital called the *Little Houses*; and the *Royal Hospital* for the invalids.

Hotel Dieu. The hotel *Dieu* is the most antient hospital in *Paris*. It is a very large building, situate in the quarter called the *City*; but neither handsome nor convenient, the houses being too close about it for the numerous patients with which it is sometimes crowded; for the ordinary number amounts to 3000 persons, who generally lie two in a bed. It is the chief hospital for the sick in *Paris*, and receives all people that are brought hither, whether natives or foreigners. The sick are attended by the nuns of S. *Austin*, with great care and tenderness. In the hospital of *Charity*, the friars of S. *John* perform the same offices as the nuns do in the former.

Hospital General. The hospital *General*, is a vast pile of building which owes its foundation to the president *de Bellièvre* and Mr. *Foquet*. The king's edict for its establishment bears date in 1656. The archbishop of *Paris*, the chief president of the parliament, and the attorney general, are perpetual governors of this hospital. In this great inclosure there are six distinct houses, one for poor old women and girls; another for poor families and foundling children; the others for poor lying in women, beggars, vagrants, &c. the whole number amounting to about 11,000 persons, who are made to work when they are well; and

taken

taken care of in their illnefs. Particularly there are near three thoufand girls, who work, fome at lace-making others at embroidery and tapeftry. The greateft part of them are foundlings. The church which was defigned by *Liberal Bruant*, is fufficiently large and beautiful.

In the hofpital called the *Little Houfes*, the curious have nothing to fee but mad people, as in our *Bedlam*. It was eftablifhed in 1557, and the attorney-general has the chief direction of it. The *Petites Maifons*.

The *Royal Hofpital of Invalids*, in the quarter of *S. Germain*, for the wounded, infirm, and aged foldiers, is much the moft magnificent of any in *Paris*. *Lewis* XIV. founded it in 1671, and finifhed it in 1678, under the direction of *Liberal Bruant*, a famous *French* architect, who imitated in this building the pope's palace of *Monte Cavallo* at *Rome*. As to the conftruction of this edifice, the outward form is a regular fquare, which covers an extent of ground of feventeen arpents. The whole is compofed of five handfome quadrangles, built of hewn-ftone, the largeft of which is in the middle of the reft. The fquares are furrounded with piazzas and galleries above them, which make a moft noble appearance. In the refectories where the foldiers eat, moft of the famous battles and fieges that were fought in *Lewis* XIV's time, are painted on the walls. The apothecary's fhop is beautifully contrived, and well furnifhed; and the fick are attended by the fifters of *S. Lazarus*. There are ufually entertained in this hofpital 7000 men, officers and foldiers. The officers lie two in a chamber, and the private men fix or feven in a room; every one has a bed to himfelf, and may follow what bufinefs he likes. They eat in common, but each man has his portion of meat ferved up to him; The Invalids.

him; they are permitted to go abroad and negotiate their affairs twice a week. The soldiers mount guard daily at the gates of the hospital, as in a fortified town. There is a governor, a king's lieutenant, and a major. The fathers of *S. Lazarus* have the spiritual care of this place, as well as of many other royal foundations. The kitchens are worth seeing, being vastly large, and surprisingly neat. There are two churches belonging to this hospital the one internal, for the use of those of the hospital, and the other external for strangers. The external is called the new church, and is justly allowed to be one of the finest buildings in *France*. But of this church, see a description, p. 45.

The church of the Invalids.

VI. *Public* SQUARES.

Though there are several public squares in *Paris*, yet three are particularly remarkable, because of the brazen statues with which they are adorned, viz. *Place Royale*, *Place des Victoires*, and the *Place de Louis le Grand*, or *Place Vendôme*.

Place Royale. *Place Royale* was built in 1604, under the reign of *Henry* IV. at the expence of several private persons. Upon this spot formerly stood the garden and the hotel *des Tournelles*, which were built by *Charles* V. and had been the residence of the kings of *France* his successors, till the reign of *Henry* II. Then it was that *Catharine* of *Medicis* left it, and it was sold to different private persons. It is now a perfect square of 72 toises. Of each side are nine pavilions of stone and brick, of the same height and symmetry, all covered with slate. On the side next the street of *S. Lewis*, where the square is open, there is one pavilion less. The houses that form this inclosure are

FRANCE.

are not greatly ornamented without, tho' very large and handsome within. At the bottom there is a range of arcades, in the manner of a corridor, but very low. The center of the square is a large grafs plat, furrounded and inclofed with beautiful iron rails: upon each of the two gates there is a medallion of *Lewis* XIII. under whofe reign the iron-work and all the ornaments were put up. In the middle of the grafs plat is an equeftrian ftatue of *Lewis* XIII. erected on a large pedeftal of white marble. The horfe was made by *Daniel Ricciarelli* of *Volterra*, a pupil of *Michael Angelo*, and is perfectly well done. The ftatue is the work of *Biard*, and not near fo eftimable. It has been an old and trite remark at *Paris*, that the horfe of *Lewis* XIII. fhould be given to *Henry* IV. upon the new bridge, to make a compleat monument. The four fides of the pedeftal are filled with infcriptions in praife of *Lewis* XIII. and cardinal *Richlieu* his minifter.

The *place des Victoires* is fo denominated, becaufe the ftatue of *Lewis* XIV. in the middle, with four flaves enchained, denotes his victories. It was erected by the duke *de Fuillade* in 1684, at his own expence, the city contributing five hundred thoufand crowns towards it. This place is of an oval figure, none of the largeft, being only forty toifes in diameter; but there are fix ftreets that terminate in it, which renders it extremely light and open. All the buildings round it are in exact proportion; on the outfide they are adorned with a range of pilafters in the *Ionic* order, fupported by arcades. In the midft of the place is a ftatue of *Lewis* XIV. in gilt *bronze*, upon a pedeftal of white veined marble. The king is reprefented ftanding, in his habit of ceremony, ufed at his coronation, with a *Cerberus* at his

Place des Victoires.

his feet, and Victory behind him, putting a crown of laurel upon his head, and with the other hand she holds a branch of laurel and palms intermixed. The whole group is thirteen feet high, and was cast at once, thirty thousand weight of metal being employed for that purpose. Under the statue is this vain inscription, *Viro Immortali*. *To the immortal man*. The pedestal on which this group stands, is twenty-two feet high; it is adorned with *baſſo-relievos*, and large projections at the bottom. Four captives in *bronze*, as chained to the pedestal, are at the four corners, accompanied with a great number of trophies. Each of these slaves is much larger than the life. This pedestal is surrounded with iron rails six feet high. It was *Desjardins* who drew the designs of this statue, and was present at the casting of it.

Place Ven- The square by some called *La place de Louis le dome. Grand*, and by others, *Place Vendome*, is a large octagon, open towards the street *S. Honoré*, where the hotel *de Vendome* formerly stood. *Lewis* XIV. purchased it in 1681, for six hundred and sixty thousand crowns. In 1699 the place was begun, as it appears at present, after the designs of *Julius Harduin Manſart*. All the buildings are magnificent and uniform, inhabited by persons of the first quality, or by rich farmers of the revenue. The length of the square is 75 toises, and the breadth 70. Yet its greatest ornament is the fine equestrian statue in *bronze* of *Lewis* XIV. erected in the middle of the square, the 13th of *August* 1699. The king is represented in the dress of a hero of antiquity, without saddle or spurs. The statue and horse are twenty-two feet two inches high; the whole cast at once by *Balthasar Keller*, a native of *Zurich* in *Swiſſerland*, but designed by *Girardon*. Fourscore thousand weight of metal were

were employed in this work, which cost two hundred thousand crowns. The pedestal on which this horse stands, is thirty feet high, twenty-four long and thirteen broad.

VII. GATES.

They reckon twenty gates at *Paris*, but the principal ones are those of *S. Dennis, S. Antony, S. Bernard,* and *S. Martin,* which are all stately pieces of architecture, with *Basso relievos*, trophies, and inscriptions, designed as so many triumphal arches, to eternize the memory of that vain prince, *Lewis* XIV.

Gate of S. Denis. The gate of *S. Dennis* is the most beautiful in *Paris.* It was designed by *Francis Blondel,* who also wrote the inscriptions. The height of it is 72 feet and the breadth as many. The opening is 24 feet: on the sides of it are two pyramids, charged with military trophies. The upper part is open, after the manner of the ancient triumphal arches. There is a large *Basso relievo* upon the center of the side next the city, which represents the passage of the *Rhine*; and on the side next to the suburb, is the taking of *Mastricht,* with two inscriptions. 'The ornaments of sculpture were begun by *Girardon*; but upon the king's calling him off to other work, they were finished by *Anguier* the elder.

Gate of S. Antony. The gate of *S. Antony* was intended for a triumphal arch to *Henry* II. It was afterwards greatly embellished in 1671, after the designs of *Francis Blondel,* who preserved however all the antient gate, and the antient architecture of the *Doric* order. The whole building is eight toises high, and nine in breadth; it contains a great number of ornaments in sculpture, with variety of inscriptions to the memory of *Lewis* XIV. The most beautiful front is on the side of the suburb. The two rivers, there represented, the *Seine* and the *Maine*, are greatly esteemed. They were cut by *John Gougeon* for the antient gate. The statue of *Lewis* XIV. which is in the middle at top, was cut by *Gerard Van Opstat*, a *Flemish* sculptor; as were likewise the *Apollo* and the *Ceres* upon the pediments. the two statues in the niches were by *Anguier* the elder. This gate, take it altogether, is magnificent and beautiful.

The gate of S. Bernard.
The gate of *S. Bernard* took its name from a convent of *Bernardines* in its neighbourhood. It is ten toises high, and eight in breadth. The designs of it were drawn by *Francis Blondel* in 1670. On the side next the town, you see *Lewis* XIV. in high *relievo*, by *Tuby*, diffusing plenty among his subjects, with an inscription in *Latin*. The other *basso-relievo* on the side of the suburb, is by the same *Tuby*; it represents *Lewis* XIV. under the figure of a Divinity, holding the rudder of a ship, with an inscription.

The gate of S. Martin.
The gate of *S. Martin* was erected after the designs of *Peter Bullet* in 1674. It is in the form of a triumphal arch; the architecture is rustic embossed work vermiculated, with *basso-relievos* in the tympanums. Its height is about fifty feet, and its breadth as many. The sculptures that appear on this gate, were done by four eminent masters, *Desjardins*, *Marsy*, *d'Hongre*, and *Le Gros*. There are two inscriptions.

Great and little Chatelet.
The great and little *Chatelet* were the gates of *Paris*, when the city was confined to the *island of the palace*, surrounded by the branches of the *Seine*. The great *Chatelet* was, according to tradition, built by *Julius Cæsar*, of which there are

FRANCE.

are only some antique towers remaining, all the rest having been built since the year 1684. Here the courts of justice are held for the provostship and viscounty of *Paris*; and it serves likewise for a prison for criminals. The little *Chatelet* is also an antient fortress, and a prison for criminals, in the same manner as the great *Chatelet*.

VIII. BRIDGES and FOUNTAINS.

Paris has a great many bridges over the several branches of the river *Seine*. We shall here take notice only of five or six, which are the most remarkable, viz. the *Pont Neuf*, *Pont Royal*, *Pont Notre Dame*, *Le Pont au Change*, *Le Pont S. Michael*, and *Le Pont de la Tournelle*. As for the two first, they are not only extremely convenient to the city of *Paris*, but likewise form a great part of its beauty. And indeed the *Pont Neuf*, and *Pont Royal*, are two of the finest structures of the kind in *Europe*. The beauty and solidity of their construction, the fine prospect they afford, and the continual concourse of passengers, all contribute to raise our surprize.

Pont Neuf, or the new bridge, was begun in 1578, in the reign of *Henry* III. and under the conduct of *James Androuet du Cerceau*. This work having been discontinued on the account of the civil war, it was not finished till 1604, by the orders of *Henry* IV. who employed *William Marchand* the architect. This bridge is 170 toises long, and twelve broad. The breadth is divided into three parts; the middle, which serves for coaches and other carriages, is five toises wide; and the two foot-ways take up the rest. It consists of twelve arches, five on the side of the *Augustines*, and seven on the side of the *Louvre*.

Pont Neuf.

Equestrian statue of Henry IV. The equestrian statue of *Henry* IV. is a great ornament to this bridge. It was put up in 1635. The four figures in *bronze*, of slaves enchained, as well as the *baſſo relievos*, which repreſent the principal actions of *Henry* IV. were deſigned and caſt by *Franceville*. The figure of the king was done by a ſculptor, whoſe name was *Dupré*; but the horſe was by *John* of *Bologna*, a diſciple of the famous *Michael Angelo*. *Coſmo* II. grand duke of *Tuſcany*, made a preſent of it to *Mary* of *Medicis*, at that time regent of *France*.

The Samaritan. Here the little building of the *Samaritan* woman deſerves ſome notice. You may go into it, to ſee the pump, by means of which, water is conveyed to the *Louvre*, and to many other places in the town. This building was finiſhed in 1715, after the deſigns of *Coſté*; that which ſtood there in the reign of *Henry* III. having been deſtroyed in 1712. *Bertrand* cut the figure of our Saviour, below the clock; and *Fermin* that of the *Samaritan* woman. Theſe two figures, as well as the baſon in the middle, are of metal, and the colour of *bronze*, and the whole is extremely well done.

Pont Royal. *Pont Royal*, or royal bridge, is not ſo much beautified as *Pont Neuf*, but it is full as ſtrong, and enjoys as pleaſant a proſpect. It was built in the room of a wooden ſtructure, called the *Red bridge*. The deſign was by *Julius Harduin Manſard*; and the work was conducted by father *Francis Romain*, a *Dominican* friar, who began it in 1685. The length ſupported by five arches, is about ſeventy toiſes, and the breadth eight toiſes four feet, with foot-ways on the ſides, in imitation of thoſe upon *Pont Neuf*.

Pont Notre Dame. *Pont Notre Dame*, or the *Bridge of our Lady*, was built in 1507, under the direction of *Giovanni Giocondo*, a *Cordelier* of *Verona*. There was

was a wooden bridge in the room of it, which fell down in 1499. This bridge is all along loaded with houses, like *London* bridge; having thirty-four on each side. The fronts of these houses are adorned with large *terms*, which have baskets of flowers and fruit on their heads. Betwixt these *terms* are medallions, on which the kings of *France* are represented. The square gate of the *Ionic* order, which you see on the middle of the bridge, leads to the water engine. This consists of two hydraulic machines, which raise the water of the *Seine* 80 feet, to distribute it afterwards into seventeen or eighteen fountains. These machines are worth seeing. The design of the gate is *Bulet*'s, and the *basso relievos*, which represent a river and a Naiad, are by *John Gougeon*. The beautiful epigram over the gate, graved on black marble, was composed by *Santeuil*.

Water Engine.

Sequana cum primum Reginæ allabitur urbi,
  Tardat præcipites ambitiosus aquas.
Captus amore loci cursum obliviscitus, anceps
  Quo fluat, & dulces nectit in urbe moras.
Hinc varios implens fluctu subeunte canales,
  Fons fieri gaudet, qui modo flumen erat.

There are a great many other bridges in *Paris*, some with houses as the *Pont aux Changes*, and *Pont S. Michel*, &c. Others without houses, as the *petit Pont*, the *Pont de la Tournelle*, the *Pont Marie*, &c.

Tho' there are a great many cities that excel *Paris* in fountains, yet there is no piece of workmanship of the kind superior to that of the *Innocents*. It was erected in 1550 in *S. Dennis* street. This piece of work, even in its present ruinous condition, ought to be looked upon as a noble

The fountain of the Holy Innocents.

noble performance. The design of the architecture was by the abbot of *Clugny*, the same who gave the drawings of the *Louvre*. The excellent *basso-relievos*, which represent the Naiads in different attitudes, are by *John Gougeon*.

IX. COLLEGES.

<small>The University.</small>
<small>Its antiquity and colleges.</small>
The university of *Paris* gives name to that part of the town which is situated on the south side of the river *Seine*. It was founded about the latter end of the eleventh century, and their first statutes were instituted in 1215, by *Robert Corceon*, legate of the holy see, in which there is no mention made of any other faculties, but arts, philosophy, and divinity. *Innocent* III. introduced the canon law about the year 1216, and a Bull of pope *Gregory* in 1231, shews that there were physicians at that time members of this university. They did not read civil law till the last century, when lectures were instituted for the civil law and the common law of the nation; their schools being first founded only for the liberal arts. The university consisted formerly of an hundred colleges, but there are only fifty four houses at present that bear that name, and of these no more than eleven where public exercises are performed, viz. the college of *Sorbonne*, *Du Plessis*, *Harcourt*, *Beauvais*, *le Moine*, *de la Marche*, *de Lisieux*, *de Montagu*, *de Grassins*, and *Mazarin*, or the four nations. The *Sorbonne* and the college *de Navarre*, are appropriated chiefly to divinity; the schools for law are in the street *de Beauvais*; and the physicians have a fine anatomical theatre in the street *de Boucherie*, with a hall where they read lectures.

<small>The college of Sorbonne.</small>
The *Sorbonne* is esteemed one of the finest colleges in *Europe*, and of such reputation, that
the

FRANCE.

the whole university is sometimes denominated the *Sorbonne*. It received its name from *Robert de Sorbon*, a canon of the church of *Paris*, who founded it in 1252; the structure was but mean, till cardinal *Richlieu* rebuilt it in a most magnificent manner. The beautiful church has been already described, p. 49. As to the library, see what we say of it in the 11th section. This college contains apartments for thirty-six doctors. After the students have attended public lectures three years, they are qualified for the degree of bachelors, and wear lambskins and tippets two years: afterwards they are made licentiates, and these are generally opponents to such as take the doctors degree, who must answer all objections from sun-rise to sun-set.

The head of the university, who is called Rector, is always elected from the faculty of arts. He has the precedence in the university of all persons who are not princes of the blood. His habit of ceremony is a violet-coloured gown, with a mantle of ermins, and he is elected every three months. Before a person is admitted a graduate in the university, he must study five years, *viz.* two in philosophy, and three in divinity, law, or physic. The university had formerly civil jurisdiction, but they have lost most of their privileges; and other independent colleges, academies, and societies have been erected of late years by royal encouragement. Their revenues arose from a grant of the letter-office, but were resumed by the government, and only a pension of forty thousand livres allowed to the eleven colleges where exercises were held. But the duke of *Orleans*, by letters patent in 1619, raised it to 120,000 livres and upwards, which may amount to eleven thousand pounds *sterling per annum*.

The Rector

82   *The* GRAND TOUR.

Independent Colleges.
The Jesuits College.

The colleges that have no dependence on the university are the Jesuits college, and the college royal. We have already taken notice of the Jesuits college, p. 43, and have only to add here, that of all the colleges in *Paris* this is the most frequented, having a prodigious number of boarders of the first distinction. The scholars act a tragedy here once a year, in the month of *August*, attended with music and dances, and then it is that their masters make the distribution of prizes.

The College royal.

The college royal was founded by *Francis* I. about the year 1531: and the professorships were encreased by *Charles* IX. *Lewis* XIII. and *Lewis* XIV. The present building was erected by *Mary* of *Medicis*; and *Lewis* her son, laid the first stone. The professors are nineteen in number, viz. two for the *Hebrew* tongue, two for the *Greek*, two for the mathematic, two for the canon law, two for *Latin* eloquence, two for *Greek* and *Latin* philosophy, four for physic, chirurgery, pharmacy, and botany; two for *Arabic*, and one for the *Syriac* tongue.

X. Academies, Physic Garden, *and* Observatory.

Academies.

In *Paris* there are eight academies, three litterary ones, viz. the *French* academy, that of inscriptions, and that of the sciences; one of painting and sculpture, another of architecture, and three for military exercises.

The French.

The *French* academy was at first only a society of ingenious men, who met once a week at their respective lodgings for conversation; but being encouraged by cardinal *Richlieu*, they attempted the improving and polishing the *French* language, which is the end of their present meetings.

ings. This academy was established by a royal edict of *Lewis* XIII. in 1635, and consists of forty members; the king is their protector, and their device *Immortality*.—The academy of inscriptions and *belles lettres* was established in 1663, by the famous *John Baptist Colbert*; it was first designed only for composing the inscriptions of medals for the history of *Lewis* XIV; but in 1716, its province was extended to whatever regards the cultivating of polite literature. Their number is likewise limited to forty, like that of the members of the *French* academy.—The royal academy of sciences was also established by the above-mentioned *Monsieur Colbert*, in 1669, and is composed of seventy-two members, whose institution is pretty much of the same kind as that of the royal society in *London*, viz. to promote philosophy and the mathematics.—The academy of painting and sculpture, was originally formed in 1643, by cardinal *Mazarin*, but not established in its present state till 1664, by the chancellor *Seguier*, and *Monsieur Colbert*. In 1675, it was united with the *French* academy established for the same purpose at *Rome*.—The academy of architecture was established in 1671, by the said *Colbert*, minister and secretary of state. It is composed of the most eminent architects, and some engineers, who by letters patent in 1717, were divided into two classes. Besides painters and sculptors, engravers are also admitted. The most famous edifices in *Paris* have been built under the direction of this society. All these academies hold their assemblies in the *Louvre*, where they have their several apartments assigned them by the king's order.——The three academies for learning to ride the great horse, &c. are that of M. *Vandeuil*, *rue des canettes*; that of

Academy of Inscriptions.

The Academy of Sciences.

Academy of Painting and Sculpture.

Academy of Architecture.

E. 6. M.

M. du Gas, rue de l'Université; and that of *M. de la Gueriniere, rue de Tournon.*

The Physic Garden. The physic garden in the suburb of *S. Marcel*, is excellently well supplied with all kinds of plants, and maintained at the king's expence, under the direction of one of his physicians. It is somewhat longer, but not broader than that of *Oxford*, and has a good anatomy-school, well provided with skeletons, where botanic lectures are held. **The Laboratory.** In the king's laboratory every body is admitted to see the operations; and the medicines they make are given away to the poor.

The Observatory. The observatory, for the use of the academy of sciences, in their astronomical observations, was built by *Lewis* XIV, in 1667, under the direction of Monsf. *Perrault*, the king's first architect. It is a vaulted fabric, without either wood or iron-work, three stories high: you descend from it into a cave with little alleys by two hundred steps, from whence you may see quite through the top of the house to the sky, the use of which is to make most of their astronomical observations without the assistance of mathematical instruments. The stair-case leading to the halls is very much esteemed; the halls are large and beautiful, containing a vast number of models of machines and curious instruments, invented by learned mathematicians. One of these is called the hall of secrets, where a person speaking close to a wall, is heard by another at the opposite wall, without being heard by those who are in the middle.

XI. LIBRARIES.

There is not a city in *Europe*, that can boast of a greater number, and of better libraries than *Paris*.

FRANCE.

Paris. We shall only take notice of the most valuable.

The king's library is not only the first in the kingdom of *France,* but one of the richest and most voluminous in all *Europe.* King *John* left his son *Charles* V. a small number of books, tho' considerable for that time; *Charles* V. increased it to the number of nine hundred volumes, and *Charles* VI. his successor, made a further addition to it. These books were kept in a tower belonging to the *Louvre,* which is called *the Tower of the library.* Of all those books, there are not at present above five or six to be seen in the king's library; for, besides other casualties, the duke of *Bedford,* then regent of the kingdom for the *English,* carried them all off to *England* in 1423. The successors of *Charles* VII. down to *Francis* I. formed a new library: *Francis* I. found there a thousand volumes, which number he considerably augmented. *Catharine* of *Medicis* stripped the library of *Florence* of some of its choicest manuscripts, to enrich this collection. And, indeed, here are excellent manuscripts of the old *Italian* poets, as *Dante, Petrarca,* &c. But all that other kings have done, is very inconsiderable, when compared to the valuable improvements it received from *Lewis* XIV. This library is now said to contain 50,000 printed volumes, and near 40,000 manuscripts. It has likewise been enriched with the manuscripts of the count *de Brienne,* of messieurs *de Gaignieres, d'Hoziers, Baluze,* the *Abbé de Louvois, M. Colbert,* and lastly, with those of *M. J. Cangé.* Besides the vast number of books already contained in this famous library, and an annual stock for purchasing others, two copies of every book printed in the kingdom with his majesty's privilege, must be presented to the royal

royal library: so that in time it will become the most considerable library in *Europe*. Among others, there is a *Latin* bible in folio, written on vellum, in gold characters, embellished with fine designs, called the bible of *Charles the Bald*, which is thought to be nine hundred years old. There is a second tome of the new testament in large quarto, the first of which is said to be at *Cambridge*; both volumes are thought to be above 1200 years old. There is also a *Latin* bible in two volumes in folio, printed at *Mentz* in 1462. They have likewise a Mosarabic breviary and Missal, with a great multitude of very scarce books, as well in print as in manuscript. Besides books, there is a great number of other

Curiosities. curiosities, such as a marble bust of *Isis*; two lachrymatories of chrystal, &c. Here also is preserved, as a most valuable relick, the tomb of *Childeric* IV. king of *France*, embellished with divers gold medals, rings, and other pieces of antiquity. This tomb was found under ground in 1653 at *Tournay*, by some pioneers, who were at work upon the fortifications. The emperor *Leopold* made a present of it to *John Baptist de Schonborn*, elector of *Mentz*, who gave it to *Lewis* XIV. in 1664. In a separate closet are to be seen a prodigous number of prints, from the beginning of engraving; and a natural history painted in miniature, on vellum, containing in the whole about forty-two volumes. The two globes in the same place are twelve feet diameter. Cardinal *L'Estries* had them made by father *Coronelli*, a *Venetian* cordelier, and gave them to *Lewis* XIV. The celebrated cabinet of medals and antiques, that was formerly in this library, is now at *Versailles*. The librarian is *Abbé Bignon*. *Abbé Salier* is keeper of the printed books; and *M. Me-*

lot

FRANCE.

lot of the manuscripts. The library is kept in the *Hotel de Nevers*, and *Rue de Richlieu*.

The library of *S. Genivieve* consists of about fifty thousand volumes. *Maurice le Tellier*, archbishop of *Rheims*, who died in 1710, bequeathed his library, consisting of seventeen thousand volumes, all scarce chosen books, to this convent. There is a printed catalogue of it in folio. This voluminous library was collected within a few years. The fathers *Fronteau* and *Lallemande*, were the founders of it, and father *Moulinet* continued to increase it. The fine case where these books are deposited, was not finished till the year 1733. The design and contrivance is very remarkable. Here is a very curious clock that has eleven dial-plates, *viz.* the seven planets, the hour-plate, the astrolable, the dragon's-head, and that of the moon. The cabinet of rarities is as valuable as the library. Here you find all the curiosities that formerly belonged to the cabinet of *M. Pereisc*. The *Congius* you see here, was copied from the antique now at *Rome* in the *Farnesian* palace. Of the four hundred medals of the popes, which are there in bronze, *viz.* from *Martin* V. to *Innocent* XI. the greatest part of the first of them are modern, and not struck in the life-time of the popes themselves.

The library of *Mazarin* college, commonly called *the four nations*, consists of about thirty-six thousand volumes. This collection was founded by cardinal *Mazarin*, and partly by the care of *Gabriel Naudé*, his bibliothecarian. It formerly abounded in manuscripts, but at present they are all deposited in the king's library. It is open for the public two days in the week, *Mondays* and *Thursdays*, morning and afternoon.

The library of the Jesuits, Rue S. Jacques. The library of the Jesuits, *Rue St. Jacques*, consists of about fifty thousand volumes, among which there are a great many very scarce books. Monsieur *Fouquet*, minister of state, left a very considerable pension to this library; and the books which have been purchased with this money are marked on the back *F. F. Francis Fouquet.* In 1718 the library of the count *de Harlay*, counsellor of state, consisting of about one thousand volumes was added to it.

The library of the Jesuits, Rue S. Antoine. The Jesuits have another library in their college, *Rue St. Antoine*, composed of about twenty thousand volumes. The greatest part of these were a present from cardinal *Bourbon* the founder of the house. Monsieur *Huet*, the famous bishop of *Avranches*, left his library to these fathers. In this house there are several curiosities to be seen, as the chapel of *S. Ignatius* in the church; several beautiful pictures in the hall; and the late father *Chamillart*'s cabinet of medals.

The library of the abbey of S. Germain. The library of the *Benedictine* abbey of *S. Germain de Prés*, in the *fauxbourg St. Germain*, consists of about forty thousand printed volumes, and fifteen hundred manuscripts, one hundred of which are originals. Among the manuscripts, there is a psalter, or the psalms of *David*, written above twelve hundred years ago, which *S. Germain*, bishop of *Paris*, made use of. There are also the gospels of *S. Matthew* and *S. Mark*, written near nine hundred years ago, in characters of gold and silver, upon purple vellum: and a *Latin* bible in folio, which the emperor *Justinian* sent above nine hundred years ago, from the east, to king *Childebert.* The *Abbé d'Estrées* left his library to these fathers in 1718; and the *Abbé Renaudot* did the same by his.

The library of S. Victor. In the abbey of *S. Victor* there is a very numerous library, containing about forty thousand printed

FRANCE.

printed volumes, and a great many manuscripts. It is open three times a week, *Monday*, *Wednesday* and *Saturday*. Among other curiosities they shew you a very antient manuscript bible, the Koran in *Arabic*, &c.

The library of the *Sorbonne* consists chiefly of books of divinity, among which there are a great many very scarce. Here they shew you, as an extraordinary curiosity, a *Livy* translated into old *French*, perhaps in the reign of *Charles* V. in two great volumes in folio, with fine designs in miniature. The library of the *Sorbonne*.

The library of the bare footed *Augustinians*, who are otherwise called the *Little fathers*, near the *Place des Victoires*, contains about eighteen thousand volumes. It is commodiously situated, and has a great quantity of good books, but no manuscripts. Here is a cabinet of antiquities worth seeing. The religious of this house were called the *Little Fathers* from *Lewis* XIII. giving two of their order that name as he met them in the street. The library of the *Little Fathers*.

The *Fathers of the christian doctrine* near the *Estrapades*, have a very numerous library of about twenty thousand volumes. Father *Mitton*, doctor in theology, of the faculty of *Paris*, is the founder. It is open for the public on *Wednesdays* and *Fridays*. The library of the *Fathers of the christian doctrine*.

In the neighbourhood of the church of *Notre Dame*, there is a library called the *Advocates*. It stands open for public use every day in the week. But the greatest part of this collection are law-books. The library of the *Advocates*.

Among the libraries of private persons, that of cardinal *Rohan*, in the *Hotel de Sobize*, deserves particular notice. The principal part of this collection comes from the library of M. *de Thou*, the celebrated historian. It contains about four-
The library of cardinal *Rohan*.

teen

teen thoufand volumes Among other fcarce books, here is a *Servetus de Trinitate*, which the late *M. Dryander*, heretofore fecretary of the *Swedifh* ambaffador in *France*, made a prefent of to the cardinal: but the *Dialogues de Trinitate* of the fame *Servet* are not there. Thefe *dialogues* are more fcarce than his *differtation*. The librarian is the *Abbé Oliva*, an *Italian*, a man of great erudition. In 1723 he publifhed at *Paris, Poggio's* differtation on the *Vanity of Fortune*. The *hotel* contiguous to it, belongs to the prince *de Rohan*; the court is the moft beautiful and the moft regular in *Paris*. The gardens, which are open for the public, are worth feeing.

XII. PAINTINGS.

Paintings at *Paris*.

The great encouragement given by *Lewis* XIV. to the polite arts, has been a means of enriching this city with excellent paintings, the principal of which are as follows. In the *Louvre*, you begin with the queen's apartment, which is level with the hall of the hundred *Swifs*, where the cieling of the hall is painted in *frefco*, by *Francefco Romanelli*, a difciple of *Peter* of *Cortona*. The nine landfcapes on the wall are by *Bourdon*. The antichamber, and the queen's chamber, are painted in *frefco* by the fame *Romanelli*, and the figures in *ftucco* in the latter apartment are by *Girardon*. In the gallery of *Apollo*, over the window towards the water, there is a picture of the triumph of *Neptune* and *Thetis*, one of *Le Brun*'s beft pieces. The cartridges in the cieling are alfo by the fame hand. The portraits of the princes of the houfe of *Auftria*, from *Philip* IV. were painted by *Velafques*, a *Spanifh* painter, and are in the private hall of the baths. The

Paintings in the Louvre.

pictures to be seen in the hall of the academy of *Belles Lettres* are by *Coypel*, and the portraits by *Rigault*.

In the palace of the *Thuilleries*, mounting the great stair-case, you enter the king's great apartment. Many famous painters of the sixteenth century, wrought there in emulation of one another, under the direction of *Le Brun*. On the cieling of the guard-room are represented the march of an army, a battle, a triumph, and a sacrifice; and in the middle, Fame, with many other figures. The cieling of the anti-chamber represents the hours of the day and the night, by different allegorical figures. The fable of *Procris*, the statue of *Memnon*, *Clitias*, and the *Sun* going to sink into the sea, are taken from the *Metamorphoses* of *Ovid*. The cieling, which is admired in the gallery of ambassadors, was copied after that of the *Farnesian* gallery at *Rome*, painted by *Annibal Caracci*. The landscapes in the apartments on the garden-side, are by *Francisque*, and the other paintings by *Noel Coypel*. The queen's apartment was painted by *Nocret*: the queen is represented under the form of *Minerva*, but in different exercises. The apartment underneath was painted by *Mignard* of *Avignon*. The apartment of the duke of *Orleans* was painted by *Philip* of *Champagne*, who has represented the education of *Achilles*. The cieling of the hall of machines was painted by *Noel Coypel*, after the cartoons of *Le Brun*.

In the palace royal belonging to the duke of *Orleans*, there is one of the finest collections of pictures in *Europe*. The late regent of *France* was not only a great lover, but a very good judge of painting. It was he that made this collection, which is said to have cost him upwards of four millions of livres in less than twenty years. Most of

of these pictures, or at least the choicest, came from the cabinet of the queen of *Sweden*, who had them from the emperor's cabinet, when the *Swedes* made themselves masters of *Prague*. After the death of the queen of *Sweden*, they were purchased by *Don Livio Odescalchi*, nephew of *Innocent* XI. and from hence they fell into the hands of the duke of *Orleans*. It is observed, in praise of this prince, that for seven pictures, which are the seven sacraments of *Poussin*, he gave forty thousand crowns to a *Dutchman*. *Poussin* painted these seven sacraments twice; the first time for the commander *del Pozzo*; the second for Monsf. *de Chantelou*, which are those in the palace-royal. It is observed that the sacrament of marriage is not done quite so well as the rest. The duke of *Orleans* paid likewise for the picture of the resurrection of *Lazarus*, by *Sebastiano del Piombo*, forty thousand livres to the cathedral of *Narbonne*. This picture is upon wood, eleven feet ten inches high, and nine feet broad. It was sent by *Clement* VII. to *Narbonne*, where he had been archbishop. It is supposed that the designing was by *Michael Angelo*, and the execution by *Piombo*. The S. *John* in the desart is one of *Raphael*'s master-pieces. This picture is upon wood, five feet one inch high, and four feet six inches broad: it formerly belonged to the president *de Harlai*. The connoisseurs look upon the picture of the family of *Charles* I. king of *England*, as the real original by *Vandyke*. But for the satisfaction of the curious, I shall give here an exact description of the principal pieces in this famous collection.——
The cieling of the first antichamber of the great apartment, is painted by *Noël Coipel*. From thence you pass to the gallery of illustrious men, where you see the portraits of the most celebrated personages of the *French* nation, from *Abbot Suger* down

down to marshal *Turenne*, drawn by *Philip Champagne* and *Simon Vouet*, by cardinal *Richlieu*'s orders. *Vouet* painted also the chapel adjoining.—— In the antichamber where they dine, you see the buyers and sellers driven out of the temple, and the paralytic cured, by *Ciro-Ferri*; the death of the *Virgin*, *Sampson*, *Prometheus*, and a *S. Francis* in little by *Guido*; and the famous picture of the family of king *Charles* I. of *England* by *Vandyke*. In the hall of the ambassadors you see *Moses* exposed on the *Nile*, by *Poussin*; *Moses* saved from the water, by *Paolo Veronese*; *Abigail* presented to *David*, by *Guido*; the massacre of the Innocents, a famous piece, by *Le Brun*; the repose or rest after the flight into *Ægypt*, by *Pietro di Cortona*; a manger, and a flight into *Ægypt*, by *Bassano*; a conversation piece, by *Rubens*; the death of *Adonis*, by *Annibal Caracci*; with a great many landscapes, by eminent masters.—The new gallery of *Æneas* contains the history of *Æneas*, done in fourteen pictures, by *Antony Coipel*.—In the regent's chamber, the portraits over the door are, *Philip* II. by *Titian*; *Mary* of *Medicis*; *Seneydre*, and his wife, all three by *Vandyke*.—In the little gallery there is a row of cabinets, all adorned with costly pictures. In the first cabinet, you see the holy family, by *Raphael*; the seven sacraments, by *Poussin*; the striking of the rock, and the infant *Moses* treading on *Pharaoh*'s crown, by the same hand; the death of *Semele*, by *Caracci*; the education of *Bacchus*, and *Alexander the Great* indisposed, by *Le Sueur*.---In the second cabinet you see *S. John* in the desart, the holy family, and a virgin, all three by *Raphael*; the holy family, by *Barocci*; the fables of the nymph *Calisto*, of *Acteon*, and the rape of *Europa*, by *Titian*; the judgment of *Paris*, by *Rubens*; the same subject of *Calisto*, and *Venus*'s toilette,

toilette, by *Caracci*; *Jupiter* in the form of a swan with *Leda*, by *Paolo Veronese*; a *Virgin*, by *Carlo Maratti*.---In the third cabinet you see, over the door, the portraits of six cotemporary *Italian* poets, *Dante, Petrarch, Guido, Cavalcanti, Boccace, Cino da Pistoia*, and *Guitton d'Arezzo*: this picture was drawn by *George Vasari*, the same who wrote the lives of the painters, sculptors, and architects; a work very much esteemed. Within you see the communion of *S. Mary Magdalen*, a holy family, the baptism of *S. John*, the *Samaritan*, a *Noli me tangere*, and the predication of *S. John*, by *Francis Albani*; the holy family, *S. Peter*'s head, the flight into *Egypt*, the burning of *Troy*, and a holy family, by *Frederick Barocci*; the paralytic, the prodigal son, the shepherd asleep, by *Francis Bassano*; *Noah*'s ark, and the last judgment, by *Leander Bassano*; the predication of *S. John*, by *Blomaert*; a holy family, by *Bourdon*; *Hercules* whipping *Diomedes*'s horses, and a massacre of the innocents, by *Charles le Brun*; a crucifix, *S. Roche* with an angel, *S. Jerom* and *Mary Magdalen*, mount *Calvary*, the prodigal son, the unnailing of *Christ* from the cross, the *Samaritan*, the bathing of *Diana*, *Venus*'s toilette, the holy family, *S. John* asleep, *S. John* in the desart, *Danae*, *Hercules* strangling the serpents, *Venus* and *Cupid*, all by *Annibal Caracci*; a *Magdalen*, a *Noli me tangere*, *Leda*, *Danae*, the education of *Love*, a holy family, by *Antony Caracci*; the martyrdom of *S. Bartholomew*, by *Augustin Caracci*; an *Ecce Homo*, a crown of thorns, the unnailing of *Christ* from the cross, *S. Catharine*, by *Lewis Caracci*; the sacrifice of *Isaac*, a transfiguration, a player on the flute, by *Caravagio*; a sacrifice of *Isaac*, a *Sibyl*, *S. John the Evangelist*, *S. Francis*, *S. Jerome*, two landscapes,

landscapes, a carrying of the cross, by *Domenico*: a nativity, the adoration of the kings, a flight into *Egypt*, by *Durer*; a wounded cavalier, *Gaston de Foix*, *S. Peter Martyr*, *Picus* of *Mirandola*, the adoration of the shepherds, the invention of the cross, *Milo* of *Crotona*, by *Giorgione*; a *Magdalen*, *Susanna* going to bathe, *Susanna* with the old men, a virgin, *Herodias*, a *Sibylla*, *David* and *Abigail*, *S. Bonaventure*, *S. Sebastian*, by *Guido*; the representation of the Virgin, a picture of our Lady, another of *Christ*, *David* and *Abigail*, by *Guercini*; the portrait of a woman, *Sir Thomas More*, *George Lysein*, *Thomas Cromwell*, by *Holbein*; the infancy of *Jupiter*, the birth of *Bacchus*, the bathing of *Venus*, the rape of the *Sabines*, *Coriolanus*, the siege of *Carthage*, *Scipio*'s virtue, *Scipio* distributing military rewards, by *Julio Romano*; the portrait of a woman, the annunciation, a *Roman* charity, by *Lanfranco*; the unnailing of *Christ* from the cross, the prayer in the *Garden of Olives*, *Ganymedes*, the holy family, by *Michael Angelo*; *Galatea*, the Virgin and the infant *Jesus*, by *Carlo Maratti*; a *Venus* lying down, *S. Catharine*, a holy family, *Herodias*, a *Doge* of *Venice*, by *James Palma*; *Leda*, *Mars* disarmed by *Venus*, the death of *Adonis*, *Mars* and *Venus* tied by Love, Wisdom the companion of *Hercules*, Respect, Love, Distaste, Infidelity, *Mars* and *Venus*, the burning of *Troy*, the *Israelites* going out of *Egypt*, the judgment of *Solomon*, *Moses* saved, by *Paolo Veronese*; the holy family, the picture of our Lord, the blessed Virgin, *S. Joseph* and *S. Francis* together, by *Parmeggiano*; a landscape, the flight of *Jacob*, by *Pietro di Cortona*; the adoration of our Lord, the blessed Virgin and her child *Jesus*, the unnailing of *Christ* from the cross, by *Pietro Perugino*; the extasy of *S. Paul*, by *Poussin*; the portrait of an old woman, the blessed

The GRAND TOUR.

sed Virgin, *Julius* II. S. *John* in the desart, the holy family, the vision of *Ezekiel*, S. *Antony*, S. *Francis*, and several virgins, our Saviour in the tomb, the prayer in the *Garden of Olives*, the carrying of the cross, by *Raphael*; a picture of night, a landscape, the portrait of a *Flemish* woman, a burgomaster, by *Rembrant*; the dream of *Caravagio*, our Saviour in the middle of the doctors, S. *Joseph*, *Democritus*, *Heraclitus*, by *Ribera*, called the *Espagnolet*; the history of *Constantin* in twelve sketches, *Thomiris*, *Scipio*'s continency, *Ganymedes*, *Philopomene*'s adventure, *Mars* and *Venus*, *Diana* returning from hunting, the judgment of *Paris*, the history of S. *George*, by *Rubens*; the carrying of the cross, *Adam* and *Abel*, by *Andrew Sacchi*; a philosopher, *Christ* dead, *Pilate* washing his hands, *Christ* in the tomb, by *Schiavone*; the portrait of *Michael Angelo*, the unnailing of *Christ* from the cross, the resurrection of *Lazarus*, by *Sebastiano del Piombo*; *Alexander* and his physician, by *Le Sueur*; a portrait of *Henry* III. the presentation in the temple, the conversion of S. *Thomas*, a consistory, the unnailing of *Christ* from the cross, *Titian*, *Pietro Aretino*, the dukes of *Ferrara*, the suckling of *Hercules*, *Leda*, by *Tintoret*; the emperor *Otho*, count *Castillon*, *Charles* V. *Philip* II. *Clement* VII. *Acteon*, *Calisto*, human life, *Venus* in the shell, *Titian*'s mistress, the tempter, *Diana* and *Acteon*, *Vitellius*, *Vespasian*, the rape of *Europa*, *Venus*, admiring her self, *Perseus* and *Andromeda*, the education of Love, a *Mary Magdalen*, a *Noli me tangere*, *Philip* II. and his mistress, by *Titian*; the judgment of *Paris*, a women selling fresh sea-fish, a woman selling eggs, by *Vander-Werff*; the royal family of *England*, *Mary* of *Medicis*, a man with an arrow, the Virgin and the little child *Jesus*, an *English* peer, the princess of

Phalz-

Phalzburg, the earl of *Arundel*, by *Vandyke*; and four beautiful landscapes, by *Woucrman*.

The palace of *Luxemberg* is famous for its beautiful gallery, containing the history of *Mary* of *Medicis* painted within the space of two years, in twenty large pictures, nine feet broad, and ten high, by the celebrated *Peter Paul Rubens*. As there is a great deal of allegory in those pieces, which renders them somewhat obscure, 'tis proper for a stranger, to have the explication of them published by Monf. *Moreau de Mautour* in 1714, for the use of the duke of *Mantua*. In the chapel of this palace near the gallery, the paintings on wood, which are much esteemed, are by *Albert Durer*. In the hall of the Muses, the picture over the chimney, is young *David* naked, holding *Goliah*'s head, by *Guido*. In the same hall there is a picture of *Mary* of *Medicis*, by *Vandyke*. Over the chimney of the *Salle des Gardes*, there is a picture representing Riches with its attributes, by *Guido*. *Paintings in the palace of Luxemberg.*

There are a great many other remarkable paintings in *Paris*, the principal of which we shall here enumerate.—The body of the church of *Notre Dame*, as well as the choir, are ornamented with a number of scripture-pieces; the best *French* hands have been employed on them; in general, however, they are more conspicuous for number than merit. The most deserving of notice are, the visitation, by *John Jouvenet*, which he painted with his left hand, when he had the palsy: it is an excellent piece for composition and design: the representation, by *Boulogne*, our Saviour among the doctors, the assumption, and the death of S. *James*, all by *Coypel*: the adoration of the shepherds, and the adoration of the Magi, by *La Fosse*; these two pieces are much admired for the harmony of their co- *Other famous paintings in Paris.*

Vol. IV.   F   lours

lours: the apparition of Chrift to *S. Peter*, by *Mignard:* the defcent of the Holy Ghoft upon the apoftles, a very beautiful piece, by *Blanchard:* *S. Paul* burning the books of the pagans, one of *Le Sueur*'s fineft pieces: the martyrdom of *S. Peter*, by *Bourdon*, a very valuable piece: the martyrdom of *S. Andrew*, and the martyrdom of *S. Stephen*, both by the famous *le Brun*.——In the Jefuits college, *rue S. Antoine*, there is a hall filled with a great many good pictures, and among the reft you fee an *Ecce homo*, and a *S. Praxede*, by *Guido Reni*. In another hall there are four pieces by *Andrea del Sarto*.—In the Jefuits church of the *Noviciate*, there is a picture of *S. Francis Xavier*, curing a young woman, by *Pouffin*, and efteemed the beft picture in *France*.— In the paintings of the dome of the church of the *Sorbonne*, the four fathers of the church between the double arches, are in *fresco*, by *Champagne*.—In the church of the college of *Mazarin*, the great altar-piece is the circumcifion, by *Alexander Veronefe*. The other fmall pictures placed all round, are by *Jouvenet*.——In the *Carthufian* monaftery, the cloifter is adorned with pictures of an ineftimable value, reprefenting the life of *S. Bruno*, by *Le Sueur*. Some of them have been disfigured thro' malice, fo that the monks have been obliged to cover them with a kind of cafe under lock and key. In the room called the chapter, there is an admirable fine crucifix, by *Champagne*; and an excellent picture of our Saviour appearing to *S. Mary Magdalen*, under the habit of a gardener, by *Le Sueur*. In the church belonging to thefe fathers, there are feveral large pieces greatly admired; among the reft, that over the door of the facrifty, reprefenting the refurrection of *Lazarus*, is by *Boulogne* the elder. The piece over againft it, is our Saviour healing the fick, by *Jouvenet*.

The

The others are, the woman cured of the bloody-flux, by *Boulogne* the younger: the daughter of *Jaira* raised to life, by *La Fosse*: the miracle of the five loaves, by *Audran*; the *Samaritan*, by *Coypel* the father: the blind men of *Jericho*, by *Coypel* the son: the *Canaanean*, the *pool*, *Lazarus*, the *Centurion*, by *Corneille* the younger: the great altar-piece, representing our Saviour in the midst of the doctors, by *Champagne*.——In the church of the barefooted *Carmelites*, the great altar-piece is by *Quintin Varin*, of *Amiens*, master of the famous *Poussin*: this piece deserves the attention of the curious. The painting of the dome is by *Bartolet Flemal*, and very much esteemed.—In the church of the *Celestin* monks, there is a picture of the un-nailing from the cross, by *Francis Salviati*, of *Florence*, which is greatly admired.—In the church of *S. Gervaise*, they have six large pictures representing the martyrdom of *S. Gervasius* and *Protasius*; the first next the choir is by *Bourdon*; the next by *Le Sueur*; the third by *Goussé*, from *Le Sueur*'s designs; the other three over against them are by *Champagne*. It is a pity this church is so dark, that these pictures cannot be seen to an advantage. The crucifix over the door of the choir, is by *Sarrazin*; and the Virgin and *S. John*, accompanying her, are by *Buiret*. There are some other pieces of *Le Sueur*'s in a chapel, which is under the cross pile on the left hand.—In the church of *S. Nicholas du Chardonnet*, the altar-piece in the chapel of *Le Brun*, is a *S. Charles* praying before the crucifix, an admirable piece, by *Le Brun*.—In the church of the *Capuchine* nuns, *place de Vendome*, the great altar-piece representing the un-nailing from the cross, is one of *Jouvenet*'s best pieces. The altar-piece in the chapel of *Louvois*, is by *Coypel*. The altar-piece in the chapel of *Crequi*, is by *Jouvenet*.

—In

——In the new church of the *Invalids*, the first vault of the dome is distributed into twelve equal parts, in which are seen the twelve apostles painted in *fresco* by *John Jouvenet:* the second vault is painted by *Fosse:* it is the representation of heavenly glory. The four evangelists, who are placed betwixt the double arches which bear the weight of the dome, are also painted by *La Fosse*. The vault of the sanctuary was painted by *Noel Coypel*, who has represented the mystery of the trinity, and the assumption of the virgin. Here are also represented two concerts of angels; that on the east side is by *Lewis Boulogne*; and the other opposite to it, is by his brother, *Bon Boulogne*. The paintings in the chapel of *S. Jerome* and *S. Ambrose*, are by *Bon Boulogne*. That of *S. Augustin* was painted by *Lewis Boulogne*; and that of *S. Gregory*, by *Corneille.*——In the chamber *des Enquêtes*, in the *Palais*, there is an excellent picture of the woman caught in adultery, by *Bourdon*; and another of the accusation of *Susannah*, by *Le Brun*.——In the church of *S. Germain L'Auxerroi*, the pictures of *S. Vincent* and *S. Germain* in the parochial chapel, are by *Champagne*; those of the next and opposite chapel, are by *Bourdon* and *Leonardo da Vinci*.——In the church of the Capuchins, and street of *S. Honoré*, there is a beautiful picture of *Christ* expiring, by *Le Sueur*.——In the *Hotel de Bullion* there are two galleries filled with very good paintings, one by *Blanchard*, and the other by *Simon Vouet*.———Over the door of the choir of *S. Martin's in the fields*, there is an excellent crucifix, by *Sarazin*.———In the convent of the *Piopus* friars the high altarpiece is by *Le Brun*, as also another picture in the refectory.————In the church of *S. Paul*, there are two excellent pictures in the two chapels as you come in on the right hand; one the benediction

diction of the sacrament, by *Le Brun*, and the other the ascension, by *Jouvenet*.---In the Dominican church in the street of *S. James*, there is an admirable picture of the nativity of our Lady over the door of the choir, which was drawn by *Valentine*, and made a present of to this convent by cardinal *Mazarin*.---In the church of the *Nuns of the Visitation*, the altar-piece representing *S. Francis Sales*, is by *Le Brun*.——In the church of the barefooted *Carmelite* nuns, the cieling has an excellent piece of perspective representing our Saviour crucified, and the blessed virgin, by *Champagne*. Of the twelve pictures with gilt frames under the windows, the first on the right are by *Champagne*, and much esteemed. The second on the other side is *S. Mary Magdalen*, one of, *Le Brun*'s best pieces; the fifth is *Christ in the desart*, by the same hand. The great picture opposite the choir represents the annunciation, by *Guido*. In the chapel of *S. Mary Magdalen*, there is a picture of this saint doing penance, an admirable piece, by *Le Brun*.---In the church of *Val de Grace*, the painting in *fresco* of the dome, is exquisitely fine; it was done by *Mignard*, and represents the happiness of the blessed.-----In the chapel of the seminary of *S. Sulpice*, the cieling is adorned with an admirable fine picture of the assumption of the virgin, by *Le Brun*; and the altar-piece representing the descent of the Holy Ghost, is by the same hand.-----In the *Hotel de Condé*, among several other fine pieces, there is a most beautiful picture of the baptism of our Lord, by *Albano*.——In the church of the *Nuns of the Immaculate Conception*, there is a picture of our Saviour washing the feet of his apostles, one of *Tintoret*'s best pieces.

XIII. THEATRES.

There are three theatres in *Paris,* that of the opera in *Palais Royal;* that of the *French* comedians, *Fauxbourg S. Germain;* and that of the *Italian* Comedians, *rue Mauconseil.* There is also one for the comic opera, at the fairs of *S. Germain* and *S. Lawrence.*

The opera. Cardinal *Richlieu* built a theatre in his palace, where the opera is now performed; it is even said that he built it for the sake of acting a dramatic piece of his own composition. However it appeared under the name of *John Desmarets de Saint Sorlin.* The theatre belongs now to the king, having been excepted in the donation of that palace made by *Lewis* XIV. to the duke of *Orleans.* The king has granted the privilege of it to certain persons, who exhibit the representations at their own expence, and to their own profit. It is said that the income amounts to above 200,000 livres a year; but more than two thirds of it goes to defray the expences of the house. For there are above two hundred persons to mantain; singers, dancers, and fidlers. They are all paid by the manager appointed by the king. Operas were not exhibited at *Paris* till the year 1669, when the abbé *Pierre Perrin,* who had been introducer of ambassadors to *John Gaston* duke of *Orleans,* obtained a privilege for that purpose of the king. They have acted at the present theatre only since 1673, for before that time it belonged to the *French* comedians, who removed from hence upon the death of *Moliere.* The operas are performed four times a week in winter, *viz. Sundays, Tuesdays, Thursdays,* and *Saturdays;* and three times a week in summer. The price is a pistole in the balconies,

conies, seven livres ten sols in the first boxes, and the amphitheatre; four livres in the second boxes, which are also called *Paradise*; and forty sols in the pit.

The *French* comedians are upon a different footing from the actors of the opera. They have no manager, but divide daily among themselves the profits of the house. The whole company consists of thirty actors and actresses, who have very rich dresses, even better than in any other country. It is a pity that the theatre and the decorations do not answer to the magnificence of the dresses, and to the goodness of the plays. The theatre is not large; it consists only of three rows, each of which has thirty boxes, and each box may hold eight persons. The pit may contain six or seven hundred; and the theatre and amphitheatre three hundred. They act every day, except a fortnight before *Easter*, and a week after. Usually for the closure and the re-opening of the theatre, they act a sacred drama of *Corneille*, called *Polieucte*. There is also a vacation at the theatre, on the great festivals. The price in the pit is twenty sols; thirty sols in the third boxes; forty sols in the second boxes; four livres in the theatre, amphitheatre, and first boxes. This playhouse is in the *rue des Fosses* and quarter of *Luxemburg*; it was built in 1688, by *D'Orbay*, a famous architect; the cieling is painted by *Boulogne*.

The theatre for *Italian* comedies is so called, not because they are acted in *Italian*, but for being in the *Italian* manners: it is situated in the *rue Mauconseil*, at the *Hotel de Bourgogne*. This hotel where the dukes of *Burgundy* formerly resided, was given to the confraternity of the *Passion*, to represent the mysteries of religion; afterwards the *French* comedians had possession of it, and then the *Italians*. These comedians had been banished the stage above twenty years, for the too great liberty they took with private characters, even of high rank; but they were restored after the death of *Lewis* XIV. by permission of the late duke regent, and now they are called *His R. H. the duke of* Orleans's *company of comedians*. The prices at the *Italian* theatre are the same as at the *French*.

<small>Comic opera.</small> At the fairs of *S. Lawrence*, and *S. Germain*, there is a theatre for the comic opera. And every year, the beginning of the month of *August*, the *Jesuits* scholars in the college of *Louis le Grand*, perform a *Latin* tragedy. The theatre is in the great court, and very richly decorated; there is always a great deal of good company to see the performance.

XIV. Trade *and* Manufactures.

<small>Trade of Paris.</small> The trade of *Paris* consists chiefly of the manufactures of this city, which are very considerable. These are principally gold and silver stuffs, wrought silks, velvet, gold and silver lace, ribbands, tapestry, linen and glass.

<small>The Gobelins.</small> The tapestry made here, is brought to the highest degree of perfection. The house where the manufacture is carried on, took its name from one *Gobelin*, a famous dyer at *Rheims*, who came to settle here in the reign of *Francis* I. But the present royal manufactory was established in 1667, by *M. Colbert*. There used to be sometime ago about 800 workmen here, reckoning painters, sculptors, goldsmiths, embroiderers, when the celebrated *Le Brun* was their director. Though they have not such a number of hands at present, yet they have always some eminent masters. In general, you can see only the tapestry

FRANCE.

pestry upon the looms; but during the feast of *Corpus Christi*, they display abundance of beautiful tapestry, antient and modern. There are likewise several pieces of fine painting, always to be seen, which the manufacturers are at work upon. They are famous here for dying of scarlet: the beauty of it is ascribed to the quality of the water of a little rivulet that runs by, called the *Bievre*. The sieur *Dagly* of *Liege* makes a malleable varnish of his own invention, almost as beautiful as that of *China*. Here they have also an academy for designing, a model exposed, as at the academy of painting in the *Louvre*. The workmen employed in this manufacture, and even the apprentices, have very great privileges.

The manufactory of plate-glass in the *Faux-bourg S. Antoine*, was first established by M. *Colbert* in 1666. Before that time, the *French* had all their plate-glass from *Venice*, and other foreign parts. The whole business of this house is to polish the glasses, and to cover the backs with quicksilver; for they are cast at *Cherbourg*, and *S. Gobin*. Some attribute the art of casting glass for this purpose to the *French*; but now the secret is known in several other countries. There are some plates 120 inches high; but those of so large a size are taxed at a great rate; the largest and finest are in the gallery of *Versailles*. It is worth while to visit the workmen that lay the quicksilver on the backs of the glasses. The number employed at present in this manufacture is about 400. *Manufactory of plate glass.*

After the manufactory of the *Gobelins*, which is the best in *Europe* for tapestry, you should pay a visit to the manufactory of carpets at the *Savonerie à Chaillot*. Here they work carpets after the manner of *Turkey*, which are equal in goodness *The manufacture of carpets.*

ness to those brought from the *Levant*. This manufacture was begun in *France* in 1604, under the reign of *Henry* IV.

The glass-house. Without going much out of the way, you may visit the glass-house in the same neighbourhood. The glass work made here is almost equal to that made at *Venice*, or in *England*. If it be true, that they have the secret of making glasses that will stand the fire, this is an article of no small consequence.

Plaister of Paris. There is also a considerable trade in this city of the plaister of *Paris*, of which it has been lately so much the fashion to form busts and figures. It is made from a stone dug at a place called *Montmartre* in this neighbourhood. This stone does not lie in whole continued rocks, but in flat loose pieces, of different sizes, among a kind of loose marle; the finest of these pieces are as white as snow, and two or three inches in thickness, little inferior to crystal in transparence. There needs only a slight burning of these stones, to make them fit for grinding to powder; and after that the dust is wetted with common water, and made so thin that it will run; in this condition it is cast into moulds, and it presently hardens on the one part into a softer, and on the other into a firmer matter. Under the same management, the most pure and elegant mass hardens into a kind of marble, of which the slabs and tables imitating marble, with a card or book on them, are made. Nor was it discovered till lately that from this the *French* artists made their artificial marble.

Fairs. They have two great fairs every year at *Paris*, one in the *Fauxbourg S. Germain*, which begins on the third of *February*, and lasts a fortnight; and the other at *S. Laurence's* which begins

on

FRANCE.

on the festival of that saint, and ends the seventh of *September*.

XV. CABINETS of *Medals*.

There is not in all *Europe* a richer cabinet than the king's at *Versailles*. M. *Le Gros de Boze* is the keeper.----In the college of *Jesuits*, called *Louis le Grand*, there is a very curious cabinet of medals.----In the college of the same fathers, called *La Maison Professe*, there is a famous cabinet of medals of all metals and sizes, collected with great care and pains by the late father *Chamillart*.---The *Celestine* monks have a cabinet of some natural curiosities, among which are two *Egyptian* mummies well preserved.---- We mentioned the cabinet of the monks of *S. Genevieve*, when speaking of their library.---- The *Petits peres*, in the *Rue neuve des bons enfans*, have a curious cabinet of medals, antient and modern.----The *Abbé de Rothelin*, who lived in the *Rue des petits peres*, had a very fine series of silver medals in his cabinet.---Father *Mantfaucon* had a very fine series of medals, in bronze. In the abbey of *S. Germain*, where he belonged to, there is a cabinet of antiquities of this father's collecting.----M. *Genebrier*, M. D. well known for his *Dissertations on Medals*, is possessed of some that are very curious.---M. *de Valois*, of the isle of *S. Lewis*, has a great many *Greek* medals in his possession: his lady has a very curious collection of shells.--- M. *Titon du Tillet*, *Rue de la Cerisage*, author of the *French Parnassus*, keeps this monument in his own house, which deserves a traveller's notice,---The most valuble part of the curiosities which the late *M. Baudelot* died possessed of, were left to the academy of *Inscriptions*. This gentleman had several statues

statues of marble of four or five hundred years standing, more antient than those in the famous *Aurundelian* collection.—The cabinet of M. *Pajot*, of *Ons-en-Bray*, at *Bercy*, is perhaps the most curious in its kind in all *Europe*. There you find every thing that is of any consequence in the mathematical way. The house and gardens are very agreeable.

XVI. ANTIQUITIES.

The article of antiquities might be the most copious of any we have yet given, since it has furnished matter of whole volumes to several nuthors. Father *Montfaucon* has wrote the monuments of the *French* monarchy. This writer affirms, that the church of *Notre Dame*, was founded upon the ruins of a temple dedicated to *Jupiter*, which opinion seems to be confirmed by an inscription found in these later times. *De Breuil*, and several others, have wrote of the antiquities of *Paris*, to whom we refer the curious reader. But we cannot help mentioning the *Palais des Thermes*, *Rue de la Harpe*, because it is the most remarkable curiosity of its kind in all *France*.

It is the remains of a palace which the emperor *Julian* built, about 356 or 357; and seems to have been erected upon the same model as *Dioclesian*'s baths. The beauty of this edifice consists not only in its correct taste, but in its extraordinary strength; for over the vaults there are large gardens, which you enter by the fourth story of the *Hotel de Clugny*. The remainder of this antient structure consists of several arches, and a large hall. It is built of a kind of mastic (cement) whose composition is lost, with small square stones and bricks. *Adrian* of *Valois* seems to think, that several of the *French* kings of the first race, resided in this palace. Father *Mabillon* is of the same opinion. And, indeed, we find that several charters of the first kings are dated from the *Palace des Thermes.*

It is pretended that the abbey of S. *Germain des Prés*, occupies the place of an antient temple dedicated to the goddess *Isis.* The church of the *Carmelite* nuns, *Rue S. Jacques*, is said to have been a temple dedicated to the goddess *Ceres.*

XVII. PUBLIC WALKS.

There are a great many public walks in *Paris,* which in fine weather afford matter of pleasure and curiosity. Here it is that the ladies come *to see and be seen.* These walks are the garden of the *Thuilleries* : the course or ring for taking the air in coaches : the garden of *Luxemberg* : the garden of *Palais Royal* : the garden of *Condé* : the garden of *Soubize* : the king's garden; the garden of the arsenal; the gardens of the archbishop near *Notre Dame* : besides the *Place Royale*, and the avenues of the *Hotel de Breton Villiers*, where a great many people walk in the evening.

We have made mention of these gardens when speaking of the hotels they belong to. One ought to remember the plants and simples that are preserved in the king's garden. Here are professors of botany, chemistry, and anatomy. The garden of *Condé* has been shut up from the public within these few years. In the public walks, either on foot or in a coach, it is the custom to salute one another but once. The princes and princesses of the blood, and foreign ministers, take the middle track in the *Queen*'s *course.*

XVIII. Go-

XVIII. Government.

Ecclesiastical government.
Paris was a bishopric suffragan to the archbishop of *Sens*, till pope *Gregory* XV. erected it into an archbishopric at the request of *Lewis* XIII. in 1622. *Lewis* XIV. made the archbishops of *Paris* perpetual dukes and peers of *France* in 1674. The archbishop exercises a civil as well as ecclesiastical jurisdiction in the lands belonging to his see; his revenue is computed at one hundred and eighty thousand livres a year. The chapter of the cathedral consists of eight dignitaries, and fifty canons.

Civil government of Paris.
The civil government of *Paris* is distributed among several courts of justice, the highest of which is the parliament, whose jurisdiction extends over several of the neighbouring provinces, and is the last resort in all causes, where the court does not intermeddle. This parliament consists of the chief president, nine presidents, a mortier, one and twenty presidents by commission, two hundred and fourteen counsellors, with the necessary officers, as attorney, and sollicitor-general, register, &c. It is divided into nine chambers or houses, which have each their respective branches of business assigned them. They assemble in the quarter of the city, in a building called the *Palais*,

The Palais.
because it was once the ordinary residence of the *French* kings. It is said to have been built by the ancestors of *Hugh Capet*, the first *French* king of the third line, and contains a great many large halls, filled with the shops of booksellers, jewellers, and toymen. The architecture of this edifice, tho' in the *Gothic* taste, is much admired by able connoisseurs. The parliament begins to sit the 12th of *November*, and opens its assemblies with
a so-

FRANCE.

a solemn service called *the red mass*, because the members attend all in scarlet robes. The other courts in *Paris* are the chamber of accounts; the court of aids; the court *des monoyes*, which regards the coinage, weights, and measures; the court of the treasury; the court of the waters and forests; the court of the constable and marshals; the court of admiralty; the chatelet, or the ordinary court of justice for the civil government of the city, of which the provost, who is like our lord-mayor, with the four *eschevins* or aldermen, and twenty-six counsellors, are judges; the court of the *Hotel de Ville* or Guildhall, which takes an account of the city-rents, and the taxes on all provisions brought into *Paris*; and finally, the court of the consuls, which takes cognizance of all things relating to commerce, in which courts the provost (by himself or his lieutenant) presides, being nominated by the king. The *eschevins* have sixteen *quarterniers* under them, with their commissaries and other under-officers, a hundred and twenty archers or watchmen, sixty cross-bow-men, a hundred musquetiers, with a watch of foot and horse that go the rounds every night, commanded by a captain, who is called *Le Chevalier du Guet*, or knight of the watch.

Besides the civil, there is also a military government of *Paris*, which in this, and in every other province, is independent, if not superior to the civil power. The courts above-mentioned are suffered to go on without interruption, where the crown is not concerned, and while they obey the dictates of the ministry; but should they presume to dispute the king's pleasure, they would soon be made sensible of their error by a military force, *Paris* being in reality subject to a lieutenant-general. The captains of the castles or palaces

Military government.

laces of the *Louvre* and *Thuilleries* receive orders also immediately from the king; and the governors of the *Bastile* and the *Hotel des Invalides* are accountable only to his majesty.

CHAP. IV.

The Environs of PARIS.

THERE are few cities in *Europe* that have such agreeable avenues as *Paris*. It would be inconsistent with our proposed brevity to enter into a description of every place; we shall therefore give only a short account of the royal palaces, and of a few private seats that are most deserving of a traveller's notice. The royal seats are *Versailles, Marly, Vincennes, Meudon, S. Germain, Fontainebleau*, to which is generally added the abbey of *S. Denis*, already described p. 29. The private seats are *S. Cloud, Sceau, Clagny, Chantilly, Issy, Saint Maur, Bagnolet, Conflans, Maison, Montmorency*, and the pleasant seat of M. *Pajot d'Ons-en-Brai* at *Berci*.

I. VERSAILLES.

The town of *Versailles*. *Versailles* is a small town of the isle of *France*, situated on a rising ground, and champaign country, about twelve miles west of *Paris*. Under *Lewis* XIII. it was but a little village, and the castle like a plain country-house, where that prince used to keep his hunting-equipage. But his son *Lewis* XIV. being taken with the place,

made

made a city of the village, and converted the castle into one of the finest palaces of the world; having employed the famous *Mansard* many years in embellishing it. The avenue which leads to the palace, divides the town into two parts: that which stands on the left as you come from *Paris*, is called *Old Versailles*; and that on the right, *New Versailles*. *Old Versailles* comprehends the kitchen-garden, near the *Swiss*'s piece, and the convent and church of the *Recollect Friars*, which are both very plain. There are a great many hotels and good houses in this quarter, as likewise the stables of the life-guards, and several magazines. *New Versailles* contains a large square, called *Place Dauphine*, a market-place, and a parish-church. The houses are well built, and the streets wide and uniform. Not far from the market-place are the queen's stables, the square of *Bourgundy*, and the castle of water, which is a large pavilion that serves for a reservoir. The parish-church is a very handsome building, forty-seven fathom long, and eighteen broad. It is built of free-stone, very lightsome, and extremely neat. The church is served by the fathers of the mission of *S. Lazarus*, who have a large house here, founded by *Lewis* XIV. for thirty-six in community. In this quarter there are several hotels built by the lords of the court, for their conveniency during the time they reside at *Versailles*.

From *Paris* you may go to *Versailles* for five and twenty sols with the *Coche*, which sets out twice a day from the *Rue Saint Nicaise*. You may likewise go with a *carosse* or stage-coach that holds but four, for a *French* crown each; or with a post-chaise. Another way is by water for five sols as far as *Seve*, which is half way, either with the boats of *Seve* or *S. Cloud*; they set out at eight

Carriages from Paris to Versailles.

eight in the morning from *Pont Royal.* From *Seve* there is a great causeway, that carries you by the heights of *Virofle* to the great avenue of *Versailles.*

Palace of Versailles.
There are three fine avenues to the palace; the middle one leads directly to *Paris,* and is five and twenty toises in breadth; as to the other two, one leads to *S. Cloud,* and the other to *Sceau*; they all three terminate in a kind of parade, called the *Royal Square.*

Avenues.

Park-lodge.
The park-lodge, a spacious building, intended for his majesty's head-huntsman, and the other officers under his direction, stands on the side of the avenue leading to *Paris,* opposite the *Hotel de Conti,* which formerly belonged to the duke of *Vermandois.*

Stables.
The design of the stables was given by *Julius Harduin Mansart*; they are built in the form of a crescent at the upper-end of the grand avenue, on the right and left, the whole so regular and beautiful, that few royal palaces exceed them. From hence the castle appears like a magnificent theatre; and you must ascend to come at it. The outer gate is all wrought iron gilt, and about twelve feet high; it is terminated by two lanthorns, surmounted by two groups of figures; the one carved by *Marsy,* and the other by *Girardon.* A second gate, adorned with groups, separate the two court-yards; the figure of Peace was done by *Tuby,* and Plenty by *Coisevox.* The two large piles of buildings belonging to the wings, each terminated by a pavilion, are designed for the officers of the kitchen. After that, you see the fore-front and the wings of the old castle or palace; the front has a balcony, supported by eight marble columns; there are two ranges of apartments that join the two palaces.

The new palace.
The new palace is a range of magnificent apartments, which, together with its wings, forms

forms a front of above three hundred fathoms. The ridge is decorated with statues, vases, and trophies, ranged on balustrades, which run along the whole building. It is built so as to front the garden, and it is on this side that *Versailles* makes the finest appearance. The great marble stair-case surpasses any thing of the kind that antiquity can boast of. The fresco paintings were done by *Le Brun*; and the bust of *Lewis* XIV. was carved by the famous *Coisevox*. This is the entrance into the grand apartments, the furniture of which is immensely rich and magnificent.

<small>Stair-case.</small>

First you pass into the hall of plenty, painted by *Houasse*. Thence you proceed to the cabinet of antiquities and jewels, which is of an octagon figure, and enligthened by a roof in the form of a dome, and painted also by *Houasse*. Here, among other precious curiosities, they have the finest agate in *Europe*, being of three colours, and four or five inches in diameter, representing the figure of a naked emperor, carried on the back of an eagle, and crowned with victory. The escrutoire, in the middle of this chamber, contains a most magnificent collection of antient and modern medals. The first pieces were given to *Lewis* XIV. by his uncle the duke of *Orleans*, and afterwards, by much search and expence, it was made the completest collection in the world. The hall of *Venus* has some beautiful paintings, and an antient statue of *Cincinnatus*. The hall of the billiard-table is likewise adorned with fine paintings, and with *Lewis* XIV's bust by cavalier *Bernini*. The hall of *Mars* has a great number of exquisite paintings, and among the rest the family of *Darius* at *Alexander*'s feet, one of *Le Brun*'s best pieces. On the cieling the god *Mars* is represented in a chariot drawn by wolves.

<small>The grand apartments.</small>

The

The hall of *Mercury* is painted by *Champagne*, where you may fee feveral other pieces by the fame hand, and likewife fome by *Raphael*, *Titian*, and other eminent mafters. The hall of *Apollo* has fome excellent pieces, and among the reft, the four feafons by *La Foffe*, and feveral pictures, by *Guido*. The halls of war and peace are at both ends of the gallery, the former has fome fine paintings reprefenting the actions of *Lewis* XIV. by *Le Brun*.

The great gallery. From the hall of war you pafs to the great gallery, the moft beautiful and magnificent in *Europe*. It is thirty-feven fathom long, and feven broad, ending with a great arch, which leads into the forementioned halls, and adorned with two marble pillars. On the garden-fide there are feventeen windows which look into it; and on the fide of the king's apartment as many arches, filled with large pier-glaffes. Thefe arches and windows are feparated by twenty-four pilafters. The roof is excellently painted by *Le Brun*, and reprefents in allegorical or emblematical figures, part of the memorable tranfactions of the late king's reign, from the *Pyrenean* treaty to the peace of *Nimeguen*. The reft of the gallery is adorned with bufts, veffels, tables of porphyry and alabafter, and with eight antient ftatues, among which thofe of *Bacchus*, *Venus*, *Germanicus*, and *Diana* are moft efteemed.

The queens apartment. From the great gallery you may proceed directly to the queen's apartment, which is of the fame dimenfions as the king's, but of different workmanfhip, adorned with paintings of very great value, chiefly by *Vignon* and *Coypel*. Paffing to the landing place of the great marble ftair-cafe, *The king's apartment.* you come to the king's apartment, diftributed into feveral chambers. Firft you enter into the hall of guards, adorned with gilding and looking-glaffes.

FRANCE.

glasses. The next is the hall where the king dines in public, embellished with pictures of several battles. From thence you pass to the great hall, which is worthy of admiration for its riches and beauty; particularly for the cornices, with the *Mosaic* work and *basso-relievo's*. The king's bed-chamber is ornamented with a great deal of magnificence, and good order. His bed is of crimson velvet, with a beautiful and rich embroidery (sometimes of damask, and other times of gold tissue, according to the season) placed in an alcove, and inclosed with a gilded balustrade. The most exquisite pictures adorn this royal chamber, and the rest of the furniture is magnificently elegant. We shall take notice of the pictures in the council-hall in another place. The billiard-room has a noble fine billiard-table, at which *Lewis* XIV. used to play very often; it is likewise embellished with a great many excellent pictures, and with a clock of very curious workmanship. From this room you proceed to several other chambers, all finely adorned with paintings; in one of them there is a globe whose circles move just as those in the heavens do. At length you come to the little gallery, which is the last piece of the king's apartment. The cielings of this gallery, and of the two halls at the end of it, were painted by *Mignard*. This gallery is likewise full of some of the best performances of painters of the first rank. Thence you proceed to the apartments belong to the *Dauphin*, and the rest of the royal family, which consist of chambers, cabinets, halls, &c. laid out with a great deal of art.

The chapel belonging to the palace is an exceeding fine piece of architecture, built of freestone, in the *Corinthian* order, twenty-two fathom long, twelve broad, and about fourteen high.

The chapel.

high. On the top there is a fine balustrade, with eight and twenty statues. Nothing can be more beautiful or richer than the inward embellishments of this chapel. The great altar is of the finest marble. The sacristy is very neat. You ascend to the galleries by two stair-cases with iron rails, richly gilt. The king's gallery faces the great altar, over the great door, and is thirteen feet and a half wide. The two lamps are gilt in an exquisite taste, and the glasses are exceeding beautiful. The queen's gallery is on the right; and the gallery that runs round the chapel, is nine feet and a quarter wide, supported by sixteen pillars, and some pilasters of the *Corinthian* order. The balustrade is very rich and elegant. The roof is elegantly painted by eminent hands.

The gardens of Versailles. The gardens abound with master-pieces of every kind. The orangery is one of the fairest pieces of *Tuscan* architecture to be seen at *Versailles*. The design is by *Le Maitre*; but it was revised and finished by *Mansart*, though indeed with greater elegance than solidity. The eight groups of bronze, which you see in the parterre of water, and which represent eight rivers of *France*, were cast by the two *Kellers*. The vase of *Latona* has two sheafs thirty feet high; the group of marble there is by *Marsy*. The flower-garden is by *Le Notre*, and the parterre or the orangery is by *Quintinie*. The equestrian statue at the head of the *Swiss* piece, or bason, on the other side of the orangery, was made by cavalier *Bernini* for *Lewis* XIV; but not finding the work so complete as he could wish, he changed the features of *Lewis* XIV. and made a *Curtius* of it. The figure of *Autumn* in the bason of *Bacchus* is by *Marsy*, and the vase of *Saturn* by *Girardon*. The colonade is a peristyle of thirty-two columns, supported by as many pilasters in the *Ionic* order.

The

The roofs are of white marble, embellished with beautiful *basso-relievos*; in the middle is a beautiful group of marble by *Girardon*, representing the rape of *Proserpine*. The group of metal in the large bason of *Apollo*, is by *Tuby*, and reckoned one of his best pieces. The *Enceladus* is a very fine group, set up in an octogan bason; from the mouth of this giant, oppressed by the weight of mountains, flows a *Jet d'eau*, or spout of water, that rises seventy-eight feet high. *Tuby* made the bason of *Flora*; and *Renaudon* that of *Ceres*. Of the three excellent groups in the baths of *Apollo*, *Girardon* made the middle one; and *Marsy* and *Guerin* the other two. The fountain of the pyramid, is executed in bronze by *Girardon*: *Tuby* and *Le Hongre* made the two basons below; the vases you see there, were carved at *Rome*. The cascade of the canal where the nymphs are bathing, is a square, where several masks seem to spout out water for the use of those nymphs. This work is by *Girardon*; and the rivers were executed by *Le Hongre* and *Le Gros*. The dragon of the fountain that bears that name, was made by *Marsy*; the group of the bason of *Neptune* is by *Dominic Gendi*, a disciple of *Algardi*. These two last pieces surpass all the other figures at *Versailles*. The triumphal arch remains to be seen; it is built of marble of different colours, and adorned with three fine fountains. The figures are by *Tuby* and *Coisevox*; the fountains of *Victory* and *Glory*, both by *Maseline*, have a great number of decorations, which produce a very good effect. The piece of water, called the *Grand Canal*, is eight hundred fathom in length, and thirty-two in breadth; it has a traverse or cross-current of five hundred fathom, with the same breadth, which on the one side leads to the menagery, and on the other to *Trianon*.

The

The GRAND TOUR.

The menagery. The menagery is a small palace built by *Mansart*. The two apartments for winter and summer, are adorned with excellent paintings, and finely furnished with pier-glasses in gilded frames. There is a vast number of little fountains, which sprinkle those who are not upon their guard. The volery, or bird-cote, is the finest in all *France*, and best stocked. Several apartments in this palace are appointed for the breeding of animals of all kinds, from the most common to the rarest.

S. Cyr. From the menagery, there are several alleys that lead to the royal and magnificent abbey of S. *Cyr*, of the order of S. *Augustin*. It is situated in the park, about three miles from *Versailles*, and was founded by *Lewis* XIV. for the education of two hundred and fifty young ladies. The number of nuns is forty. The king has reserved the nomination of the young ladies to himself. To obtain admission, they must prove four degrees of nobility on the father's side. No girl can enter under seven years of age, nor stay there after the age of twenty years and three months. When they go out, they have either a thousand crowns in money, or one of those places which the king has the disposal of in several convents. The building is extremely fine, the architect was *Mansart*, who finished it in 1686.

Trianon. *Trianon* was built after the design of *J. H. Mansart*. This little palace may be looked upon as a kind of summer-house to the gardens of *Versailles*; it is built in an excellent taste, and is moreover embellished by the richest decorations. The front is sixty-four fathom in length, and has two returning wings, terminated by two pavilions. The finest views of the palace and park of *Versailles*, are in the great gallery, and were painted chiefly by *Cottel*. *Allegrin* has painted

the

the same subjects, and the sketch of a portico in the great saloon. There are also some of *Houasse*'s pictures in the billiard hall. The group of children, in the upper parterre, are by *Girardon*. *Tuby* carved the *Laocoon* and his sons, which stands in the garden of *Maroniers*; this is an admirable group, copied after the antique. The vases and dragons of gilt lead, which are upon the large piece of water that terminates the gardens, are extemly well wrought, and finished.

List of the principal Paintings at Versailles.

In the chapel of *Versailles*, the chapel of the Holy Sacrament is painted by *Silvester*; the chapel of *S. Lewis* by *Jouvenet*; the chapel of *S. Teresa* by *Santerre*; the chapel of the *Virgin* by *Boulogne* the younger. The principal vault painted by *Antony Coypel* represents the eternal Father in his glory. In the five first vaults of the gallery, on the right hand, as you come in, you see *S. Barnabas, S. Jude, S. Bartholomew, S. James the less*, and *S. James the greater*, all painted by *Boulogne* the younger. In the sixth vault, on the same side, *Boulogne* the elder has represented the vision of *S. Paul*. The saints, *Peter, Andrew, Philip, Simon, Matthias*, and *Thomas*, are also by the same hand. *La Fosse* has painted the resurrection in the vault of the *Chevet*. In the vault of the king's gallery, *Jouvenet* has represented the descent of the *Holy Ghost*.

<small>Paintings in the chapel of *Versailles*.</small>

The great gallery was painted by the famous *Le Brun*. The largest picture in the middle of the vault is in two parts; one is the king, taking upon him the administration of affairs; and the other, the antient pride of the neighbouring people, in 1661. The second picture on the left hand

<small>Paintings in the great gallery.</small>

hand of the great saloon, is the king taking a resolution to wage war against the *Dutch* in 1671. The third, on the right of the great saloon, is the king arming by land and sea in 1672. The fourth, on the left of the great saloon, is the king attacking *Holland* in 1672. The fifth, which fills the whole vault, is the passage of the *Rhine* in 1672. The sixth, over the arcade of the saloon of war, is the league of *Germany*, *Spain* and *Holland*, in 1672. The seventh, on the side of the great saloon, is *Franche comté* re-conquered, in 1674. The eighth, which takes up the whole vault, is the taking of *Ghent*, in 1678. The ninth, over the arcade of the saloon of peace, is *Holland* accepting of peace.

<small>Small pictures of the gallery.</small> The small pictures of the gallery, in the key of the vault, are, 1. the relieving of the people during the famine in 1662. 2. the edict against duels, in 1661, 3. The peace of *Aix-la-chapelle* in 1668. 4. The war for the queen's right in 1667. 5. The police, established at *Paris* in 1665. 6. The acquisition of *Dunkirk* in 1662.---On the side of the looking glasses, 1. *Holland* succoured in 1665. 2. The defeat of the *Turks* in *Hungary*, in 1664. 3. The re-establishment of navigation in 1663. 4. The finances put into order in 1662. 5. The establishing of the hospital of the invalids, in 1674. 6. The renewing the alliance with the *Swiss*, in 1663.----On the side of the windows, 1. The insult of the *Corsicans* repaired, in 1664. 2. The pre-eminence ceded by *Spain* to *France*, in 1662. 3. Justice reformed, 1667. 4. The polite Arts protected in 1663. 5. Embassies from the extremity of the earth, in 1686. 6. The junction of the two seas, begun in 1666, and finished in 1680.

The

FRANCE.

The pictures that may be seen, during the winter, in the king's apartments at *Versailles*, are as follow.---In the guard-room, over the chimney, a battle painted by *Parocel*.---In the dining-room, over the chimney, a battle much esteemed, by *Pietro di Cortona*.--- The eleven pictures representing sieges, by *Parocel*.---In the king's antichamber, over the door, a nativity, *Esther* before *Ahasuerus*, and *Christ* in the tomb; all three by *Paolo Veronese*. Over another door, a picture by *Bassano*. Over the chimney, a repose, after the flight into *Egypt*, by *Gentileschi*. Over the door, the entering into the ark, by *Bassano*; *Bethsheba* and *David*, by *Paolo Veronese*; *Judith* and *Holophernes*, by the same hand.--In the bed chamber, over the door, the marquis of *Aitonne*, by *Vandyke*; *S. John*, by *Caravaggio*.---In winter, *S. John* the evangelist, by *Raphael*; a *David*, by *Domenicini*; over the door, a *Magdalen*, by *Alexander Veronese*; a portrait by *Vandyke*. Over the cornish, *S. John* the evangelist, by *Valentini*; the marriage of *S. Catherine*, by *Alexander Veronese*; *S. Luke* the evangelist, *S. Matthew*, *Christ* paying tribute to *Cæsar*, *S. Mark*, all four by *Valentini*. ---In the council-cabinet, over the door, a little *Pyrrhus*, and a *Bacchanalian*, both by *Poussin*; the departure of *S. Peter* and *S. Paul*, by *Lanfranco*; *Christ* healing the blind men of *Jericho*, by *Poussin*.---In the periwig closet, three pictures over the door, representing menageries, by *Bassano*.---In the clock-chamber, over the chimney, the elevation of *Christ* on the cross, by *Le Brun*. Over the door, the *Samaritan*, by *Guido*; the marriage of *S. Catherine*, by *Nicolo*; *Rebecca*, by *Coypel*; the daughters of *Jethro*, by *Le Brun*. Over the door, *Adam* and *Eve*, by *Albano*; *Christ* carrying the cross, by *Mignard*; *Latona* and the peasants, by *Albano*;

Pictures in the king's apartments in winter.

the marriage of *Moses*, by *Le Brun*; *Moses* taken out of the waters, by *la Fosse*.——In the antichamber of the king's little apartments, over the door, *Moses* spurning away the crown of *Pharaoh*, the descent of manna, a holy family, the rapture of *S. Paul*, the *Arcadian* shepherds, the plague, *Moses*'s rod changed into a serpent, all seven by *Poussin*; a nativity, by *Bassano*; the good *Samaritan*, by *Molle*; *Venus* and *Vulcan*, by *Mignard*; *Angelica* and *Medor*, by *Molle*; *S. Bruno*, by the same.——In the king's little apartment, over the door, *Diana* returning from the chase, by *Breugle*. Over the chimney, silence, by *Le Brun*; the incredulity of *S. Thomas*, by *Mutian*; a landscape and figures, by *Banboccio*; a holy family by *Poussin*; a small virgin, by *Guido*; a nativity, by *L. Caracci*; a landscape and concert, a silence, the preaching of *S. John*, all three by *A. Caracci*; the Virgin and *Christ*, with many angels, by *Andrew Azio*; a small virgin, by *Guido*. Over the door, the view of *Fontainebleau*, by *Vendermeulen*; the view of *Vincennes*, by the same; the players on the violin, by *Giorgione*; a small landscape and an hermit, by *Caracci*; the resurrection, by the same; the sacrifice of *Abraham*, by *Holbein*; a muse, by *Giorgione*; a small landscape, by *Paul Bril*.——In the saloon, over the door, the views of *S. Germains*, and of *Versailles*, both by *Vandermeulen*; the annunciation, by *L. Caracci*; the bearing of the cross, by *Rotenamer*; a nativity, by *Josephin*; *Circe*, *Ulysses*, and his companions; by *Albani*; the preaching of *S. John*, by the same; the marriage of *S. Catharine*, by *Parmeggiano*, the martyrdom of *S. Stephen*, by *Corneille Pollain*; ditto, by *A. Caracci*; the siege of *Rochelle*, by *Claude Lorrain*; the sacrifice of *Abraham*, by *Caracci*; the annunciation, by *Albani*; *Biblis*, by

FRANCE.

by the fame; the virgin and *Jesus*, by *Domenicini*; *Parnassus* and the *Muses*, by *Perin del Vago*; the eternal Father in his glory, by *Albani*; *Absalom*, by *Caracci*; a holy family, by *Raphael*; *Apollo* and *Daphne*, by *Albani*; *Christ* healing a fick perion, by *Paolo Veronese*; *Christ* in the tomb, by *Vandyke*; landfcapes and wafherwomen, by *Caracci*; the paſs of *Susa*, by *Cl. Lorrain*; *Venus* and the *Loves*, by *Julio Romano*; a landfcape of *S. John* preaching, by *Ph. Napolitan*; a fair, by the fame; the baptifm of our Lord, by *Albani*.---In the cabinet of fhells, *Herodias*, by *Giorgione*; a landfcape, by *Cl. Lorrain*; *Henry* II. by *Jannet*; the adoration of the wifemen, by *Paolo Veronese*; *S. Cecilia*, by *Mignard*; *Joseph* and *Potiphar*, by *Albani*; *S. George*, by *Raphael*; a virgin, by *Mignard*; the flight into *Egypt*, a landfcape, by *Adamo*; *S. Michael*, by *Raphael*; the fair farrier, by *Leonardo da Vinci*; *Griſſal*, by *Raphael*; a virgin, in a garland of flowers, by *Francy*; *Christ* and the apoſtles; by *Paolo Veronese*, a landfcape, by *Cl. Lorrain*; the portrait of *Henry* IV. by *Porbus*.

In the gallery, over the door, a carrying of the croſs, by *Paolo Veronese*; *Jocunda*, by *Leonardo da Vinci*; the baths of *Diana*, by *Albani*; the fenſual man, by *Correggio*; *S. Francis*, by *Domenicini*; heroic virtue, by *Correggio*; *Loves* in a garland of flowers, by *Domenicini*; the virgin and *Christ*, by *Titian*; the un-nailing from the croſs, by *Titian*; *S. Cecilia*, by *Domenicini*; the circumciſion, by *Julio Romano*. An *Ecce homo*, by *Guido*; a holy family, by *Parmeggiano*; the union of deſign and colour, by *Guido*; the charity of *Battus*, by *Albani*; a *Magdalen*, by *Guido*; a holy family, by *Raphael*; the virgin and *S. Elizabeth*, by *Leonardo da Vinci*; the nativity, by *A. Caracci*; *Herodias*, by *Solario*; a ſmall nativity,

Paintings in the gallery.

nativity, by *A. Caracci*; Omphale, by *L. Caracci*; *S. Paul*'s trance, by *Domenicini*; the espousal, by *Corregio*; the virgin and rabbit, by *Titian*; the *Castilian*, by *Raphael*; the assumption of the virgin, by *Poussin*; a portrait, by *Raphael*; our Lord's prayer in the garden, by *Guido*; the portrait of *John Bellini* and his brother, by *J. Bellini*; a portrait, by *Leonardo da Vinci*; a holy family, by *Albani*; a virgin, greatly esteemed, by *Raphael*; *S. Francis*, by *A. Caracci*; a portrait, by *Carafalo*; a portrait, by *Julio Romano*; the annunciation, by *Albani*; a portrait, by *Holbein*; a small landscape, by *Paul Brill*; an oval virgin, much esteemed, by *Guido*; a virgin and *S. John*, by *Raphael*; Hope, by *Mignard*; a virgin, much esteemed, by *Correggio*; *S. Catharine*, by *da Vinci*; Faith, by *Mignard*; the virgin and *S. Catharine*, by *Guido*; a portrait, by *Holbein*; a repose after the flight into *Egypt*, by *Corneille*; a head, by Sir *Antony More*; a virgin and *Jesus*, after *Correggio*; a portrait of *Anne of Cleves*, by *Holbein*; a virgin and *Christ* asleep, by *Guido*; *S. Jerome*, by *Guercini*; a *Mary Magdalen*, by *Titian*; the martyrdom of *S. Stephen*, by *A. Caracci*.

Paintings in the king's great apartment. — In the state-chamber, over the door, a virgin, by *Vandyke*. Over the chimney in summer, the portrait of *Lewis* XIV. by *Rigault*; Hercules on the funeral pile, by *Guido*; Hercules fighting the Hydra, by the same; *S. Francis* in an extasy, by *Valentini*; *Thomiris*, by *Rubens*; Hercules and *Achelous*, by *Guido*; the *Centaur* and *Dejanira*, by the same. Over the door, the portraits of the *Palatine* princes, by *Vandyke*. — In the bed-chamber, in summer, over the door, a charity, by *Blanchard*; *Christ* in the sepulchre, by *Titian*; the holy family, by *Raphael*; the marriage at *Cana*, by *J. Bassano*;

an

an assumption, by *A. Caracci*; *S. Sebastian*; by the same; the virgin, *Christ*, and *S. Agnes*, by *Titian*; the pilgrims of *Emmaus*, by *J. Bassano*; a *S. Michael*, by *Raphael*. Over the door, a woman wishing good luck, by *Caravaggio*.---- In the concert-room, in the winter, over the door, the virgin and *S. Peter*, by *Guercini*; the pilgrims of *Emmaus*, by *Paolo Veronese*.---First gallery, a nativity, by *Dosse*; a virgin by *Mignard*; over the chimney, a virgin, *Christ* and *S. John*, by *Paolo Veronese*. Second gallery, a virgin, by old *Palma*; an *Ecce homo*, by *Mignard*. In summer, the family of *Darius*, by *Le Brun*. Over the door, *S. John* in the desart, by *Raphael*.---- In the next chamber, *Iphigenia*, by *la Fosse*; an angel guardian, by *Feti*.----In the saloon of the cabinet of medals, *Christ* healing the woman of the bloody flux, by *Paolo Veronese*. In summer a nativity, by *Gaudentio*; the flight into *Egypt*, by *Guido*; a virgin and pilgrims, by *Poussin*---- In the great saloon, the *Pharisees* feast, by *Paolo Veronese*.---In the cabinet of medals, a virgin, *Christ*, and *S. John*, by *Raphael*; the marriage of *S. Catharine*, by *Paolo Veronese*; a virgin, by the same; the virgin, *Christ*, and *S. Michael*, by *L. da Vinci*; the virgin and *Christ*, by *Andrew Mantagne*; *Christ* on the cross, by *Paolo Veronese*; a virgin, *Christ*, *S. George*, and *S. Benedict*, by *Paolo Veronese*; the angel leading *Tobias*, by *Andrea del Sarto*.—In the apartment of the duke of *Orleans*, in the bed-chamber, over the door, a portrait, by *Raphael*; a portrait in its shift, by *Vandyke*; a circumcision, by *Dosse*; a virgin, *Christ*, *S. John*, and *S. Antony*, by *Palma*; *Christ* in the sepulchre, by *J. Bassano*; *Christ* on the cross, by *Dorigny*. Over the door, two soldiers, by *Feti*. In the closet, the portrait of *Joan* of *Sicily*, by *Raphael*; a *Circe*, by *Guercini*; *Titian*'s mistress, by by *Titian*; the triumph of *Titus*, by *J. Romano*; the portrait of *Pontorme*, by *Raphael*; *Judith* holding the head of *Holofernes*, by *L. Justrus*.

Pictures in the cabinets de la Surentendante des Batimens. The pictures not shewn in the king's apartments, are kept in the cabinets *de la Surintendante des Batimens*, where among others you may see, the four elements, by *Albani*; a virgin, *Christ* and *S. John*, by *L. da Vinci*; a country wedding, by *Rubens*; a large landscape, by *Domenicini*; the ghost of *Samuel* appearing to *Saul*, by *S. Rosa*; the four seasons, by *Poussin*; several other pictures by the same; a *Susanna*, by *Tintoret*; *Venus* and *Adonis*, by *Paolo Veronese*; *Apollo* and *Daphne*, by *Carlo Maratti*; a virgin and *Christ* asleep, by the same; a large landscape, by *Paul Brill*; a *Susannah*, the judgment of *Daniel*, the judgment of *Solomon*, all three by *Valentini*; *Timocleas*, by *Domenicini*; *Venus* and *Mars*, by *L. Justrus*; *Christ's* baptism, by the same; a sea port, by *Cl. Lorrain*; *Mary* of *Medicis*, by *Vanayke*; the portrait of queen *Margaret*, by *Rubens*; *Moses* taken out of the water, by *Paolo Veronese*; the nativity of the virgin, by *Paolo Veronese*; a virgin, *Christ*, and *S. Martina*, by *Pietro di Cartona*.

Pictures at Trianon. At *Trianon*, in the grand saloon, you see *Juno* and the rape of *Orithya*, by *Duverdier*. The pictures of flowers and vases in the three next pieces, are by *Baptiste* and *Fontenai*.---In the second hall, there are two pictures of nymphs, by *Blanchard*.---In the third hall, you see *Venus* at her toilet, by *Boulogne* the elder; Cupid asleep, by *Mignard*; the judgment of *Midas*, by *Corneille* the elder; *Venus* and *Adonis*, and *Venus* with the loves over the doors, by *Boulogne* the younger; art and nature, by *Boulogne*; the elder; *Orpheus* awakened at the approach of *Iris*, over the chimney, by the same hand.---In the fourth hall, you

FRANCE.

see *Diana, Endymion,* and *Mercury,* by *Houasse;* *Juno* menacing *Io*, and *Mercury* cutting off the head of *Argus,* by *Duverdier; Hercules* alone, and *Hercules* with *Juno,* by *Noel Coypel.*----In the fifth hall, are *Zephyrus* and *Flora,* by *Jouvenet;* and the four views of *Versailles,* by *Martin* the elder.--- In the first room of the next apartment, you see *Narcissus, Cyanea, Alpheus,* and *Arethusa,* by *Houasse.*---In the second, *Thetis* and *Flora,* by *Coypel; Juno* and *Flora,* by *Boulogne* the elder. Over the doors are morning, noon, evening, and night, by *Martin* the elder.--In the third, you see six pieces of the history of *Apollo,* painted by *Noel Coypel, Jouvenet,* and *Boulogne* the younger.----Over the chimney of the first room, in the apartment of the late Monseigneur, is a *S. Luke,* by *la Fosse.*---In the anti-chamber, there is a *S. Mathew,* by *Mignard;* and a *S. Mark,* by *la Fosse.*---In the ice chamber, you see a *S. John* in the isle of *Patmos,* one of the best pieces of *Le Brun;* and four landscapes, by *le Lorrain.*

List of the Statues at Versailles.

In the great court of *Versailles,* on the right, *Iris,* by *Housseau; Juno,* by *Desjardins; Zephyr,* by *Roger; Vulcan,* by *Errard;* a cyclop, by *Maniere;* another cyclop, by *Droville.* On the left, *Ceres,* by *Tuby, Pomona,* by *Mazeline; Flora,* by *Masson; Neptune,* by *Buister; Thetis,* by *Le Hongre; Galatea,* by *Housseau.*-- About the pediment of the grand front, *Hercules,* by *Girardon; Mars,* by *Marsy.*--On the right of the grand front, *Victory,* by *Espingola; Africa,* by *Le Hongre; America,* by *Renaudin;* Glory, by *Renaudin;* Authority, by *Le Hongre;* Riches, by *Le Hongre;* Generosity, by *Le Gros;* Strength, by *Coisevox;* Plenty, by *Marsy.*---On the left of

Statues belonging to the palace.

the grand front, Fame, by *Le Comte*; *Asia*, by *Masson*; *Europe*, by *Le Gros*; Peace, by *Renaudeu*; Diligence, by *Raon*; Prudence, by *Masson*; *Pallas*, by *Girardon*; Justice, by *Coisevox*; Riches, by *Marsy*.---In the great gallery, the *Venus* of *Arles*, a *Bacchus*, a *Venus, Germanicus, Diana*, a *Priestess, Urania*, a *Vestal*, these eight are antiques.--Upon the great landing-place, *Silenus, Antinous, Apollo, Bacchus*, all four in brass, cast by the *Kellers*; *Diana*, by *Roger*; *Apollo*, by *Raon*.

Statues in gardens. The half moon of *Apollo*'s bason. On the right, *Titus, Antinoüs*, Plenty, *Apollo*, all four antiques; *Orpheus*, by *Franqueville*; *Augustus*, and a Senator, antiques.--On the left a Senator, *Agrippina, Juno*, Victory, *Titus, Hercules, Brutus*, all seven antiques.----*Termes* on the right, *Vertumnus*, by *Le Hongre*; *Juno*, by *Claron*; *Jupiter*, by the same; *Sirinx*, by *Maziere*; the binding of *Proteus*, by *Solds*.---*Terms* on the left, *Pomona*, by *Le Hongre*; *Bacchus*, by *Raon*; Spring, by *Arsis* and *Maziere*; *Pan*, by *Maziere*; *Ino* and *Melicerta*, a group, by *Graniere*.---In the great alley, on the left, *Achilles* discovered by *Ulysses*, by *Vigier*; an Amazon, by *Buret*; a *Dido*, by *Pouletier*; a *Fawn*, by *Flaman*; *Venus*, coming out of the bath, by *Clairion*; Fidelity, by *Le Fevre*; *Milo* of *Crotona*, an admirable piece, by *Puget*; *Castor* and *Pollux*, by *Coisevox*; a dying *Myrmillo*, by *Monier*; the *Pythian Apollo*, by *Mazeline*; *Urania*, by *Carlier*; *Mercury*, by *Melo*; *Antinous*, by *Le Gros*; *Silenus* holding *Bacchus*, by *Maziere*; *Venus* with the beautiful thighs, by *Clairion*; *Tiridates*, by *Deindré*; Fire, by *Dandré*; Lyric Poetry, by *Tuby*; *Aurora*, by *Marsy*; Spring, by *Maniere*; *Water*, by *Le Gros*; *Cleopatra*, by *Vancleve*.---On the right, *Artemisa*, by *Le Fevre*; *Cyparissa*, by *Flaman*; *Venus* of *Medecis*, by *Fremery*; the emperor *Commodus*, by *Jouvenet*;

Jouvenet; *Jupiter*, by *Granier:* Knavery, by *Le Comte*; *Andromeda* and *Perseus*, by *Puget*; *Cinna* and his Wife, by *Espingola*; the Nymph in the Shell, by *Coisevox*; *Jupiter* and *Ganymede*, by *Laviron*; *Urania*, by *Fremery*; *Commodus*, by *Coutoux*; *Fauſtina*, by *Renaudin*; *Bacchus*, by *Granier*; a *Fawn*, by *Hurtrel*; *Tigranes*, by *Eſpagnandel*; *Antinous*, by *La Croix*; Melancholy, by *Le Perdrix*; Air, by *Le Hongre*; Evening, by *Desjardins*; Noon, by *Marſy*; *Europe*, by *Mazeline*; *Africa*, by *Guerin*; Night, by *Raon*; the Earth, by *Maſſou*; Paſtoral Poetry, by *Granier*; *Autumn*, by *Renaudin*; *America*, by *Cornu*; Summer, by *Hutinot*; *Winter*, by *Girardon.*—— Terms; the river *Acheloüs*, by *Maziere*; *Pandora*, by *Le Gros*; *Mercury*, by *Vancleve*; *Plato*, by *Rayol*; *Circe*, by *Maniere*; *Hercules*, by *Le Comté*; a Bacchanal, by *de Dieu*; a Fawn, by *Houzeau*; *Diogenes*, by *Eſpagnandel*; *Ceres*, by *Pouletier*; *Apollonius*, by *Melo*; *Iſocrates*, by *Granier*; *Theophraſtus*, by *Hurtrel*; *Lyſius*, by *de Dieu*; *Ulyſſes*, by *Maniere.*——The orangery, *Lewis* XIV. by *Deſjardins*; an *Iſis* of touch-ſtone, antique.—The north parterre, *Venus*, the baſhful, by *Coiſevox*; the Rotator, by *Fremery*; Heroic Poetry, by *Drouilly*; a Flegmatic Perſon, by *Eſpagnandel*; Satyric Poetry, by *Buiſter*; *Aſia*, by *Roger*; a Sanguine Perſon, by *Jouvenet*; a Choleric Perſon, by *Houzeau.*——The Dragon's Fountain; *Fame* writing the king's life, by *Domenico Gendi*; *Fauſtina*, by *Fremery*; *Berenice*, by *Eſpingola*.

II. MARLY.

The palace of *Marly* is ſituated in a park near the river *Seine*, three miles from *Verſailles*, and fifteen from *Paris*. It was built by *Lewis* XIV.

and the celebrated *J. H. Manfart* drew the defign of it. The body of the building is fquare, being one and twenty toifes each way. The four fronts are equal, each with a flight of fteps, adorned with groupes and vafes. The palace contains one large pavilion, which is in the midft of twelve others of a fmaller fize. The principal pavilion confifts of one great hall in the form of an octagon, which you enter by four porches: the whole building is in an admirable tafte, as well as the gardens. There was formerly a fuperb cafcade, which has been deftroyed on account of the too great expence to fupply it. The great hall, a room famous for its beauty and extent, is in the *Ionic* order, and adorned with four chimneys, over which are painted the four feafons; *Spring* is by *Antony Coypel*; *Summer*, by *Boulogne* the younger; *Autumn* by *La Foffe*; *Winter* by *Jouvenet*. The four porches which lead to this fine faloon, are adorned with pictures by *Vandermeulin*, reprefenting the fieges of feveral towns. In the firft porch are *Luxemburg*, and the taking of *Luxemburg*; in the fecond porch *Maftricht*, *Cambray*; in the third porch, *Tournay*, *Oudenarde*: in the fourth porch, *Valencienne* and *Douay*. In the king's antichamber are to be feen the taking of the following towns, by the fame painter; *viz. Narden, Loo,* and *Utrecht*. In the chamber are the fieges of *Ipres* and *Condé*. In the cabinet, *Salins* and *Joux*. In the cabinet formerly belonging to *Madame de Maintenon*, he has alfo painted *Gray* and *Friburg*. *Martin* the elder painted in the apartment of the duchefs of *Orleans*, the following places; *viz. Rees, Orfoy, Wefel,* and fort *Schenck*; and in that occupied by *Madame de Maintenon*, the towns of *Aire* and *Duesburg*. In the upper gardens called *Belveder*, there are four admirable groupes; *viz. Mercury* carrying off *Pandora*, by *Boulogne*: the *Laocoon, Hercules,* and *Diana*, cast by the *Kellers*. But the greatest curiosity of *Marly*, is the admirable machine which conveys the water from *Marly* to *Versailles*; the chevalier *de Ville* was the inventor of it, and a branch of the river *Seine* turns the wheels. This machine raises six hundred and forty cubical inches of water to the height of sixty fathom, from whence by an aqueduct of five hundred fathom it is carried into the reservoir of *Versailles*: it is said to cost the king five and twenty thousand pounds *sterling per annum*, to keep it in repair.

III. VINCENNES.

Vincennes is an antient castle or palace situated in the isle of *France*, on the east side of *Paris*, in the midst of a wood, where the citizens of *Paris* divert themselves with walking and other exercises. It was begun in 1183, by *Philip Augustus*, and the work carried on by several princes, some of whom chose it for their residence. Under *Lewis* XIV. it was repaired and beautified in 1660, when two constructions were added towards the park, which contain various apartments. The architect was *Lewis le Vau*; and *Manchole*, an excellent *Flemish* painter, decorated the inside. The palace has a spacious court with a stately chapel, and pleasant walks; it is also surrounded with a good ditch, a wall, and eight square towers. The avenue from hence to *Paris*, was planted by cardinal *Mazarin*. The gallery was built by *Mary* of *Medicis*, and contains some good paintings. The cieling of the king's apartment is painted by *Champagne*; and the cieling of the queen's, by *Seve*. *Michael Dorigni*, the son-in-law of *Simon Vouet*, was also employed there. The great gate towards the park is an excellent piece of architecture, built in the form of a triumphal arch, and adorned with the *Doric* order. There is an oak here, under which *S. Lewis* used to administer justice to his subjects. The holy chapel at *Vincennes*, though a *Gothic* structure, is much admired. The glass windows were painted in a peculiar manner by *John Cousin*; and this is reckoned an excellent thing in its kind. There is also a very pleasant convent of *Minims* in the forest, founded by *Charles* VIII. One of its principal curiosities is an excellent picture of the day of judgment, by the abovementioned *John Cousin*, which is to be seen in the sacristy belonging to that convent.

IV. MEUDON.

Meudon. *Meudon* is a small town six miles from *Paris*, remarkable for a royal palace, where the late dauphin (the present king's grand-father) used commonly to reside. This palace stands on an eminence in the midst of a forest: it has a most beautiful avenue that leads to it, three quarters of a mile in length; on the right is a convent; with a pleasant garden belonging to the *Capuchins*, and on the left the vineyards of *Meudon*. The palace was begun by *Philip de L'Orme*, who built it for the cardinal of *Lorrain*: afterwards it came into the possession of *M. de Louvois*. At the death of this minister, the king exchanged *Choisy* upon *Seine*, which had been left to the dauphin by mademoiselle *d'Orleans*, for *Meudon*. The improvements made by his royal highness, rendered it one of the finest residences in all *France*. At the entrance of the court of the palace there is a large pile of building on the right, and another on the left, which open in form of a semicircle, but are disjoined from the body of the house. In the

the middle of the front is a lofty advanced building with a portico, which you enter by three doors. Above it runs an order of architecture, confisting of arches and pillars finely defigned, and above them another order, accompanied with pilafters. The wings are not fo high as the principal building, and each of them is terminated by a fquare pavilion. The infide of this palace was adorned with the richeft furniture, and with a fine collection of ftatues, paintings, medals, and other antiquities, which were removed upon the death of the late dauphin, and great part of them fent to his fon *Philip* king of *Spain*. *Martin* the elder painted the gallery. The front towards the garden confifts likewife of a lofty advanced building, with wings confiderably lower, which terminate on the right and left, with two pavilions of the fame height with the body of the building. The gardens of this place are much admired for their fine walks, parterres, canals, and waterworks. Adjoining to the gardens there is a fpacious park, furrounded with a brick wall, and adorned with woods, bafons, and refervoirs of water. The woods are cut through and divided by beautiful ridings.

V. S. Germains.

S. *Germains*, commonly called *S. Germains en* S. Germains. *Laye*, is a fmall town of the ifle of *France*, in the diftrict of *Mantois*, fituated on a high hill, at the foot of which runs the *Seine*, about twelve miles to the weftward of *Paris*, and one from *Verfailles*. It is remarkable for the royal caftle The caftle, or palace, which was bugun by *Charles* V. and enlarged and beautified by fucceeding princes, but efpecially by *Lewis* XIV. who was born here. The palace is built in the form of a caftle, and

fur-surrounded with a dry ditch. A magnificent stone gallery runs round the middle of the whole structure, which is of an oval figure, and the roof is covered with thin flat free-stone instead of tiles. The chapel is remarkable for an excellent altar-piece, representing the Lord's Supper, by *Pouſſin*. The prospect from the castle is admirable, especially towards the river and the plains, having *Paris*, *S. Denis*, and *Marli*, within sight. There is a curious mall in this castle, with square pavilions built all along, for the conveniency of the players and spectators. Among the improvements made to this place by *Lewis* XIV. he added the terrass of above three thousand paces in length, the grand parterre, and the valley-garden. There are abundance of dry grottos, which afford pleasant retreats in the summer, and several wet ones, with curious water-works, and artificial birds, which make an agreeable sound. In one of the grottos there is a virgin playing on the organs, whose eyes are so artificially moved, that she seems to be alive; in another place there is an *Orpheus* playing on the lute, and keeping time, while the beasts, birds, woods and rocks seem to follow him, with several representations of the like nature, all put into motion by water. The adjacent forest contains upwards of five thousand acres, and is cut through with an infinate number of large ridings, well replenished with game, which renders it a most agreeable situation for hunting. It was in this castle that the late king *James* resided with his court during his exile, and here he died in 1701. His body was afterwards interred in the monastery of the *Engliſh Benedictins* in *Paris*.

Town of S. Germains. The town of *S. Germains* is well peopled, which is owing to the goodness of the air, and the privileges they enjoy. The houses are high and

and well built. There are some squares, with several hotels; among the rest, that of the duke of *Noailles*, which is neatly furnished, and has some handsome gardens. The town has only one parish, an hospital, and some convents, which are those of the *Recollects*, the *Ursuline Nuns*, and the barefooted *Augustinians*, who live in the forest.

VI. FONTAINEBLEAU.

Fontainebleau is a small town of the *Gatinois*, in the isle of *France*, so called because of its fine waters; it is situated in the middle of a forest three miles from the river *Seine*, twelve from *Melun*, and forty-two from *Paris*. There are only three or four streets in the town (all filled with public inns) which terminate in the castle. The *French* kings have chosen this for a hunting-seat, by reason of its situation proper for that diversion. The castle or palace contains some magnificent piles; yet it is a very irregular piece, having been built at several times without any order or symmetry. The old palace was first built by *Lewis* VII. in 1137, but improved by *Francis* I. *Henry* IV. and chiefly by *Lewis* XIV. As you approach the palace, you pass through the court of offices to come to the court of the old castle, known by the name of *Donjon*, and built by *Francis* I. Here you see the front of the great gate of the draw-bridge, supported by several marble pillars, and some ornamental statues. The architecture of this old castle is much esteemed. Round the court there are a great many small turrets and galleries; but the greatest curiosity of this part of the building is a small cabinet adorned with some beautiful pictures, and a chapel whose cieling is admired for its workmanship.

Fontainebleau.

The old palace.

From

138   *The* GRAND TOUR.

The new palace. From the old castle you pass on to the court of fountains, which is adorned with a great many fine brass and marble statues, and a bason where you see several statues, spouting water. This court answers to three sides of a building, which form another palace, so that there are four castles or palaces, and as many gardens in *Fontainebleau*. This here is most esteemed for the beauty of its apartments and galleries. The hall of the hundred *Swiss* is painted in *fresco*, by *Primaticio*, *Maitre Roux*, and *Salviati*. The gal-

The galleries. lery of the stags is a hundred paces long, and runs all along the orangery: it is enriched with paintings representing all the royal palaces, and the finest country-seats in *France*. These palaces are separated from one another by very large horns of stags that have been killed in this forest. Near this gallery you see another small one, where *Henry* IV. is beautifully represented with all his court in their hunting equipage. Above is the queen's gallery, adorned with several pictures representing the victories of the latter kings of *France*. From this gallery you pass to the cabinet of *Clorinda*, enriched with beautiful paintings, containing the history of *Tancred* and *Clorinda*.

The royal apartments. From this cabinet you proceed to the queen's apartment, remarkable for its cieling and gildings: afterwards you pass through the queen's bed-chamber to come to the king's apartment, which is adorned with some very good paintings, particularly *Jocunda*, and a queen of *Sicily*, by *Leonardo da Vinci*, and the portrait of *Michael Angelo* drawn by himself. From thence you pass to the gallery of *Francis* I. where are several paintings representing the history of this prince: but the frescoes are now very much damaged. The little cabinet towards the pool-garden is

enriched

enriched with some exquisite paintings; and the cieling is admired for the elegant taste of the carving and gilding. Next you must see the gallery of the antients, adorned with the representation of several pieces of antient history, which are somewhat effaced. Thence you descend by the great stair-case, facing the court of the white horse, to see the royal chapel, which is called the church of the *Trinity*, and belongs to the *Mathurin* friars. The paintings of this church are by *Freminet*, a famous *Parisian* painter: the high altar is richly adorned, the cieling beautifully gilded, and the pavement of the finest marble. On a wing of the court of the white-horse, is the gallery of *Diana*, or of the labours of *Ulysses*, where the history of this hero is painted beautifully in *fresco*, by *Primaticio*. *The chapel.*

After the apartments you must see the gardens, where the orangery is most deserving of your attention. Among several brass statues in the middle of a large bason, you see a *Diana* stopping a stag by the horns, surrounded by four hounds; a *Hercules*; a serpent between two children; and a *Cleopatra*. The pool garden is surrounded with several canals, which have very large fish, especially carp. This pool is bordered with beautiful alleys, in the middle of which is an octagon cabinet. Next you proceed to the pine-garden, and thence to the parterre of the great garden, where you have a most beautiful prospect of the castle. In the middle is a large bason, in which there rises an aquatic rock, which pours out its waters in a most wonderful manner. To the right of this parterre you see a piece of water level with the ground, in the middle of which is a most beautiful statue of *Apollo*. The grottos and cascades are next to this parterre at the entrance of the park, which is divided in the middle by a large canal. *The gardens.*

The

The walks along the alleys of this park are most delightful, being inclosed with palisadoes of a surprizing height, and extending further than your eyes can reach. The forest of *Fontainebleau* was anciently called the forest of *Bievre*, and contains upwards of six and twenty thousand acres; it is of a round form, and the palace stands in the centre.

VII. S. CLOUD.

S. Cloud.   S. *Cloud* is a small town of the isle of *France*, pleasantly situated upon the river *Seine*, about six miles west of *Paris*. This town was erected into a duchy and peerage in 1674, by *Lewis* XIV. when *Francis de Harly*, archbishop of *Paris*, and his successors, were created perpetual dukes and
The town. peers of *France*, with the title of S. *Cloud*. It is a very antient place, and was originally called *Nogent*, which name it changed to honour the memory of *Clodoald* or *Cloud*, third son of *Clodomir* king of *Orleans*, and brother of *Clovis* II. In the collegiate church they preserve the relics of S. *Cloud*, and the heart of *Henry* IV. who was killed here in 1589, by *James Clement*, a Dominican friar. They have likewise a very good manufacture of earthen-ware, and a stone-bridge over the *Seine* consisting of fourteen arches. This town is much frequented by the citizens of *Paris*, who come hither by water on Sundays and holidays to divert themselves.

The palace.   But the principal curiosity of S. *Cloud* is the palace belonging to the duke of *Orleans*, which for situation, waters, woods, architecture, sculpture, and paintings, is reckoned one of the finest in the kingdom. It is situated at the side of a mountain, at the foot of which the river *Seine* pleasantly glides. The avenue to the palace is upon the declivity of the hill, adorned with three

fine

fine walks of trees, having the town on the right, and the park on the left. This avenue terminates at the *basse-court*, from whence you proceed to the great court at one of the angles, because of the irregularity of the ground. The palace consists of a large advanced building in the middle of the front, and two wings, each of them flanked with a pavilion. The apartments are extremely magnificent, and richly furnished; the paintings especially are vastly admired, being reckoned *Mignard*'s best pieces. Before you enter the guard-hall you may see the billiard-room on the right, the cieling of which is most beautifully adorned with paintings and gildings. The great hall before the gallery is remarkable for the amours of *Mars* and *Venus*, represented in several beautiful pictures. The famous gallery of *Apollo* and its two halls, from whence there is a fine prospect of *Paris* and the adjacent country, are decorated with every thing that can render a place charming and pleasant. The most admired pictures in this gallery are the royal palaces and castles, the birth of *Apollo* and *Diana*, the rising sun, the *Zephyrs* shedding the morning dew, *Aurora* in her chariot with *Cupid* strewing flowers before her, *Apollo* inventing music, *Climene* presenting *Phaeton* to the sun, *Apollo* and Virtue, *Circe* and *Cupid*, *Icarus* falling, and especially the Four Seasons, which are exquisitely drawn. Of the eight *bas reliefs* in *cameos*, in the gallery, with gilt frames, the two largest are, *Marsyas* challenging *Apollo*, and *Apollo* causing *Marsyas* to be flead. The two lesser, are *Apollo* with the Sibyl kneeling before him; and *Apollo* with *Æsculapius* by him. The other four *bas reliefs* placed in the other half of the gallery, are the metamorphosis of *Ceronis*, of *Daphne*, of *Clitia*, and of *Cyparissa*. Towards the left of the further
end

end of this gallery, there is a small hall, adorned with a cieling elegantly painted. The great cabinet is enriched with an infinite number of singular and valuable curiosities, collected with great care and expence, and ranged with the greatest order and taste. The chapel is small, but very beautiful.

The gardens. The gardens are disposed with a great deal of art. Their situation is quite charming; for the river *Seine* running close under them, forms a beautiful and large canal, which waters a long terrass, planted with rows of trees. These gardens are embellished with groves, saloons, basons, water-works, and especially with grand cascades. The upper gardens are very spacious: on the top of the hill there are several large pieces of water, distributed into spouts and sheafs, and diversified in several manners. The park is almost twelve miles in circumference. The orangery, the labyrinths, and the basons, have each their particular merit: but the greatest beauty of all are the two admirable cascades, which are reckoned a master-piece in their kind, and very well deserve a traveller's attention; the highest was designed by *Le Pautre*, and the second by *J. H. Mansard*.

VIII. P r i v a t e S e a t s.

Choisy. *Choisy* lately belonged to the princess of *Conti*, second dowager; it was called *Choisy Mademoiselle*, because it was formerly in the possession of *Mademoiselle de Montpensier*. It belongs now to the king, who has improved the buildings; and it is called *Choisy Le Roy*, so that it ceases in some measure to be a private seat. The house is very beautiful and richly adorned. The gardens are extremely fine; among others the eight statues

statues copied by *Anguier*, from antiques at *Rome*, are greatly admired.

Sceaux is a seat belonging to the duke of *Maine*. In the apartments and gardens there is abundant matter to satisfy the curious. The *Aurora* painted in the pavilion, called by the name of *Le Brun*, is by that famous artist, as are also the fine paintings in the chapel, where he has represented the antient law fulfilled by the new. *Sceaux.*

Clagny near *Versailles*, is a seat belonging to the duke of *Maine*'s son; it was built by *Lewis* XIV. for Madame *de Montespan*. The designs are by *Francis Mansart*. The whole house is in a very good taste, but the court and stair-case are most remarkable. The small pieces of cannon in one of the halls are a present from the officers of the city of *Paris* to the duke of *Maine*, when he was admitted great master of the Ordnance. *Clagny.*

The house, which the princess, of *Conti*, second dowager, had at *Issy* is very fine, both in regard to the architecture, which is in a very good taste, and to the furniture, which is extremely rich. The gardens are very beautiful. The name of the village of *Issy* is said to be derived from the goddess *Isis*, who had a temple there. *Issy.*

S. Maur is a seat belonging to the duchess dowager of *Bourbon*. The taste, the magnificence, and the delicacy so much admired in the *palais de Bourbon* at *Paris*, which was built by this princess, may serve to give us an idea of her country-seat. The situation is extremely pleasant. *S. Maur.*

Bagnolet belongs to the duchess of *Orleans*. The house is large and agreeable; the gardens are well laid out, and of a very great extent. You cannot see this house without a ticket, which is not difficult to obtain. *Bagnolet.*

The

Confians. The house of *Confians* belongs to the archbishop of *Paris*. The whole inside is magnificent, yet the gallery deserves chiefly the attention of the curious. The gardens are extremely pleasant, and the little grotto that opens to the river is inimitable.

Maisons. There are few houses in the neighbourhood of *Paris*, equal to *Maisons* in magnitude and beauty. It belongs to M. *de Maisons*, one of the first and wealthiest families of the law. The whole is remarkably curious, and among the rest, the door on the garden-side, which is wrought with infinite labour. The gardens are also perfectly beautiful and very large.

Montmorency. The house of M. *Croizat* at *Montmorency*, is one of the pleasantest in the neighbourhood of *Paris*. Besides the merit of the architecture which is correct, the cieling painted by *La Fosse* is greatly admired. This famous artist has there represented *Phaeton* asking his father to let him drive his chariot. It formerly belonged to M. *Le Brun*, and the gardens which answer to the beauty of the building, were designed by him. In the church of *Montmorency* there is a tomb of the *Constable* of that name, reckoned one of the finest monuments in *France*.

CHAP. V.

Journey from Paris *to* Italy.

THOSE who intend to travel from *Paris* to *Italy*, must set out for *Lyons*, to which city there are three different routes, viz. two post-roads, and a third used by the *Diligence*. Again there are four different routes from *Lyons* to *Italy*;

the

FRANCE.

the first and plesantest, but longest about, is by *Marseilles* and *Toulon*, at either of which places there are daily opportunities of vessels going to *Genoa*; but if you dont like the sea, you may proceed by the post-route from *Aix* to *Nice*, and thence by land to *Genoa*, or any other part of *Italy*: the second somewhat shorter, is by *Geneva* and *Swisserland*: the third still shorter is by *Grenoble* and *Briançon*: and the fourth as short as the preceding, is by *Pont Beauvoisin*. The *Diligence* from *Paris* to *Lyons* sets out every other day from the *Hotel de Sens*, near the *Ave Maria*; the price to each passenger seventy-five livres. For your baggage you pay five sols a pound, except twenty-five pounds, which you have free. There are likewise coaches at the same place that set out every third day at four in the morning, and winter and summer go through *Burgundy*. You have also water carriages from *Paris* to *Lyons*; the fare to each passenger is thirty-five livres, and you are ten days upon the road.

The first route from Paris *to* Lyons *by* Moulins.

PARIS	Posts.	Puy la Laude	1
Ville-Juif	Post royal.	Montargis	1
Fromenteau	1½	La Commodité	1½
Essonne	1½	Nogent	1
Ponthierry	1⅝	Bezards	1
Chailly	1	La Buissiere	1
FONTAINEBLEAU	1½	Belair	1
Bouron	1	Briarre	1
NEMOURS	1	Ousson	1
Glandelle	1	Bony	1
La Croisiere	1	Neury	1
Fontenay	1	La Celle	1
			Cosne

Cosne	1	Varennes	1
Maltaverne	1	S. Geran	1½
Pouilly	1	La Palice	1½
Meuves	1	Droiturier	1
La Charité	1	S. Martin d'Estreaux	1
Barbeloup	1	Pacaudiere	1
Pougues	1	S. Germain l'Espinace	1½
NEVERS	1½	Roanne	1½
Magny	1½	L'Hospital	1
Villars	1	S. Siphrorien de Lay	1
S. Pierre le Monstier	1	La Fontaine	1½
Chantenai	1	Tarare	1½
Villeneuve	1½	La Croisette	1
La Perche	1	La Bresle	1
MOULINS	1	La Tour	1½
Sannes	1	LYONS Post royal	1½
Bessay	1		
Eschirolles	1	In all sixty-five posts.	

The second post route from Paris *to* Lyons, *by way of* Dijon *in* Burgundy.

You follow the preceding route as far as *Fontainebleau*, where you turn off towards *Burgundy*.

FONTAINEBLEAU	Posts.	Vermanton	1½
Moret	1½	(and in a chaise 2 posts)	
Faussart	1½	Petit Lissard	2
Villeneuve la Guiare	1	Lucy le Bois	1
Pont sur Yonne	1½	Cussy les Forges	1½
SENS	1½	Rouvray	1
Villeneuve le Roy	1½	Maison neuve	1½
Ville Vallier	1	Vitcaux	2
Joigny	1	Chaleure	1½
Bassou	1½	Pont de Panis	1½
AUXERRE	1½	La Cude	1
S. Brice	1	DIJON	1

Le

FRANCE.

La Baraque	1½	MACON	1½
Nuys	1	Maison blanche	2
Beaune	1½	S. George de Renant	1½
Chaigny	1	Villefranche	1
CHALLON	2	Les Echelles	1½
Senneçey	2	La Chaux	1
Tournus	1	LYONS	Post royal
(and in a chaise a post and a half)			
S. Albin	2	In all fifty-nine posts.	

The third route from Paris to Lyons, by the Diligence.

	English miles.		
PARIS		S. Aubin	3
CHARENTON	3	D. Joigny	3
Villeneuve S. George	9	Bassou	9
Mongeron	1½	Rezende	3
Lieursain	7½	AUXERRE	6
D. Melun	9	Saint Brice	6
Le Chatelet	6	Cravant	6
Valence	6	S. Vermanton	3
Moret	6	Sersy le Sec	6
Faussart	6	Luci le Bois	6
Villeneuve la Guiare	6	Vessy	3
Champigny	4½	Souvigny le Bois	1½
La Chapelle	1½	Cussy les forges	4½
Vilmanoche	1½	Rouvray	6
S. Pont sur Yonne	1½	D. La Roche en Breni	3
S. Denis	6	Cheritan	6
SENS	3	Saulieu	3
La Maison blanche	3	Maupas	9
Villeneuve le Roy	6	Pouché	4½
Armaux	4½	Joué	1½
Villecarriere	1½	S. Arnay le Duc	3
Villesien	3	La Cauche	4½
		Yvry	

The GRAND TOUR.

Yvry	4½	Mâche	4
La Rochepot	6	S. Macon	4½
S. Aubin	3	Creche	6
Chaigny	3	La Maison blanche	4½
S. Fargeux	6	Belleville	6
D. Chalon	3	Villefranche	6
Drou	1½	Anse	3
Senecey	7½	Les Echelles	3
Tournus	6	Le Marechal	4½
Montbelet	6	Lyons	0 4½

The first route from Lyons *to* Italy, *by the way of* Marseilles, Toulon, *and the county of* Nice.

Lyons	Posts	Montelimart	1½
S. Fons	Post royal	Donzere	1½
S. Saphorin d'Ozon	1	Pierrelatte	1
Vienne	1½	La Palu	1
Auberive	1½	Pont S. Esprit	1
Peage de Roussillon	1	Bagnols	1
S. Rambert	1½	Le Begude S. Laurent	1½
S. Valier	1½	Pujeau	1
Tein	1½	Avignon	1
Sillart	1	S. Andiol	2
Valence	1	Orgon	1
Paillasse	1½	Pont Royal	2
Loriol	1½	S. Canat	1½
Laine	1½	Aix	2

Here you may either proceed to *Marseilles* and *Toulon*; or turn off to the left, and go directly to *Nice*.

FRANCE.

Route from Aix to Marseilles and Toulon.

	Posts		
AIX		Cuges	1½
Pin	2	Bausset	2
MARSEILLES	1½	TOULON	2
Aubagne	2		

Forty-seven posts from *Lyons* to *Toulon*.

Route from Aix to Nice.

	Posts		
AIX		Muy	1
Rousset	2	FREJUS	1¾
Pourcieux	1½	L'estrelles	2
Tourves	1½	Cannes	2
Brignolles	1	ANTIBES	1
La Cabasse	1	Loup	1
Luc	1	NICE	1
Vidauban	1		

Eighteen posts from *Aix* to *Nice*.

The second route from Lyons to Italy, by the way of Geneva.

	Posts		
LYONS		S. Marlin du Frene	1
Mirebel	Post royal and a half	Nantua	1
		S. Germain le Joux	1
Montluel	1	(and in a chaise a post and a half)	
Valbonne	1		
Chateaugaillard	1½	Chatillon	1
S. Jean le vieux	1	Coulonges	2
Cerdon	1	(and in a chaise 2 posts and a half)	
(and in a chaise a post and a half)		Pougny	1
		Saconnay	

Saconnay	1	GENEVA	1

Sixteen posts from *Lyons* to *Geneva*.

The third route from Lyons *to* Italy *by* Grenoble *and* Briançon.

LYONS	Posts	(in a chaise 2.)	
Bron	Post royal	La Frette	2
S. Laurent des Mures	1	Rives	1¼
Verpilliere	1½	Voreppe	1¼
Bourgoin	1½	GRENOBLE	1½
Eclofes	1¼		

Thirteen posts from *Lyons* to *Grenoble*.

At *Grenoble* the post road ends, by reason of the mountains; you must therefore hire horses to carry you to *Bourg d'Oisans*, which is 27 miles from *Grenoble*, and from thence you proceed in the same manner to *Briançon*, which is 27 miles from *Bourg d'Oisans*. From *Briançon* you go to *Pignerol*, the first town in *Piedmont*.

The fourth route from Lyons *to* Italy, *by* Pont de Beauvoisin *and* Savoy.

This route is the same as the preceding as far as *Bourgoin*, where you break off to the left, to take the road of *Savoy*.

Bourgoin	Posts	Gas	1
Vacheres	1	Pont de Beauvoisin	1
La Tour du Pin	1		

Nine posts from *Lyons* to *Pont de Beauvoisin*.

This

FRANCE.

This is the last town of *France* on the frontiers of *Savoy*. It is situated within six miles of the *Rhone*, on the river *Giers*, which separates *Savoy* from *France*. The river divides it into two parts, which are joined by a bridge. The inhabitants make a considerable profit by the vipers they take in the adjacent country. From hence you must proceed to *Montmeleian*, and thence by *S. John de Maurienne* and *Susa* to *Turin*, according to the route pointed out in the 6th chapter of the third volume of this work, p. 167.

Remarkable places in the first route from Paris *to* Lyons.

Fountainebleau has been described in the preceding chapter, p. 137.

I. NEMOURS.

Nemours is a city of the isle of *France*, in the district of *Gatinois*, in east longitiude 2. 45. latitude 48. 17. It is situated between two hills, on the river *Loin*, and consists principally of one large street, in which there is a market-place, and the old priory of *Malta*; this last is likewise the parish church of the town, and dedicated to *S. John*. In this priory they pretend to have part of the upper jaw of *S. John the Baptist*, brought from *Jerusalem* by *Lewis* VII. The town is on this side of the *Loin*, which you pass on a large bridge, that gives its name to the suburb on the other side of the river. They have a castle on the banks of the *Loin*, with several high round towers, which serve for prisons. This city was erected into a duchy in 1404, and gave title to the illustrious house of *Nemours*, but has returned to the crown since the death of the last duchess, who was princess of *Neufchatel*. Without the town there is a nunnery of the *Cistercian* order, called *Our Lady*

Lady of Joy, where you may see the tomb of the ancient counts of *Nemours*. There are likewise two other handsome convents, one of the nuns of *S. Mary*, and the other of *Reccollect* friars.

Montargis. From *Nemours* you proceed to *Montargis*, a town of *France*, in the province of *Orleanois*, and territory of *Gatinois*, in east longitude 2. 45. latitude 48. It is the capital of the *Gatinois*, pleasantly situated on the *Loin*, not far from the place where the canal of *Orleans* falls into this river. The town is not large, but having been burnt down in 1528, it is handsomely rebuilt, and has a castle situated on a hill, which commands the town and the neighbouring country. The great hall of this castle is very considerable, being 28 fathom 2 feet long, and eight fathom four feet broad. The parish church is dedicated to *S. Mary Magdalen*. They have two convents of men, and four of women. The town is called *Montargis le Franc*, because of its privileges, being the seat of an election, bailiwic, and provostship.

Briare. *Briare* is a town of *France*, in the government of *Orleanois*, and district of *Gatinois*; in east longitude 2. 45. latitude 47. 40. situated on the river *Loire*. It has nothing considerable in its self, consisting only of one long street filled with inns, and smith's shops, being the great thouroughfare to *Lyons*. But it gives name to the famous canal which joins the *Loire* and the *Seine* by means of the *Loin*. This canal was begun under *Henry* IV. and finished under *Lewis* XIII. by the care of Cardinal *Richlieu*. It extends thirty three miles in length to *Montargis*, from whence another of fifty four miles has been dug to *Orleans*, which together with the *Loire*, form an irregular polygon.

Cosne. *Cosne* is a town of *France* in the government of *Orleanois*, and province of *Nivernois*, situated on
the

FRANCE.

the banks of the little river *Noaim*, not far from the *Loire*, in a fruitful and pleasant country. It is surrounded with ditches, but very indifferently built. The avenues of the market-place indeed are pretty spacious, and much the agreeablest part of the town. The suburbs are almost equal to it in bigness, and much superior in beauty. *Cosne* is separated from *Berry* by the *Loire*, and has a very good trade in cutler's ware, and founding of cannon.

La Charité is a town of *France* in the government of *Orleanois*, and territory of *Nivernois*, situated on the declivity of a pleasant hill near the *Loire*, over which it has a handsome stone bridge. It is half way between *Lyons* and *Paris*, and had its name from the liberality of the monks of *Cluny* to poor pilgrims and strangers who passed this way. There is a priory here of the abovementioned order, which has the lordship of the town, both as to temporals and spirituals. The choir and refectory of the monks deserve your curiosity, the former has some curious representations of animals in *Mosaic* work. There are some good houses in the town, together with a large market-place. The inhabitants are famous for glass-work, in which they carry on a pretty good trade.

Pouges is only a village; but its mineral waters have rendered it more famous than a great many towns. It is situated at the foot of a mountain, and the mineral source is within two hundred paces of the village.

II. NEVERS.

Nevers is the capital of the *Nivernois*, in the kingdom of *France*, and government of *Orleanois*, in east longitude 3. 15. latitude 46. 50. situate on the river *Loire*, which here recieves the little river *Nievre*, from whence this city derives it name. It is a place of great antiquity, supposed to be *Cæsar*'s *Noviodunum in Æduis*, where he erected magazines for his armies. *Francis* I. made it a duchy and peerage, in 1521, in favour of *Francis* of *Cleve*, to whom it came by marriage. It devolved afterwards to the house of *Mantua*, and then to the *Palatine* family, who in 1651, sold it to cardinal *Mazarin*. The cardinal obtained a title of duke and peer for his nephew *Philip Mancini*, in whose family it still continues. The town is fortified with walls, defended with many high towers and deep ditches, and is the seat of a bishopric, suffragan of *Sens*, as likewise of a bailiwic, and chamber of accounts. There is a stone bridge on the *Loire*, with twenty arches, a draw-bridge on each side, and towers to defend them. The cathedral is dedicated to *S. Cyr*. There are eleven parishes in the town, and a great many religious houses. The Jesuits college near the gate *des Ardeliers* is a handsome structure. The palace of the dukes of *Nevers* has a large front between two great towers, with a court on one side, and a garden on the other. Here it was that *John Casimir* king of *Poland* died the 16th of *December* 1672. Near this palace stands the convent of *Cordeliers*, who have a magnificent church, in which the tombs of duke *John*, and *Catharine* of *Bourbon*, on the right; and those of *Lewis* of *Gonzaga* duke of *Nevers*, and *Henrietta* of *Cleves* his wife, merit your attention. This town is famous for its glass-manufacture, and earthen-ware; and is said to contain about eight thousand inhabitants.

S. Pierre le Monstier. *S. Pierre le Monstier* is a town of *France*, in the government of *Orleanois*, and district of *Nivernois*, situated between the *Allier* and the *Loire*, about

about half way between *Nevers* and *Moulins*. The town is small, though noted for a presidial court, on which *Nevers* depends. As it stands at the foot of a lake, and is surrounded on every side with mountains, except towards the south, the air is consequently unwholesome. There is a very considerable priory here, of the order of *S. Benedict*; whose prior is lord of part of the town.

III. Moulins.

Moulins is a city of *France*, and capital of the *Bourbonois*, in the government of *Lionnois*, in east longitude 3. 16. latitude 40. 33. It is situated in the middle of a beautiful plain, on the *Allier*, and derives its name from the number of mills, which were formerly in this neighbourhood. The improvements it has recieved of late years are so considerable, as to render it one of the handsomest and richest cities in *France*. The town is walled and defended with towers, of no great extent itself, but it has large suburbs. The antient dukes of *Bourbon* made this place their ordinary residence, where they built a noble castle, which is still admired for its beauty. It is built of a free stone, has some very good paintings, and is situated on an eminence, from whence there is a beautiful prospect of the river, the town and the adjacent country. The *Palais* or court of justice is a new building, where they have a presidial, which depends on the parliament of *Paris*. The generality of *Moulins* consists of nine elections; but in spirituals the town depends on the bishop of *Autun*. The great church dedicated to our Lady, is reckoned a handsome structure. In the *Carthusian* monastery out of the town, the church, the cloysters, and the gardens are particulrrly worth seeing. There are several

several other churches and convents of men and women, but the most curious is that of the nuns of the visitation, whose church is adorned with fine marble, and handsome paintings. You must not forget the magnificent tomb of the great duke of *Montmorency*, who was beheaded at *Toulouse*, the 30th of *October* 1632. This monument was erected by his duchess, and is deservedly admired both for materials and art. The town is famous for its medicinal waters, which are much of the same nature as those of the *Bath* and *Aix la Chapelle*. The suburb of *Allier* is filled with cutlers, whose work is vastly esteemed, and brings a considerable trade to the town. The inhabitants are said to enjoy great privileges, to be very courteous, and speak good *French*.

Roane.

Roane is a town of *France* in the government of *Lyonois*, and territory of *Forez*, in east longitude 4. latitude 46. situated on the *Loire*, where this river begins to be navigable. The conveniency of its situation, whereby goods may be brought by water from *Lyons*, has rendered it a very flourishing place. There are a great many rich merchants here, who have several beautiful houses. The Jesuits of this town have a handsome college.

You may embark at *Roane* to descend the *Loire*, in covered boats called *Cabanes*, to *Orleans*, *Tours*, *Angers*, and even as far as *Nantes*.

Tarare.

Tarare is a small town of the *Lyonois*, very much taken notice of by travellers, because of its high mountain, three miles long, and extremely difficult to pass. You descend as far as the village of *La Fountaine*, and then you ascend by a very rugged road and through a great wood till you come to *Tarare*.

IV. Lyons.

FRANCE.

IV. LYONS.

Lyons is the capital of the *Lyonois* in the king- <small>Lyons.</small>
dom of *France*, situated at the confluence of the
rivers *Rhone* and *Soane*, in east longitude 4. 55.
latitude 45. 50. It is a place of great antiquity, <small>Antiquity.</small>
whose origin is variously reported, but the most
probable opinion supposes it to have been at first
a colony, settled there in the time of *Augustus*,
by *Lucius Munatius Plancus*, the *Roman* governor of that country. Its situation in the middle
of *Europe*, and on two fine navigable rivers, the
beauty likewise of its buildings and walks, the
greatness of its commerce and manufactures, the
many privileges it enjoys, being the capital of the
government of *Lyonois*, the seat of an archbishop
primate of *Gaul*, as also of a presidial, a generality, a seneschal's jurisdiction, and a chamber of
money or mint; all this together renders it the
second city of this great and flourishing kingdom.

Lyons is divided as it were, into two towns by <small>Situation.</small>
the *Soane*, which runs through the middle. It
takes up the declivity of two hills, with the level
ground between these hills, and the rivers *Rhone*
and *Soane*. For the civil government, it is divided into thirty wards, each of which has its
proper officer. The town is encompassed with
large suburbs, and has an old strong castle cut out
of a rock, and therefore called *Pierre-encise*, where
state prisoners are kept. The hills, and the
natural temper of the climate, make it very
warm in the summer, in so much that the windows are generally of oiled paper, which keeps
out the heat better than glass, but takes off from
the beauty of the buildings. The streets are <small>Buildings.</small>
narrow, but the houses very high, and of a white
stone, like our *Portland*. There is a stone-bridge

over

The GRAND TOUR.

Bridges. over the *Rhone*; and three handsome bridges, one of them stone, over the *Saone:* that over the *Rhone* has twenty large arches, and is 260 fathom long; in the middle of it there is a cross, which divides the *Lyonois* from the *Dauphiné*. The town has six gates, as many great squares, four suburbs, thirteen parish churches, fifty monasteries, and about 100,000 inhabitants.

The Cathedral. To take a survey of the curiosities of this city you must begin with the cathedral, which is dedicated to *S. John Baptist*, and stands in the lower part of the town near the river *Saone*, having a great square before it, adorned with a fountain. The curious esteem it one of the best structures in *France*, though very plain, and without ornament; it was built on the ruins of an antient temple, dedicated to *Augustus*. The archbishop is primate of *Gaul*, and has 48,000 livres a year. The dean and canons take the title of counts, and must prove their nobility by four descents. Their church-service is somewhat different from that of other places in *France*; they must say it all by heart in *Gregorian* song, and without organs. The cupboard near the altar is reckoned a curious piece, consisting of two antient fragments, one of marble, very well wrought, and the other in the *Gothic* taste. The clock on the right side of the choir is esteemed a most curious piece of mechanism, and was made by *Lippius*, a mathematician of *Basil*. The chapel of *Bourbon*, though in the *Gothic* taste is worth seeing; it was built by cardinal *Bourbon* archbishop of *Lyons*, who lies here interred in a marble tomb.

Other churches and convents. Next to the cathedral comes the collegiate church of *S. Paul*, which was built by saint *Sacerdos* towards the middle of the sixth century.

Opposite

Opposite to *S. Paul* is the church of *S. Laurence*, where you may see the tomb of the famous *Gerson*, chancellor of the university of *Paris*. The church of *S. Irenæus* is very antient; here is a chapel and a well, in which they preserve the relics of a great number of martyrs. At the entrance of the church there is a fine piece of *Mosaic*, with eight verses expressing the death and number of those martyrs. The collegiate church of *S. Just* is very rich; the nave and the front were elegantly rebuilt in 1703, after the designing of Sieur *de la Monce:* it stands near the church of the *Minims*, who have a handsome convent. *S. Nisier* is a parochial and collegiate church, which was formerly the cathedral: the great door is very curious; the choir has several pictures representing the life of Christ, which are all, except four, by *Thomas Blanchet:* the picture of the flagellation is by old *Palma*. In the subterraneous chapel of this church, *S. Photinus* is said to have assembled the primitive christians in time of persecution. The *Dominican* church in the *Place Confort* is worth seeing, because of a very valuable picture of *S. Thomas* the apostle, by *Salviati*, and of the many monuments of great men, who lie here interred. The church of the *Cordeliers* was founded by *Charles* VIII. and *Anne* of *Britany*. These fathers have the head of *S. Bonaventure* in a fine silver busto. In the convent they shew the room where this saint died, which is converted into a chapel, said to have been designed by *Michael Angelo*, but painted by old *Stella*, and supported by four great pillars of fine grey marble of one piece. The altar-piece is greatly esteemed; it represents *S. Francis*, and was drawn by *Vannius*.

The Jesuits have three houses at *Lyons*, two of which are colleges. The little one is in the quarter

The Jesuits college.

quarter de Fourviere; in the church there is a very beautiful picture of Christ in the desart, by *Stella*. The great one, situated below the square *de Terraux*, is one of the most magnificent colleges in the kingdom, being an excellent piece of modern and regular architecture, in the form of a perfect square. The court is admired for its paintings, representing the arms of every province of *France*, and the entire history of the city of *Lyons*. The church is a very handsome structure, dedicate to the *Holy Trinity*. The library is magnificently built in the form of a T. at the expence of the family of *Villeroy*; it is reckoned one of the best in the kingdom, consisting of about forty thousand volumes. They have here a cabinet of medals and other antiquities, as *Roman* and *Egyptian* idols, unextinguishable lamps, talismans, &c. collected by *Pere la Chaise*, and an excellent observatory, designed and built by father *John* of *S. Bonnet*. The chapel of the congregation of this place is very rich.

Abbey of D'Aisnay. The abbey of *D'Aisnay* without the town is one of the richest of the province. The church and cloysters have nothing extraordinary in their architecture, but are famous for several antiquities. This was formerly the college called *Athenæum*, erected for the improvement of the *Greek* and *Latin* tongue by the emperor *Caligula*, who is said to have ordered such as were overcome when they contended for the prize of eloquence, to be thrown into the *Rhone*, which *Juvenal* alludes to by the following verse.

Aut Lugdunensem Rhetor dicturus ad aram.

The church of *D'Aisnay* is built on the ruins of the antient temple dedicated to *Augustus* by
Lucius

Lucius Munatius Plancus, at the conflux of the *Rhone* and the *Soane*. The pillars, which support at present the roof of the choir, are some of the remains of that antient edifice. It was consecrated about six hundred years ago, by pope *Paschal* II: at the bottom of the great altar, you see a *Mosaic* piece, representing this pope with the following verse almost defaced by time; *Hanc ædem sacram Paschalis papa dicavit*. Under the choir they shew a subterraneous chapel dedicated to *S. Photinus* and *S. Blandina*. Over the gate of the church there is a *basso-relievo* in marble, with this inscription, *Matri Augustæ Philenus Egnatius Medicus;* which father *Menestrier* in his history of the city of *Lyons* supposes to have been a votive offering of the abovementioned physician, to the goddess *Abundance*, under the title of *Mater Augusta*.

The *Carmelites* have two convents, one near the *Place de Terraux*, and the other in a very agreeable situation, on the banks of the *Seine*, where they have a terrass from whence there is a charming prospect. In the cloysters there are some good paintings, and among the rest the last judgment, a very extraordinary piece, and well coloured. Their chapel has an altar piece, all of marble, curiously wrought. The *Carthusians* have also a fine terrass, from whence you have a beautiful view of the town. Their refectory is a handsome room, beautified with many curious pieces of painting. Their cloysters are very spacious, and in their gardens which lie on a declivity, near the *Saone*, they have vineyards that produce excellent wine. The church called *Our Lady of Fourvier*, was formerly a temple of *Venus*. The convent of the *Carmelite* nuns was built by the family of *Villeroy*, at a royal expence; the high altar is surprisingly magnificent. The altar-

_{The Carmelites.}

_{The Carthusians.}

_{The Carmelites.}

altar-piece is the un-nailing of Christ from the cross, reckoned one of *Le Brun*'s best pieces. The tabernacle was made at *Rome* after the designs of cavalier *Bernini*. The chapel of the founders is reckoned a master-piece, where the monument of the family of *Villeroy* is greatly admired. The convent of the *Recollects* is famous for a noble vault, which supports their house, and in some measure upon which it leans. This piece of architecture is greatly extolled; it was built in 1648 by brother *Valerian*, a religious of the same order. The other churches and convents most worthy notice are, the fathers of the oratory, the Celestins, the barefooted *Carmelites*, the fathers of *S. Antony*, the nuns of the Visitation, and the convent of *S. Elizabeth*, where you see a beautiful picture by *Stella*, and another in needle-work by the nuns, which is reckoned a master-piece.

The Recollets.

Town-house.

The town-house of *Lyons* is one of the most magnificent and most regular buildings of that kind in *Europe*; it stands in the square *des Terraux*, and is built all of white stone in a quadrangular figure: it was begun in 1647, and finished in 1655. The front is flanked with two great square pavilions, and adorned with a gilt balcony, supported by two beautiful columns of porphyry in the *Ionic* order. Its principal entrance is embellished with a great many fine pillars, which form a spacious and most magnificent portico. As you come into this portico, you see the busts of several *French* kings; mounting a few steps you may read on antient tables of brass the harangue pronounced by the emperor *Claudius*, who was then only censor, before the *Roman* senate, in favour of the inhabitants of *Lyons*. These tables were found accidentally in 1528, by workmen who were digging in the

FRANCE.

the hill of *Sebastian*. The stair-case leading to the apartments is esteemed an accomplished work, enriched with beautiful paintings, by *Thomas Blanchet*, representing the burning of *Lyons* under *Nero*, which is said to have happened by lightning. This stair-case leads to a magnificent hall, admired for its bigness and paintings. From thence you go through a little gallery, into another hall, where you see the portraits of all the *French* kings that bore the name of *Lewis*; the cieling is adorned with some good pieces of perspective. Among several other halls, you ought to see that where the provost of the Marchands, and the Eschevins assemble. The different courts of justice are held in this town-house, where they have each their seperate chambers, and exercise their respective jurisdiction. 'Tis here also the merchants meet, to concert together about commercial affairs.

The hospital for the sick is a very large edifice, situated along the *Rhone*, and consisting of a pavilion in the middle of four great halls. The work-house, called the *Hospital of Charity*, is a noble structure, consisting of nine courts, where 1500 poor people are constanly employed. The granaries where they preserve their corn, are a large pile of buildings, and much admired by strangers. The custom-house stands on the great key, close to the river, where all the goods that come to *Lyons* are visited. Just by, you may see the silk-mills, which are made in such a manner, that a single woman may turn one of them with ease; they are fastened together, and one mule generally turns seven or eight mills. They have an arsenal likewise in this city, well furnished with all necessary implements of war. *The arsenal.*

The hospital. *The workhouse.* *The Granaries.* *The customhouse.* *The silkmills.*

The principal squares are *Bellecour*, now called *Place de Louis le Grand*, *La Place de Terraux*, and *Place Confort*. The square of *Bellecour* is *The squares.*

much

much the handsomest, being adorned with very good houses, and a fine alley of trees, terminating at one end with the *Rhone*, and the other with the *Soane*. It has taken its new name from an equestrian statue of *Lewis* XIV. which was cast at *Paris* after the model of *Coisevox*, and stands in the middle of the square. The two marble figures on the pedestal representing the *Rhone* and the *Soane*, were made at *Paris* by *Coutoux* the elder. The square *Des Terraux* is next in rank to *Bellecour*; it is adorned with a very beautiful fountain in the middle, and with the royal nunnery of S. *Peter* on one side, and the town-house on the other. In the *Place Confort*, there is a triangular obelisk, erected in honour of *Henry* IV. on which the name of God is engraved in four and twenty languages.

Antiquities Besides those already mentioned, there are a great many other remains of antiquity in the city of *Lyons*. Near the gate of *Veze*, they discovered some years ago an antient mausoleum, supported in the nature of an altar by four columns, and whose architecture seemed to be of the age of *Augustus*. As there was no inscription found with it: various opinions were handed about concerning this tomb; but the most probable is that of father *Meneftrier*, viz. That it was a monument in form of a temple or altar, consecrated to the memory of one of *Augustus*'s priests, called *Amandus*, by two of his freed-men, whom he left his heirs. This conjecture is supported by an inscription somewhat to this purpose, which is still preserved in the house of the count *de Chalmazel*. This antient monument, after having escaped the fury of barbarous ages, was shamefully destroyed by the magistrates of *Lyons* in 1707.—The aqueducts of *Mark Antony*, a *Roman* quæstor, and friend of *Julius Cæsar*, are another curiosity worth seeing. These aqueducts

ducts are without the gates of *S. Juſt*, and built entirely of square stone. Some years ago, as they were digging in the neighbourhood, they found part of the ruins of the burning of *Lyons* under *Nero*, among the rest two leaden pipes half melted, which distributed the water of the aqueducts. These pipes are now preserved in the cabinet of the Jesuits college.------ Near the mountain of *S. Juſt*, in the vineyard of the *Urſuline* nuns, there is a reservoir built by the *Romans*, to preserve the water of these aqueducts; this reservoir is 45 feet long and 44 broad and the wall is three feet thick.--In the isle of *S. Barbe* there are several considerable ruins, and, among the rest, some *low relieves* of tombs in a very good taste: one of them represents the four seasons; and another *Bacchus*, with the gods *Sylvanus*, *Pan*, and *Faunus*. --- In the vineyard of Monſ. *Caſſaire*, as they were digging in 1676, they discovered the face of a wall lined with mosaic work; but the workmen, in endeavouring to clear away the rubbish, spoiled a great part of the figures. The pavement however, which is 20 feet long, and ten broad, by good luck remained entire. It is composed all of mosaic, or of what the ancients called *Teſſelatum*, *Sectile*, or *Vermiculatum Pavimentum*. The middle has a square three foot high, and four broad, representing a group of four very ingenious and emblematical figures. The other curiosities at *Lyons* are, the palace, the arsenal, the three forts, *viz. Pierre-Cize*, (already mentioned) fort *S. John*, and fort *S. Clair*; the house *des Antiquailles*; the statue of Monſ. *de la Roche*; the curious cabinet of the late M. *Nicolas Grollier de Serviere*; *la Claire* and *la Duchere*, two country-houses without the gate of *Veſé*; the high-roads of *Agrippa*; the ancient amphitheatre in the inclosure of the *Minims*; the

god

god *Mithra*, formerly adored at *Lyons*, and now shewn in the *Hotel de Chevrieres*; the nuns of the imperial palace; and especially the antient altar, which was discovered in 1704, in digging on the mount of *Fourviere*, with an inscription, and the head of a bull in *demi-relief* on one side, and the head of a ram without an inscription on the other. The learned suppose this monument to have been erected to preserve the memory of a *Taurobolus*, or the sacrifice of a bull in honour to of the goddess *Cybele*.

Trade. The trade of *Lyons* is very considerable, for which it is advantageously situated on the rivers *Rhone* and *Saone*, and in the neighbourhood of *Swifferland*, *Italy*, and *Germany*. The chief branch of their commerce is in silks and rich stuffs; their silk they have raw from *Sicily*, *Naples*, *Florence*, and the other towns of *Italy*, as also from *Languedoc* and *Provence*; and after they have manufactured it, they send it to most parts of *Europe*. In these manufactures they formerly employ'd 20,000 men, but at present not near so many, since other nations have begun to set up silk manufactures. They print likewise abundance of books, with which they furnish the mart of *Frankfort*, and other parts of *Europe*, but this trade is also upon the decline. They have four annual fairs, with a great many immunities, as also a conversator of their privileges, who determines disputes among the merchants.

Public inns. They have a great many handsome Inns at *Lyons*, the principal of which are the *Three Kings* and *The Dauphin*. There are likewise several good ordinaries, where you may dine very reasonably.

Stage-coach to Paris. The stage-coach from *Lyons* to *Paris* sets out from the *Rue de Flandre*, every other day, at four in the morning. You pay seventy-five livres for your

FRANCE.

your place, and five fols *per* pound for your baggage, except twenty-five pounds which you have free.

Remarkable places in the second route from Paris *to* Lyons.

Leaving *Fontainebleau*, the first place you come to is *Moret*, a small town of the *Isle of France*, and district of *Gatinois*, situated at the confluence of the rivers *Seine* and *Loin*, in E. long. 2. 55. lat. 48. 22. It is surrounded with pretty good walls, and has a very antient castle, which has only one small tower, covered with a terrafs. The great church dedicated to *Our Lady*, is a tolerable building.---*Pont-sur-Yone* is a small town on the right side of this river, within two leagues of *Sens*. It is a modern place, and contains nothing remarkable.

Moret.

I. SENS.

Sens is a city of *France*, capital of the province of *Senonois*, in the government of *Champaign*, in E. long. 3. 23. lat. 48. 6. It is a place of great antiquity, known to the *Romans* by the name of *Senones*, and *Agendicum Senonum*. It is pleasantly situated in a fine plain on the rivers *Yonne* and *Vanne*, over the first of which there is a large stone bridge. Most of the streets are watered with streams which come from the little river *Vanne*. There are thirteen parishes in the town, but it is not so populous as large. This city is the seat of an archbishop, and has likewise a presidial and a bailiwic, one of the most antient in *France*, which depends on the parliament of *Paris*. The cathedral of *S. Stephen*, a magnificent

Sens.

ficent structure with two great towers, is equal in bigness to *Notre Dame* at *Paris*, but better built. At the foot of the altar there is a golden table enriched with precious stones, upon which are engraved, in *Baffo-relievo*, the four evangelists, with S. *Stephen* on his knees in the middle of them. The tombs of the *Sallezards*, of the archbishop of *Sens*, and the bishop of *Angouleme*, are worth seeing, because of the marble figures, which are well done. The chapels round the choir are very handsome; and the windows are much admired for the paintings, done by *John Coufin*, who was born at *Coucy* near *Sens*.

Villeneuve le Roy. *Villeneuve le Roy* is a small town of the district of *Senonois* in *Champagne*, situated on the river *Yonne*, over which it has a stone-bridge. Some will have this to be the *Vellaudunum*, mentioned by *Cæsar*.

Joigny. *Joigny* is a small town of *France*, in the government of *Champagne*, and district of *Senonois*, in east longitude 3. 28. latitude 47. 55. It is pleasantly situated near the banks of the river *Yonne*, on the declivity of a hill, surrounded with thick walls, and large towers. The great church is a handsome building; there is likewise a large square in the town, a good stone-bridge, and a castle.

II. AUXERRE.

Auxerre. *Auxerre*, in Latin *Antifiodurum*, is the capital of the district of *Auxerois* in *Burgundy*, in east longitude 3. 35. latitude 47. 40. It is situated partly on a hill, partly in a valley, and watered by the river *Yonne*. The river brings some trade to the town, which is moreover the seat of a presidial, bailiwic, election, and of a bishop, suffragan of *Sens*. It is adorned with handsome squares,

FRANCE.

squares, and a great many fountains and churches. The cathedral of *S. Stephen* is a magnificent structure, with a fine choir and a lofty tower. The bishop's palace is an elegant building. The abbey of *S. Germain* is famous for the bodies of many holy prelates, which are preserved in the grottos built in 850 by *Conrad*, brother of the empress *Judith*, and abbot of *S. Germain*. There are a great many convents of men and women within and without the town, besides a college of Jesuits, and a commandery of the knights of *Malta*. The episcopal seminary is governed by the fathers of *S. Lazarus*.

III. D I J O N.

Dijon is the capital of the duchy of *Burgundy*, in the kingdom of *France*, in east longitude 5. 5. latitude 47. 15. It is situated between two small rivers which surround it, viz. the *Ouche* and the *Suson*, at the entrance of a vast plain. It is a town of great antiquity, said to have been founded by the emperor *Aurelian*, who gave it the name of *Divio* or *Divionum*, to appease the Gods for having destroyed a town where *Hercules*, and some other heathen deities, were worshipped. It is now one of the most considerable cities in the kingdom, being the seat of a parliament, appointed by *Lewis* XI. in 1477, as also of a presidial, a chamber of accounts, a court of money, and a generality. The city is large and well built; the streets well paved, wide, straight, and lightsome. It is surrounded with strong walls and deep ditches, and fortified with twelve bastions. There are four gates; close to that which goes by the name of *William*, stands the castle, built by *Lewis* XI. and fortified with four large round towers, and two ravelins.

Marginal notes: Dijon. Situation. Buildings.

The town has three suburbs, that of the gate of *Ouche*, that of *S. Nicholas*, and that of *S. Peter*. Without the gate of *Ouche*, there is a fine alley of trees, which carries you to *Beaune*. As you go out of *S. Peter*'s gate, you see the course, almost a mile long, and planted with four rows of trees; this leads you to a great park, embellished with parterres and labyrinths, and terminated by a terrass on the banks of the *Ouche*, over which is a bridge that communicates with the castle of *Colombiere*.

Churches. There are seven parochial churches in *Dijon*. That of *S. Michael* is remarkable for the beauty of its portal, adorned with sculptures. The front of *Notre Dame* is very handsome, and principally noted for its clock. The church of *S. John* is observable for having no pillars to support the roof. Behind the choir of *S. Benignus*, there is a very antient building of a round figure, supported by a hundred and four pillars, and lightened only from the top, which is supposed to have been a heathen temple dedicated to all the Gods, like the *Pantheon* at *Rome*. It is now converted into a Christian church. The church called the *Holy Chapel* is remarkable for a host, which is said to have shed blood upon being pierced with a knife by a Jew; and for the escutcheons of the knights of the order of the *Golden Fleece*, which are painted in the choir. The Jesuits have a fine college, and a good library, which is open to the public. The *Carthusian* monastery without the town is one of the richest and handsomest in *France*; their choir is remarkable for two beautiful marble tombs of *Philip the Bald*, and *John* his son, both dukes of *Burgundy*. They have a vast number of other religious houses of both sexes in *Dijon*, a house likewise for penitent courtesans, a seminary for young ecclesiastics; and three large

large hospitals, one for orphans, another for indigent travellers, and a third for poor sick people.

Near the holy chapel is an antient palace, in which the dukes of *Burgundy* formerly resided, and where the governor of the province, when he comes to *Dijon*, is used to lodge. Part of it has been lately repaired, and a new magnificent hall added to it, where the states of the duchy of *Burgundy* hold their assemblies. There is a handsome square, with piazzas before this palace, and in the middle an equestrian statue of *Lewis* XIV. made of brass, at *Paris*, by *Le Hongre*. The palace or court where the parliament of *Dijon* assembles, is also an antient building. In the front there is a portico supported by four columns. *Charles* IX. built the great hall, which has several shops on each side. The great chamber for hearing causes was built by *Lewis* XII. and is remarkable for its beautiful cieling. About a mile from *Dijon* is the little town of *Talon*, where the dukes of *Burgundy* once resided.

Nuys is a small town of the duchy of *Burgundy*, situated in a plain on a brook called *Mexin*, about half way between *Dijon* and *Beaune*. It is surrounded with walls and ditches, and has the title of bailiwic, with a court subject to that of *Dijon*. And yet it consists only of one large street, which is filled with nothing hardly but coopers, because of the great quantity of wine that grows in the neighbourhood. These wines, and those of *Beaune*, are esteemed the best in *Burgundy*.

Beaune is a town of *Burgundy* in *France*, in east longitude 4. 50. latitude 47. It is situated on the little river of *Bougeoise*, in one of the pleasantest and most fruitful parts of the kingdom. The town is neatly built, of an oval figure,

figure, surrounded with walls and ditches, 780 fathom in circumference. It has four gates, two parish churches, besides three in the suburbs, and a college where the fathers of the oratory have the instruction of youth. The collegiate church of our Lady is reckoned one of the most famous in *France*; the great altar is adorned with a table, enriched with diamonds, a present of the dukes of *Burgundy*. The work on which the organ is fixed, is admired as a curious piece of architecture. The church of the *Carthusians* is a modern building, adorned with handsome statues and pictures. The hospital of *Beaune* is reckoned one of the best buildings of the kind in *France*, and was founded by *Rollin* chancellor of *Philip the Good*, duke of *Burgundy*. The wines in the district of *Beaune*, are esteemed all over *Europe*; the most exquisite are those of *Volnet*, *Mulsant*, and *Pommard*.

The abbey of Citeaux. Not far from *Beaune*, is the famous abbey of *Citeaux*, where the general of the *Cistertian* order resides. It had its name from a great number of cisterns dug there under ground, and was founded by *Otho* I. duke of *Burgundy*, in 1098.

IV. CHALLONS.

Challons. *Challons* (commonly called *Challons sur Saone*, to distinguish it from a town in *Champagne*, named *Challons sur Marne*) is the capital of the territory of *Challons* in the duchy of *Burgundy*, in east longitude 5. latitude 46. 40. This is a place of great antiquity, as appears from several statues, inscriptions, and the ruins of an amphitheatre. It is very agreeably situated on the river *Saone*, in a large fruitful plain, surrounded by by a wall, and defended by a castle. Here the Saone forms an island; over it there is a bridge of wood and another of stone. It is divided into the old and new town; the latter incloses the former, which consists only of three long streets, beginning at the stone-bridge, and ending at the gate of *Beaune*. In the middle street, which is the largest, you may see the palace of the bailiwic, a modern building situated near the river. *Challons* is the seat of a bishop, who is suffragan of *Lyons*. The cathedral dedicated to S. *Vincent* has some monuments of the antient counts of *Challons*. The town-house, the Jesuits college, and the commandery of S. *Stephen* and S. *John*, are worth seeing. There is a very agreeable walk to the castle, from whence you have a delightful prospect.

Tournus is a small town of the district of *Ma-* connois in the duchy of *Burgundy*, situated on the right bank of the river *Saone*. The town is of an oblong figure, and contains a collegiate church, two parishes, a convent of *Recollects*, and another of *Benedictins*, whose abbot is lord of the place. The adjacent country is one of the pleasantest and most fruitful parts of all *Burgundy*.

Tournus.

V. MACON.

Macon is the capital of the district of *Ma-* connois in the duchy of *Burgundy*, in east longitude 4. 55. latitude 46. 22. This is a very antient town, situated on the declivity of a hill, on the west side of the river *Saone*, over which there is a fine stone bridge, which joins it to the suburb of S. *Laurence*. The town extends itself in the form of a crescent, and contains about six thousand people. The streets are narrow and ill-

Macon.

ill-paved. It is the seat of a bishop suffragan of *Lyons*, as also of a presidial, and a governor, who is the king's lieutenant. The cathedral, dedicated to S. *Vincent*, is a dark old building, but is famous for its harmonious chimes. The episcopal palace, situated in the square of the old castle, is reckoned a handsome structure. There are several religious houses of both sexes, a handsome college of Jesuits, and two good hospitals. The wines of *Macon* are in great esteem all over *France*.

Villefranche.

Villefranche is a small town, the capital of the district of *Beaujolois*, in the government of *Lyonois*, in *France*, in east longitude 4. 45. latitude 46. *Humbert* IV. lord of *Beaujeu*, the founder of this town, in order to draw inhabitants, granted the particular privilege to husbands of beating their wives, even to the effusion of blood, so that death did not ensue. It is situate on the *Morgon*, which falls into the *Saone* about three miles lower down. The town consists chiefly of one very handsome street with a pleasant fountain in the middle, from whence you may easily see the two gates. It is fortified with good walls, and deep ditches, has a collegiate church, an academy, an election, a bailiwick, and a magazine of salt. There is a very particular custom in the district of *Villefranche*, that in harvest time, the poor people go and cut down the corn without leave of the proprietors, and take the tenth sheaf to themselves in payment for their trouble. This is called *La Cherpille*, and has been long complained against by the proprietors, but in vain.

Trevoux.

Those who have a mind to see the principality of *Dombes*, must pass the *Saone*, before they come to *Villefranche*, in order to go to *Trevoux* the capital. This principality belongs to the duke of of *Maine*, and has a parliament which is held at *Trevoux*. Here is a handsome college of Jesuits, a deanery, a good printing-house, and several religious houses of both sexes. The *Chambre du tresor*, the *Hotel de Monnoye*, and the governor's palace, are the buildings most deserving of notice. The journal of arts and sciences, under the name of *Trevoux*, is wrote by the Jesuits of *Paris*, who also composed the dictionary of that name. *Trivortium*, the *Latin* name, is owing to its having been built upon the spot, where one of the high roads made by *Agrippa* in *Gaul* divided itself into three.

Remarkable places in the third route, by the Diligence from Paris to Lyons.

Setting out from *Paris* the first place you come to is *Charenton*, a small town in the isle of *France*, situate a little above *Paris*, at the conflux of the *Seine* and *Marne*, in east longitude 2. 30. latitude 48. 45. It was remarkable for a handsome church, where the protestants of *Paris* performed their worship before the revocation of the edict of *Nants* in 1685, when it was rased to the ground, and a nunnery erected in 1703 in the same place. The road from *Paris* as far as *Mongeron* is through a fine level country. At *Villeneuve S. George* you change horses. From *Mongeron* to *Lieursain* you go through the forest of *Senar*. At *Lieursain* you change horses, and from thence you travel through a plain and two little woods, one on the right and the other on the left, till you come to *Melun*, where the coach stops to dine.

Melun is a town of the isle of *France*, situate on the river *Seine*, in east longitude 2. 45. latitude 48. 30. It is a place of great antiquity,

Charenton.

Melun.

supposed

supposed to be the *Melodunum* of *Cæsar*. In form and situation it exactly resembles *Paris*, the river *Seine* forming an island in the middle, and dividing it into three parts, which have a communication by bridges. It is fortified with a castle, encompassed with large suburbs, and has the title of a viscounty. There are several handsome churches in the town, an abbey dedicated to *S. Peter*, and some other religious houses. Here are likewise the ruins of an antient temple dedicated to the goddess *Isis*. The inhabitants have a good trade in corn, flower, wine, and cheese, which they send to *Paris* by the river *Seine*.

From *Melun* to *Moret* (a town described in the preceding route) the road is through heaths, thickets, and the forest of *Fountainebleau*, except about a mile and half of champain country, as you come out of *Melun*. Towards *Valence*, there is a wood called the wood of *Valence*. From *Moret* to *Fauffart*, you pass through a valley; the rest of the road as far as *Auxerre*, is all through a fine plain. At *Pont sur Yonne* the coach sets up for all night. The next morning you set out early and pass through *Sens*, a city already described in the preceding route. At *Maison blanche* you change horses, and from thence you come to *Villeneuve le Roy*, described also in the preceding route. You change horses again at *Villecarriere*, and dine at *Joigny*, a town of *Champagne*, described in the preceding route. At *Baffou*, *Regende*, and *Auxerre*, you change horses. *Auxerre* has been described in the preceding route.

From *Auxerre* to *Vermeton* you continually mount and descend, the country being very uneven. At *S. Brice* you change horses, and lie at *Vermenton*. The next morning you set out early, and

and in the way to *Sercy le Sec* you go through a little wood, which is reckoned very dangerous, and so is the wood on the other side of *Sercy le Sec.* From *Lucy le Bois* to *Souvigny* you pass through another wood, which is no way dangerous. Between *Souvigny* and *Cuffy*, there is a great pool surrounded with woods, called the pool of *Tobias*, which is reckoned a very dangerous place. At *Cuffy* you change horses, and between that place and *La Roche En Breni*, you pass through the woods of *Empoignepain*, otherwise called *La Grurie*, where you must be upon your guard. At *La Roche* the coach stops to dine; and from thence to *Saulieu* the road is all through woods and thickets, till you come within a mile of *Saulieu*, where you change horses. *Saulieu* is a small town in the duchy of *Burgundy*, situate on a rising ground, surrounded with walls and ditches. It has two gates, and five suburbs, which are larger than the town. There is a public college, and a small hospital in this place, which is subject in temporals as well as spirituals, to the bishop of *Autun*. Near *Maupas*, there are two places, one called *le petit bras de fer*, and the other *la maison de champs*, the passage through which is reckoned dangerous. From *Maupas* to *Arnay le Duc*, it is all a good road, except through the wood of *Joul*. At *Pouché* you change horses, and set up for all night at *Arnay le Duc*.

Arnay le Duc is a small town of the duchy of *Burgundy*, in the district of *Auxois* on the river *Arroux*, and one of the seats of the bailiff of *Auxois*. There are three gates to the town, to each a suburb, and but one parish church. At the further end of the suburb of *S. James* there is a little priory of the order of *S. Benedict*, whose church is very antient; the prior has jurisdiction in the town. There is an hospital here, and a free

Saulieu.

Array le Duc.

free school under the direction of the Jesuits of *Autun*. From hence you set out early and go through *Canche*; from this last place to the borough of *Ivry*, the road is through woods and thickets. In the neighbourhood of *Ivry* some years ago, they discovered an antient column, which was supposed to have been erected in memory of a victory obtained by *Cæsar* over the *Helvetians*. This column belongs to *M. de S. Micault*. At *Yvry* you change horses, and are obliged to have a relais of ten, because of the bad road from hence to *Rochepot*, where you pass through the great bog called *de la Fiole*. From *Rochepot* to *S. Aubin*, the road is very narrow all through vineyards, as also from *S. Aubin* to *Chagny*. At *Chagny* you change horses, and from thence to *Challons* the road is through woods which take the name of *Chagny*. At saint *Fargeux* you see the end of the forest of *Beauregard*, which is forty five miles in circumference.

At *Challons*, a city described already in the preceding route, the coach stops to dine. From thence to *Senecy* the road is through a wood called *la Grole*. Between *Senecy* and *Tournus* there is a great heath. *Tournus* has been already described in the preceding route; from thence you proceed to *Macon*, described likewise in the same place, and there the coach sets up for all night. From *Macon* to *Maison Blanche* the road is very narrow. Near *Maison Blanche* you pass through a valley, and thence come to a large heath. From *Villefranche* to *Lyons* the road is good, except through some thickets towards *Eschelles* and *Le Marechal*.

FRANCE.

Remarkable places in the first route from Lyons *to* Italy, *by* Marseilles *and* Toulon.

From *Lyons* you may go down as far as *Avignon* by water; for there are boats that descend the *Rhone* almost every day, and move with great expedition on this rapid river. Travelling by land you come to *S. Saphorin*, a small town about seven miles distant from *Vienne*, and famous for its post-asses, which go from hence to *Lyons*, and perform their stages as well as horses, but will not be driven an inch farther by any means whatever.

I. Vienne.

Vienne is the capital of the territory of *Viennois*, in the government of *Dauphiné* in *France*, in east longitude 4. 44. latitude 45. 35. This is one of the most antient towns in *Europe*. *Julius Cæsar* resided here a considerable time, and made it his magazine for provisions and arms. As a proof of its antiquity, there are still the remains of an amphitheatre, and some other *Roman* ruins. It is still a flourishing city, being the capital of the lower *Dauphiné*, and the seat of an archbishopric, bailiwic, and presidial, which depends on the parliament of *Grenoble*. It is situated on the *Rhone*, and covered by high mountains, which confine it to the banks of that river. This situation is not very pleasant; and besides the streets are narrow, uneven, and ill-paved. But the neighbouring fields on the side of *Avignon*, and the banks of the *Rhone*, are exceeding beautiful. It is about five miles in circumference, including a mountain on which were two strong castles in the time of the *Romans,* now called *Pipet & la Baffiere,* and of which there are still some considerable remains. The little river *Jere,* which falls from the rocks between these two castles into the *Rhone,* divides the town into two unequal parts; these communicate with one another, by means of two bridges. The smallest includes the priory of *S. Martin,* and the church of *S. Severus,* adorned with a square tower. In the other part, at the foot of the castle of *Pipet,* there is a convent of Capuchins, and a handsome college of Jesuits. Descending from thence through some narrow streets, you see a chapel called *Our Lady of Life,* which is said to have been the *Prætorium* of *Pilate,* governor of this town. Over the door there is a stone ball with this inscription, *Hoc est pomum sceptri Pilati,* They pretend likewise to shew the house where *Pontius Pilate* lived during his exile, (for he is said to have been banished hither by *Tiberius*) the tower where he was imprisoned, and the lake where he is reported to have drowned himself. The cathedral dedicated to *S. Maurice* is a magnificent *Gothic* structure, and stands upon an eminence to which you ascend by upwards of twenty steps. It has neither hangings nor pictures, but is quite plain, like that of *S. John* at *Lyons.* The walls of the cloyster are built of pieces of figured columns, which are supposed to be the remains of an antient amphitheatre. There are seven parishes in *Vienne,* two collegiate churches, and several religious houses of men and women; the two collegiate churches of *S. Peter* and *S. Stephen,* and the *Benedictin* abbey of *S. Andrew* are the most worthy of notice. The archbishop's palace is a good convenient building. Near it is the hall called the *Clementine,* from the constitutions made there by *Clement* V. at the time of the general council. The abbey of *S. Peter* is very antient; here, as well as in other churches, there are a vast number of antient inscriptions. This city is famous for several councils, as likewise for abolishing the order of the *Templars*, and for the institution of the feast of the sacrament. The inhabitants have a very considerable trade in paper, iron, and steel wares, but especially in sword blades, the water of the little river *Jere* being said to have a particular virtue to perfect the temper of steel. Five hundred paces from the gate of *Avignon*, there is an antient pyramid called the *Needle*, made of very hard stones without any cement. There is no inscription, but it is generally believed to have been designed for the tomb of some antient *Roman*.

In your way from *Vienne* to *Valence*, you pass through *S. Rambert*, a small town of the *Viennois* on the *Rhone*. Thence you proceed to *S. Valier*, also a little town of the *Viennois*, pleasantly situated in the fruitfullest part of the country. Thence you come to *Thein*, a large town of the same district of *Viennois*, situated on the river *Rhone*. It is mentioned in *Theodosius*'s maps by the name of *Tegna*, and is remarkable chiefly for that excellent wine, known by the name of *Hermitage*, from an hermitage situated on that fruitful hill. It is said that there are some gold mines upon this spot.

Over against *Thein*, on the other side of the *Rhone*, stands the little town of *Tournon*, in the government of *Languedoc*, and territory of *Vivarez*, in east longitude 4. 45. latitude 44. 50. It is situated on the side of a mountain, at the bottom of which runs the *Rhone*. The most remarkable building is the Jesuits college, which was founded here by cardinal *Tournon* in the sixteenth century. The college, is a handsome

Tournon.

piece

piece of modern architecture, very agreeably situated on the banks of the *Rhone*, and adorned with a beautiful church and excellent library. This town has several other monasteries, as likewise a castle, with the title of a county, belonging to the family of *Vantadour*, and extends its jurisdiction over seventy-two parishes.

II. VALENCE.

Valence. *Valence* is a city of *France*, and capital of *Valentinois* in *Lower Dauphiné*, in east longitude 4. 50. latitude 45. It is a place of great antiquity, said to have been a colony of the *Romans*, who gave it the name of *Valentia*, because of its strength. 'Tis now a large well-built town, situated on the *Rhone*, and the see of a bishop suffragan of *Vienne*. It is divided into two parts, the town and the borough; the latter lies in a bottom watered with rivulets, and enclosed with double walls and ramparts. From thence there is a gentle ascent to that part called the town, which is built on a small platform, where the streets are very narrow and winding. Here you see the abbey of *S. Ruff*, which is a fine *Gothic* building. Proceeding a little further you come to the market-place, called *La Pierre*, or the stone, because the measures made use of for corn are hollow stones. A handsome wide street carries you from hence to the great square, where stands the cathedral, a noble structure, dedicated to *S. Apollinaris*. The churches of *S. Peter* and *S. John* are remarkable for their antiquity, particularly the church of *S. John*, which was a *Roman Pantheon*. In the cloysters of the *Cordeliers*, they shew the skeleton of a giant called *Buardus*, sixteen feet high. They have an university here which was removed from

Grenoble

FRANCE.

Grenoble in 1452, by *Lewis* XI. The town has, among other jurisdictions, that of a seneschal and a presidial. The neighbouring country is extremely pleasant, the hills lying about it in the form of a crescent on the one side, and the *Rhone* with its beautiful meadows being open to it on the other.

Montelimart is a small town of *Lower Dauphiné*, situated on the little river *Robion*, about a mile from the *Rhone*, in a fertile plain. There is a citadel here which stands on an eminence. The town is well built, and pretty populous, being a great thorough-fare to *Catalonia*, *Provence*, and *Italy*. The collegiate church is subject to the immediate jurisdiction of the see of *Rome*. They have several convents of men and women, among which, that of the Jesuits is the most remarkable. The neighbouring territory is noted for its excellent wine.

Pont S. Esprit is a small town of *Languedoc*, six miles distant from *Palu*, situated on the right bank of the river *Rhone*, in east longitude 4. 45. latitude 44. 20. The streets are narrow and the houses indifferently built. The stone bridge over the *Rhone* is one of the finest in *Europe*, being eight hundred and forty yards long, and five yards sixteen inches wide, sustained by twenty-six arches. It is said to have been built by a monk, with the offerings made by devout people, at a church or chapel dedicated to the Holy Ghost, out of compassion to the misfortunes of so many people who had been drowned in the *Rhone*, which runs here with incredible rapidity. It was begun in the year 1265, and finished about the year 1309. They have a strong citadel at the foot of it, consisting of four royal bastions, this being a very important pass.

From

Orange.

From *Pont S. Esprit* you may go to *Orange*, and thence to *Chateauneuf* and *Avignon*. *Orange* is the capital of the principality of that name in the province of *Dauphiné*, in east longitude 4. 46. latitude 44. 10. It is situated in a fine large plain watered with a vast number of little rivulets, on the east-side of the river *Rhone*. This town made a considerable figure in the time of the *Romans* by whom it was called *Aurosio Cavarum*, and *Secundanorum Colonia*, being the garrison of their second legion. They adorned it with several buildings, whereof there are still some ruins left; particularly of an amphitheatre, a circus, an aqueduct, a public bath, and a triumphal arch almost intire, dedicated to *Marius*. This town and principality were formerly subject to the princes of *Orange*, but were yielded to *France* by the peace of *Utrecht*, tho' the title is still retained by the house of *Nassau*. It is now a bishop's see, suffragan of *Arles*, and has a court of finances, a mint, and an university, founded by *Raymond* V. prince of *Orange*, in 1364. The country is pleasant, abounding with corn and fruit, but liable to frequent winds.

III. AVIGNON.

Avignon.

Avignon is a city of *Provence* in *France*, and capital of the county of *Venaissin*, in east longitude 4. 40. latitude 43. 50. situated on the east-side of the river *Rhone*. This is a very antient city; the *Romans* called it *Avenio Cavarum*. After a great many revolutions, it came to the pope, under whose jurisdiction it still continues. Pope *Clement* V. removed the pontifical see hither in 1309, where his successors lived till 1371. 'Tis now a fine large city, surrounded with a stone wall, rather beautiful than strong, and with ditches filled

filled in some parts with water. Pope *Sixtus* V. made it the see of an archbishop, before which it was suffragan of *Arles*. It has some stately buildings, and very agreeable avenues. The cathedral, dedicated to the *Virgin Mary*, is a noble structure, remarkable for its great altar, the tombs of several popes and bishops, and for the chapel of our Lady, which is admirably well painted. The treasure of the Sacristy is worth a traveller's curiosity. The palace of the vice-legate was the residence of the pope, when the see was at *Avignon*; the great hall is adorned with good paintings, as also the chapel, and the other aparments. The little palace belonging to the archbishop is a handsome structure. The church of the *Celestins* is a magnificent building, in which there is a picture of the carrying of the cross in mosaic work reckoned a master-piece in its kind. The tomb of *S. Benezet*, a little sheperd, who built the bridge of *Avignon*, is a curious piece. In one of the halls of the convent there is a large skeleton, admirably well painted by king *René*, and said to represent a beauty whom he admired. On the coffin, a long side of it, there is a painted cobweb, which you would take for a real one, unless you touched it. The chapel of the *black Penitents* at the *Cordeliers*, is adorned with excellent paintings of *Mignard* of *Avignon*. Among other curiosities in their church you may see the tomb of *Laura*, whom *Petrarch* has immortalized by his verses. This tomb was erected by *Francis* I. who likewise wrote the epitaph. The Jesuits have two colleges, both of which are handsome buildings. The church of *S. Martial*, belonging to the *Benedictins*, has several fine marble tombs; and in that of *S. Didier* there is a beautiful tomb of cardinal *Peter Damianus*, adorned with marble statues. They have an university, which was

founded

founded in 1303, by *Charles* II. king of *Jerusalem* and *Sicily*, and count of *Provence*. The civil government is administered by the vice-legate, the rota, and the viguier. The *Jews* have a synagogue here; they are miserably poor, and deal chiefly in old clothes. There is a wooden bridge here upon the *Rhone*, which is almost gone to ruin for want of repair. In the little borough of *Villeneuve*, the other side of the bridge, there is a handsome convent of *Carthusians*, whose church is much admired for its paintings. Not far from *Avignon* is the fountain of *Vaucluse*, where the little river *Sorgue* has its source, inclosed with hills and mountains, which form the valley of *Vaucluse*. Here it was that the famous *Petrarch* fixed his *Parnassus*, and composed the most part of his works in praise of the beautiful *Laura*, with whom he fell in love in this country. Near this same source they shew you some ruins, which they call *the castle of Petrarch*.

IV. A I X.

Aix.

Aix is the capital of *Provence* in *France*, in east longitude 5. 25. latitude 43. 30. situated in a plain on the little river *Arc*, almost surrounded with fruitful hills, and watered with several fountains. This city is said to have been built by *Caius Sextius Calvinus*, a *Roman* consul, who called it *Sextia*, from his own name; and *Aquæ*, because of the hot-baths and other springs in the neighbourhood. 'Tis now a large well built city, said to resemble *Paris* the most of any town in the kingdom, for the beauty of its buildings, the politeness of the inhabitants, its spacious squares, and beautiful fountains. This city has a parliament which was settled by *Lewis* XII. in 1501; likewise a chamber of accounts, a court of aids, a

seneschal's

seneschal's jurisdiction, a generality, a mint, and an university. It is also the seat of an archbishop, who is always chancellor of the university. The cathedral dedicated to *S. Saviour* is a fine *Gothic* building, remarkable for a beautiful font of marble, and some handsome tombs. The chapter of *S. Saviour* is one of the most considerable in *France*. The square of the *Dominicans* is very beautiful; here stands the palace where the parliament and courts of justice are held. In this palace there is a chamber in which the kings of *France* are painted on square compartments. The Jesuits church and college are handsome structures of modern architecture. The chapel of the congregation is very beautiful, being noted for eight large statues by the famous sculptor *Puget*; the altar-piece, representing the annunciation, is admired by connoisseurs for its composition, and the beauty of colouring. In the square of *Orbitello* there is a course consisting of three fine walks of trees of a great length, with elegant uniform buildings on each side of it, and embellished with fountains. The town house is a handsome building, remarkable for one of the finest clocks in *France*, and for a public library. The market-place is large, and well supplied with provision of all sorts. In the church of the *Fathers of the Oratory*, the high altar is worth attention; the architecture is of the *Corinthian* order, and the six pictures decorating it are by *Mignard*; there are also some other good pieces by the same hand. In a little chapel in the court-yard, belonging to those fathers, there are about twenty curious pictures of the life of *Christ*, and different saints, by a famous old painter of this city, named *Daret*. In the chapel of the *white Penitents*, there is an admirable *bas relief* of white marble, representing

our

our *Lady of Piety*, said to be done by *Michael Angelo*. On the cieling of this chapel there is a picture of the resurrection by *Daret*,, which is extolled as a master-piece. The nuns of the *Visitation* have a handsome church and convent. The church and convent of the *Dominican* friars are worth seeing; In the cloyster are painted all the great men of the order. From the library you have a very pleasant prospect of the neighbourhood of *Aix*: the refectory and the kitchen are extremely well contrived. In the church of the *Carmelites* you see a very remarkable picture, drawn by the good king *René*. In the church of the barefooted *Carmelites*, there are three pictures by *Daret*. The priory of the knights of *Malta* is remarkable for its tombs, and for the curiosities of the sacristy. In the suburb of the *Cordeliers*, there is a great square, where they drink the mineral waters, which were discovered the beginning of this century. By the medals, and other antient monuments found here, it appears to be the place where *Sextius*'s baths were situated. In 1705, they discovered a stone three feet long, and a half wide; on this stone was an altar with a *Priapus* of an extraordinary size, and these three letters, *I. H. C.* that is, *in hortorum custodiam*, or *Jucundo hortorum custodi*. Here the *Carthusians* have a handsome church. The course without the gate of *S. Lewis* is terminated by the front of the church of the *Recollects*, which makes a very pretty appearance. In the garden there is a curious grotto. The hospital, called *la Charité*, is a handsome commodious building.

V. Mar-

FRANCE.

V. MARSEILLES.

Marseilles is a city and port-town of *Provence* in *France*, situated on a fine bay of the *Mediterranean*, in east longitude 5. 20. latitude 43. 15. It is a place of great antiquity, generally said to have been founded by the *Phocians*, about 586 years before *Christ*. 'Tis now one of the largest, handsomest and most trading cities in the kingdom, situated at the bottom of a hill, which rises in the form of an amphitheatre as it recedes from the sea. The harbour is one of the best and safest in the *Mediterranean*, and the usual station of the *French* king's gallies, but will not admit of ships of above five or six hundred tuns. It is of an oval form, and surrounded with a key 1400 paces long, on which are built the finest houses in the town. The entrance of the port is narrow, and shut with a chain, which lets only one vessel in at a time.

The town was much enlarged by the late king, and well fortified with walls, bastions, and ditches; it has six gates, whereof that called the *Royal* is very well built, and ornamented with the statues of S. *Lazarus* and S. *Victor*. The citadel is near the harbour, commanding the whole town; and its fortifications reach to the mouth of the port. The magazines of arms and warlike stores are said to equal any in *Europe*. Here you may see the great hospital for the slaves, and the arsenal consisting of six large pavilions, and as many fronts, with a great square for building the galleys. Within canon reach of the *Tetragon* that commands part of the town, there is a fort called *Notre Dame de la Garde*, from whence the inhabitants can espy the ships out at sea. This fort is built on the top

top of a mountain, on the ruin of an antient temple of *Venus* called *Ephesium*. On this mountain they shew you a mine of soap; it whitens linen like artificial soap, which it greatly resembles. Here the Jesuits have lately built a very curious observatory.

Buildings. *Marseilles* is a very populous city, being said to contain 100,000 inhabitants. It is the see of a bishop, suffragan of *Aix*, of a court of admiralty, a viguiery, a seneschal's jurisdiction, and a bailiwic. It is divided into the old and new town; the old stands on an eminence above the port, where the streets are narrow and dirty, and the houses very indifferent. On the other hand, the new town is perfectly well built, particularly the street called the *Course*, which is one of the finest in *Europe*, the houses on each side being uniform and magnificent, and between them a charming walk of trees. The cathedral dedicated to *S. Lazarus* is a dark old building in the old town, said by some to have been dedicated to *Venus*, and by others to *Diana* of *Ephesus*. The treasure of this church is very considerable; and there are still some large pillars on which the idol is said to have stood. Here is a piece of marble with an *Arabian* inscription, said to be the epitaph of some *Mahometan* priest. In the chapel behind the choir you see a beautiful representation in demi-relief of *Christ* in the sepulchre, all of white earthen ware. Our Lady *de Acoules* is a fine large church, which was antiently a temple dedicated to the goddess *Pallas*. The church of *S. Saviour* was consecrated to *Apollo*. The abbey of *S. Victor* of the order of *S. Benedict*, is a handsome large edifice, situated at the foot of the citadel, and inclosed with walls like a castle. The church is famous for a subterraneous grotto in which *S. Mary Mag-*

The Course.

Cathedral

Other churches.

dalen

FRANCE.

dalen is said to have lived six or seven years. In the monastery there is a great number of tombs and antient inscriptions. The *Carthuasins* are within half a league of the town.

Town-house. The town-house is situated on the port opposite the galleys; 'tis a neat, though not a large building. The most remarkable beauty of this edifice are the town arms on the frontispiece, carved by the famous *Puget*.

Trade. The trade of this city is the most considerable of any place in the *Mediterranean*. They have several manufactures of their own, but the royal manufactory of silk surpasses the rest.

Neighbourhood. As you approach *Marseilles* towards the sea, you have a very agreeable prospect. The town appears like a great terrass raised on the sea-shore, before which you see the isles of *If*, *Rattoneau*, and *Pomegues*, which are only three miles off. In each of these isles there is a strong castle, and a *Lazaretto* for performing quarantine. On the land side, you behold one of the finest plains in *Europe*, in which there are very near six thousand country houses called *Bastides*, belonging to the merchants and tradesmen of *Marseilles*. These *Bastides* consist of a small pavilion, with a garden or vineyard, whither the inhabitants retire from the noise of the town.

From *Marseilles* to *Toulon* the road is stony and mountainous; the mountains are so perpendicularly high, and hang over in some places, that they look dismal as well as barbarous and extremely barren. In the road to *Toulon* you pass through the little town of *Aubagne*, which has the title of a barony, and belongs to the bishop of *Marseilles*.

VI. TOULON.

VI. Toulon.

Toulon. Toulon is a city and sea-port of *Provence* in *France*, in east longitude 6. latitude 43. 5. It is a place of great antiquity; *Telo Martius* the tribune settled a colony there, and called it by his own name. The kings of *France* finding it a commodious harbour, pitched upon it as their principal arsenal in the *Mediterranean*. To *Lewis* XIV. it owes its fine docks, yards, founderies, and the finishing of its fortifications.

Buildings. This city is the see of a bishop suffragan of *Arles*, the station of the royal navy, and the seat of a viguier. It is of no large compass, but well built, and adorned with many handsome **The Cathedral.** churches and religious houses. The cathedral is remarkable for the chapel of our Lady. The Jesuits have a handsome house, with a seminary for the chaplains of the navy. The finest street in the town is that of *S. Mignaud*, beginning from the key, and containing among other build- **The town-house.** ings the town-house, remarkable for the two stone *Terms* on the side of the great gate, which were cut by the famous *Puget*, and raised the admiration of cavalier *Bernini*. Almost opposite the town-house, is the house of the said *Puget*, built after his own designs, which shews that he was as indifferent an architect, as he was excellent in sculpture and painting. On the ceiling of this house he has painted the Destinies in a man- **Harbour.** ner as strikes all connoisseurs. The harbour extends the whole length of *Toulon*, and has always a considerable number of men of war. The key is very uniform, and all paved with bricks.

Magazines. The magazines and offices which the late *French* king erected for the navy, are worthy the curiosity of travellers. These offices consist,

1. Of

1. Of the rope-yard; 2. The school for the marine-guards; 3. The hall of arms; 4. The artillery-park. 5. The store-house. 6. The foundry; 7. The royal bake-house, &c. The machine for putting the masts in ships at the old dock near the chain, is the admiration of all that see it.

At *Toulon* and *Marseilles* there are vessels almost every day bound for *Genoa* or *Leghorn*. But those that chuse to proceed by land, must go from *Toulon* to *Pignan*, and from *Pignan* to *Vidauban*, where you fall in with the post road from *Aix* to *Nice*, as mentioned p. 149.

Remarkable places in the route from Aix to Nice.

Brignole is a small town of *Provence*, with a bailiwic, a seneschal, a judge-royal, and a viguier. 'Tis a very antient place, as appears by several inscriptions. It is also noted for it's fine fruit, particularly prunes, which are transported to the *Levant*.

Brignole.

Frejus is a city of *Provence* in *France*, situate at the mouth of the river *Argens*, about a mile from the sea, thirty-five miles north east of *Toulon*, and thirty south west of *Nice*. It is a place of great antiquity, *Julius Cæsar* being said to have given it the name of *Forum Julii*. At present it is a bishop's see, who is temporal as well as spiritual lord of the place, and suffragan of *Aix*. The town has some old fortifications, but is very indifferently built, and in a ruinous condition. The amphitheatre of *Frejus*, which they call here the *Arenes*, deserves notice. Not far from hence, in the church of the *Dominicans*, you may see an admirable statue of the infant *Jesus*, made

Frejus

Vol. IV.   K   of

of wood, washed with paint, which was taken on board a *Spanish* vessel.

On the road from *Frejus* towards *Canes*, you see the remains of an old *Roman* aqueduct, that carried the water seven leagues. To *Canes* you climb all the way on the sides of great stony mountains, thick covered with pines and firs.

Antibes. *Antibes* is a port town of *Provence*, situate on the *Mediterranean*, in east longitude 7. latitude 43. 40. This is the last town in *Provence*, towards the frontiers of *Italy*, and was formerly called *Antipolis Julia Augusta*. The town is pretty well built, surrounded with walls, and defended by a strong citadel. The harbour is very safe, but too shallow. The parish church is called *Notre Dame de la place*.

Road from Antibes to Nice. From *Antibes* to *Nice* the roads are very bad, through rugged mountains, bordered with precipices on the left, and by the sea to the right. Between *Antibes* and the village of *S. Laurent*, you pass the little river *Loup*, which falls into the *Mediterranean*. The village of *S. Laurent* is famous for its excellent wine. At a hundred paces from thence you pass the river *Var*, which rises in the *Alps*, and empties itself in the *Mediterranean* in the neighbourhood of *Nice*. Here, it is divided into three branches, which are so many torrents that separate the county of *Nice* from *Provence*.

Bye-places in the route from Lyons to Italy by the way of Nice.

Most travellers that pass through *Avignon* or *Aix*, make it their business to visit the famous and antient city of *Arles*. The road from *Aix* to *Arles* is through the little town of *Salon*, and a plain called *De Crau*, one and twenty miles long.

FRANCE.

long, where you meet only with two inns, and a chapel called by the name of *S. Martin.* The town of *Salon* is situated in *Provence,* in east longitude 5. 5. latitude 43. 33. about eighteen miles from *Aix.* It is famous for the birth of the noted astrologer *Nostradamus,* whose tomb, with an epitaph by his wife, is in the church of the *Cordeliers.* There is a collegiate church in the town, and a few convents. On a little hill in the town you see an antient castle, where they have a garrison of invalids.

I. ARLES.

Arles is a city of *Provence* in *France,* in east longitude 4. 45. latitude 43. 32. situated on the east bank of the *Rhone,* upon a very uneven ground, and almost surrounded by a morass, which renders the air unhealthful. Its antiquity appears from its having been a colony of the *Romans,* and the seat of their empire in *Gaul.* 'Tis now a large and a flourishing city, the seat of an archbishop and seneschal. The cathedral dedicated to *S. Trophimus,* is a vast *Gothic* structure. The high altar has a fine tabernacle of silver embellished with several figures, in a good taste. Opposite to the cathedral stands the church of *S. Mary the greater,* on the left hand the bishop's palace, and on the right the town-house. The latter is an elegant regular building, and finely situated. There are six parishes in this city, and a great many religious houses of men and women. They have a bridge of boats over the *Rhone,* which joins the town with the suburb called *Tranquetaille.*

There is no city in *France* so remarkable for antiquities as *Arles,* insomuch that it is generally called a second *Rome.* the principal of these are 1. A noble obelisk of granite marble, supposed to have been brought hither in *Tiberius*'s reign. It is all of one stone, fifty two feet high, and seven

seven feet diameter in the base, like those of *Rome*, only it has no hieroglyphics. 2. The ruins of an amphitheatre, which was built by the *Romans*, and, as some pretend, by *Julius Cæsar*. It is of an oval form, and a hundred and ninety-four fathom in circumference; the longest diameter of the area seventy-one fathom, and the shortest fifty-two. The porticos are three stories high, built with free-stone of a prodigious size; every story contains sixty arches, which still remain. The area within-side has been filled with houses, and many of the arches demolished. 3. The burying-place of the *Elysian Fields*, where the heathens buried their dead, is situated on a very agreeable hill without the town: their tomb-stones are known by the two letters .D. M. which signify *Diis Manibus*. 4. In the parish of the archiepiscopal palace on the great stair-case, and in the hall, there are several curious remains of antiquity, as busts, fragments of statues, *basso-relievo's*, and lachrymal urns. Hard by, there are also some remains of the antient *Thermæ*, or hot-baths. 5. There is a great vault going from hence to *Nimes*, which was used by the *Romans*. The other antiquities consist of columns, busts, pedestals, aqueducts, niches, with some remains of the capitol, and the temples of the false gods: for a complete description of all these curiosities see *Monsi. Seguin's Histoire des antiquités d'Arles*.

S.Maximin. *S. Maximin* is a small town of *Provence*, situated to the eastward of *Aix*, on the river *Argens*, in a plain surrounded with mountains, eighteen miles from *Aix*, twenty four from *Toulon*, and six from *S. Beaume*. The place is famous for a convent of *Dominicans*, where, according to tradition, they preserve part of the body of *S. Mary Magdalen*. The church is a fine *Gothic* building, full of rich ornaments, and remarkable for some
excellent

excellent paintings; the high altar passes for one of the best in *France*.

S. Beaume is a name given to a very high rock, where *S. Mary Magdalen* is supposed to have spent thirty years in doing penance. The grotto where this saint is said to have resided, is inclosed with an iron grate, having a large number of lamps before it night and day. Near it is a fountain, which runs on every side of the rock, except where the saint is said to have rested. Just by this grotto they have built a pretty little church, and a convent for eight of the fathers of *S. Maximin*. From hence devout people ascend to the holy pillar, whither it is said that the saint was lifted up seven times a day by angels.

S. Beaume.

Remarkable places in the route from Lyons *to* Italy *by the way of* Geneva.

In this route you meet with no place worth notice, till you come to *Geneva*, of which city we have given a description already in this work, vol. iii. p. 181.

Remarkable places in the route from Lyons *to* Italy *by* Grenoble *and* Briançon.

I. GRENOBLE.

Grenoble is the capital of *Dauphiné* in *France*, in east longitude 5. 28. latitude 45. 12. pleasantly situated on the river *Isere*, in a fruitful plain, at the foot of a mountain which produces excellent wine. This city was enlarged and beautified by the emperor *Gratian*, who called it *Gratianopolis*, from whence comes the present name *Grenoble*. It is generally ranked among the chief cities of the kingdom for the number of its houses, churches, and other buildings. 'Tis the seat of a bishop

Grenoble.

bishop suffragan of *Vienne*, as likewise of a parliament instituted in 1453, and of a chamber of accounts, a mint, a bailiwic, and a generality. The river *Isere* divides it into two unequal parts, the largest of which is much the finest. The streets are wide, and well paved, and most of the public buildings very handsome. The episcopal palace, built by the late bishop Cardinal *Le Camus*, is a beautiful structure. The *Hotel de Lesdiguiere*'s is a large building, no way remarkable for its external beauty, but very convenient and magnificent within. The gardens are pleasant, and open for the public. At *S. Clare* you see the beautiful tomb of the constable of *Lesdiguiere*'s lady and her daughter. The collegiate church of *S. Andrew* is remarkable for its lofty tower, in form of a pyramid, and for a very curious tomb. The church of the *Dominicans* is one of the most antient in the town; in the middle of the choir you see the tomb of *Andrew*, son to *Humbert* the last prince of *Dauphiné*, whom this prince let fall out of the window as he was playing with him. The wood-work in the choir is reckoned a master-piece in its kind. The governor's palace, fortified with some towers, is a large and magnificent structure, from whence there is a beautiful prospect of the river and the adjacent country. The house of the marquis of *Canillac*, is a modern edifice, deservedly esteemed for the beauty of its architecture. There are two bridges over the *Isere*, one of stone and the other of wood, which join the great with the little town. The latter is called *la Parriere*, and consists only of one large street, that stretches along the river, beginning at the gate of *S. Laurence*, and ending at the gate of *France*, where you see a mall of several rows of trees on the banks of the *Isere*.

Most

Most travellers, in going by *Grenoble*, embrace the opportunity of paying a visit to the *Grand Chartreuse*. This is a famous monastery, situated seven miles north-east of *Grenoble*, upon a high rock. 'Tis a magnificent, but irregular structure, having been built at different times. It was founded by *S. Bruno* in 1086, and here the general of the order keeps his residence. The church is beautifully adorned, as also the public apartments for the reception of strangers, and especially the great hall, where you see some good paintings. In the chapel of our Lady at the bottom of the valley, there are some beautiful pictures, but particularly that of *S. Bruno* kneeling before the cross. These fathers entertain such as visit them, with great civility.

The *Grand Chartreuse*.

Briançon is the capital of the *Briançonois* in *Dauphiné*, in east longitude 6. 20. latitude 44. 50. 'Tis a pleasant city, situated at the foot of a rock, upon which there is a very strong castle: and at the conflux of two small brooks, the *Doire* and the *Ance*, which give name to the river *Durance*. Some reckon the situation of *Briançon* the highest of any city in *Europe*. The town is naturally strong, and the fortifications much improved, since the *French* have been obliged to surrender *Exiles* and *Fenestrelles* on the frontiers of *Piedmont*, to the king of *Sardinia*. They have a handsome parish-church, three convents, and a bailiwic. The manna of *Briançon* is very much esteemed; being a kind of white sweet gum, which falls from a particular kind of pine-trees during the heat of summer. About six miles from hence lies a rock called *Pertuis Rastan*, or the pierced rock, thro' which a way was cut to facilitate the passage from *Italy* to *Gaul*, and supposed by some to be the work of *Hannibal*, by others of *Cæsar*, and by others of *Cottius*, a brave prince

Briançon.

of the *Gauls*, whom the *Romans* took into their alliance, and from whom these mountains received the name of *Alpes Cottianæ*. Upon the front of the gate you see this inscription, *D. Cæsari Augusto dedicata, salutate eam*; by which 'tis supposed that the statue of that emperor was placed over it.

Pignerol. From *Briançon* you may enter *Italy* by *Pignerol*, proceeding first to the village of *Sezane*, nine miles from *Briançon*, thence to the little town of *Perouse*, which gives its name to one of the valleys of the *Vaudois*, and is eighteen miles distant from *Sezane*; thence nine miles farther to *Pignerol*. *Pignerol* is a town of *Italy* in the province of *Piedmont*, in east longitude 7. 15; latitude 44. 45. situated on the river *Chizon*, ten miles south-west of *Turin*, at the foot of the *Alps*, and the confines of *Dauphiné*. The town is small, but populous, and extremely well fortified by the king of *Sardinia*, since the treaty of *Utrecht*. It is defended by a citadel, on the top of the mountain, near which is the castle of *Perouse*, which was built at the entrance of the valley of that name.

CHAP. VI.

Journey from Paris to Strasburg.

THE route from *Paris* to *Strasburg* is by *Challons* in *Champagne*, from whence you may either proceed to *Metz* and *Verdun*, or you may go by the way of *Nancy* and *Luneville*. The coach from *Paris* to *Strasburg* sets out on *Saturdays* at seven in the morning, from the *Hotel de Pompone*

FRANCE.

pone in the *Rue de la Vererrie*; you pay fifty-five livres for your place, and five sous *per pound* for your baggage. There are likewise daily conveniences of berlins and chaises for *Strasburg* and other parts of *Alsace*.

First route from Paris *to* Strasburg *by* Metz *and* Verdun.

	Posts		
PARIS		*Islettes*	1
Bondy	Post royal	CLERMONT	1
Verigalant	1	*D'Ombale*	1
Claye	1	VERDUN	1½
MEAUX	2	*Manheule*	2
S. Jean	1	*Harville*	1
La Ferté	1	*Marsiatour*	1
Nanteuil sur Marne	1	*Gravelotte*	1
Chezy	2	METZ	1½
Chateau-Thierry	1	*Horgne*	1½
Paroy	1	*Solgne*	1
Dormans	1½	*Delme*	2
Port à Binson	1	*Vic*	2
La Cave	1	*Bourdonnaye*	1½
Epernay	1	*Azondange*	1
Plivaux	1	*Heming*	1½
Jalons	1	*Sarrebourg*	1
Mastogne	1	*Honmartin*	1
CHALLONS	1	*Phalzburg*	1
NotreDame de L'Epine	1	*Saverne*	1½
Belay	1½	*Wiltem*	1½
Orbeval	1½	*Stissen*	1
S. Menehoud	1	STRASBURG	1½

In all fifty-five posts and a half.

K 5   Second

Second route from Paris *to* Strasburg *by* Nancy *and* Luneville.

This route is the same as the preceding as far as *Challons*, where you leave *Verdun* on the left, and take the following route to *Nancy*.

	English miles.		*English* miles.
CHALLONS.		TOUL	6
Coupinville	12	*Velain*	6
Polsesse	12	NANCY	6
Nettancourt	9	*S. Nicholas*	6
Bar le Duc	12	LUNEVILLE	6
Ligni	9	*Binnamini*	9
S. Aubin	9	*Blamont*	9
Void	9	*Heming*	12
Layes	6	SARREBOURG	6

The remainder from *Sarrebourg* as in the preceding route.

Remarkable places in the first route.

Meaux. *Meaux* is a city of *France*, and capital of the district of *Brie Champenoise* in *Champagne*, in east longitude 3. latitude 49. This is a very antient city, the seat of a bishop suffragan of *Paris*, of a bailiwic, and an election. 'Tis pleasantly situated on the river *Marne*, over which there is a stone bridge. They have a very good trade in corn and cheese of *Brie*; but the town is indifferently built, and the streets narrow. The cathedral, dedicated to *S. Stephen*, was reckoned a fine building, before the *English* destroyed one of its towers. The bishop's palace has a spacious court and handsome stair-case. Among the religious

religious houses the abbey of *S. Farin* is the most deserving of notice.

La Ferté is a small town of *Brie Champenoise* *La Ferté.* situated on the conflux of the *Marne* and *Morin*. They have a handsome wooden bridge over the river, and a very good castle.

Chateau-Thierry is another small town of *Brie* *Chateau-* *Champenoise* in *France*, situated on the *Marne*. *Thierry.* It is pretty well built, has several churches, and is strong by its situation. They have a good castle on an eminence, from whence there is a delightful prospect.

I. CHALLONS.

Challons, called *Challons sur Marne*, to distin- *Challons.* guish it from *Challons sur Soane* in *Burgundy*, is the capital of the *Challonoise* in *Champagne*, in east longitude 4. 35. latitude 48. 55. In the time of the *Romans* this was one of the chief towns of *Gallia Belgica*; now 'tis the seat of a bishop suffragan of *Rheims*, as likewise of a presidial and bailiwic, and of the intendant of *Champagne*. The bishop is one of the three ecclesiastical counts and peers of *France*. *Challons* is pleasantly situated on the river *Marne*, by which it is divided into three parts, the town, the isle, and the borough, which have a communication with one another by bridges. The streets are large, and the houses well built. The cathedral dedicated to *S. Stephen*, is noted for its two beautiful towers; and the town-house is a neat building. The river *Marne* affords the inhabitants, who have a pretty good trade in cloth, linen, and corn, a great conveniency of transporting their goods to *Paris*. Without the town there is a most delightful walk, called the *Jard*, with trees planted on each side, extending for three miles as far as the bishop of

K 6 *Challon's*

Challons's house, which is much esteemed for the beauty of its gardens and canals. Some *French* writers are of opinion that in the neighbouring plains *Attila* was defeated by *Ætius* the *Roman* general.

S. Menehoud. *S. Menehoud* is a small town of *Champagne*, in the country of *Argonne*, situated on a morass between two rocks, and defended by a good castle.

Clermont. *Clermont* is a small town of *Champagne*, with the title of a county, in east longitude 5. latitude 49. 10. situated on a hill, whose foot is watered by the river *Air*.

II. VERDUN.

Verdun. *Verdun* is a city of *French Lorrain*, and capital of the bishopric of that name, in east longitude 5. 10. latitude 49. 14. It is situated on the *Maese*, which forms here several little islands, and renders it extremely pleasant. The citadel has the command of the whole town, whose walls are very strong. The cathedral is a large *Gothic* building: the great altar of the first choir is beautifully adorned; and the second choir is paved with *Mosaic*. The episcopal palace, and the townhouse, are handsome buildings; in the latter the clock deserves particular notice. The Jesuits have a beautiful college, in the street called *La Moisée*, and a little farther are the houses of the richest merchants of the town. They sell a great quantity of comfits in *Verdun*, and particularly their aniseeds are held in great reputation.

III. METZ.

Metz. *Metz* is a city of *French Lorrain*, and capital of the bishopric of that name, in east longitude 6. latitude 49. 16. It is a large wealthy town, situated

FRANCE.

situated at the conflux of the *Moselle* and *Selle*, and seized by *France*, together with the cities of *Toul* and *Verdun*, in 1552. The *French* have made it the seat of a bishop suffragan of *Treves*; as also of a bailiwic, and a parliament. The town is about nine miles in circumference, has three gates and two bridges, and is extremely well fortified. The cathedral dedicated to *S. Stephen*, is an antient noble pile, and remarkable for a font of an intire piece of porphyry, ten feet long. *Metz* is one of the *French* towns where the *Jews* have liberty to reside. They are obliged for distinction to wear cloaks winter and summer, and have a considerable trade. There are several arches and other monuments of antiquity in and about this city, especially at *Jouy* about three miles from hence.

From *Metz* you may go to *Nancy*, and from thence by *Luneville* to *Strasburg*. The route from *Metz* to *Nancy* is as follows. From *Metz* to *Corny*, post and a half; from *Corny* to *Pont-a-Mousson*, post and a half: from *Pont-a-Mousson* to *Belleville*, post: from *Belleville* to *Nancy*, post and a half. The only remarkable place in this route is *Pont-a-Mousson*, a small town of *Lorrain*, with the title of a marquisate, in east longitude 5. 50. latitude 49. situate on the river *Moselle*. There is a bridge here over the *Moselle* from whence the town had part of its name, and the other part from the ruins of the neighbouring castle of *Mousson*. It has two abbeys, several handsome churches, and an university founded by *Charles* cardinal of *Lorrain*, in 1573.

But to return to the direct route from *Metz* to *Sarrebourg*.

Sarrebourg is a small town of *Germany* in the circle of the *Lower Rhine*, and electorate of *Triers*, in east longitude 6. 15. latitude 49. 46.

Route from Metz to Nancy.

Pont-a-Mousson.

Sarrebourg.

It

It is situated on the river *Saar*, seven miles south of *Triers*, and consists only of one great street, with houses built in the *German* manner. The fortifications are pretty good, as likewise some of the public buildings, particularly the castle, the town-house, *S. Nicholas*'s hospital, and the commandery of *S. John*.

Phaltzburg.   *Phaltzburg* is a small town of *Germany*, with the title of a principality, in the landgraviate of *Alsace*, in east longitude 7. 20. latitude 48. 20. situated at the foot of the mountains of *Vosges*, near the river *Zinzel*, which falls into the *Saar*. Being an important pass, because of its situation on the frontiers of *Germany*, it was well fortified by *Lewis* XIV. who built here a strong citadel.

Saverne.   *Saverne*, by the *Germans* called *Zabern*, is a small town of *Germany*, in the landgraviate of *Alsace*, in east longitude 7. latitude 48. 30. It is thought to be *Antonin*'s *Tabernæ*, and is situated at the foot of a mountain, on the river *Soor*, which fills the ditches on one side; and on the other there is a great morass. There is only one great street in the town, and about one thousand three hundred inhabitants. The bishop of *Strasburg* is lord of *Saverne*, and has a handsome castle built by *Egon* of *Furstemberg*; the garden belonging to it is very pleasant.

IV. STRASBURG.

Strasburg.   *Strasburg* is a large and populous city of *Germany*, in the circle of the *Upper Rhine*, and capital of the landgraviate of *Alsace*, in east longitude 7. 35. latitude 48. 38. Its situation is in the middle of a fine plain, at the conflux of the rivers *Ill* and *Breusch*, which a mile below fall into the *Rhine*. It was an imperial city till 1682, when

when it was surprized by the *French*, who are its present masters. 'Tis the see of a bishop, who is suffragan of *Mentz*, and has 300,000 livres a year, the greatest revenue of any prelate in *France*.

The river *Ill* divides the town into two parts, called the old and new. Over this river there are two stone-bridges, and four of wood. The town is of a very large circumference, strongly fortified with walls and out-works. The citadel consists of five bastions and five half moons, with several other works contrived by marshal *Vauban*. The streets in general are narrow, but the houses extremely well built. The number of inhabitants is reckoned twenty eight thousand, part *Protestants* and part *Roman Catholicks*, though the latter seem to have now the majority. The cathedral dedicated to our Lady, is perhaps the finest *Gothic* building in *Europe*. The portal is quite magnificent, and the high altar built by cardinal *Fürstemberg*, is extremely beautiful. The tower, reckoned by some the highest in the whole world, is built in the form of a pyramid. It is 574 feet high, curiously built of carved stone, and has 662 steps from bottom to top. But that which is most admired, is the great clock, finished in 1573, by the famous *Habrecht*, remarkable for shewing the motions of the planets, the increase and decrease of the moon, with the motion of the sun through the signs of the zodiac; but a great part of the mechanism has been for some time out of order.

The town-house is a large square edifice terminated by two advanced pavilions, the front of which is ornamented with antient painting; the inside answers in every respect its external beauty. The episcopal palace, as well as those
of

of the governor and the intendant, are worth seeing; as also the city hospital, and that of the garrison. We should not forget the anatomical amphitheatre, the public granaries, and the arsenal, remarkable for preserving the armour in which the great *Gustavus Adolphus* king of *Sweden* was killed. The theatre is a handsome structure, and extremely commodious. In summer there is a great resort of company to a place in the neighbourhood, called the *Green-tree*, where they have a variety of all manner of diversions. In the neighbourhood of *Strasburg* there is a wooden bridge over the *Rhine*, about half a mile long. The stage coach from *Strasburg* to *Paris*, sets out from *S. John's street* on *Tuesday* morning. You pay fifty five livres for your passage, and five sous *per* pound for baggage.

Road from Strasburg to Basil. From *Strasburg* you may proceed to *Basil* and *Geneva*, by the route pointed out in the second volume of this work, p. 366, 367.

Remarkable places in the second route from Paris *to* Strasburg.

Toul. *Toul* is a city of *Lorrain*, in east longitude 5. 42, latitude 48. 45. It is situated on the river *Moselle*, but has no other fortifications than a single wall. The town is pretty large, and the seat of a bishop, who has the title of count, and is suffragan of the archbishop of *Triers*.

Nancy. *Nancy* is the capital city of *Lorrain* in *Germany*, in east longitude 6. latitude 48. 44. It is situated in a large plain, near the river *Meurte*, and divided into two parts, the upper called the old town, and the lower called the new. The old town contains the duke's palace, which has a magnificent entrance, leading to a fair court, surrounded with piazzas; the gardens about it

FRANCE.

are exceeding fine. The new town is much larger and better built. In this part are the courts of judicature, the town-house, several churches and monasteries, and a fine college of Jesuits. By the treaty of *Vienna* between *France* and the emperor *Charles* VI. the duchy of *Lorrain* was settled for life upon *Staniflaus*, father to the present queen of *France*, and to devolve to this crown upon the death of that prince.

Luneville is a small town of *Lorrain*, in east longitude 6. 26. latitude 48. 36. situated in a very pleasant part of the country, and remarkable only for being the residence of king *Staniflaus*.

Luneville.

CHAP. VII.

Journey from Paris *to* Basil.

THERE are two different routes from *Paris* to *Basil*; the first, which is likewise the shortest, by *Langres*, and the second by *Dijon* and *Besançon*. Again, there are two routes to *Dijon*, the first and shortest is that which we have already given in this volume, p. 146. the second is by *Langres*. There is a stage-coach from *Paris* to *Besançon*, *Dole*, and other parts of *Franche Comté* or the county of *Burgundy*, which sets out from the *Hotel de Sens*, in summer on *Fridays*, and on *Thursdays* in winter, at six in the morning, and goes through *Dijon*. It is nine days on the road in summer, and eleven in winter; each passenger pays forty two livres as far as *Besançon*, and four sous *per* pound for his baggage. There is another coach that sets out from the same place for *Dijon* on *Mondays* and *Wednesdays* in summer, and on *Mondays* and *Thursdays* in winter,

winter. Each passenger pays thirty livres for his person, and three sous *per* pound for his baggage.

From *Besançon* to *Paris* the coach sets out from *Rue S. Vincent* opposite the seminary on *Wednesdays* in summer, and *Tuesdays* in winter. Each person pays thirty-six livres for his place, and four sous *per* pound for his baggage. From *Dijon* to *Paris* the coach sets out on *Wednesdays* and *Fridays* in summer, on *Mondays* and *Fridays* in winter; it is seven days on the road in summer, and eight in winter.

First route from Paris *to* Basil, *by the way of* Langres.

PARIS	Posts	LANGRES	1½
Charenton	Post royal	*Griffonottes*	1½
Gros Bois	1½	*Faybillot*	1
Brie-Comte-Robert	1	*Saintrey*	1½
Guignes	2	*Combeau Fontaine*	1½
Mormans	1	*Port sur Saone*	1½
Nangis	1½	*Vesoul*	1½
La Maison Rouge	1	*Calmoutier*	1
PROVINS	1½	*Lure*	2
Nogent sur Seine	2	*Ronchamps*	1
Granges	2½	*Frayet*	1
Grés	1½	BEFFORT	1
TROYES	2	*Chavanne*	1½
Montieramé	2	*Alkirk*	1½
Vandœuvre	1½	*Trois Maisons*	1½
Bar-sur-Aub	2	*S. Louis* near *Hunningen*	1½
Suzbiencourt	2	BASIL	1
CHAUMONT	1½		
Vesigne	1½		

In all fifty-two posts and a half from *Paris* to *Basil*.

Second

Second route from Paris *to* Basil, *by the way of* Dijon *and* Besançon.

The shortest way from *Paris* to *Dijon*, has been already given, p. 146. The other is the same as the preceding as far as *Langres*.

LANGRES	Posts	*Saint Wit*	1½
Protboy	2	BESANÇON	2
Thil	2	*Roulans*	1½
Norge le Pont	1½	*Beaume les Nones*	1
DIJON	1	*Clerval*	1½
Genlis	1½	*S. Maurice*	1½
Auxonne	1½	*Montbeliard*	1½
DOLE	1½	BEFFORT	1½
Orchamps	1½		

From *Beffort* to *Basil* as above.

From *Beffort* you may proceed to *Strasburg* by the following route.

Beffort	Posts.	*Ostheim*	1
La Chapelle	1½	*Schelestat*	1½
Aspach	1½	*Benfeld*	1½
Isenheim	2	*Feggersheim*	1½
COLMAR	1½	STRASBURG	1½

Or else you may take the following road from *Beffort* to *Strasburg* by *Huningen*.

BEFFORT	Posts.	*Otmarsheim*	1½
Chavanne	1½	*Fessenheim*	1½
Alkirk	1½	*Briesheim*	1½
Trois Maisons	1½	*Markelsheim*	1½
S. Louis near *Huningen*	1½	*Freimheim*	2
		Krafft	1½
Groskempt	1	STRASBURG	2

Remark-

The GRAND TOUR.

Remarkable places in the first route from Paris *to* Basil, *by* Langres.

Charenton has been mentioned, p. 175.

Brie-Comte-Robert. *Brie-Comte-Robert* is a small town of the district called *Brie Françoise*, in the isle of *France*, situated near the river *Jere*, in a very fruitful country. There is a parochial church here, remarkable for a very high steeple, and a convent of *Minims*. Before you come to *Brie-Comte-Robert*, you pass through the village of *Gros Bois*, where you should see the fine seat and park belonging to Monsieur *Chauvelin*, and the beautiful monastery of the monks of *Camaldula*.

Provins. *Provins* is a town of *France*, situated on the *Morans* and the *Vousie*, in the province of *Champagne*, and district of *Brie Champenoise*, in east longitude 3. 20. latitude 48. 35. The town is small, consisting chiefly of two main streets. The priory of *S. Ayou* is remarkable for its treasure. The collegiate church of *S. Quiriac*, our Lady of *Val*, and the abbey of *S. James* are worth seeing. *Provins* was formerly the capital of the whole country, and the residence of their counts; the old castle where these counts lived, is still existing. The town is noted for its excellent roses, of which they make a conserve. At about three miles from *Provins*, you come to the forest of *Sourdun*, which continues till you come within four miles of *Nogent sur Seine*.

Nogent sur Seine. *Nogent sur Seine* is a small town of *France*, in the province of *Champagne*, and district of *Senonois*, in east longitude 3. 33. latitude 48. 26. It is a very pleasant place, situated on the river *Seine*, over which it has a handsome bridge. Its situation is convenient for trade, of which it enjoys a considerable share. The great church dedicated

to

to *S. Laurence*, is remarkable for the harmony of its chimes; the top of the steeple is ingeniously built.

I. Troyes.

Troyes, the antient *Urbs Tricaſſina*, is a city of *France*, in the province of *Champagne*, and capital of the diſtrict called *Champagne Proper*, in eaſt longitude 4. 5. latitude 48. 15. It is ſituated on the river *Seine*, in a very fruitful plain, ſurrounded alſo with a wall and ſome other old fortifications. The town is large and pretty well built; it is the ſeat of a biſhop, ſuffragan of *Sens*, a bailiwic, and a preſidial. The cathedral dedicated to *S. Peter* is a fine *Gothic* building. Not far from the cathedral ſtands the abbey of *S. Lupus*, in which they preſerve the head of that ſaint, in a caſe all covered with diamonds. The collegiate church of *S. Stephen* is a handſome building, remarkable alſo for its treaſure, and a great number of manuſcripts. As you enter the church of the *Dominicans*, you ſee a ſtatue of *S. Dominic*, greatly eſteemed. The ſtalls of the choir, and the glaſs windows of the library are alſo admired. In the church of *S. Pantaleon* you ſee ſeveral excellent ſtatues by *Francis Gentil*, ſome beautiful pictures, and glaſs windows of ſurpriſing beauty. The college is under the direction of the fathers of the Oratory, in whoſe library there are ſome curious manuſcripts, among the reſt the letters of *Abelard*, thoſe of pope *Clement* IV. and a *Horace* ſaid to be eight hundred years old. At the *Cordeliers* there is a very good library, which is open three times a week for the public. The town houſe is a handſome building, conſiſting of a large front with two wings. Before the gate ſtands a marble ſtatue of *Lewis* XIV.

Troyes.

almoſt

The GRAND TOUR.

a moſt beautiful performance, by the famous *Girardon,* a native of this town, to which he ſent it as a preſent. The town contains about fifteen thouſand ſouls, and carries on a very good trade in linen, of which it has a conſiderable manufacture, as likewiſe in cloth, toys and ſmall ware.

Bar-ſur-Aube. *Bar-ſur-Aube* is a very antient town of *Champagne* in *France,* in the diſtrict of *Baſſigny,* in eaſt longitude 4. 40. latitude 48. 15. This place is ſo called from its ſituation on the river *Aube,* at the foot of a very pleaſant hill, *Barrum* in the old *Gaulois* ſignifying a port. It is very indifferently built, but remarkable for its excellent wine. On a neighbouring hill you ſee the remains of a caſtle, ſaid to have been deſtroyed by the *Vandals.* There is a convent here of *Iriſh* Capuchins, who ſeem to be well reſpected in the neighbourhood, and are very civil to their countrymen that paſs this way.

Clairvaux. About ſix miles from hence ſtands the abbey of *Clairvaux,* in the bottom of a valley ſurrounded with woods, founded by *S. Bernard.* The abbot's apartment, and the church, are worth notice.

Chaumont. *Chaumont* is the capital of the diſtrict of *Baſſigny* in *Champagne,* in eaſt longitude 5. 15. latitude 48. 12. ſituated on a hill, which ſtretches to the banks of the *Marne.* The Jeſuits have a good college, and a very elegant church. The nuns of *S. Benedict* have likewiſe a handſome church. There is an old caſtle here, in which the counts of *Champagne* formerly reſided.

II. LANGRES.

Langres. *Langres* is a city of *France,* in the province of *Champagne,* and diſtrict of *Baſſigny,* of which ſome reckon it the capital, in eaſt longitude 5. 22.

latitude

FRANCE.

latitude 48. It is situated on a hill near the river *Marne*, in the midst of a pleasant fruitful country, just on the confines of *Lorrain* and *Franche Comté*. By the *Latins* it was called *Lingones*, and *Andomatunum Lingonum*. The ramparts are covered with a kind of roof, by which means you may walk round the town, without being wet in time of rain. 'Tis the see of a bishop suffragan of *Lyons*, who is spiritual and temporal lord of this city, and one of the three ecclesiastical dukes and peers of *France*. There is a pretty large square in the town, to which they have given the name of *Champbeau*. As you enter this square you see two parochial churches, of *S. Amatre* and *S. Martin*; and not far from thence the house of the fathers of the oratory, and afterwards the episcopal palace. The cathedral dedicated to *S. Martin*, is a fine *Gothic* building, but a little too dark; it has a curious treasure, and some handsome tombs. In the choir you see several stones, which were antiently made use of in Pagan sacrifices. The Jesuits have a fine church and college. *Langres* is famous for cutler's ware; and is likewise the seat of a presidial and bailiwic, which depend upon the parliament of *Paris*.

From *Langres*, you come to *Vesoul*, a little neat city of *Franche Comté*, twenty-one miles north from *Besançon*. *Lure* is a famous abbey on the river *Ougnon*.

Vesoul.

Beffort is a small town of *Alsace*, in east longitude 7. latitude 47. 35. situate at the foot of a mountain; it is a great thorough-fare from *Franche Comté* to *Alsace*, and belongs to the duke of *Mazarin*. It is divided into the old and new town, has a good castle on an eminence, and its fortifications were greatly improved by marshal *Vauban*. *Hunningen* and *Basil*, have been described in the second volume, p. 382. 383.

Beffort.

Remarkable

Remarkable places in the second route from Paris *to* Basil, *by* Dijon *and* Besançon.

This route is the same as the preceding, as far as *Langres*; this city and *Dijon* have been already described, the first p. 214. the second p. 169.

Auxonne.   *Auxonne* is a small town of *Burgundy* in *France*, in the district of *Dijonois*, in east longitude 5. 22. latitude 47. 15. It is pleasantly situated on the river *Saone*, over which there is a handsome bridge. The fortifications were repaired in 1673. It is now the seat of a bailiwic, and has one parish church, two nunneries, and a convent of Capuchins.

Dole.   *Dole* is a city of *France*, in the province of *Franche Comté*, in east longitude 5. 25. latitude 47. 10. It is a very antient town, pleasantly situated on the river *Dou*, in a fruitful country called the valley of *Love*. The streets are wide and regular, and filled with handsome edifices. Among these, the most worthy of notice are the palace in which the parliament used formerly to meet, a magnificent and well furnished structure; the palace of the chamber of accounts; the house which belonged to the university; the college of *S. Jerom*; and especially that of the Jesuits. The church of our Lady is the most considerable in town. *Dole* is the seat of a bailiwic, and a chamber of accounts. Among the antiquities of this town they reckon the square *des Arenes*, where the *Romans* formerly exhibited their public spectacles and combats. Not far from the fountain of *Gougeans*, there are two aqueducts of the same time. At the neighbouring village of *Joue*, they have springs of mineral waters, which are very much esteemed in that country.

FRANCE.

I. BESANÇON.

Besançon is the capital of *Franche Comté* in *France*, in east longitude 6. latitude 47. 20. This is a very antient city, called by the *Latins Vesuntio*. It is situated on the river *Dou*, which divides it into two parts, one of which is called the high, and the other the lower town, and are joined by a stone bridge. The town is surrounded by a strong wall, and other fortifications, built by *Lewis* XIV. There is also a strong citadel, which commands the whole town, and stands on a steep rock. The streets are large and regular, the houses well built of free-stone, and covered with slate. *Besançon* is the see of an archbishop, who has the title of prince of the empire; it is also the seat of a parliament or chief tribunal of the province, of an university, of a bailiwic, a presidial, and a court of money. The cathedral dedicated to S. *John*, is reckoned a handsome building. The town is very populous, and has seven parish churches, two chapters, two abbeys of men and two of women, a seminary, a college of Jesuits, seven convents of friars, five of nuns, five handsome fountains, an hospital for the education of poor children, and another general hospital, which is a handsome building. The church of the *Carmelites*, the fountain of *Neptune* opposite that church, the town-house, with the brazen statue of the emperor *Charles* V. before it, the governor's palace, the fountain just by with the nymph spouting water out of her nipples, the palace of cardinal *Granvelle*, and the tomb of *James* of *Bourbon* at the nuns of S. *Clare*, are the principal things that deserve a traveller's notice. This city is remarkable for several monuments of antiquity. The gate of the cloyster of S.

(margin notes: Besançon. Situation. Antiquity. Fortifications. Seat of an archbishop. Churches. Antiquities.)

VOL. IV.   L   *John*

John the Great, is the remains of a triumphal arch erected in honour of the emperor *Aurelian*. Without the walls you see the ruins of an amphitheatre, about a hundred and twenty feet in diameter. The mountain *Chandane*, on the other side of the river, is a place where formerly they sacrificed to *Diana*, which made them give it this name, being as it were *Campus Dianæ*. There are still the remains of a *Pantheon*, which the inhabitants call the *Pillars*; likewise the remains of a great aqueduct; and several places in the neighbourhood that have taken their names from the encampments of the antient *Romans*, thus *Chamars*, as much as to say, *Campus Martis*: Chamuse, *Campus Musarum*: Chailla, *Campus Lunæ*, &c.

Montbeliard.

Montbeliard is the capital of a county of that name, in *Franche Comté*, in east longitude 6. 45. latitude 47. 35. It is situated on the frontiers of *Alsace* and *Franche Comté*, at the foot of a rock, on which there is a very strong citadel. The town likewise is pretty well fortified, but within side it consists of only two or three streets, which run in a direct line from the gate of *Basil* to that of *Vesoul*. The houses are generally of freestone, and three or four stories high. The church of *S. Martin* is a curious piece of architecture; for tho' it is very long and broad, it is neither vaulted at top, nor supported by pillars. This city, with the county of the same name, upon the death of the last prince of the branch of *Wirtemberg Mombeliard* in 1723, devolved to the duke of *Wirtemberg Stutgard*.

CHAP.

FRANCE.

CHAP. VIII.

Journey from Paris *to* Bourdeaux *and* Bayonne.

THIS is one of the longest, most curious, and most convenient tours a traveller can take thro' *France*; being a journey of about one hundred and seventy leagues, thro' a fruitful, populous country, where the roads are very good, and you meet with the best of accommodation in the public inns. It is the road generally used by those who go from *Paris* to *Madrid*; for the other by *Perpignan*, which we shall give in the next chapter, is much the longest about. The stage coach sets out from *Paris* to *Bourdeaux* and *Bayonne*, on *Tuesdays* at six in the morning, from the *Rue Contrescarpe*. Passengers pay sixty livres for their place as far as *Bourdeaux*, and five sous *per* pound for baggage. Those that take places for *Bayonne*, pay fourscore livres, and seven sous *per* pound for baggage.

The post route from Paris *to* Bourdeaux *and* Bayonne, *thro'* Orleans, Blois, *and* Poictiers.

	Posts		
PARIS		Etrechy	1
La Croix de Berny	Post royal 1½	Etampes	1
		Montdesir	1
Longjumeau	1½	Monerville	1
Linas	1	Angerville	1
Arpajon	1	Boisseau	1
Bonne	1	Toury	1

Chateau

Chateau Gaillard	1	Coué	1
Artenay	1	Chaunay	1
Cercottes	1½	Sauſay	1½
ORLEANS	1½	Bannieres	1
S. Memin	1	Villefagnan	1
Clery	1	Fond des Marais	1
Lailly	1	Aigre	1
S. Laurent des eaux	1	Gourville	1
Nouant	1	S. Cibardeau	1
Saint Diéy	1	Villars Marangé	1
BLOIS	2	Chateau-neuf	1½
Chouſy	1¼	Nonnaville	1
Veuve	1½	Barbeſieux	1½
Haut chantier	1	Reignac	1½
AMBOISE	1	La Grolie	1½
Bordes	1	Chevanceau	1
La Friliere	1	Montlieu	1
TOURS	1½	Cherſac	1
Carrez	1½	Pierre Brune	1
Montabſon	1	Cavignac	1
Sorigny	1	Bois Martin	1
S. Catherine	1	Cubſac	1
S. Maure	1	Carbon blanc	1
Beauvais	1	BOURDEAUX	1½
Ormes S. Martin	1	Gradignan	1½
Ingrande	1½	L'Eſtaule	1
Chatelleraut	1	Putz de la Gubatte	1
Barres de Nintré	1	Barps	1
Tricherie	1	L'Hoſpitalet	1
Clan	1	Belin	1
Grand Pont	1	Muret	1
POITIERS	1	Hiſpotey	1½
Croutelle	1	Bouchaire	1½
Ruffigny	1	Belloc	1½
Vivonne	1	La Harie	1½
Minieres	1½	L'Eſperon	1½

Caſtets

FRANCE.

Castets	2	*La Cabanne*	1
Majex	2	*Ondres*	2
Monts	1½	BAYONNE	1½
S. *Vincent*	1		

Route by the stage-coach from Paris *to* Bourdeaux *and* Bayonne.

B. signifies the Place where you stop to take a *Buvette*, as the *French* call it, or a cup of refreshment; D. the place where you stop to dine; S. where you sup.

PARIS	*English* miles.	S. *Port de Pile*	12
B. *Seaux*	6	D. *Chatelleraut*	12
S. *Dauphin*	18	S. *Tricherie*	9
D. *Etampes*	18	D. *Clan*	6
B. *Angerville*	18	S. POITIERS	6
S. *Toury*	12	D. *Lusignan*	15
B. *Cercottes*	21	S. *Chenay*	12
D. ORLEANS	9	D. S. *Leger*	9
S. *Clery*	12	B. *Briou*	6
B. S. *Laurent des eaux*	12	S. *Ville Dieu*	6
D. S. *Diey*	12	D. *Varaise*	9
S. BLOIS	12	S. *Escoyeux*	9
D. *Veuve*	18	D. SAINTES	9
S. AMBOISE	12	S. *Pont*	12
D. *Bleré*	6	D. *Petit Niort*	12
S. *Faux*	9	S. S. *Aubin*	6
D. *Mantelan*	9	B. *Blaye*	6

The coach stops at *Blaye*, and goes no further; wherefore passengers are obliged to take water for themselves and their baggage, as far as *Bourdeaux*, boats being always ready for that purpose.

The GRAND TOUR.

	English miles.		
S. Bourdeaux	21	D. Maroife	9
S. Caftres	12	S. Roquefort	12
D. Langon	12	D. Mont de Marfan	12
S. Bolac	9	S. Tartas	12
		D. Dax	15

At *Dax* the coach stops and goes no further; so that you must either take horses from thence to *Bayonne*, or go by water. With horses the route is thus: from *Dax* to *S. Vincent*, twelve miles; from *S. Vincent* to *Ondres* twelve miles; from *Ondres* to *Bayonne*, twelve miles. By water the passage is twenty-one miles; and there are boats always ready for Passengers.

Route from Bayonne to Madrid.

France		Segnoreda	3
Bayonne	Posts.	Bribiefca	2
Bidars	1½	Caftel de Peones	2
S. Jean de Luz	1½	Quintanapalia	3
Orogne	1	Burgos	3
		Zara in	2
Spain		Madrigalejo	3
	Leagues	Lerma	2
Iron	2	Baabon	3
Oijarfun	4	Aranda	4
Urniete	2	Orombia	3
Toloza	3	Frefnillo	3
Villa Franca	3	Caftillejo	2½
Zegama	3	Sumofiera	3
Galereta	3	Buitrago	3
Udicana	2½	Cavanillas	4
Victoria	3	S. Augoftino	4
La Puebla	3	Alcoviendas	3
Miranda	2½	Madrid	3
Meugo	2		

Remarkable

FRANCE.

Remarkable places in this Journey.

Etampes is a small town in the province of the isle of *France*, in east longitude 2. 15. latitude 48. 25. It is situated on the river *Juine*, in the middle of pleasant meadows, and vineyards. The great church, the collegiate of our Lady, and S. *Martin*, are the principal buildings. There is likewise an antient castle, whose foundations are said to to be laid by *Robert the First*.

I. ORLEANS.

Orleans is a city of *France*, capital of the province of *Orleanois*, situated on the river *Loire*, in a very pleasant country, in east longitude 2. latitude 47. 55. This is a very antient city, originally founded, as 'tis said, by the *Druids*, and beautified by the emperor *Aurelian*, who gave it the name of *Aurelianum*. 'Tis now one of the largest and pleasantest cities in *France*, the see of a bishop, suffragan of *Paris*, and gives title of duke to the first prince of the blood. The streets are neat and broad, and the houses in general are fair and beautiful, though antient. The town is fortified after the antient way, and has six gates. The cathedral is a fine *Gothic* structure, remarkable for one of the handsomest and highest steeples in *Europe*. The town-house is a noble structure, with a lofty tower, erected by *Charles* VII. in 1458. The palace of justice is likewise a good edifice. There are twenty-two parishes in the town, and a great number of religious houses. There is a large handsome stone-bridge of sixteen arches over the river, leading to one of the suburbs, which stands upon an island. Upon this bridge, which is 170 fathoms long, stands a brazen

zen statue of the blessed Virgin, with king *Charles* VII. kneeling on one side of her, and *Joan* of *Arc*, called the *Maid* of *Orleans*, on the other. They have an university here, which is resorted to chiefly for the study of the law. The inhabitants are remarkable for speaking *French* in its full perfection. This city is also the seat of a generality, a presidial, a bailiwic, and a chamber of money.

S. Memin. From *Orleans* you proceed to *S. Memin*, a small town on the *Loiret*, remarkable for a rich abbey, and for the fertility of its soil, which produces the wine *de Genetin*. From thence you go *Clery.* to *Clery*, a small town of the *Orleanois*, celebrated for the collegiate church of our Lady, which was rebuilt and considerably enriched by *Lewis* XI. who is here interred in a stately monument.

II. B L O I S.

Blois. *Blois* is the capital of the territory of *Blasois*, in the province of *Orleanois* in *France*; in east longitude 1. 20. latitude 47. 35. This is one of the pleasantest cities in *France*, agreeably situated on the declivity of a hill, on the north bank of the river *Loire*, and surrounded with a most beautiful fertile country. Over the river there is a handsome stone-bridge, which joins the suburb called *Vienne* to the town. On the bridge there is an inscription, shewing that *Henry* IV. rebuilt it, in 1598. The castle of *Blois*, where some of the *French* kings have kept their courts, is a sumptuous building, begun by *Lewis* XII. and finished by succeeding princes. The west side, begun by *Gaston* duke of *Orleans*, under the direction of the celebrated *Francis Mansard*, is a magnificent structure, though left unfinished. The pictures in the apartments, the gallery of the

stags,

stags, the water-works, and statues, are deserving of notice. The Jesuits have a handsome college; and the front of their church is adorned with three orders of architecture. The town-house is a handsome building; as likewise the cathedral dedicated to *S. Stephen.* Here are the remains of a *Roman* aqueduct, into which three men may ride abreast. *Blois* is the see of a bishop, the seat of a chamber of accounts, and a presidial. The *bons Crétiens* pears, and *Perdrigon plumbs* of *Blois,* are much valued; and here the *French* tongue is spoke in its greatest purity.

Four leagues from hence is the royal palace of *Chambor,* built by *Francis* I. where Marshal *Saxe* resided after the last war. The great stair-case is extremely curious; the apartments are noble, and the gardens answer the magnificence of the building. On a pane of glass in one of the closets you read the following verses cut by *Francis* I. with a diamond.

Chambor.

> *Souvent femme varie,*
> *Mal habil qui s'y fie.*

Amboise is an antient town of the province of *Tourraine* in *France,* in east longitude 1. 30. latitude 49. 40. situate on the river *Loire,* over which there is a handsome stone bridge. The town is small, consisting only of two parishes, and two streets; but is famous for a fine old castle, embellished and enlarged by *Charles* VIII. who was born and died here. Without the town there is a very pleasant walk, between two rows of trees, called the *Courfe.*

Amboise.

L 5   III. Tours.

III. Tours.

Tours.

Tours is the capital of *Tourraine* in *France*, in east longitude 45 min. latitude 47. 25. It is a large handsome town, situate in a plain, on the south side of the *Loire*, between this river and the *Cher*. Most of the houses are built of fine white stone; the streets are spacious and vastly clean, which is owing to the several rivulets that form six public fountains. The fortifications round the town take in a vast compass, including the suburbs, but are not very regular. The castle consists of several round towers, situate at the extremity of the bridge over the *Loire*; which bridge has nineteen arches. Tours is the see of an archbishop. The cathedral dedicated to *S. Gatien*, is the largest in the kingdom, remarkable for a beautiful chapel of our Lady, and a very curious clock. The library belonging to this church is enriched with some curious manuscripts of great antiquity; among the rest the Pentateuch in capital letters, a thousand years old; the four Gospels in *Saxon* letters, said to have been written by *S. Hilary* of *Poitiers*, twelve hundred years ago. The next church in rank is that of *S. Martin*, whose tomb is behind the great altar. There are a great many handsome convents in the town, the principal of which are, the Jesuits near *S. Saturnin*, the Dominicans behind the church of *S. Peter*, the Cordeliers in the *Rue S. Catherine*, the abbey of *S. Martin* opposite the great square of *Haumont*, and the abbey of *Murmoutiers* in the suburb of *S. Simphorian*. The key upon the river, is the most beautiful part of the town; and the mall near the gate of *S. Stephen*, is esteemed one of the finest in *France*, being a thousand paces long. One of the gates of *Tours* goes by the name of *Hugon*, from an earl of *Tours* of that name, a very wicked prince, whom the superstitious vulgar imagined to walk the streets by midnight to terrify the inhabitants; the *French* Protestants were first called *Hugonots*, because of their midnight assemblies in some caves near that gate. At a place called *Pleſſis-les-Tours*, is a royal palace, built by *Lewis* XI. who died there; it stands between a large park and handsome gardens: here is also a collegiate church with a convent of *Minims*, whose situation is most delightful. The conveniency of the *Loire* renders *Tours* a trading town, especially in silk stuffs, of which they have an excellent manufacture. Not far from *Tours* is the village of *Langes*, famous for its melons.

Ingrande is a small town, situated on the *Loire*, part of it belonging to *Anjou*, and part to *Britany*, which ends here. They have a pretty good trade, by their communication with *Nants*; and there is a custom-house, where goods and baggage are examined very strictly. *Chatellerault* is a small town of *Poitou*, situated on the river *Vienne*, in east longitude 35. latitude 46. 45, This place is famous for its cutler's ware, and for a fine stone bridge over the *Vienne*, being 230 paces long, 66 broad, and consisting of nine arches. Near this town are found little stones, which cut and polished look like diamonds.

IV. POITIERS.

Poitiers is the capital of the province of *Poitou*, in *France*, in east longitude 15. latitude 46. 40. This is one of the largest and most antient cities in the kingdom, situated on a rising ground, on the left bank of the little river *Clain*. 'Tis the seat of a bishop, a seneschal's court, a presidial, generality, court of finances, and a chamber of money. No town in *France*, except *Paris*, surpasses this in bigness; but within the compass of the walls there are a great many gardens, meadows, and corn-fields. However, it has twenty-four parochial churches, five abbeys, several convents of friars, and of nuns, two seminaries, and three hospitals. The cathedral is an old *Gothic* building, dedicated to *S. Peter*. Here is an antient marble with a curious inscription, which may be seen in *Mabillon*'s *Diplomatica*; it was taken some years ago from the church of *S. John*, which most antiquarians suppose to have been a Pagan temple. The collegiate church of *S. Hilary* is immediately subject to the pope. Here they show a stone, which consumes dead bodies, as they say, in twenty-four hours; and a hollow stump of a tree, into which they pretend that madmen being put, recover their senses. The famous nunnery of *S. Croix* was founded by *Radegonde* queen of *France*, in the sixth century. The seats of the choir have each a picture done on copper, which are reckoned very curious; they were made a present of by *Philip* prince of *Orange*, to his sister who was lately abbess. The church of *Notre Dame la Grande*, is said to have been built in the reign of *Constantine*, whose equestrian statue has been erected on one of the outward walls. In the middle of the *Place Royale*, there is a pedestrian statue in brass of *Lewis* XIV. with proper ornaments. They have an university in this town of some credit, founded by *Charles* VII. in 1431. The Jesuits college is a very handsome building, as also the hall where the judges sit. There are several monuments of *Roman* antiquities in and about the town, as that of the palace of *Gallien*, the castle of *Maubergeon*, an amphitheatre, a triumphal arch,

which

FRANCE.

which still serves for one of the city gates, and the remainder of an aqueduct at a place out of town, where the Capuchins have an hermitage. Within a mile of the town, there is a large stone called the *pierre levée*, of which they tell a great many idle stories: antiquarians suppose it to have been the burying place of the antient *Picts*. About six miles from *Poitiers*, in the year 1357, *Edward the black prince* obtained the famous victory over king *John* of *France*.

Vivonne is a small town of *Poiton*, situated on the river *Clain*, and adorned with a castle. *Vivonne.*

Barbesieux is a small town of *Saintonge*, on the frontiers of *Angoumois*. It is situated in a very fertile country, though at some distance from any river. *Lewis* XIV. gave it the title of a marquisate, in favour of one of *Louvois*'s sons. It has two parishes, and a convent of Cordeliers. *Barbesieux.*

V. Bourdeaux.

Bourdeaux is the capital of the *Bourdelois*, and of all *Guienne* and *Gascony*, in west longitude 40. latitude 44. 50. This is one of the largest and richest cities in the kingdom, situated on the west side of the river *Garonne*, fifty miles south of the mouth of that river. The town and suburbs lying in the form of a crescent about the river, make a capacious harbour for small ships. It is surrounded by an old wall and towers; but its principal defence consists in three strong forts, *viz.* the *Trumpet Castle* situated at the entrance of the *Quay*, the castle of *Haa*, and *Fort S. Lewis*, or *S. Croix*, all antient castles, enlarged and improved by Marshal *Vauban*. The town in general is none of the most beautiful, the streets being narrow, and the buildings old; but the suburb of *Chastron* is very large, and adorned with magnificent

ficent buildings. In the new hospital without the town, there is a famous manufactory, especially of lace. They reckon five thousand houses in the city and suburbs, and upwards of forty thousand souls. Here are several monuments of *Roman* antiquity, such as the remains of an amphitheatre, the *Low Gate*, the *Palais Tutele*, the *Palais Gallien*, the fountain of *Duge*, and divers aqueducts. *Bourdeaux* is now the seat of an archbishop, an university, of a parliament established here in 1462, as also of a generality, a mint, a seneschal's jurisdiction, and a court of admiralty. The principal modern edifices are, the cathedral dedicated to *S. Andrew*, one of the fairest in *France*; the archiepiscopal palace, near the ramparts, a magnificent building; the church of *S. Michael*, the Jesuits college, the Carthusian convent, the Cordeliers church, the church and convent of the Dominicans, and the hospital. The place where the parliament assembles, which is said to be an old *Roman* structure; the university, the church yard of *S. Surin*, the town-house, the arsenal, the custom-house, the mint, are likewise worth a traveller's notice. Besides the university, there is an academy established here in 1713, which has distinguished itself in the culture of polite learning. They have a fine quay, where vessels unload, the tide rising here upwards of two fathom. From the walk of *S. Eulalia* on the ramparts, you have a most beautiful prospect. Their foreign trade is very considerable, consisting chiefly in wine, of which they sell in time of peace, seldom less than an hundred thousand tuns annually.

VI. BAYONNE.

Bayonne.

Bayonne is a city of *Gascony*, in *France*, in west longitude 1. 20. latitude 43. 30. This is a very

very antient town, situated at the conflux of the rivers *Nive* and *Adour*, about fifteen miles north of the confines of *Spain*, and about three from the sea. It recieved its name from the *Basquish* words *Baia* and *Ona*, which signify a good bay. The whole town was strongly forified in the late reign by Marshal *Vauban*, and is moreover defended by a very good citadel. *Bayonne* is tolerably large and populous, and is a bishop's see suffragan of *Ausch*. The harbour is good, but of difficult access. They wine trade of *Bayonne* is very considerable; hither also the *Spaniards* bring their wool over the mountains on mules, and take sugars in return. Timber for shipping, is also brought down the rivers in floats from the *Pyrenean* mountains to *Bayonne*, and sent from thence to *Brest* and other ports.

From *Bayonne* you proceed to S. *John de Luz*, a pretty large town of the county of *Labourd* in *Gascony*, situated near the sea, at the mouth of the *Urdacuri*. The inhabitants are said to be good ship-carpenters, and expert at the whale and cod fishery. Near this place lies the *Isle of Pheasants*, in the middle of the river *Bidassoa*, which divides *France* from *Spain*, and being equally claimed by both princes, was pitched upon for a treaty of peace between those crowns, in 1659, called the *Pyrenean* treaty, from the *Pyrenean* mountains, which begin in this neighbourhood.

S. *John de Luz* is the last town of *France*; from thence you may either proceed to *Spain*, or you may return to *Paris* by the way of *Languedoc*, *Provence*, *Dauphiné*, the *Lyonnois* and *Burgundy*. The route from *Paris* to *Spain* thro' *Languedoc*, shall be given in the next chapter.

Remar-

Remarkable places in the coach route from Paris to Bayonne.

Most of the places worth description in this route are the same as those in the post route. The following is a short account of such as are different.

Saintes. — *Saintes* is a city of *France*, in the province of *Guienne*, capital of the territory of *Saintonge*, in west longitude 36. min. latitude 45. 50. This is one of the oldest cities in *Gaul*, and is now the seat of a bishop suffragan of *Bourdeaux*, and a presidial. It is situate on the river *Charente*, about twenty miles to the eastward of the ocean. The city is large, but indifferently built. The cathedral of *S. Peter* is a very antient structure, said to have been built by *Charlemagne*. They have a great many considerable monuments of *Roman* antiquities, as, a triumphal arch, supposed to have been erected in the reign of *Tiberius*, the ruins of an amphitheatre, several aqueducts, and a capitol.

Blaye. — *Blay* is a little town, in the province of *Guienne*, situated on the *Garonne*, in west longitude 45. min. latitude 45. 7. —This town has a citadel and two strong forts, one of which is erected on an island in the middle of the river, and the other on the opposite shore, called *Fort Medon*, from its standing in a district of that name. The passage of the river is secured by these forts, so that no ship can come up and down the river without their permission.

Langon. — *Langon* is a small town of the government of *Guienne*, in the district of *Bassadois*, situated on the *Garonne*, and noted for its excellent white wine.

Dax. — *Dax* or *Daques*, is a city of *France*, capital of the territory of *Les Landes*, in the province of *Gascony*, in west longitude 1. latitude 43. 45. This is a very antient

antient place, formerly called *Aquæ Augustæ*, a name it took from the hot springs in the middle of the town, which were much esteemed in the time of the *Romans*. It is situated on the river *Adour*, and defended by a castle, with some other antient fortifications. The town is populous, and has some trade. 'Tis likewise a bishop's see, suffragan of *Auche*, and has a seneschal's court, with several religious houses. At a very little distance from *Dax*, upon an eminence, is the parish church of *S. Paul*, behind which is a cavern, remarkable for an extraordinary phenomenon. There are three antient tombs of marble in it, the middle one larger than the other two; at the full moon the biggest is full of water, and the two little ones are empty; but at the wane of the moon, it is *vice versa*; and what is more extraordinary, there does not appear any opening in the tombs thro' which this water should pass.

CHAP. IX.

Journey from Paris *to* Narbonne *and* Perpignan.

THE preceding route from *Paris* to *Bayonne* is much the shortest way to *Madrid*; the following is the pleasantest, as it goes thro' *Languedoc*. There are two different roads from *Paris* to *Narbonne*, one by *Limoges*, *Perpignan*, and *Toulouse*, and the other by *Lyons* and lower *Languedoc*. Again, there are two different roads to *Limoges*, one the nearest, by *Orleans*; and the other, further about by *Moulins* and *Clermont*.

Route from Paris *to* Narbonne *and* Perpignan, *by* Orleans, Limoges, *and* Touloufe.

From *Paris* to *Orleans,* fce p. 219.

	Pofts		
Orleans		Souillac	2
La Ferté	2½	Peyrat	1½
Chaumont	1½	Pont de Rodes	2
Chateau-vieux	1	Pelaquoy	1½
Milliance	1½	Cahors	1½
Remorentin	1½	L'Hofpitalet	1
Villefranche	1	Caftelnau	1
Dun le Poillier	1½	Melieres	1
Graffay	1	S. Remans	1
Vatan	1	Montalban	1½
L'Epine fauveau	1½	La Baftide	1
Chateauroux	2½	Griffelles	1
Loitier	1½	S. Jorry	1
Argenton	1½	Courtanfoul	1
Fay	1½	Toulouse	1
Boifremond	1	Caftanet	1
Boitmandé	1	Baffiege	1
Montmagné	1	Villefranche	1
Mortrolles	1	La Baftide d'Anjou	1
Razes	1½	Caftelnaudary	1
La Maifon Rouge	2	Alzonne	2
Limoges	1½	Carcassonne	1½
Boiffeil	1	Barbeyrac	1½
Pierre Buffiere	1	Mons	1
Magnac	1	Lezignan	1
Fregefond	1½	Villedaigne	1
Uferches	2	Narbonne	1
Barriolet	1½	Sijean	2
Donzenat	2	La Palme	1
Brives	1	Salces	2
Creffenfac	2	Perpignan	1½

FRANCE.

From hence to *Mont Louis*, the laſt town belonging to *France*, on the frontiers of *Spain*.

Prades	4	*Mont Louis*	2
Aulette	1½		

Thoſe who chuſe to take the ſhorteſt way from *Toulouſe* to the frontiers of *Spain*, when they come to *Carcaſonne*, muſt leave *Narbonne* on their left, and proceed directly to *Mont Louis*, the laſt town belonging to *France*, on the frontiers of *Spain*; the route from *Carcaſſonne* is as follows.

CARCASSONNE		Aunat	2
Limoux	2	Puyvalador	1½
Couiſſa	2	Mont Louis	1½

Route from Paris to Limoges by Moulins and Clermont.

You follow the route from *Paris* to *Lyons* by *Moulins*, as far as *Eſchirolles*, p. 145. which makes 45 poſts and a half.

	Poſts		
Eſchirolles		Croc	1½
S. Pourçain	1½	Pont Charraut	1
Vernet	1	Felletin	1
Gannat	1½	La Valiere	1
Aigueperſe	1	Compeix	1½
RIOM	1½	La Brugiere	1½
CLERMONT	1	Sauviat	1
Pont Gibaut	2	S. Prieſt de Taurion	1½
Pont au mur	1½	LIMOGES	1½
S. Avy	1½		

The remainder to *Toulouſe* and *Perpignan* as in the preceding route.

Route from Paris *to* Narbonne *and* Perpignan, *by* Lyons *and* Lower Languedoc.

From *Paris* you go to *Lyons*, according to the route, p. 145. From *Lyons* to *Pont S. Esprit*, according to the route, p. 148.

Pont S. Esprit	Posts	Montpelier	1¼
Bagnols	1	*Fabregues*	1
Connaut	1	*Gigean*	1
Valiguieres	1½	*Liujian*	1
Remoulins	1¼	*Villemagne*	1
S. Gervafy	1	Pfzenas	1¼
Nismes	1	*Begude de Jordy*	1
Uchaut	1	Beziers	1½
Lunel	1½	*Niffan*	1
Colombiere	1	Narbonne	2

From *Narbanne* to *Perpignan* as in the First route.

Remarkable places in the route from Paris *to* Narbonne, *by* Limoges *and* Toulouse.

La Ferté.   *La Ferté,* commonly called *La Ferté Senneterre,* is a large borough in the province of *Orleanois,* with the title of duchy and peerage, remarkable for a handsome palace built by Marshal *de la Ferté,* adorned with a fine park and beautiful gardens. *Chaumont,* is a borough in the county *Remorentin.* of *Sologne,* situate on the river *Calne.*----*Remorentin,* is a small town situate on the river *Saudre,* in the territory of *Blafois,* and famous for its woolen manufacture. This is said to be a very antient place; and the inhabitants pretend that *Cæsar* built a tower here, of which there are

still

still some considerable remains. They have a manufacture of serge and cloth, which is used for the cloathing of the troops.-----*Chateau-roux* is a large town of the duchy of *Berry*, situate on the river *Indre*, within sixteen leagues of *Bourges*. It contains four parishes, a collegiate church, a convent of Cordeliers, an abbey of Benedictins, a fine castle, and a park belonging to prince *Condé*, who is lord of the town. *Lewis* XIII. erected it into a duchy and peerage. The castle was built by *Raoul le Large*, whence by corruption it was called *Chateau-roux*. The suburb of *Martins* is full of weavers, who make a cloth called *drap de Berry*.-----*Argenton* is a small town of the duchy of *Berry*, in east longitude 1. 35. latitude 46, 40. It is situate on the river *Creuse*, which divides it into the upper and lower town

I. LIMOGES.

Limoges the antient *Lemovica*, is a city of *France*, in the province of *Guienne*, and capital of the *Limosin*, in east longitude 1. 22. latitude 45. 52. 'Tis a large populous city, situated near the river *Vienne*, partly in a valley, and partly on the declivity of a hill. It is rather long than broad, and surrounded with a wall and deep ditches. 'Tis also the seat of a bishop suffragan of *Bourges*, a generality and presidial. The streets are generally narrow and crooked, and the houses ill built, the roofs projecting so far into the street that you can scarce see the sun at noon day. The cathedral dedicated to *S. Stephen*, is said to have been built by the *English*; but is not yet finished. The nunnery called *La Regle*, is a handsome building. The abbey of *S. Austin* is a very convenient house, most pleasantly situated.

The

The collegiate church of *S. Martial*, reckoned the apostle of the country, is remarkable for its clock; the hours are struck by the figure of death The parochial church of *S. Michael*, has a very high steeple, said to have been built by the *English*. The seminary is a fine stone structure, built after the model of *S. Sulpice*, but the court is larger. The houses are well built, covered with slate, and very clean. The inhabitants are not very polite, nor very rich; the poorer sort make bread of chesnuts, as there is not much corn in the country: when they get other bread, they eat so greedily, that a *Limosin* is used in *France* as a synonimous term for a glutton.

Userches.   *Userches* is a town of *France*, in the province of *Guienne*, and territory of *Limosin*, in east longitude 1. 32. latitude 45. 30. It is seated on the top of a high rock, at the bottom of which runs the river *Vesere*, which has occasioned the proverb, *He that has a house at* Userches *has a castle in* Limosin. There is a very rich abbey of Benedictin monks in this town—*Brives* is a

Brives.   small town of the *Lower Limosin*, situated on the river *Curreze*, which forms in the neighbourhood the finest landscape in the province. The town is called *Brives la Gaillarde*, by reason of the beauty of its situation, the fertility of the soil, and the number of its inhabitants. 'Tis the seat of a presidial, and a seneschal. The parish churches of *S. Martin*, and *S. Sernin*, are worth seeing, as also the college, and the convent of *S. Anthony* of Padua.

II. Cahors.

Cahors.   *Cahors* is the capital of the territory of *Quercy*, in the province of *Guienne*, in *France*, in east longitude 1. latitude 44. 25. This is a very antient

tient town, situate in a peninsula formed by the river *Olt*, over which there are three stone bridges. It is regularly fortified, being surrounded with thick walls, which inclose the peninsula, and the suburb *la Bar*. *Cahors* is the see of a bishop suffragan of *Bourdeaux*, and has likewise a presidial, and a seneschal's jurisdiction. The episcopal palace is the handsomest building in the town. There is an university here, which was founded in 1332, by pope *John* XXI. native of this town, and a shoemaker's son. The town in general is poor, and does not contain above eight thousand souls. There are still the remains of an amphitheatre, built of small square stones.

III. MONTAUBAN.

Montauban is a city of *France*, in the province of *Guienne*, and territory of *Quercy*, in east longitude 1. 5. latitude 44. This is a large, well built, populous town, situate on a hill, at the bottom of which runs the river *Tarn*. It was built in 1144, by *Alphonsus* I. count of *Toulouse*, and is now the seat of a bishop suffragan of *Toulouse*, as also of a generality, a court of aids, and a presidial. 'Tis divided into three parts, viz. *Ville Bourbonne*, the *Old Town*, and the *New Town*. The first is separated from the other two by the river, over which there is a fine stone bridge. This was one of the cautionary towns given by the crown to the Protestants; it held out an obstinate siege against *Lewis* XIII. in person, in 1629, who took it at length, and demolished its fortifications. It now contains about eighteen thousand souls, and has a pretty good silk and woollen manufacture. The principal places worth viewing are the bishop's palace,

lace, the griffon fountain, and the *Falese* which is an agreeable walk on the banks of the *Tarn*.

IV. TOULOUSE.

Toulouse. *Toulouse* is the capital of *Languedoc* in *France*, in east longitude 1. 5. latitude 43. 40. This is a place of great antiquity, being mentioned in history as one of the most flourishing towns of *Gaul*. 'Tis now one of the most considerable cities in the kingdom, the seat of an archbishop, of an university, noted chiefly for the study of the law, Situation. and a parliament. The situation of this city is extremely pleasant, in a large fruitful plain, on the river *Garonne*, which divides it into two unequal parts; these communicate by a beautiful stone bridge, designed by *Mansard*, and terminating with a fine triumphal arch, on which *Lewis* Buildings. XIV. is represented. The whole city contains about eighteen or nineteen thousand families. The streets are large and handsome; and the town walls, as well as the houses, are built of brick. The episcopal palace is one of the most magnificent in *France*.

Churches. The cathedral dedicated to *S. Stephen* is a beautiful building, remarkable for several handsome chapels, a large bell, and a very beautiful choir. The church of *S. Saturnin*, first bishop of *Toulouse*, is a large magnificent edifice, but very dark; it is valued by the inhabitants chiefly for its treasure of relics; the shrine of *S. George* is of immense value. The parish church of *Dalbade* is one of the handsomest in town, and was formerly a heathen temple dedicated to *Apollo*. The convent of the Cordeliers has some handsome paintings in the cloysters, representing the life of *S. Francis*. The Dominican convent is famous for its organ, its rich sacristy, and for the

the body of *S. Thomas* of *Aquin*; they have also a vault remarkable for drying dead bodies. The Carmelites have a curious painting in their cloyster, representing the history of *Charles* VI's delivery out of a wood, when he had lost himself a hunting. The chapel of the company of blue penitents, built by *Lewis* XIII. is one of the most regular in *Europe*. The *Dorade*, belonging to the Benedictins, is noted for the *Mosaic* paintings in the choir, the organ, and the baptistry. There are a great many colleges belonging to the university, but few of them are frequented. The college called the *Esquille*, was finished in 1555; it has a beautiful front 45 fathom long. The Jesuits college is a large and beautiful edifice; here they have a most beautiful piece of sculpture, by *Bachelier*, representing *Hercules* in his cradle, strangling the serpents. Their *Maison Professe* is remarkable for the marble tomb of *Henry* duke of *Montmorency*, who was beheaded at *Toulouse* in the reign of *Lewis* XIII. The other religious places worth viewing are the *Chartreuse*, the bare-footed Carmelites, and the Minims.

The town-house is a magnificent building, which they call the capitol, and the eschivins or consuls, they call Capitouls, there are several good apartments in this edifice, and some handsome paintings, particularly in the hall called the great consistory, the entry of *Lewis* XIV. into *Toulouse* in 1659; opposite to which is a white marble statue of *Clemence Isaure*, who founded the floral games. In the hall on the left hand, are the portraits of the Capitouls, and over the door an excellent picture representing *Clemence Isaure*, and the floral games of *Toulouse*, with a landscape of the city; at the other end of the hall is a fine picture of *Toulouse*, represented under the

Other Public Buildings.

the figure of *Pallas*. In the gallery you see the busts of all the illustrious natives of *Toulouse*, and at the bottom a bust of *Lewis* XIV. adorned with trophies. In another hall are four beautiful pictures, the subjects of which are taken from the history of *Toulouse*. One is by *Boulogne* the elder, another by *Jouvenet*, the third by *Coypel*, and the fourth by *Peter Rivals*. Near the townhouse is the arsenal, which is also worthy of notice. The parliament of *Toulouse*, is the second in the kingdom; it was instituted in 1443, by *Charles* VII. The court where they assemble was the antient palace of the counts of *Toulouse*. There was a feast of floral games instituted in this city by the abovementioned lady *Clemence Isaure* in 1324, for the encouragement of poetry, with prizes of three golden flowers. This feast
Academy. or company was erected into an academy of *Belles Lettres* by *Lewis* XIV. Along the *Garonne*, there is a handsome quay, with a course consisting of a fine walk of trees. The garden of *Frescati*, and the curious mill of *Bazacle* deserve to be also seen.

Trade. *Toulouse* is extremely well situated for trade, lying almost half way between the *Mediterranean* and the ocean, and near the west end of the
Royal Ca- *Royal Canal*. This is a stupendous work, designed to convey goods from the bay of *Biscay* to the gulph of *Lyons*, in fifteen days, without any danger, by forming a communication betwixt the two seas, by the help of the *Garonne*. It extends fifty-three *French* leagues in length, and is in most parts thirty feet broad; it was begun by *Lewis* XIV. in 1660, and finished in 1680, under the direction of *Picquet* the engineer and his sons. And yet this city is neither rich nor populous, the genius of the inhabitants being more turned to the pursuit of civil employments,

ployments, than to commerce. The trade of *Toulouse* consists chiefly in *Spanish* wool, coarse hangings, and stuffs made of silk and wool. There are still the remains of an amphitheatre, *some* temples, aqueducts, and a capitol. The honour of building a capitol was conferred by the *Romans*, only on their largest colonies; that of *Toulouse* till the thirteenth century, was used as a town-house, from whence their eschivens were called Capitouls. Antiquities.

Castelnaudary is a town of *Upper Languedoc*, in the district of *Lauragais*. It is situated in a fruitful plain, and watered with the little river or bason of the canal of *Languedoc*. The roofs of the houses project very far into the streets, so as to render them vastly dark. The collegiate church, and that of the Carmelites, are the principal places worth seeing. The above-mentioned famous canal of *Languedoc*, begins in this neighbourhood; it is formed by the junction of the *Aude*, which falls into the *Mediterranean*, and the *Garonne*, which empties itself into the ocean. You cross the *Aude* over a stone bridge, and on an eminence you discover *the stones of Norouse*. The honest inhabitants of that country relate, that a poor woman going along with seven small stones in her apron, flung them separately into the field, saying that these stones would increase, so as to join one another, when women laid aside all modesty; they now are either joined or very near it; so that we may say of this story, that the prophecy is pretty nigh fulfilled. Castelnaudary.

V. CARCASSONNE.

Carcassonne is a town of the province of *Languedoc* in *France*, in east longitude 2. latitude 43. 20. This is an antient city, as appears by the old Carcassonne.

old manuscripts still kept there, written on the bark of trees, linen, and such other materials. It is situate on the river *Aude*, which divides it into two parts, the upper and lower, both joined by a stone bridge. The upper is called the city; it stands on a hill, encompassed with a double wall, and has moreover a strong castle. The lower part is called the town, and is very well built; the streets are spacious and regular, terminating in a square, from whence you see the four gates of the town. *Carcassonne* is the see of a bishop, suffragan of *Narbonne*, of a seneschal, and a presidial. The cathedral is remarkable only for its antiquity; but the other churches, convents, and public buildings, especially the town-house, and the palace of the presidial, make a handsome appearance. The inhabitants have a great woolen manufacture.

VI. NARBONNE.

Narbonne is a city of *France*, in the province of *Languedoc*, in east longitude 2. 40. latitude 43. 18. This is a very antient city, which the *Romans* made the capital of this part of *Gaul*, called *Gallia Braccata*. At present 'tis the see of an archbishop, who is president of the states of *Languedoc*. It is situate in a bottom, almost surrounded with mountains, on a canal called *Robine*, which affords it a communication with the *Canal Royal* and the river *Aude* on one side, and on the other with the *Mediterranean*, from whence it is but six miles distant. The fortifications are destroyed, but the ramparts are left standing, and serve for the inhabitants to walk on. The canal divides it into two parts, the town and the city; from the city you pass to the town over a bridge, which has houses built on it on

both

both sides, inhabited by principal merchants. The cathedral is an old *Gothic* structure, remarkable for the boldness of its architecture, for a beautiful picture of *Lazarus* raised from the dead, and a fine organ. The archbishop's palace is a kind of fortress, encompassed with large square towers. In the garden there is an antient tomb of white marble, and also a marble niche, through which the Pagan priests uttered their oracles by a square hole in the middle of the niche. The other places most deserving of notice are the collegiate church of *S. Paul*, remarkable for its fine tapestry; the collegiate church of *S. Sebastian*, built by *Charlemaign*; and the church of the Carmelite nuns, famous for the beauty of the marble of the high altars and chapels. The seminary merits also the attention of the curious, being a very handsome building. The air of this city is unwholsome, because of the adjacent lakes and pools; though antiently when these were well drained, they had a very good air. There are some ruins still extant of their antient magnificence, *viz.* of a capitol, an amphitheatre of marble, aqueducts, &c.

VII. PERPIGNAN.

Perpignan is the capital of *Roussillon*, in east longitude 2. 35. latitude 43. This city is situated on the river *Tet*, about three miles to the westward of the sea, partly on a hill, and partly in a bottom. It was taken by the *French* from *Spain* in the last century, and confirmed to them by the *Pyrenean* treaty. The fortifications are very regular; and the town is moreover defended by a strong citadel. 'Tis a bishop's see, who is suffragan of *Narbonne*; and the seat of an university. The cathedral dedicated to *S. John* is a fine

fine large old edifice, whose choir is inclosed with white marble. The *Ostensorium*, in which they expose the sacrament, weighs above four hundred marks. There are several other churches, convents, and hospitals in the town; as also, two colleges of Jesuits, and a seminary. The town house is remarkable for a large clock; and the great market place for a handsome fountain. The inhabitants are a mixture of *French* and *Spaniards*, and speak both languages indifferently.

Prades.   *Prades* is a small town situated in a very pleasant country, near the river *Tet*. The town is neatly built, and subject to the abbey of *La Grasse*. Without the walls, there is a pleasant convent of *Mont Louis.* Capuchins.— *Mont Louis* is the last town belonging to *France*, in the county of *Roussillon*, situate in the *Pyrenean* mountains, upon the right of the neck of *La Perche*, and upon an eminence which commands the bridge of the river *Tet*, and makes the separation betwixt *Cerdagne* and *Conflent*. It is a pretty little town, built and fortified by *Lewis* XIV. in 1681, to which he added a fine citadel, and made it one of the strongest fortresses on the side of *Spain*.

Remarkable places in the route from Paris *to* Limoges, *by* Moulins *and* Clermont.

This route as far as *Moulins* has been already described from p. 151, to p. 155.

S. Pourçain.   *S. Pourçain* is a small town of the *Bourbonnois*, situate on the river *Sioul*, which a little lower falls into the *Allier*. In the parish church of *S. George* there is a statue of an *Ecce Homo*, which is reckoned a master-piece. It is all of one stone, even the cord that ties him, which in some places seem to be knotted with as much ease as *Gannat.*   a riband. — *Gannat* is a small town of the *Bourbonnois*,

Lonnois, situate in a very fruitful country. They have only one large street; but there is a handsome square, and some good churches.—*Aigue-* *Aiguesperse. sperse* is the first town of *Auvergne* coming from the *Bourbonnois*, when you enter into one of the most beautiful countries in the world. The town is small, consisting of only one street, yet it has two collegiate churches. In one of them called the *Holy Chapel*, there is an admirable fine picture of *S. Sebastian*. In the same place there is a curious piece of architecture in perspective.

I. RIOM.

Riom is a town of *France*, in the province of *Riom Lionois*, and territory of *Auvergne*, in east longitude 3. 13. latitude 45. 50. It is situated on a small eminence, from whence there is a most agreeable prospect. 'Tis the capital of the duchy, has a seneschal's jurisdiction, a generality, one of the most considerable presidials in *France*, an election, a mint, and consular jurisdiction. The high street is very broad and long, extending from one end of the town to the other; and the houses are in general well built. Most of the churches are handsome structures. There are three considerable chapters in the town; the building of that of the Holy Chapel is much esteemed.

II. CLERMONT.

Clermont is the capital of *Auvergne*, in the pro- *Clermont* vince of *Lionois*, in *France*, in east longitude 33. 20. latitude 45. 42. This is a large city, situate on a small eminence, in a very pleasant country, between the rivers *Artier* and *Bedat*. By the *Romans* it was called *Arverna Civitas*. 'Tis

'Tis now the seat of a bishop, a presidial, and a court of aids. The town is rich and populous, but the streets are narrow, and the houses very dark. The cathedral is a stately fabric; round the choir there are figures in *relief* representing the history of the Old Testament. The collegiate church of our Lady *Du Port*, the *Course*, the seminary, and the Jesuits college, are worth seeing; as also the palace of the presidial, the bishop's palace, the court of aids, the abbey of *S. Alyre*, &c. Abundance of *Roman* medals, and other antiquities, are frequently dug up near this city. In the suburb of *S. Alyre* there is a fountain that has a petrifying quality. Within a league of *Clermont* is *Pui de Dome*, one of the highest mountains in *Auvergne*, where *M. Pascal* made his experiments on the weight of the air. Leaving *Clermont* you meet with nothing worth description, till you come to *Limoges*. From *Limoges* to *Narbonne* and *Perpignan*, you have been directed by the preceding route.

Remarkable places from Pont S. Esprit to Narbonne *and* Perpignan.

Bagnols. We have already given a description of *Pont S. Esprit*, page 183. *Bagnols* is a small town of *Lower Languedoc*, in the diocese of *Usez*, situate on the river *Cese*, in a very fruitful territory. The streets are narrow and dirty. The town contains a priory, which is the parish church, with three convents of men, and two of women. The great square in the middle of the town is one of the finest in *Languedoc*. The river *Cese*, which passes by it, is said to carry a golden sand.

I. NISMES.

I. Nismes.

Nismes is a city of *France*, in the *Lower Languedoc*, in east longitude 4. 26. latitude 43. 40. This is a very antient city, by the *Romans* called *Nemausis*, from the woods that antiently surrounded it; and noted for a colony fixed here by *Augustus*, immediately after the battle of *Actium*. 'Tis now the seat of a bishop, suffragan of *Narbonne*, a presidial, and a seneschal. Its situation is extremely pleasant. On the hill towards the west end of the town, *Lewis* XIV. built a citadel, composed of several bastions. The town is large, containing above twelve thousand families; the streets are spacious, and the houses generally well built. The cathedral dedicated to the blessed Virgin, is an old *Gothic* building. The Jesuits have a handsome modern church. The finest part of the town is near the great market-place; the streets that terminate in this quarter, are very handsome, as also those near the Jesuits college. The course is a very pretty place, just opposite the cathedral. The inhabitants have considerable manufactures both of silk and wool, in which they carry on a good trade.

The many antiquities of the city of *Nismes* render it, in some measure, a second *Rome*. But there is none that more deserves the attention of the curious, than the amphitheatre. It is of an oval figure, having two rows of arches, which form two rows of galleries, one over the other, consisting of sixty arches each, being 115 fathom in circumference. The entrance is by four doors, placed east, west, north, and south. The whole edifice consists of three orders of archi-

architecture, built of large stones, as durable as marble, without mortar or plaister. The area in the middle of the theatre, where their combats and shews were exhibited, is an hundred feet in diameter, filled up at present with little houses of tradesmen. The outside is adorned with columns and handsome cornishes; and on several of the stones are *basso-relievos.*—From the amphitheatre you go to see the *Square-house,* an admirable piece of *Corinthian* architecture. This building is seventy-four feet long, and about forty-two broad; it has six columns in the front, and ten on each side. On the ceiling there are several figures, which are much esteemed by antiquarians. This building was formerly a Pagan temple, called the *Basilica* of *Plotina,* to whom it was dedicated by the emperor *Adrian;* but *Lewis* XIV. gave it to the *Augustinian* friars, who have made a handsome church of it.—Without the walls on the top of a high hill, there is an antient building, called the great tower. It was of a prodigious height, in form of a pyramid, and seems to have been designed for a watch-tower, for the sea is said to have come up formerly to the foot of this hill. 'Tis built of small square stones, well cemented.—Here also are the ruins of the temple of *Diana,* of a square form, and built of large stones, supported by columns, adorned with chapiters, architraves, and niches in the walls for the idols.

Pont du Guard. Those who travel for pleasure should not neglect seeing the famous *Pont du Guard* in this neighbourhood.---*Pont du Guard* is nine miles north of *Nismes,* and justly reckoned one of the noblest and compleatest monuments of *Roman* magnificence, having been built by the *Romans* to support an aqueduct that brought water to the city

city of *Nismes*; This admirable structure, lies over the river *Gardon*, and is indeed three bridges, one upon another, which join two mountains together. On the banks of the river *Gardon*, there are two mountains, each of them fifteen fathom high, over which the aqueduct is carried. The whole work is of the *Tuscan* order, formed of three rows of arches, one over another, all built of free-stone, of the same consistency as the amphitheatre of *Nismes*. The lowest bridge which lies over the river *Gardon*, has six arches, each of them fifty-eight feet wide; it is fourscore and three feet in height, and four hundred and thirty-eight feet in length. The second bridge is supported by eleven arches, each of which has fifty-six feet in diameter, and sixty-seven feet in height. The third stands upon thirty-five arches, each of which has seventeen feet in diameter; it supports the aqueduct, and is five hundred and fourscore feet and a half in length. The whole height of the bridges, from the river which runs under the lowermost arch, to the top of the uppermost, is 186 feet. The whole length of the aqueduct, taking in all its windings, is no less than twenty-seven miles.

II. Montpellier.

Montpellier is a city of *France*, in the province of *Languedoc*, in east longitude 3. 50. latitude 43. 37. This is a small but handsome city, situated on a hill, at the foot of which runs the river *Lez*, six miles from the *Mediterranean*: they have a pleasant prospect of the sea to the southward, and of a fine country to the northward. It had the name of *Mons Puellarum*, from an hermitage which stood here before the city was built in the eighth century, inhabited by

Montpelliers

Situation

two young women, of whose sanctity the people had a great opinion. The river *Lez* receives the small river *Merdanson*, which fills part of the town ditches. *Lewis* XIII. built here a citadel, flanked with four royal bastions. One of the gates of the town is built after the model of a triumphal arch, on which are several *basso-relievos* and inscriptions expressing the memorable actions of *Lewis* XIV. The houses are for the most part of free-stone, and well built; the streets are narrow and crooked, but kept pretty clean. This city is the see of a bishop, and the seat of a generality, a presidal, a court of aids, a chamber of accounts, and a mint. In the cathedral dedicated to *S. Peter*, there are three pictures of the life of this saint, the middle one of which is by *Sebastian Bourdon*. The church of our Lady, one of the three parish churches, is remarkable for its steeple, the high altar, and the chapel of our Lady. The Jesuits have a handsome college. The bishop's palace is a sightly structure, all of free-stone. The town-house is admired for its beautiful halls, most elegantly painted. The *Peyrou* is a delightful walk without the town; the states of *Languedoc* ordered a fine equestrian statue to be cast at *Paris* in brass, by *Coizevox*, and erected it on this spot on a handsome pedestal of marble. On the terrass of *Canourgue* the better sort of people meet in summer evenings, to hear the concerts and serenades. The inhabitants are polite and sociable; their women are the handsomest in *France*, and extremely agreeable in company. The trade of this town is considerable, for they have a large silk manufacture, and another of wool; they likewise whiten great quantities of wax, which they bring from the *Levant*, and have a good trade in skins, cotton, verdegrease,

strong-

Fortifications.

Buildings.

Walks.

Trade.

strong-waters, brandy, cinnamon waters, &c. as also in vermilion, and confection of alkermes.

Montpellier is famous for its university, and par- University. ticularly for its physical school, frequented by students from all parts of *Europe*. The foundation of this university is ascribed to the disciples of *Averroes* and *Avicenna* in 1196, but it was not perfectly established till 1220. Without the town, lies the king's physic garden, well stored with medicinal herbs. The number of apothecaries in this small city is incredible; some say near two hundred. Vast numbers of consumptive people flock hither from all parts of *Europe*, especially from *England*, to breathe this air, which is said to have a good effect upon bodies of a moist and phlegmatic temperament. About 12 miles from *Montpellier*, on the lake of *Latte*, stands the little town of *Frontignan*, famous for its muscate wine.

Pezenas is a small town of *France*, in the pro- Pezenas. vince of *Langeudoc*, in east long. 3. 12. lat. 43. 30. It is situated on an eminence, on the river *Peyne*, in a most fruitful pleasant country. The agreeable avenues to the town, the pleasant walks, the handsome squares adorned with fountains, and the neatness of the buildings, render it one of the prettiest towns in *France*. They have a collegiate church, with a college of the priests of the oratary. The air is very wholesome, and the climate temperate. The inhabitants have a woolen manufacture, and sell a considerable quantity of cloth in fair time.

III. Beziers.

Beziers is a city of *Lower Languedoc*, in east Beziers. longitude 3. latitude 43. 25. This is a very antient place, having been made a *Roman* colony called

called *Beterræ*, in the time of *Julius Cæsar*. 'Tis now the seat of a bishop suffragan of *Narbonne*, as also of a presidial and a seneschal. It stands on a hill, at the foot of which runs the little river *Orbe*. The royal canal passes likewise in its neighbourhood. The town is large and well built, so as to pass for one of the prettiest in *France*, but is not proportionably populous. The church of S. *Nazarius* is small for a cathedral. The Jesuits college founded in 1599, is a handsome building. From the terrass before the cathedral there is a most charming prospect, extending over the valley, through which the river *Orbe* passes; and the hills beyond it form a kind of amphitheatre, covered with olives and vineyards. You see here the ruins of a *Roman* amphitheatre.

CHAP. X.

Journey from Paris *to* Bourges.

YOU must follow the route from *Paris* to *Lyons* p. 145, as far as *La Charité*, which is 3.1 posts. From *La Charité* you proceed thus:

	Posts.		
La Charité		*Nohant*	1½
Charentonay	1½	BOURGES	1½
Beaugis	1½		

Bourges. *Bourges* the atient *Biturecæ*, is the capital of the territory of *Berry*, in the *Orleanois*, in east longitude 2. 30. latitude 47. 10. fifty miles south-west of *Orleans*, and about an hundred and five south of *Paris*. It is situate betwixt two small

small rivers, the *Evre* and the *Orron*, upon a hill that gently descends to the banks of those two rivers, which almost surround the town. It is a large well-built city, the see of an archbishop, and an university, which is not much frequented. The town is pretty full of gentry, ecclesiastics, and students, but has very little trade, which is the reason of its not being populous. The whole town is divided into four wards, *de S. Bourbonnoux, d'Orrons, de S. Sulpice,* and *de S. Prive*; which contain 16 parishes and five chapters. The cathedral dedicated to *S. Stephen,* is one of the finest Gothic structures in *France*. On each side are two fine steeples, the old one called *la Toure Sourde,* and the new one built in the beginning of the 16th century. The latter is one of the highest and best structures in *France*; the design was by *William de Peilevoisin,* a famous architect at that time. The other, called the *Tour Sourde,* is supported by a pillar of a prodigious thickness, and by a vaulted arcade, which is esteemed a master-piece in architecture. The holy chapel was built in 1400, and is greatly admired. The townhouse is a handsome edifice, built by *James Coeur* king *Charles* VII's goldsmith, for his own dwelling house; it cost him 135,000 livres, a great sum in those days. The archiepiscopal palace would be one of the finest in *France,* if the plan of *M. Pheypeaux,* archbishop of this see, was continued. The square of *Bourbon* is the largest in the town, where formerly the amphitheatre stood. The design of the seminary is extremely beautiful. The Jesuits college is a large magnificent building. The *Capuchins* are in the suburb of *Bourbonnoux,* and have a very handsome avenue to their convent. There is a very fine walk which begins at the gate of *S. Michael*. Without the gate of *Orran* is the king's garden, with a pleasant walk. It was in this city *Charles* VII.

of

of *France* resided, when the *English* being masters of the rest of the kingdom, he was in derision called king of *Berry*.

CHAP. XI.

Journey from Paris *to* Rochelle *and* Rochefort.

FROM *Paris* you must go to *Poitiers*, according to the route given, p. 219. There is a stage-coach that sets out from *Paris* to *Rochelle* and *Rochefort*, from the *Rue Countrescrape*, every *Friday* at eight in the morning. You pay fifty livres for your place, and five sous *per* pound for baggage, and are generally nine days upon the road. The post route from *Poitiers* to *Rochelle* is as follows.

	Posts.		
POITIERS		*Niort*	1½
Croutelle	1	*Rohan-Rohan*	1
Colombieres	1½	*Mosay*	1
Lusignan	1	*Courson*	1
Ville Dieu du Perron	1¾	*Nouaillé*	1
La Motte	1	*Dompierre*	1
S. Maixent	1	ROCHELLE	1
Ville-Dieu du Pont de Vaux	1		

Remarkable places in this journey.

Lusignan. *Lusignan* is a town of *France*, in the province of *Poitou*, under the meridian of *London*, latitude 46. 30. It is situate on the little river *Vonne*, and was famous in former times for its castle, which

which was reckoned one of the strongest in *France*, built by *Hugh* II. surnamed the beloved, lord of *Lusignan*. The vulgar imagine it was built by a fairy, half a woman and half a serpent, named *Melusine*, of whom they tell a thousand idle stories. This castle held out for the Calvinists, when the duke of *Montpensier* took it, after a siege of four months in 1574, and levelled it to the ground.

S. Maixent is a small town of *Poitou*, which *S. Maixent.* took its name from an antient hermit who lived in the time of *Clovis*. Thus from an inconsiderable hermitage it became a handsome town. The hermitage has been changed into an abbey of the order of *S. Benedict*. The town is agreeably situate on the river *Sevre*, and is indifferently built. Here they have a considerable manufacture of fine serges; and in the district they drive a good trade in corn and cattle.

Niort is a town of *France*, in the territory of *Niort.* *Poitou*, in west longitude 30 min. latitude 46. 22. It is situate on the banks of the river *Sevre*, which is navigable from hence to the sea. In the suburb they have a quay, where small vessels come to unload their cargoes, consisting chiefly of spices, salt and fish. The town in general is well built; in the high street, you see the town-house, adorned with a very large clock. The other principal things worth notice, are the church of our Lady, famous for its high steeple, and the strong castle flanked with four large towers. The market-place is one of the largest in *France*. The town has a considerable manufacture of woolen stuffs, and shamois leather.

I. ROCHELLE.

Rochelle is a city and port town of *France*, in *Rochelle.* the province of *Orleanois*, and territory of *Aunis*, in west longitude 1. 5. latitude 46. 7. It is situate

tuate on the *Bay of Biscay*, six miles south-east of the isle of *Ré*, and twelve north-east of *Oleron*, in the middle of a morass, which adds to the strength of the fortifications made here by the famous engineer *Vauban*. The town is of a square figure, and about three miles in circumference. Most of the streets are drawn in a direct line, and the houses adorned with porticos. *Rochelle* is at present a bishop's see, suffragan of *Bourdeaux*. The Jesuits college is a very handsome building. The pleasantest part of the town is the *Rue du Temple*. The town-house stands in the *Rue saint Yon*. The *Palais* or court of justice, in the *Rue de Conseil*, is a handsome building, as also the church of *S. Lewis*, which is in the great square of the castle. There is a presidial in the town, and a sovereign court for the salt-houses of the west. The harbour is bordered round with a large quay built of free-stone, in which the tide rises four fathom, so as to admit of vessels of 200 tuns. They have several manufactures in the town, the principal of which are the refining and baking of sugar, and the distilling of brandy and strong waters. But nothing turns so much to their account as their salt, which is made by the sea water. The foreign trade of *Rochelle* is very considerable. This city is famous for the siege its protestant inhabitants maintained against *Lewis* XIII. when they were obliged at length to surrender, the 8th of *October* 1628. At low water you may see the remains of the famous digue made by cardinal *Richlieu*, which hindered the *English* from throwing succours into the town. From *Rochelle* there is a stage-coach that sets out for *Paris*, every *Thursday* at six in the morning, from the canton *des Flamans*, near the new gate. You pay fifty livres for your place, and five sous *per* pound for baggage; the coach is nine days upon the road.

La

FRANCE.

La Rocher is an inn, and the only house upon the road betwixt *Rochelle* and *Rochefort*. They reckon it only two leagues between *Rocher* and *Rochefort*, but they are such long leagues, that *Rocher* may be reckoned half way.

II. ROCHEFORT.

Eighteen miles to the left of *Rochelle*, as you come from *Paris*, stands *Rochefort*, a port town of *France*, in the province of *Guienne*, and territory of *Saintonge*, in west longitude 1. latitude 46. It is a fine large town, situate on the river *Charente*, about five miles from its mouth. Before the year 1664, it was but an inconsiderable village; but *Lewis* XIV. upon discovering that there was depth sufficient in the *Charente* for the largest vessels, and that a good harbour, which was very much wanted for the royal navy, might be made at the mouth of that river, ordered a town to be built, which he surrounded with a wall and other modern fortifications. Here he erected an arsenal and magazines, and gave all manner of encouragement to his subjects to build and settle; so that 'tis now a handsome town, and the best provided to accomodate the royal navy of any upon the coast, except *Brest*. The entrance of the river and the port is defended by several forts, that render it inaccessible to an enemy by sea. The principal places worth seeing are, the royal dock, the magazines, the foundery, the arsenal, the manufacture of sail cloth, the hospital for disabled seamen, the intendant's house, the square of the Capuchins, and the beautiful *Hotel des Cazernes*, where three hundred sea-officers are maintained and instructed at the king's expence.

From *Rochefort* you may go to *Bourdeaux*, by the way of *Saintes*, *Royan*, and *Blaye*. From *Saintes* to *Bourdeaux*, see p. 221, 232.

CHAP.

CHAP. XII.

Journey from Paris *to* Breſt, *thro'* Tours *and* Nants.

THE road from *Paris* to *Breſt* is by *Angers*; but there are two ways to *Angers*, one by *Amboiſe*, *Tours*, and *Saumur*; the other by *Rambouillet*, *Chartres*, and *La Fleche*.

Route from Paris *to* Breſt, *thro'* Saumur *and* Nants.

The route from *Paris* to *Tours*, ſee p. 219.

	Poſts		
Tours		*Mauves*	$1\frac{1}{2}$
Luynes	$1\frac{1}{2}$	Nants	$1\frac{1}{2}$
Pile S. Marc	1	*Temple*	2
Langets	1	*Lamoire*	$1\frac{1}{2}$
Trois Volets	$1\frac{1}{2}$	*Pontchateau*	$1\frac{1}{2}$
Chouzé	$1\frac{1}{2}$	*La Roche Bernard*	2
S. Catharine de l' Iſle Anger	1	*Muſillac*	$1\frac{1}{2}$
Saumur	1	Vannes	$2\frac{1}{2}$
S. Martin de la Place	1	*Auray*	2
Roſiers	1	*Hennebond*	$1\frac{1}{2}$
Meniſtré	1	*L'Orient*	1
La Dagueniere	$1\frac{1}{2}$	*Quimperlay*	$2\frac{1}{4}$
Angers	1	*Roſpourden*	$2\frac{1}{2}$
La Roche au Breuil	1	Quimpercorentin	2
S. George ſur Loire	1	*Chateaulin*	$2\frac{1}{2}$
Chantocé	1	*Le Fou*	2
Varades	2	*Landernau*	2
Ancenis	$1\frac{1}{4}$	*Guypava*	1
Ouden	$1\frac{1}{2}$	Brest	1

FRANCE.

Route from Nants to Brest, through Rennes.

	Posts		
NANTS		Lamballe	1½
Curet	2	Etangles	1
Pavillon	1	S. BRIEUX	1
Nosay	1½	Chatelaudrin	2
Derval	1½	Guingamp	1½
Breharaye	1	Goismormant	1
Roudun	1½	Belle isle	1
Bout de Landes	1	Pontir	1
RENNES	1½	Pontou	1
Passe	1	Morlaix	2
Bedée	1½	S. Egonec	1
Montauban	1	Landivisiau	1
S. Juan	1	Landernau	1½
Broon	1	Guypava	1
Langouedre	1	BREST	1

Route from Paris to Brest, Chartres and La Fleche.

	Posts		
Paris		La Ferté Bernard	2
VERSAILLES	2	Conneré	2
the first royal		S. Marc	1
Trappes	1	MANS	1½
Connieres	1	Guesselard	2
Rambouillet	1½	Fouille tourte	1
Maintenon	2½	LA FLECHE	2
CHARTRES	2	Bourgneuf	2½
Courville	2	Pelouailie	1½
La Louppe	1½	ANGERS	1
Nogent le Routrou	2½		

The remainder as in the preceding route.

Remarkable

The GRAND TOUR.

Remarkable places in the first route.

This route as far as *Tours* has been already described chap. VIII. p. 223.

Luines is a small town, which bore the name of *Maillé*, before it was erected into a duchy and peerage, in favour of *Albert de Luines*, in 1621. It has two parishes, and about 2000 inhabitants. In the collegiate church are the tombs of the antient lords of *Maille*. There is a strong castle here, with a large tower. Two leagues further you come to the castle of *S. Mark*, where you see a pillar of bricks so hard as to be cannon proof. It is called *La pile de S. Mark*, and by the tradition of the country, it was built by *Cæsar*. —*Langets* is a small town upon the north of the *Loire*, where you see a pretty good castle, built by *Peter de Bruffe*, minister to *Philip the Bold*. This place is famous for its melons, which are exquisitely good.

I. SAUMUR.

Saumur is a town of *France*, in the duchy of *Anjou*, under the meridian of *London*, latitude 47 17. It was antiently called *Salvus Murus*, deriving the name of *Murus* from the wall or rock under which it was built. The town is agreeably situated on the river *Loire*, over which it has two handsome bridges. The suburb of our lady of *Ardeliers*, is a large street along the river, at the end of which there is a church of the same name, much frequented by pilgrims; it is served by the fathers of the oratory, who have a large community; the royal college is also under their direction. The castle on the top of a rock, consists of several round towers of free stone, in the middle

middle of which there is a handsome apartment for the governor. The town was heretofore more populous by one half; at present it does not contain above five thousand inhabitants. This diminution is owing to the suppression of the protestant academy, and the abolition of their religion. There are still some manufactures in the town, the principal of which are the refining of sugar, and those of hard-ware and toys. Within half a mile is the abbey of *S. Florent*, remarkable for its pleasant situation.

II. ANGERS.

Angers is the capital of the province of *Anjou*, in west long. 30 min. latitude 47. 30. This is one of the largest and handsomest cities in *France*, pleasantly situated at the confluence of the little *Loir*, the *Sarte*, and the *Mayenne*. Part of the town stands on the side of a hill, and the rest in the plain watered by the *Mayenne*, which divides *Angers* into two pars. That on the side of the hill is the largest, and communicates with the other by a very large bridge. The whole town is surronded by a wall and antique fortifications, commanded by a castle situate on a steep rock. The number of houses in the town are said to be nine thousand, which contain thirty-six thousand inhabitants, divided into sixteen parishes, twelve within the walls, and four in the suburbs. The city is a bishop's see, suffragan of *Tours*. The cathedral dedicated to *S. Maurice*, is a noble structure, remarkable for one of the finest steeples in *France*, which is supported by the foundation of two other steeples, one on each side, and seems suspended in the air. The roof of the church is high and broad, and yet has never a pillar to sustain it. In the church-yard of the collegiate church of *S. Julian* there is a large stone urn, which contained the ashes of a Pagan lady with this inscription, *Uxori optimæ Tit. Flavius Aug. lib. Asiaticus.* In the collegiate church of *S. Peter*, the statues of *S. Peter* and *S. Paul* are very antient and extremely beautiful. The town-house is a handsome building, being the work of *Peter Poyet*, mayor of *Angers*. In the garden belonging to it there is a statue of *Lewis* XIV. erected by the town in 1685. There is a very good university in *Angers*, frequented chiefly for the study of law. The annual procession of the sacrament in this city, is very pompous. The seminary is a handsome building whose foudation was owing to *M. Pelletier*, bishop of *Angers*. In the suburb of *Bresigny*, you may see the famous quarries of *Angers*, by which they are supplied with those excellent slates that cover their houses, and from whence *Angers* has the name of the *Black Town*.

Chantocé is a barony situated on the right bank of the *Loire*.——*Ancenis* is a little town of the province of *Britany*, situate on the frontiers of *Anjou*. The town is prettily built, well peopled, and belongs to the family of *Bethune Charrost*.

III. N A N T S.

Nants is a city of *France*, in the province of *Britany*, in west longitude 1. 30. latitude 47. 15. This is a large populous town, situated on the *Loire* and the *Ardre*, about thirty miles to the eastward of the ocean. It is surrounded by a wall, and other fortifications, and defended by a castle. Along the river side there is a fine key, on which stand the merchants houses. Over the river there is a handsome stone-bridge, from whence

FRANCE.

whence you have a charming prospect. This city was formerly the residence of the dukes of *Britany*, and now is the see of a bishop, suffragan of *Tours*. The cathedral, dedicated to S. *Peter*, is a fine *Gothic* structure, remarkable for the tombs of several of the antient dukes of *Britany*. The church of the Carmelites is famous for the magnificent tomb of *Francis* II. the last duke of *Britany*, done by *Michael Colombe*. In the parish church of S. *Nicholas*, over the high altar, there is a glass window, whose painting is extremely admired; it represents the fifty-six miracles of Christ. The other principal buildings are, the Jesuits' college, the episcopal palace, and the town-house. This city has as great a foreign trade as most in the kingdom; though ships of burden cannot come so high up the river, because of the sands, but are obliged to unload their merchandize into hoys and lighters at *Port-Launai*, fifteen miles off, near the mouth of the river. The principal trade of the merchants of *Nants* is to *America* and the *West-Indies*, whither they send annually about fifty sail, from sixty to three hundred tun, laden with all manner of provisions and necessaries for the plantations, and make their returns in sugar, cocoa, ginger, cotton, wool, indigo, hides, tortoise-shells, &c. The country round about *Nants* feeds great herds of cattle, of which they make a considerable advantage. Near the city is a famous hermitage, situated on a rock, from whence there is a fine prospect of the town, the *Loire*, and the adjacent country.

IV. VANNES.

Vannes is a city of *France*, in the province of *Britany*, in west longitude 2. 37. latitude 47. 40. This is looked upon as one of the most antient

tient towns of the province, and is still a bishop's see, suffragan of *Tours*. It is situate about six miles from the sea, and watered by two little rivers, which unite their streams, and form a pretty harbour, capable of admitting vessels of 200 tuns. The key is built of free-stone, as also the mole, which advances into the middle of a small morass, round which there are several handsome houses, belonging to wealthy merchants. This part, called the *Market Suburb*, is much larger than the town, from which it is separated by a ditch and walls, and is remarkable for a very handsome mall. The town itself is populous, but indifferently built, the streets being very narrow, except that which leads from the gate towards the sea to the town-house. The other principal buildings are the cathedral, the grand hospital, the Jesuits' college, the Capuchins, the Dominicans, and the Ursulines. The bishop is temporal lord of part of the town.

Auray.   *Auray* is a small sea-port of *Britany*, consisting properly of only one street, and a large key: it has a tolerable trade, and is famous for a handsome convent of Carthusians.

Hennebon.   *Hennebon* is a small town of *Britany*, situate on the river of *Blavet*, six miles from the sea, from whence the tide flows high enough into the town, to admit of vessels of 150 tun. It is divided into the new, the old, and the walled town. The parochial church is dedicated to our Lady, near which there is a handsome square. The wall that separates the town from the river, is bordered with a large key, built with free-stone.

Port Louis.   Three miles from *Hennebon* stands *Port Louis*, a port town of *France*, in the province of *Britany*, in west longitude 3. 6. latitude 47. 42. It is situate on the *Bay of Biscay*, at the mouth of the river *Blavet*, and sometimes called by that name.

name. 'Tis defended by a very strong castle, built on rocks, which form a peninsula, entirely occupied by the town, at the end of which there is a large ditch, which is filled with water from the sea. The harbour is very commodious, and receives the largest vessels, being a station for the royal navy, and for the ships of the *French East-India* company.

L'Orient, or port *L'Orient*, is a fortress and sea-port town of *France*, in west longitude 3. 15. latitude 47. 42. It is situate in the province of *Britany*, at the mouth of the river *Blavet*, opposite to *Port Louis*, being the station of the *French East-India* ships, from whence it lately obtained the name of the eastern port, or port *L'Orient*.--- *Quimperlay* is a small town, situate among mountains, in a peninsula formed by the junction of the two little rivers *Isole* and *Elle*, which form a port capable of receiving large boats. The key has several warehouses, and the town is pretty populous.

V. QUIMPERCORENTIN.

Quimpercorentin is a city of *France*, in the province of *Britany*, in west longitude 4. latitude 48. This is a handsome city, situate at the conflux of the *Oder*, and another small river called *Benaudet*. Its present name comes from its walls, (for *Quimper*, in the language of the *Bas Bretons*, signifies surrounded with walls) and from *Corentin* its first bishop. The town is tolerably large, a place of some trade, and the see of a bishop, suffragan of *Tours*. The cathedral dedicated to the blessed Virgin is a handsome structure. The other principal buildings are, the episcopal palace, the Jesuits' church and college, and the church of the Cordeliers, where are several tombs of the dukes of *Britany*.

VI. BREST.

VI. BREST.

Brest.

Brest is a sea-port town of *France*, in the province of *Britany*, in west longitude 4. 30. latitude 48. 25. The town is situated on an emicence, on the north side of a fine bay, called *Brest* or *Cameret Bay*. The streets are narrow, and the houses ill built. The parish church of S. *Lewis* is a beautiful structure, which cost above three hundred thousand livres. The Jesuits have a very handsome house, and a pleasant garden; they have also a seminary here for bringing up chaplains for the navy. The harbour is the best the *French* have in the ocean, being able to contain five hundred sail of ships. Here the *French* king lays up one of his squadrons of men of war: none of these are of the first rate, the entrance of the harbour, called the *Goulet* or *neck*, being too shallow and rocky to admit them; which is, however, a security against an enemy's fleet. Their largest ships are always built and laid up at *Toulon*. The town and the entrance of the harbour are extremely well fortified. Along the harbour they have built a very fine quay, on which they have their magazines. On the other side is the beautiful church of our Lady of Recovery, in a very large suburb, where they have a strong tower opposite the castle that commands the entrance of the port. The yards and magazines are considerable.

Remarkable places from Nants to Breſt, by the way of Rennes.

Rennes is the capital of *Britany*, of which ſee a deſcription in the next chapter.---*Lamballe* is a borough ſuppoſed to be the capital of the *Ambiliates*, mentioned by *Cæſar*. It is divided into the upper and lower town; in the laſt there is a large ſtreet inhabited by tanners and dyers.

S. Brieux is a port town of *Britany* in *France*, in weſt longitde 2. 50. latitude 48. 40. It ſtands in a bottom, near the mouth of the river *Gouat*, ſurrounded with mountains, out of ſight of the ſea, tho' within a mile and a half of it. The town has neither wall nor ditch, and yet is the ſee of a biſhop. The houſes are pretty well built, the ſtreets regular, and the churches and ſquares make a handſome appearance.---*Morlaix* is a port town of *France*, in the province of *Britany*, in weſt longitude 4. latitude 48. 37. It ſtands on a little river to which it gives its name, and will admit only of ſmall veſſels. The road at the mouth of the river is much frequented, having very good anchorage. The church of *Notre Dame* is a curious old building; the hoſpital is one of the fineſt ſtructures in the province.

Remarkable places in the ſecond route.

Rambouillet is a borough of the province of *Beauſſé*, within twelve miles of *Nogent le Roy*. It is remarkable for a very large caſtle, in which *Francis* I. died the 31ſt of *May*, 1547, and now belongs to the count of *Touloſe*, who has repaired and embelliſhed it, ſo that it may paſs for one of the fineſt buildings in the neighbourhood of *Paris*.

Paris. There is a very large garden and park, with a foreſt containing 28,271 arpens of land.

Maintenon. ---*Maintenon* is alſo a borough in the province of *Beauſſe*, with a caſtle ſituate on the river *Eure*, in a valley between two mountains. This is the place that gave a new name to Madame *Scarron*, ſo famous under the reign of *Lewis* XIV. that lady having purchaſed it of the family of *Angennes*. It now belongs to the duke of *Noailles*, who married *Françoiſe Aubigné*, Madame *Maintenon*'s niece. This borough is remarkable for an aqueduct, built here by *Lewis* XIV. There is a collegiate church dedicated to *S. Nicholas*, and two pariſhes.

I. CHARTRES.

Chartres. *Chartres* is the capital of the *Chartrain* or *Beauſſe Proper*, in the province of *Orleanois*, in *France*, in eaſt longitude 1. 32. latitude 48. 27. This is a large town, ſituated on the river *Eure*, which divides it into two parts, whereof the largeſt ſtands on an eminence. It is very well inhabited, but not handſome, the ſtreets being narrow, and the buildings old. This city is now a biſhop's ſee, the ſeat of a preſidial, a bailiwick, and an election. The cathedral is one of the fineſt *Gothic* ſtructures in *France*, remarkable for its two ſteeples of ſtone, which are admirably well built. The myſteries of the life of our Saviour are carved round the choir, and by able ſculptors are looked upon as a maſter-piece. The inhabitants have a tradition, that this was once a temple of the *Druids*, who dedicated it *Virgini pariturae*. The ſeminary is alſo a handſome ſtructure. There are ten pariſhes in the city and ſuburbs, and a great many religious houſes. Among other charitable foundations, they have an hoſpital here for a hundred and twenty blind people. There is a handſome

some quay along the river *Eure*, and a pleasant walk, where you see the church of *S. Julian*, built on a vault over the river.

Nogent le Rotrou, is the capital of the dutchy of Perche, in the province of *Orleanois*, in east longitude 3. 33. latitude 48. 26. 'Tis a small, but rich and populous town, situated on the little river *Huisne*, and remarkable for its manufactures of leather, linen, and serge. It belongs to the family of *Bethune Orval*.

II. MANS.

Mans is the capital of the dutchy of *Maine*, in the province of *Orleanois*, in *France*, in east longitude, 5 min. latitude 48. 6. It is situate on an eminence, at the foot of which runs the river *Sarte*, which here unites its stream with the *Huisne*. Formerly it was much larger than it is at present; though it is still a considerable city, being a bishop's see, and containing about 15,000 inhabitants. The four principal streets are tolerably handsome, but the rest are narrow and crooked. In the city and its four suburbs, there are fourteen parishes, four abbeys, four convents of men, four of women, three collegiate churches. The cathedral, dedicated to *S. Julian*, its first bishop, is a fine old building, remarkable for its choir, where are several considerable tombs, and a clock that passes for a master-piece. The other principal structures are, the episcopal palace, the tower of *Orbitello*, the palace of the presidial, and the town-house.

III. LA FLECHE.

La Fleche is a town of *France*, in the province of *Orleanois*, and territory of *Anjou*, under the meri-

meridian of *London*, latitude 47. 40. This is a small but handsome town, pleasantly situated in a beautiful plain on the little *Loire*. 'Tis the seat of a presidial and election, and contains a great many beautiful buildings. The whole town consists only of one parish, but has six thousand inhabitants. The streets are large and regular, and the houses well built. The great church dedicated to *S. Thomas*, is worth seeing. Over the river is a fine stone bridge, which leads to the suburb of *Beffrie*, whose entrance is defended by a small castle. The town house, and the palace of the presidial, are handsome buildings, as also the palace of the marquis of *Varenne*, adorned with a beautiful garden and fine water-works. But the greatest curiosity of *La Fleche*, is the famous college of Jesuits, built by *Henry* IV. in 1603, after the model of the palace of *Escurial* in *Spain*. In the middle of the college stands their church, which is built after the *Italian* taste; and at the side of the great altar there is a monument, with the above-mentioned prince's statue, whose heart is buried in the chapel with that of *Mary* of *Medicis*, his queen. The governor's palace, situated at the entrance of the high street, is a handsome structure, extremely well furnished. There are two pleasant walks for the people of the town, the mall, which is pretty large, and the *Pre-Luneau*, on the banks of the *Loire*.

CHAP.

FRANCE.

CHAP. XIII.

Journey from Paris *to* Rennes *and* S. Malo.

	Posts		
PARIS		Ribay	2
VERSAILLES	Two posts, 1st Royal	Mayenne	2
		Martigny	2
Neauphles	2	Laval	2
La Queue	1	La Gravelle	2½
Houdan	1½	Vitré	1½
Dreux	2	Chateaubourg	1½
Nonancourt	1½	Noyal	1
Verneuil	2	RENNES	1½
S. Maurice	1½	La Meziere	1½
Mortagne	2½	Hedé	1
Mesle sur Sarthe	1½	S. Dominieu	1
Menilbrou	1	S. Pierre de Pleguen	1
ALENÇON	1½	Chateauneuf	1½
S. Denis	1½	S. MALO	1½
Prez-en-paille	1½		

There is also another route from *Paris* to *Rennes* by following the route from *Paris* to *Angers*, page 261, as far as *Mans*, from whence you proceed thus.

	Posts		
MANS		La Gravelle	2½
Gueffelard	2	Vitré	1½
Malicorne	2	Chateaubourg	1½
Sablé	2	Noyal	1
Meslay	2½	RENNES	1½
Laval	2½		

Remarkable places in this journey.

Versailles has been already described p. 112.

Dreux. *Dreux* is a small town of *France*, in the province of *Orleanois*, and territory of *Chartres*, in west longitude 1. 25. latitude 48. 45. It is situate on the *Blaise*, and has a ruinous castle on the declivity of a hill. The town is in general well built, surrounded with old walls and deep ditches. It has four gates and four suburbs, with several churches and convents, a commandery of *Malta*, and an hospital.—*Mortagne* is

Mortagne. a town of *France*, in the province of *Orleanois*, and territory of *Perche*, in east longitude 50. min. latitude 48. 40. It is situate near a rivulet, which which begins to form the river *Huisne*, and is pretty large and well peopled. The collegiate church is dedicated to *All Saints*, and the parish church to our Lady. Not far from hence stands the

La Trappe. famous abbey of *La Trappe*, of the *Cistercian* order, founded in 1140, by *Rotrou* count of *Perche*, and reformed in the last century by the *Abbé de Rancé* The monks are obliged to perpetual silence, to live upon vegetables, bread and cyder, with several other practices of austerity. Strangers are received here with great civility.

Alençon. *Alençon* is a city of *Lower Normandy* in *France*, under the meridan of *London*, latitude 48. 32. It is situate on the river *Sarte*, near the borders of *Perche*, in a large fruitful plain. The walls are flanked with antique towers: The castle is also very antient. Most of the streets are wide, and the houses well built. There is only one parish church, dedicated to our Lady, in which you may see the tombs of the dukes of *Alençon*. The great gate of this church is an excellent piece of workmanship. There are several monasteries

nasteries of both sexes in the town, and a handsome college of Jesuits.

Mayenne is a small city of *France*, in the province of *Orleanois*, and territory of *Maine*, in west longitude 45. min. latitude 48. 20. It is situate on an eminence, at the bottom of which runs a river of the same name. There is only one large street in the town, and two parishes. Most of the other streets are small and narrow, and the houses but poorly built. They have a bridge about twelve feet long, which joins the town to the suburb of *S. Martin*.   *Mayenne.*

Those who have a mind to see Mount *S. Michael*, in their way from *Paris* to *Brest*, must take the following route when they come to *Alençon*.   *Mont S. Michael.*

La Ferté Macé	8 leagues	*Ducey*	6
Domfront	4	*Mont S. Michael*	4
Mortain	5		

Domfront is a small town with the title of County, situate on the river *Mayenne*. Within two leagues of this town is the beautiful abbey of *Loulay*.--*Mortain* is a small town, which used to give title to the youngest sons of the dukes of *Normandy*. It is of very difficult access, being surrounded on all sides with steep rocks.--Mount *S. Michael* is a fortress of *France* in the province of *Normandy*. in west longitude 1. 32. latitude 48. 38. It is situated on a rock 300 feet high, in a bay of the sea, formed by the coasts of *Normandy* and *Britany*. It stands about nine miles to the westward of *Avranches*, in the middle of a large strand of fine sand, which is covered twice in four and twenty hours at high water, and consequently there is no coming at it by land but at low water. The town of *S. Michael* is very well

The GRAND TOUR.

well built, strongly fortified, and contains about a hundred houses. To add to the strength of the place there is a strong castle, where the burghers mount guard in time of peace, but the king sends them regular troops in time of war. Here is also a famous abbey of Benedictins, on the very top of the rock, in the form of a cross, founded in 966, by *Richard* I. duke of *Normandy*. The monastery is a very handsome structure, where you are to take particular notice of the great altar, the church, the chapel of the Trinity, the treasure, and the machine for drawing up, from the bottom of the rock, all sorts of provisions that come by sea. The prior of the abbey is governor of the place in time of peace, and keeps the keys of the town and castle.

But continuing your journey directly to *Brest*, from *Mayenne* you come to *Laval*, a town of the province of *Maine*, and general government of *Orleanois* in *France*, situate on the river *Maine*. It is surrounded by a wall, and other antique fortifications of very little strength. There are two parochial churches in the town, two collegiate ones, with several religious houses. This town was taken by scalade in 1446, by the famous *Talbot*, earl of *Shrewsbury*. The inhabitants have a very considerable linen manufacture.

I. RENNES.

Rennes is a city of *Britany* in *France*, in west longitude 1. 45. latitude 48. 5. This is a very antient city, the capital of the dutchy and province of *Britany*, the see of a bishop, and the seat of the parliament of the province. It is situated on the river *Vilaine*, by which it is divided into two parts, upper and lower, that com-

communicate by bridges. Not long ago it was almost burnt down, since which time it has been built to an advantage, the streets being made much wider, and the houses better, so that it passes now for one of the prettiest cities in *France*. The cathedral, dedicated to S. *Peter*, is a large building, with two very high spires. The other churches most worthy of notice are, the church and abbey of S. *George*, the church and abbey of S. *Meleve*, remarkable for its garden called *Thabor*; the church of the Visitation; the church and convent of the *Dominicans*; and the sumptuous church and college of *Jesuits*. The palace where the parliament meets, has four large pavilions, which include a great court surrounded with galleries and shops; the halls are spacious, and the chambers adorned with rich tapestry. The great stair-case of this building is reckoned a master-piece of architecture. The square before the palace is surrounded with handsome houses, and a convent of *Cordeliers*. Besides the great square, there is another called the *Pompe*, where the houses are supported by portico's, in the middle of which you see a handsome fountain. They have a tower in the town, which is said to have been formerly a heathen temple. This tower is near the *Champ Jaquet*, which is the great market-place, where stands the court of the presidial. The river *Vilaine* carries large boats, that come up with the tide as far as port S. *Ives*, where it waters a beautiful plain, and from whence it enters *Rennes*, under three large bridges, the handsomest of which is the middle one, called *Pont Neuf*.

II. S. MALO.

S. *Malo* is a city and port-town of *France*, in the province of *Britany*, in west long. 2. latitude

48. 40. This town is not above five hundred years old, and is now the fee of a bishop, suffragan of *Tours*, and one of the principal keys of the province. It is situated on a rock called *S. Aaron*, surrounded by the ocean, but joined to the continent by a long causeway, the entrance of which is defended by a strong castle. The town is extremely well fortified, especially that part contiguous to the causeway. The garrison turn twelve large dogs out of the gates every night, to prevent a surprize The cathedral, dedicated to *S. Vincent*, stands in a square of this name, where are likewise the episcopal palace, and the town-house. The high street that crosses the square of *Cohue*, has some handsome houses inhabited by wealthy merchants. Most of the other streets are narrow, and the houses ugly, belonging chiefly to people who live in time of war by privateering, or to common mariners. The harbour is one of the best on the coast, but of difficult access, and will not admit of large vessels. The arsenal and the powder magazines, are worth seeing, near which is the platform of *S. Saviour*, planted with cannon, from whence you may go to the platform of *S. Francis*, at the mouth of the harbour, where you have a pleasant prospect of the vessels coming in and going out.

CHAP. XIV.

Journey from Paris *to* Rouen, Caen, *and* Cherbourg.

FROM *Paris* to *Rouen* there are two different routes, one by *Pontoise*, and the other by *Mante*. There is also a stage coach from *Paris* to *Rouen*, and from *Rouen* to *Paris*; each

FRANCE.

each passenger pays for his place twelve livres. If you chuse a cheaper way, you may go with the coach to the little town of *Poissy*, for ten sous; then from *Poissy* you go by water to the village of *Roboise*, which is 27 miles distant, for ten sous: from *Reboise* to the village of *Bonnieres*, you have three miles to walk, or you may ride it for six sous: from *Bonnieres* to the village of *Roule*, you have fifteen miles, which cost you ten sous: from *Roule* to port *S. Ouen*, which is fifteen miles, you have horses, such as they are, for 30 sous; and from port *S. Ouen* to *Rouen*, you go by water for three sous. But this is wretched and disagreeable travelling.

Route from Paris *to* Rouen *by* Pontoise, *and from* Rouen *to* Caen *and* Cherbourg.

	Posts		
PARIS		*Bourgachart*	1½
S. DENIS	Post royal	*Rougemontier*	1
Franconville	1	*Ponteau de Mer*	1½
Pontoise	1½	*Pont l' Eveque*	3
Bordeau de Vigny	2	*Dive*	2
Magny	1½	CAEN	3
S. Clair	1	*Breteville*	1½
Tilliers	1	BAYEUX	1½
Ecouis	2	*Formigny*	2
Bourgbaudoin	1½	*Issigny*	1½
La Forge Feret	1	*Carentan*	1
ROUEN	1	*S. Mere Eglise*	1½
Moulineaux	1 royal and ½ simple	*Valognes*	1½
		CHERBOURG	2

Route from Paris to Rouen by Mante.

	Posts		
PARIS		Bonnieres	1¼
S. GERMAINS	2	Vernon	1½
	the 1st royal	Gaillon	1½
Trielle	1½	Vaudreuil	2
Meulan	1	Port S. Ouin	1¼
Mante	1½	ROUEN	1

But the shortest way from *Paris* to *Caen* is by *Evreux* and *Lisieux*, thus:

	Posts		
PARIS		La Commanderie	2
VERSAILLES	2	La Riviere	2
	the 1st royal	Marché neuf	1
Neauphle	2	Duranville	1
La Queue	1	L'Hotellerie	1
Houdan	1½	LISIEUX	1½
Dreux	2	S. Aubin	1
Nonancourt	1½	Moux	2
Damville	1½	CAEN	2
EVREUX	2		

You may also go to *Evreux* by *Mante* thus:

	Posts		
PARIS		Mante	1½
S. GERMAIN	2	Bonnieres	1¼
	the 1st royal	Passy	2
Trielle	1½	EVREUX	2
Meulan	1		

Remarkable places in the first route.

S. Denis has been already described in this volume, page 29. From *S. Denis* you proceed to *Pontoise:* when you come to *Franconville* you descend

descend a high hill, and fall afterwards into a causey that goes to *Pontoise*. Near *Franconville* stands the famous nunnery of *Maubuisson*.

Pontoise is a town of the isle of *France*, in east longitude 2. 6, latitude 49. 5. It is situated on the river *Oyse*, upon the descent of a hill, which extends to the banks of the river. The town is commanded by a castle, in the outer court of which there is a collegiate church. Over the *Oyse*, there is a bridge of fourteen arches, from whence it take its name of *Pons ad Æsiam*. It consists only of two parishes, but has several religious houses, as the Cordeliers, the Carmelites, the Ursulines, and the abbey of *S. Martin*; which last, as also the palace called the *Vicariat*, are worth seeing. The principal trade of the town is in corn, which is brought hither from *Picardy* by the river. — From *Pontoise* you proceed to *Magny*, a small town of the isle of *France* in the *Vexin Françoise*. The houses are generally well built, and the streets regular. There is only one parish church, which is dedicated to our Lady; but they have some convents of men and women and a good hospital. The adjacent country produces a great deal of corn, in which the trade of the inhabitants chiefly consists.

I. ROUEN.

Rouen is the capital of the province of *Normandy* in *France*, in east longitude 1. 6. latitude 49. 30. This is one of the largest, richest, and most populous cities of *France*, pleasantly situated on the north bank of the *Seine*, encompassed on three sides with hills, and open only towards the river. From these hills three little rivers fall, the *Aubette*, the *Renelle*, and the *Robec*, which serve to cleanse the streets, and for the several uses

uses of the tradesmen and manufacturers. The town is surrounded by a wall, with some antique towers. The gate called *du Bac*, near the bridge, is a fine piece of architecture. Though it is populous, containing sixty thousand souls, yet it is not very large, the streets being narrow. 'Tis the see of an archbishop, and the seat of the parliament of the province. They reckon thirty-six parishes in the town, several hospitals, thirty-five fountains, a great many public squares, fifty-six religious houses, with a fine college of Jesuits. The cathedral dedicated to our Lady is one of the handsomest *Gothic* structures in *France*, remarkable for the tombs of several kings, princes, prelates, and noblemen, particularly those of *Henricus* junior, and his brother king *Richard* I. The fine monument of *Charles* V. of *France*, which stood formerly in the middle of the choir, was lately removed from thence, when the choir was repaired, to the south side of S. *Mary*'s chapel, behind the altar. The great bell of this church called *George d'Amboise*, from a cardinal and archbishop of that name, and by whose orders it was made, is reckoned one of the largest in the kingdom, and said to weigh 36,000 weight. Belonging to the church there is a good library, which is open for the use of the public. The archbishop of this city has the privilege of setting at liberty every year a criminal condemned to die, who carries in procession, with great solemnity the shrine of S. *Romanus*. The church of S. *Ouen*, belonging to the royal Benedictin abbey, is one of the most complete and most elegant *Gothic* buildings in *Europe*, remarkable for the delicacy of its pillars, its fine painted glass windows, its choir, the workmanship of the open iron-work called *Grilles de fer*, and for the great tower in the centre. In the grand portal

portal of the church of *Notre Dame de la Ronde*, there is a statue of the Virgin much esteemed, as likewise the copper angel in the middle of the choir. In the church of *S. Goddard* the glass windows are greatly admired: here you see the tomb of *S. Romain* of one single stone of jasper. The Jesuits' college is one of the best houses they have in *France*. The convent of the Carthusians, about three miles out of town, and that of the barefooted Carmelites, are worthy of particular notice. The palace where the parliament hold their assemblies has several chambers adorned with beautiful tapestry, and fine paintings, a great many of which are done by the famous *Jouvenet*. The great hall of this palace resembles *Westminster-hall* in having no pillars or columns to suppport it. Travellers should not forget going to see the square *aux Veaux*, where the celebrated maid of *Orleans* was burnt by the *English* for a witch, and where the *French* have erected a statue to her memory. Along the river there is a beautiful quay, with a fine walk. At the beginning of this quay stands the old palace or castle, said to have been built by our king *Henry* V. It is flanked with eight large round towers, and strong walls, defended with deep ditches full of water. Here you see the custom-house, and the exchange, where the merchants meet. But the greatest curiosity on the quay is the beautiful bridge of boats, which rises and falls with the tide, is paved with stones, and opens for the passage of large vessels; it was contrived in 1626 by *Nicholas Bougeois*, an Augustinian friar of *Paris*. At the other end of the bridge is the suburb of *S. Severe*, where they have a considerable business in bleaching linen, and in making earthen ware. Just below this wooden bridge are the ruins of a very fine

fine stone bridge, built by the empress *Maud*, daughter of *Henry* I. king of *England*. The mall is also in this suburb, and the course. The trade of this city is very considerable, vessels of three hundred tons being able to come up from the sea to the quay, and unload their merchandise. They have a very pretty play-house in *Rouen*, where you are well entertained. At the house of Mr. *Fortevilk*, *procureur general* at *Rouen*, you see the fine basso relievos, representing the magnificent interview of *Henry* VIII. and *Francis* I: they are of marble in five compartments. The city has several good butchers markets, and great plenty of meat. Here are several fruit and herb markets, and fountains in different parts of it. The common drink of this town, and of all *Normandy*, is cyder, for they have little or no wine of their own growth. The corporation of *Rouen* consists of a mayor and six aldermen, the mayor being elected every three years. The neighbourhood of this city is extremely pleasant.

Pont-audemer. — *Pont-audemer* is a small town in *Normandy*, where you see a pretty market-place. It is surrounded with walls, and has four gates.

II. C A E N.

Caen. — *Caen* is the capital of the *Lower Normandy*, in west longitude 25 min. latitude 49. 20. This is a large populous city, the second of the duchy of *Normandy*, situate at the confluence of the rivers *Orne* and *Odon*, in a fine, fruitful plain, about six miles south of the *British* channel. The city contains sixty streets and twelve parishes: the inhabitants are computed at near forty thousand souls. It is the seat of at intendant, and of an university founded by *Charles* VII. in 1452. The *Normans* first made this town considerable,

William

William the Conqueror having laid the foundation of their castle. This same prince and his queen built two abbeys here; the Conqueror that of *S. Stephen*, in which he was afterwards interred, and his queen that of the Trinity, in which she was buried. The stately monument of the Conqueror in the church of *S. Stephen*, was destroyed by some dissolute soldiers, who also threw the Conqueror's bones away with great derision; and now there is only an epitaph upon the ground on a flat black marble. The monastery is a fine stone building, consisting of two large squares, one of which has been lately rebuilt. In a room near the refectory, they shew you several modern pictures; and over the chimney a portrait, as they pretend, of *William* the Conqueror, but more likely of *Henry* VIII. The church of the *Trinity*, founded by *Matilda*, the Conqueror's wife, for Benedictin nuns, is remarkable for its magnificence and beauty. The church of *S. Peter* is the best in *Caen*. The next is that of *S. John*, whose steeple is much admired for its architecture; on the high altar piece is the baptism of Christ, one of *le Brun*'s best pieces. The church of *S. Nicholas* is likewise a large and handsome building. There are nine convents of men, and seven of women, the principal of which are those of the Cordeliers, the Ursulines, and the nuns of the Visitation. The town house, built on the bridge of *S. Peter*, is a very large edifice, with four great towers. The royal square is one of the finest in *Normandy*, being large, well paved, and adorned with handsome houses on three sides. In the middle of this square stands the statue of *Lewis* XIV. in the *Roman* dress, on a marble pedestal, and surrounded with an iron balustrade. The Jesuits have a magnificent church near the ramparts, from whence you discover the

two

two *Courſes*, planted with trees, in a beautiful meadow along the river *Orne*. The other public buildings moſt worthy of notice, are the caſtle, the wall with four towers built by the *Engliſh*, the epiſcopal palace belonging to the biſhop of *Bayeux*, the hotel called the *grand Cheval*, the office of the exchequer, and the new buildings of the univerſity. This univerſity is in a very flouriſhing condition, conſiſting of three colleges, *du Bois*, *du Clontiers*, and *des Arts*, to which they have aſſociated the Jeſuits' college. There is alſo an academy, of very great reputation, where young gentlemen are boarded, and taught *French*, mathematics, muſic, fencing, riding the great horſe, &*c*. *Caen* has a provoſtſhip, a preſidial, a vicounty, an office of the finances of the admiralty, and other royal tribunals.

III. BAYEUX.

Bayeux.   *Bayeux* is a city of *Normandy* in *France*, in weſt longitude 50 min. latitude 49. 20. It is ſituate on the river *Aure*, about five miles from the ſea. 'Tis the ſee of a biſhop, and contains fifteen pariſhes, but very little people. The cathedral dedicated to our Lady, is one of the largeſt and fineſt in the province, being particularly remarkable for its three high ſteeples. The outſides of the weſt, north, and ſouth doors, are adorned with exſtreme fine baſſo relievos in ſtone, which by ſome travellers are ſuppoſed to relate to *William* the Conqueror. In this church is preſerved the famous hiſtorical tapeſtry, which with great exactneſs, repreſents every particular circumſtance of the expedition of *William* the Conqueror into *England* in 1066. It is one foot eleven inches in depth, and two hundred and twelve feet in length; it goes exactly round the nave of the

the church, where it is annually put up on *S. John's* day, and continues there during the octave. The ground of it is white; the men, horses, and all the other figures are in their proper colours. This tapestry is carefully locked up in a large wainscot press, in a chapel on the south side of the cathedral. Besides the parish churches, there are several religious houses of both sexes, and a magnificent college of Jesuits. The missionaries of *S. Lazarus*, have a very handsome seminary, which has been lately built. The bishopric of *Bayeux* is one of the richest in *France*.

Issigny is a borough of *Normandy*, at the mouth *Issigny.* of the little river *Vire*. This borough has a small harbour much frequented because of its salt houses, and salt-butter, and also its cyder, in which it drives a considerable trade.—*Carentan* is a small *Carentan.* town of *Normandy* in *France*, in west longitude 1. 15. latitude 49. 20. It is situate on two little rivers called the *Ouve* and *Carentey*, within nine miles of the sea. Toward the great suburb there is a strong castle, with a handsome square, surrounded with very good houses, and supported by piazzas.—*Valogne* is a town of *Lower Normandy*, *Valogne.* situate in the diocese of *Coutances*, on a little rivulet, about nine miles from the sea, and twelve from the *Hogue*. There are no walls to the town, and the castle is quite demolished. They have two parishes, a collegiate church, and a convent of Cordeliers.

IV. CHERBOURG.

Cherbourg is a port town of *France*, in the pro- *Cherbourg.* vince of *Normandy*, in west longitude 1. 40. latitude 49. 45. This is a very antient town, situate at the extremity of the diocese of *Coutances*, on a bay of the *English* channel. The harbour, which

which is opposite to *Hampshire* in *England*, admits of vessels of three or four hundred tuns. 'Tis the seat of an admiralty, but its fortifications were demolished by order of *Lewis* XIV. in 1689. The parochial church is a handsome building, remarkable, among other things, for the tomb of *Mauger*, archbishop of *Roan*, who was banished to *Guernsey* because of his irregular life. They have a very considerable manufacture of cloths, serges, and stuffs. At *S. Gobino*, a place in the neighbourhood, there is a great manufacture of glass, which is afterwards polished at *Paris* in the suburb of *S. Antony*.

Remarkable places in the second route.

S.Germains. *S.* Germains has been already described in this
Mante. volume, p. 135. *Mante* is a small town of *France*, in the province of the isle of *France*, in east longitude 1. 45. latitude 49. It is situate on the ri-*Seine*, which forms abundance of little islands hereabouts. The town is indifferently built, but remarkable for a fine stone bridge over the *Seine*, of thirty-nine arches, and a handsome monastery of Celestins. There is a little hill within the jurisdiction of this city, that produces the best wine
Vernon. in *France.*— *Vernon* is a small town, situate on the *Seine*, in a very agreeable valley, in the diocese of *Evreux*. It has an hospital for the poor, a collegiate church, several convents, and a bailiwie. The castle, which is very antient, has a tower of
Gaillon. free stone of a very extraordinary height.—*Gaillon* is a small country town, near which the archbishop of *Rouen* has a fine palace. It is situated on a very high hill, and commands a most delightful prospect for many miles. This palace was built by cardinal *Amboise*, archbishop of *Rouen*, and is reckoned one of the most magnificent seats

in

in *France*. Not far from thence is a famous Carthusian monastery, over the door of which is written *Chartreuse Bourbon-lez-Gallion:* it is a magnificent stone building; the library, the church, the treasury, and the large monument, of the family of *Soissons-Bourbon*, deserve particular notice.

Remarkable places in the direct route from Paris *to* Caen.

I. Evreux.

Evreux is a city of *France*, in the province of *Normandy*, in east longitude 1. 12. latitude 49. 5. This is a very antient town, the see of a bishop, and the capital of the county of *Evreux*, situate in a fruitful plain on the river *Iton*. It contains eight parishes, and two famous abbeys, one of men, and the other of women, with several other religious houses. The cathedral is a fine *Gothic* building, in the middle of which there is an octagon dome, called the lantern, erected by *Lewis* XI. On the top of this lantern there is a very high steeple, delicately formed, with a pyramidical termination. The high altar of the church belonging to the nuns of Our Saviour, is magnificently decorated, and worthy the attention of the curious. The convent of the Capuchins is one of the handsomest of their whole order. Near the town-house, and just by the fish market, you see a clock, which is reckoned a master-piece; it' was made by the *English* when they were in possession of this country. This city is the seat of a bailiwic, a presidial, election, and other jurisdictions. The palace of *Navarre* belonging to the duke of *Bouillon*, and that of *Condé*, belonging to the bishop of *Evreux*, are well worth seeing.

The GRAND TOUR.

II. Lisieux.

Lisieux is a city of *Normandy*, in east longitude 16. min. latitude 49. 14. situate at the confluence of two small rivers, the *Orbiquet* and *Lezon*, partly on a hill, and partly in a valley. It is the see of a bishop suffragan of *Rouen*, and is surrounded by a wall, and some antique towers. There are four gates to the town, and four suburbs. The cathedral is a fine old building. The episcopal palace is a beautiful structure; the staircase, the chapel, and the gardens merit particular notice. The nunnery called *L'Abbaye aux Dames*, founded by *Henry* II. duke of *Normandy*, and king of *England*, has been lately rebuilt and a magnificent new church erected, on which there is a handsome dome. Among the several religious houses, the convent of the Trinitarians is the most considerable. Their church is a handsome structure; the high altar is decorated with five large statues, which are admired by the curious. The ornaments of the sacristy are also worth seeing. The college and seminary are a fine modern building. The Dominicans have a very handsome church, adorned with some good pictures.

Bye places in the first route.

Thirty-six miles south of *Cherburg*, stands *Coutances*, a port-town of *Normandy*, and capital of *Coutantin*, in west longitude 1. 32. latitude 49. 10. This town, antiently called *Constantia*, or *Cosedia*, is pleasantly situate among meadows and rivulets about six miles distant from the sea. By the remains of a *Roman* aqueduct, and other antient ruins, it appears to be a place of

great

great antiquity. 'Tis the see of a bishop suffragan of *Rome*, and has a magnificent cathedral, esteemed one of the finest pieces of *Gothic* architecture in *Europe*. The trade of this town is very inconsiderable, and the fortifications are quite demolished. They have several religious houses, and two parochial churches.

About twenty-four miles south of *Coutances*, *Avranches.* stands *Avranches*, a city of *Lower Normandy*, situate near the sea coast, on the top of a mountain, at the foot of which runs the river *See*. 'Tis a bishop's see, suffragan of *Rouen*, and has a fine old cathedral dedicated to *St. Andrew*. There are three parochial churches in the town, an abbey, and several convents of both sexes. The learned *Huetius* was bishop of this city.

Twelve miles to the eastward of *Cherburg*, *Barfleur.* stands the town of *Barfleur*, in west longitude 1. 15. latitude 49. 47. This was formerly one of the most considerable ports of *Normandy*, but the harbour is now filled up with sands, and there remains only a small bason. Here part of the *French* fleet commanded by Admiral *Tourville*, was burnt by the *English*, the day after the victory obtained by Admiral *Russel*, near *Cape la Hogue*, in 1692. *La Hogue* is a village in the neighbourhood, from whence the most north-west cape or promontory of *Normandy* takes its name.

CHAP. XV.

Journey from Paris *to* Havre de Grace, *and* Dieppe.

THOSE who intend to go from *Paris* to *Havre* or *Dieppe*, must pass through *Rouen*, the route to which city we have given in the preceding chapter. From *Rouen* to *Havre* the route is as follows.

ROUEN	Posts	Forges	2
Vieufs	2	*La Botte*	1½
	the 1st royal	HAVRE DE GRACE	2
Caudebec	1½		

From *Rouen* to *Dieppe*, and thence to *Abbeville*, and *Lille*, the post route is as follows.

Rouen	Posts	*Freffenville*	1½
Cambres	1½	ABBEVILLE	2
	the 1st royal	*Auxy le Chateau*	2½
Toftes	1½	*S. Pol*	2¼
Ofmonville	1⅓	*Bethune*	3
DIEPPE	1¼	*Waquet*	2
La ville d'Eu	3	*Lille*	2

From *Abbeville* to *Calais* you will find the route in this volume, p. 23. A stage coach goes from *Rouen* to *Dieppe* in one day, and stops to dine at an inn called *Toftes*, about half way. Passengers pay six livres a piece for their places.

Remarkable places in the route from Rouen *to* Havre de Grace.

Caudebec.   *Caudebec*, is a city of *Normandy*, in east longitude 45 min. latitude 49. 32. It is situate on the north side of the river *Seine*, at the foot of a mountain covered with woods. The town is small but populous, having a considerable trade by means of the *Seine*, and a very good manufacture of hats. The parish church is a handsome building; the stone gallery that supports the organ, is a bold piece of architecture.

There

FRANCE.

There is a convent of Capuchins, and another of women. This place is also the seat of a bailiwic, a presidial and election.

Havre de Grace is a port town of *Normandy*, in east longitude 10 min. latitude 49. 30. This is a small fortified town, situate in a large plain at the mouth of the river *Seine*. It is almost of a square figure, divided into two parts by the port, surrounded by a wall and other works, and defended by a very strong citadel. The situation of this place at the mouth of the *Seine*, as also the conveniency of its harbour, and its foreign trade, render it one of the most important places in the kingdom.

Havre de Grace.

The coach route from *Rouen* to *Havre* is a little different from that of the post. From *Havre* you go to *La Fontaine*, 9 miles: from thence to *Cler*, 3 miles: from thence to *Caudebec*, 9 miles: from thence to *L'isle bonne*, 18 miles: from thence to *Harfleur*, 9 miles: from thence to *Havre*, 9 miles. In this route the only remarkable place not already described is *Harfleur*.

Harfleur is a port town of *France*, in the province of *Normandy*, in east longitude 15 min. latitude 49. 30. It is situate on the little river *Lezarde*, near the mouth of the river *Seine*. Its antiquity appears from the causeway from hence to *L'isle bonne*, which is said to have been made by *Cæsar*. Since *Havre* has been so much frequented, this place has been upon the decline, its fortifications being destroyed, and the harbour choaked up, so as to admit only of small boats. There is only one parish in the town; the church is not finished, otherwise it would be a handsome building. The glass windows are full of painted figures. This town was taken by the *English* a little before the battle of *Agincourt*.

Harfleur.

The GRAND TOUR.

Remarkable places in the route from Rouen *to* Dieppe.

DIEPPE.

Dieppe is a port town of *Upper Normandy*, in *France*, in east longitude 1. 15. latitude 49. 55. It is situate on the north east coast of *Normandy*, at the mouth of the little river *Arcquey*. In the year 1694, it was almost destroyed by a bombardment from the *English* fleet, since which time it has risen with greater beauty out of its ashes. It is of a triangular figure, and strongly fortified; though the works are very irregular, occasioned by the unevenness of the ground. The streets are wide and even, and the houses well built of bricks. The town is separated from the sea by a long wall, and a very deep ditch. The harbour is one of the most considerable on the coast, but will not admit of ships of great burden. The castle is a very antient building, where the governor resides, and from whence there is a charming prospect. The town is adorned with a great number of handsome fountains. The churches of *S. James* and *S. Remigius*, are large handsome buildings. There are several religious houses of both sexes, and two colleges, one of Jesuits, the other of the Fathers of the Oratory. The inhabitants are chiefly mariners, and computed at about thirty thousand souls. They have a very good trade, particularly in lace, and different kinds of ivory-work, and toys. Within half a league of *Dieppe*, you see the remains of an ancient camp, which the tradition of the country affirms to have been made in *Cæsar's* time.

CHAP.

CHAP. XVI.

Journey from Paris *to* Rheims *and* Sedan, *in the way to* Luxemburg.

A Stage coach sets out from *Paris* to *Rheims* on *Saturdays* and *Mondays*, at seven or eight in the morning; the fare to each passenger fifteen livres. The following is the post route.

PARIS	Posts	*Braine*	2
Bourget	Post royal	*Fisme*	1½
Menil	2	*Joncherry*	1
Dammartin	1	REIMS	2
Nanteuil	1½	*Isle*	2
Gondreville	1¼	*Rethel*	2
Villers Cotterets	1½	*Chênele Pouilleux*	3
Vertefeuille	1¼	SEDAN	2⅖
SOISSONS	1⅓		

Remarkable places in this journey.

Dammartin is a large borough of the isle of *Dammartin*. *France*, belonging to the house of *Bourbonne Condé*. It is so called from one of its former lords of the name of *Martin*. There is a parish church dedicated to S. *John Baptist*, and a collegiate church to our Lady.

Nanteuil, called the *Hautdoin*, has borrowed *Nanteuil*. its name from the person that built the castle, which forms the principal beauty of the place. There is a handsome monastery here of *Benedictins*, of the congregation of S. *Maur*. *Villers-* *Villers-* *Cotterets* is a small town of the dutchy of *Valois*, *Cotterets*. in the isle of *France*, situate in the forest of *Rets*, from whence it takes its name. The only remarkable thing is the castle. The parish church is served by the monks of *S. Norbert*, who have an abbey here. There is also a monastery without the town; and six miles from thence, as you go out of the forest, you see the abbey of *Valsiry*, also of the order of *S. Norbert*.

I. SOISSONS.

Soissons.

Soissons is a city of the isle of *France*, in east longitude 3. 21. latitude 49. 28. This is a large populous city, supposed to be the *Noviodunum* of *Cæsar*, situate in a pleasant fruitful valley on the river *Aisne*. During the first race of the *French* Kings, it was the capital of the kingdom, and now is a bishop's see suffragan of *Rheims*. The town is surrounded with a wall and other fortifications, and defended by an antique castle, flanked with great round towers. It is in general well built, and is the seat of a bailiwic, a presidial, and an election. The cathedral dedicated to *S. Gervase* and *Protase*, is remarkable for one of the most considerable chapters of the kingdom. The bishop in the absence of the archbishop of *Rheims*, has the privilege of crowning the *French* kings. There are twelve parishes in this city, and six abbeys, with several other religious houses, among which the abbeys of our Lady and *S. Medard* are the most deserving of a traveller's notice. In the church of the abbey of our Lady, there are two antient tombs of marble, each about five or six feet long, and three high, and both adorned with curious figures and representations; it is probable these monuments were erected under one of the sons of *Constantine*, or some succeeding prince, but to whom is very uncertain. There is also an academy of *Belles Lettres* in *Soissons*, which is in great repute. The inhabitants have a

good

good trade in corn, the adjacent country being very fruitful; the walks by the river side are extremely pleasant.

Fifmes is a small neat town of *Champagne*, in the district of *Rhemois*, situate a little above the confluence of the *Nore* and the *Vesse*. The country from hence to *Rheims* is hilly, but abounding with corn, beasts, and grass.

II. R H E I M S.

Rheims is the capital of the province of *Champagne* in *France*, in east longitude 4. latitude 49. 20. This is one of the most elegant cities in *France*, situate in the middle of a large plain, on the river *Vesse*, and encompassed with a wall about three miles in circumference. The houses are in general well built, the streets wide, and the churches and other public buildings magnificent. 'Tis a very antient city, as appears by the several *Roman* monuments that have been found here of late years; and it is even mentioned by *Cæsar*, under the name of *Civitas Rhemorum*, as one of the most potent cities in *Gaul*. 'Tis now the see of an archbishop, who has the privilege of consecrating the kings of *France*, and is the first duke and ecclesiastical peer of the realm. The cathedral, dedicated to our Lady, is a magnificent old building, remarkable for the architecture of the front, and the beautiful figures in relievo, with which it is adorned. It is said to have been built by *Clotildis*, the wife of *Clovis*, the first christian king of *France*. The ceremony of the *French* king's coronation is always performed in this cathedral, by the archbishop, assisted by the bishops of *Laon* and *Langres*, who are also dukes and peers; by the bishops of *Beauvais*, *Noyon*, and *Chalons*, who are counts and peers; and by six of the lay nobility, *viz.* the dukes of *Burgundy, Guienne* and *Normandy,* and the counts of *Thoulouse, Champagne* and *Flanders.* The church of S. *Nicaise,* is the largest building in *Rheims* next to the cathedral; its front and the two steeples are worth particular notice. The abbey of S. *Remy* is a spacious building with a fine large *Gothic* church, in which are the tombs of *Carloman,* brother of *Charlemagne, Lewis de Outremer, Lothaire,* and *Lewis* V. who were of the line of *Charlemagne.* In the treasury of this abbey, they preserve a great many relics, and among the rest, the pastoral staff of *S. Remi,* whose tomb is beautifully adorned with sculptures, pillars, and statues, and in the middle of them you see the bust of *Lewis* XIII. in his robes of state. In this tomb is also preserved the holy phial, containing the oil used at the coronation of their kings, which oil, according to the tradition of the *French* nation, was brought from heaven by a white dove, at the consecration of *Clovis* I. The library belonging to this abbey is copious, and well chosen. There are several handsome squares in the city, and a magnificent town-house, before which you see an equestrian statue of *Lewis* XIII. The religious houses are pretty numerous, among which the Cordeliers and Dominicans are worth seeing. They have an university, which was founded in 1547, by *Charles,* cardinal of *Lorrain,* archbishop of this city. The company of *Harquebuziers* of *Rheims* is very considerable; they perform their exercise in a garden assigned for that use, where they have erected a pedestrian statue of *Lewis* XIV. The antiquities of this city particularly merit a traveller's attention, among which the triumphal arch, dug up in 1677, is the most remarkable. This arch was formerly the northern gate, supposed to be erected to the honour

FRANCE. 29

honour of *Julius Cæsar*; or according to others, of *Julian the Apostate*, when after the conquest of the *Germans*, he passed by *Rheims* in his way to *Paris*. It is composed of three arches of the Corinthian order, that in the middle being thirty-five feet high, and twelve broad, the basso relievo's of which represent a woman with a cornucopia, to shew the fertility of the country; the four children near her, represent the four seasons, and the other twelve, the twelve months. The other two arches are each thirty feet high, and eight broad. The bas-reliefs of that on the right, represent *Remus* and *Romulus* sucking a wolf, with the shepherd *Fastulus* and *Laurentia* his wife, standing by them. On the third arch, *Leda* is seen in *Jupiter*'s embraces, metamorphosed into a swan, and *Cupid* holding a lighted torch in his hand. Near this arch are the remains of an antient *Roman* castle: about two hundred paces from the town, you may see the ruins of another triumphal arch, and within the town, not far from the university, are the remains of an amphitheatre. The inhabitants of *Rheims* have a considerable trade in wine, as also in different kinds of woolen and silk stuffs. The gingerbread of *Rheims* is likewise very much esteemed.

Rethel is a town of *France*, in the province of *Champagne*, in east longitude 4. 24. latitude 49. 31. It is the capital of a dutchy, situate on the river *Aisne*. The town is but poorly built, having only one parish and a convent of Capuchins. The castle is very antient, and almost falling to ruin. *Rethel* was originally only a fort, built by the *Romans* to secure the passage of the *Aisne*; they built likewise a large tower in this place which is still remaining. Near this town a memorable

Rethel

O 6 battle

battle was fought between the *French* and *Spaniards* in 1650, in which the former gained the victory.

Sedan is a town of *Champagne* in *France*, in east longitude 4. 45. latitude 49. 46. This is the capital of a principality of the same name, situate on the *Maese*, six miles from *Bouillon*, and fifteen from *Charleville*. Its situation on the frontiers of the territory of *Liege*, *Namur*, and *Limburg*, renders it a place of great importance, and one of the keys of the kingdom. It is extremely well fortified, and defended by a strong citadel. The great church is near the cornmarket; and that of the Jesuits, which is a handsome building, stands towards a great square. The castle is situate on a rock, surrounded with large towers and strong walls: here you see a most beautiful magazine of antient arms. The governor's palace is opposite the castle. From the ramparts you have a most agreeable prospect of the *Maese*, and the neighbouring country. Tho' the town is but small, yet it is full of tradesmen, as tanners, weavers, dyers, and others, the manufacture of fine cloth in this city employing a great number of hands. The principality of *Sedan* formerly belonged to the duke of *Bouillon*, who was obliged in the beginning of the last century to resign to the crown in exchange.

CHAP. XVII.

Journey from Paris *to* Lille *and* Valenciennes.

A Stage coach sets out from *Paris* to *Lille*, on *Tuesdays* and *Fridays*, from the street of *S. Denis* at the great square. Passengers pay twenty-five

FRANCE.

five livres for their place, and three livres *per* pound for baggage. From *Paris* to *Valenciennes*, you go with the *Brussels* coach, which sets out on *Wednesdays* and *Saturdays*. We shall give here the post routes, and the routes used by the stage coach.

Post route from Paris to Lille.

	Posts.		
PARIS		*Roye*	1¼
Bourget	Post Royal.	*Fonches*	1
Louvres	1¼	*Marché le Pot*	1
La Chapelle	1½	*Peronne*	1½
SENLIS	1	*Sailly*	1½
Pont S. Maixence	1½	*Herville*	2
Bois de Liheu	1½	ARRAS	1½
Gournay	1	*Lens*	2
Cuvilly	1	*Carvin*	1
Conchy les Pots	1	LILLE	2

The post route from Paris to Valenciennes.

You follow the preceding route as far as *Peronne*, where you take the road to *Cambray*.

	Posts.		
PERONNE		CAMBRAY	1
Fins	1½	*Bouchain*	1¼
Bons-Airs	1½	VALENCIENNES	2

The coach route from Paris to Lille.

	Leagues.		
PARIS		S. *Peronne*	5
D. *Louvres*	6	D. *Bapaume*	5
S. SENLIS	4	S. ARRAS	5
D. *Gournay*	8	D. *Pont à Vendin*	5
S. *Roye*	6	S. LILLE	5
D. *Mieucourt*	5		

The coach route from Paris *to* Valenciennes.

Paris	Leagues.	D. *Ham*	4
D. *Louvres*	6	S. S. *Quentin*	5
S. Senlis	4	D. *Catelet*	4
Verberie	3	S. Cambray	4
D. Compiegne	4	D. *Appe*	4
S. Noyon	5	S. Valenciennes	4

Remarkable places in the post route from Paris *to* Lille.

Louvres.   *Louvres* is a borough of the isle of *France*, commonly called *Louvre en Parisis*. The castle, and the adjacent country are very agreeale.

I. Senlis.

Senlis.   *Senlis* is a town of the isle of *France*, in east longitude 2. 30. latitude 49. 10. It is situate in a pleasant country, on the river *Nonette*, six miles from *Chantilly*, and twenty-seven from *Beauvais*. 'Tis of an oval figure, has some old fortifications, seven parochial and two collegiate churches. The inclosure of the old town is a *Roman* work, of a wonderful solidity. Formerly it was called *Sylvanectum*, and is now a bishop's see, suffragan of *Rheims*. The cathedral, dedicated to our Lady, was founded by *S. Regulus*, the first bishop. The steeple of this church is one of the highest in *France*; the church is remarkable for the figures on the right side of the front. They pretend that the collegiate church of *S. Regulus* was built on the ruins of an antient temple consecrated to *Berecynthia*. There is an abbey of the order of *S. Austin* in the town, and several other religious houses.

FRANCE. 303

houses. They have likewise a bailiwic, a presidial, and an election.

Pont-Sainte Maixence, is a small town of the isle of *France*, situate on the river *Oyse*, over which there is a bridge. Though the town is small, yet it has a considerable trade, particularly in wood and corn.—*Roye* is a small town of *Picardy*, situate near the source of the *Moreuil*, twelve miles from *Noyon*. It has a collegiate church dedicated to *S. Florent*.

Peronne is a town of *France*, in the province of *Picardy*, in east longitude 3. latitude 50. It is a small, but strong and populous town, situated in a morass on the river *Somme*. They give it the name of *Virgin*, because it was never taken. The fortifications are the work of the Chevalier *De Ville*. There is a collegiate church in the town, with three parishes, and a college belonging to the fathers of the Trinity.

Leaving *Peronne* you proceed to *Arras*, a description of which city, with the rest of the places in this route, you may see in the first volume, p. 299, and 302.

Remarkable places in the post route from Paris *to* Valenciennes.

We have already observed that this route is the same as the foregoing, as far as *Peronne*. From *Peronne* you proceed to *Cambray*, a description of which city we have given in the first volume, p. 242. that of *Valenciennes* is in the same volume, chap. xi. p. 240.

The GRAND TOUR.

Remarkable places in the coach route from Paris *to* Lille.

The places worth defcription in this route, are the fame as in the poft route from *Paris* to *Lille*, except *Bapaume*.

Bapaume, is a fortified town of the province of *Artois*, in the *French Netherlands*, in eaft longitude 3. latitude 50. 10. It is fituate on the confines of *Picardy*, in a country where there are neither rivers nor fountains, and this want of water was its principal fecurity againft an enemy. In the town they had only fome deep wells, but *Foulon* the engineer difcovered not long ago a very fine fpring within a quarter of a league of the town, and brought the water to *Bapaume*, where they have erected a handfome fountain, and adorned it with the pedeftrian ftatue of *Lewis* XV. You enter the town by two ftreets directly oppofite; the infide is regularly built, but the ftreets are ill paved. There are two public fquares, one under the caftle, and the other in the middle of the town. The firft is the moft regular of the two, the two great ftreets terminating upon it from the two gates. The town has four or five churches, and is ftrongly fortified, part of the works having been contrived by the famous *Vauban*.

The coach route from Paris *to* Valenciennes.

The remarkable places have been defcribed already in the firft volume of this work, chap. xi, which contains a journey from *Bruffels* to *Cambray* and *Paris*.

THE
EUROPEAN
ITINERARY.

THE EUROPEAN ITINERARY.

PART *the* FIRST.

Regulation of the Posts according to the present State of Italy, 1756.

THE Posts all over *Italy* are from eight to ten Miles. In the following Itinerary they are all exactly described, according to the latest Regulations. We have also specified, in the Margin, where one Prince's or State's Territory begins, and where another ends. This will have two great uses; *First,* Gentlemen will not take more money into a neighbouring State than is necessary to defray the expences of their journey to it, since there it will be useless to them. *Secondly,* They will be upon their guard, not to lodge at Night where two States border, for there most Robberies and Murders are committed, as the Offenders in half an

Hour

Hour may get out of the reach of Justice from that Territory where the Fact is committed.

All over *Italy*, the Postmaster will make Strangers pay for each Chaise after 24 Hours *Italian* Reckoning, that is, after Sun-set, at the Rate of a Post and a half, and the same for a Saddle-horse. And if a Courier or Servant is dispatched upon any express, he will be obliged to pay for two Horses.

The Price of Post-chaises and Saddle-horses each Post, over all the States of Italy.

In the Kingdom of *Naples*, for a Chaise, each post   *carleens* 11
For a Saddle-horse   *carleens* 5
In the *Ecclesiastic State*, for a Chaise, each post   *paoli* 8
Saddle-horse   *paoli* 3
In the Dukedom of *Tuscany*, for a Chaise, each post   *paoli* 8
Saddle-horse   *paoli* 3
In the States of *Lucca*, for a Chaise, each post   *paoli* 8
Saddle-horse   *paoli* 3
In the State of *Genoa*, for a Chaise, each post   *paoli* 15
Saddle-horse   *paoli* 5
In *Piedmont*, for a Chaise, each post   *paoli* 15
Saddle-horse   *paoli* 5
In the Dukedom of *Milan*, for a Chaise, each post   *paoli* 14
Saddle-horse   *paoli* 5
In the Dukedom of *Parma*, for a Chaise, each post   *paoli* 8
Saddle-horse   *paoli* 4

ITALY

In the State of *Modena*, for a Chaise, going to *Bologne* paoli 8
Saddle-horse paoli 4
The Road going from *Modena* to *Massa*, for each Chaise paoli 10
Saddle-horse paoli 5
The Road going from *Reggio* to *Mantua*, for a Chaise paoli 10
Saddle-horse paoli 5
The Road going from *Modena* to *Mantua*, for a Chaise each post paoli 15
Saddle-horse paoli 5
The Road from *Modena* to *Ferrara*, for a Chaise, each post paoli 15
Saddle-horse paoli 5
In the State of *Venice*, without a Billet, each Chaise lires 16 10
With a Billet, for a Chaise, each post lires 11
Saddle-horse lires 5 10

The Value of the Sequin *in the several Towns of* Italy.

At *Naples* the *Florentine* Sequin goes at carleens 26
The *Roman* Sequin goes at carleens 24½
At *Rome* the *Florentine* Sequin goes at paoli 21
The *Roman* Sequin goes at paoli 20½
At *Bologna* the *Florentine* Sequin goes at paoli 21
The *Roman* Sequin goes at paoli 20½
At *Ferrara* the *Florentine* Sequin goes at paoli 22
The *Roman* Sequin goes at paoli 21½

At

At *Venice* the *Venetian* Sequin goes at
   lires 22

The *Florentine* Sequin goes at   lires 21 7½
The *Roman* Sequin goes at   lires 21
At *Florence* the *Florentine* Sequin goes at
   paoli 20
The *Roman* Sequin goes at   paoli 19½
At *Lucca* the *Florentine* Sequin goes at paoli 20
The *Roman* Sequin goes at   paoli 19½
At *Genoa* the *Florentine* Sequin goes at lires 13 6
The *Roman* Sequin at   lires 13 2
At *Turin* the *Florentine* Sequin goes at
   lires 9 15
The *Roman* Sequin at   lires 9 8 4
At *Milan* the *Florentine* Sequin goes at
   lires 15
The *Roman* Sequin at   lires 14½
At *Mantua* the *Florentine* Sequin goes at
   lires 44 2
The *Roman* Sequin at   lires 43 3
At *Modena* the *Florentine* Sequin goes at
   paoli 20
The *Roman* Sequin at   paoli 19½
At *Parma* the *Florentine* Sequin goes at
   paoli 20
The *Roman* Sequin at   paoli 19½

ITALY. 311

JOURNEY *from* Rome *to* Naples.

At Rome *you must provide a passport.*

ROME		Ecclesiastical State.
Torre di Mezza Via	post royal	
Marino	post	
Fajola	one third	
Velletri	one third	
Casa Fondata	one fifth	
Sermoneta	one third	

Here you pay at the Pass.

Case Nove di Sezze	post
Piperno	one third
Maruti	post
Terracina	post
Fondi	post and half

Here you enter the Kingdom of Naples.

Itri	post	Kingdom of Naples.
Mola	post	

Here you are visited by the custom-house officers.

Garigliano   post

Here you pass the river in a large boat, paying for each chaise 13 *carleens.*

St. Agata	post
Francolisi	post
CAPUA	post

Here the governor examines the passport.

Aversa	post
NAPLES	post

JOURNEY *from* Naples *to* Messina, *passing through* Salerno, Rotonda, Cosenza, Monteleone *and* Reggio.

At Naples *you provide yourself with a passport.*

NAPLES		Kingdom of Naples.
Tor del greco	post royal	
	Nocera	

Nocera de Pagani	post
SALERNO	post
Taverna Pinta	post
Evoli	post
Scorzo	post & half
Auletta	post & half
Sala	post & half
Cafal Nuovo	post
Lago Negro	post
Lauria	post
Cafteluccio	post
Rotonda	post
Caftro Villari	post
Efaro	post
Regina	post
COSENZA	post
Belito	post
Martorano	post
St. Biagio	post
Fondaco del Fico	post
NONTELEONE	post
St. Pietro di Melito	post
Drofi	post
Seminara	post
Paffo di Salona	post
Fiumara di Muro	post
Catona	post
REGGIO	post
MESSINA	post

Here ends the Kingdom of *Naples* and *Calabria*; on this fide the pofts are not well regulated all the way, fo that it is much cheaper and better to hire a boat at *Naples* for any gentlemen who defign to make a tour to *Meffina*.

ITALY.

Communication of the above-mentioned road from *Scorzo* to *Matera*.

Scórzo		Kingdom of Naples.
Vietre	post	
Tito	post	
Potenza	post	
Tolva	post	
Monte Peloso	post	
Matera	post	

JOURNEY *from* Naples *to* Ottranto, *passing through* Barletta, Bari, *and* Lecce.

NAPLES		Kingdom of Naples.
Marianella	post & half	
Cardinaro	post & half	
Avellino	post & half	
Dente Cane	post & half	
Grotta Miranda	post	
Ariano	post	
Savignano	post	
Ponte Bovino	post & half	
Ardona	post & half	
Cerigniola	post & half	
St. Cassano	post	
BARLETTA	post	
BISEGLIE	post	
GIOVENAZZO	post	
BARI	post & half	
Mola di Bari	post & half	
St. Vito	post	
MONOPOLI	post	
Fasciano	post	
Ostumi	post & half	
St. Vito della Macchia	post	
Masagne	post	

VOL. IV.   P   St. Pietro

St. Pietro della Macchia	post & half
LECCE	post
St. Pietro in Galatina	post & half
OTTRANTO	post & half

From Lecce to Ottranto *the posts are not regulated, but you may find horses all the way.*

Communication of the above-mentioned road from *Ariano* to *Troia* and *Ardona*.

Kingdom of ARIANO
Naples.

Taverna Tre Fontane	post
Troia	post
Ardona	post

Another communication of the above-mentioned road from *Cerigniola* to *Bari*, passing through *Andria*.

Kingdom of CERIGNIOLA
Naples.

Canossa	post
Andria	post
Quarata	post .
Ruvo	post
BITONTO	post
BARI	post

Another Communcation of the above-mentioned road from *Bari* to *Taranto*.

Kingdom of BARI
Naples.

Turri	post
Gioia	post
Motola	post
Masafra	post
TARANTO	post

JOUR-

ITALY.

JOURNEY *from* Naples *to* Rome, *by* Vettura.

	Italian miles.	
NAPLES		Kingdom of Naples.
Aversa	eight	
CAPUA	eight	
Here they examine the passport		
Juselletto	twelve	
Dionello	ten	
St. Germano	thirteen	
Monte Cassino	two	
Ciperano	ten	Ecclesiastical State.
Franssinone	ten	
Fiorentino	nine	
Valmontone	seven	
Cava Nova	eight	
ROME	fifteen	

In all a hundred and twelve miles.

You generally hire a chaise for a Sequin a day, and you go from Naples to Rome in four days and a half. Remember to provide yourself with a passport.

JOURNEY *from* Rome *to* Bologna *by* Loretto.

ROME		
Prima porta	post royal	Ecclesiastical State.
Malborghetto	one third	
Castelnuovo	one third	
Rignano	post	
Civita Castellana	post	
Borghetto	one third	
OTRICOLI	one third	
NARNI	post	
TERNI	post	
Strettura	post	
SPOLETO	post	

Ecclesiastical State.	Le Vene	post
	FOLIGNO	post
	Case Nove	post
	Seravalle	post
	Ponte della Trave	post
	Valcimara	post
	Tolentino	post
	MACERATA	post & half
	Sanbuchetto	post
	LORETTO	post
	Camurano	post
	ANCONA	post
	Case brugiate	post
	Sinigaglia	post
	Marotta	post
	FANO	post
	PESARO	post
	Cattolica	post
	RIMIMI	post & half
	Savignano	post
	Cesena	post
	FORLI	post
	FAENZA	post
	IMOLA	post
	St. Niccolo	post
	BOLOGNA	post & half

JOURNEY *from* Foligno *to* Florence *through* Perugia.

State of the Church.	FOLIGNO	
	Madonna degli Angeli	post
	PERUGIA	post
	Toricelle	posts two
	Camoccia	posts two
State of Florence.	AREZZO	posts two
		Levane

ITALY.

Levane	post
Pian del fonte	post
FLORENCE	post

JOURNEY *from* Rome *to* Civita Vecchia *and* Florence.

ROME		Ecclesiastical States.
Storto	post royal	
Baccano	post	
CIVITA VECCHIA	posts two	
Monte Rosi	post	
Ronciglioni	post	
The Mountain of Viterbo	post	
VITERBO	one third	
MONTE FIASCONE	post	
Bolsena	post	
St. Lorenzo	one third	
Acquapendente	one third	
Ponte Centino	post	
Radicofani	post & half	
Ricorsi	post	State of Florence.
La Scala	post	
Tornieri	post	
Buonconvento	post	
Monterone	post	
SIENNA	post	
Castiglioncello	post	
Poggibonzi	post	
Tavernelle	post	
St. Casciano	post	
FLORENCE	post	

JOURNEY *from* Florence *to* Leghorn.

FLORENCE		State of Florence.
La Lastra	post royal	
Pontormo	post	

	St. Romano	post
	Fornasette	post
	PISA	post
	LEGHORN	posts two

JOURNEY *from* Poggibonzi *to* Pisa *and* Leghorn.

State of Florence.	POGGIBONZI	
	Castel Fiorentino	post
	St. Romano	posts two
	Fornasette	post
	PISA	post
	LEGLORN	posts two

JOURNEY *from* Leghorn *to* Florence *through* Pisa *and* Lucca.

State of Florence.	LEGHORN	
	PISA	posts two
	LUCCA	posts two
	Borgo Bugliano	posts two
	PISTOJA	posts two
	Poggio Chiano	post
	FLORENCE	post

JOURNEY *from* Foligno *to* Fano *thro'* Nocera.

Ecclesiastical State.	FOLIGNO	
	Pontecentesimo	post
	NOCERA	post
	Gualdo	post
	Sigillo	post
	Scheggia	post
	Canziano	one third
	Cagli	one third
	Acqualagna	post
	FOSSOMBRONE	post

Calci-

ITALY.

Calcinello	post
FANO	post

Journey *from* Florence *to* Bologna.

FLORENCE		State of Florence.
Fonte Bon	post	
Caſſagolo	post	
Montecarelli	post	
Cavallajo	post	
Filigare	post	
Lojano	post	
Pianoro	post & half	Eccleſiaſtical State.
BOLOGNA	post & half	

Journey *from* Bologna *to* Turin, *through* Modena, Parma *and* Piacenza.

BOLOGNA		
Samoggia	post & half	Eccleſiaſtical State.
MODENA	post & half	
Robiera	post	
REGGIO	post	State of Modena.
St. Ilario	post	
PARMA	post	
Borgo St. Donnino	posts two	State of Parma.
Fiorenzolo	post	
PIACENZA	posts two	
Caſtel St. Giovanni	posts two	
Bron	post	
Voghera	posts two	State of Piedmont.
TORTONA	post	
ALEXANDRIA	posts two	
Felizano	post & half	
Annon	post	
ASTI	post	
Gubellone	post	
St. Michele	post	

	Poverino	post
	Truffarello	post
	TURIN	post

JOURNEY *from* Bologna *to* Ferrara *and* Venice.

Ecclesiastical States.	BOLOGNA	
	St. Giorgio	post & half
	St. Carlo	posts two
	FERRARA, *here you pass the* Po.	post & half
	ROVIGO, *here you pass the* Adige.	posts two
State of Venice.	Moncelese	posts two
	PADUA	post & half
	Dolo	post & half
	Fusina	post & half

From hence you go by water five miles to Venice.

JOURNEY *from* Bologna *to* Milan, *thro'* Modena, Parma *and* Piacenza.

Ecclesiastical State.	BOLOGNA	
	Samoggia	post & half
	MODENA	post & half
State of Modena.	Robiera	post
	REGGIO	post
	St. Ilario	post
State of Parma.	PARMA	post
	Borgo St. Donnino	posts two
	Fiorenzola	post
	PIACENZA	posts two
	Zurlesco	posts two
	Loli	post
	Melegnano	post
State of Milan.	MILAN	post

JOURNEY *from* Bologna *to* Mantua *and* Verona, *through* Modena.

Ecclesiastical State.	BOLOGNA	
	Samoggia	post & half
	MODENA	

Modena	post & half	State of Modena.
Here you pass the Panaro.		
Bon Porto	post	
Mirandola	posts two	
Concordia	post & half	
St. Benedetto	post & half	
Here you pass the Secchia.		
Mantua, *here you pass the* Po.	post & half	State of Mantua.
Rouerbella	post	
Verona	posts two & half	

Journey *from* Milan *to* Mantua.

Milan		State of Milan.
Melegnano	post	
Lodi	post	
Zurlesco	post	
Pizzighittone	post	
Cremona	post	
Pieve di St. Giacomo	post	
St. Pier Medicale	post	
Bozzolo	post & half	
Castellacio	post & half	State of Mantua.
Mantua	post	

Journey *from* Modena *to* Ferrara.

Modena		State of Modena.
Bon Porto	post	
Fanale, *here you pass the* Reno.	posts two	
Ferrara	posts two	Ecclesiastical State.
On this road the posts are not regulated.		

Journey *from* Modena *to* Massa.

Modena		
Sacollo	post & half	
In Paullo	post & half	State of Modena.
Castel Novo di Graffignana	post & half	
Massa	post & half	

P 5 *From*

From Caſtel Novo di Graffig-
nana *to* Lucca   poſts three

JOURNEY *frm* Modena *to* Mantua, *through*
Reggio *and* Guaſtalla.

State of Modena.	MODENA	
	REGGIO	poſts two
	Guaſtalla	poſts three
	The poſts are not regulated from Guaſtalla.	
State of Mantua.	Borgoforte	poſts two
	MANTUA	poſts two

JOURNEY *from* Ferrara *to* Mantua, *through*
Oſtiglia.

Eccleſiaſti- cal State.	FERRARA	
	Palantone	poſt
	Maſſa	poſt
	Oſtiglia	poſt
	Governal	poſt
State of Mantua.	MANTUA	poſt
	On this road the poſts are not regulated.	

JOURNEY *from* Venice *to* Mantua, *through*
Eſte *and* Caſtellaro.

From Venice *to* Fuſina, *by water, five miles.*

State of Venice.	Dolo	poſt & half
	PADUA	poſt & half
	Moncelese	poſt & half
	Eſte	poſt
	Bevilacqua	poſt & half
	Sanguineto	poſt & half
	Caſtellaro	poſt & half
State of Mantua.	MANTUA	poſt & half

VOYAGE *from* Milan *to* Turin.

State of Milan.	MILAN	
	St. Pietro Lelmo	poſt

Buffa-

Buffaloro	post	State of Piedmont.
Novara, *here you pass the* Ticin	post	
VERCELLI	post & half	
St. Germano	post	
Ziano	post & half	
Chivasco	post & half	
Settimo	post	
TURIN	post	

JOURNEY *from* Venice *to* Milan, *through* Verona, Brescia *and* Vaprio.

From Venice *to* Fusina *five miles.*

Dolo	post & half	State of Venice.
PADUA	post & half	
Slesega	post	
VICENZA	post	
Montebello	post	
Caldier	post & half	
VERONA	post	
Castel Novo	post & half	
Desenzano	post & half	
Ponte St. Marco	post	
BRESCIA	post & half	
Ospitaletto	post	
Palazzolo	post & half	

Here you pass the Oglio.

Cavernago	post	

Without passing by Bergamo, *you shorten the way half a post.*

		State of Milan.
Vaprio	posts two	

Here you pass the Adda.

Colombarolo	post
MILAN	post & half

VOYAGE *from* Venice *to* Pontieba, *in the way to* Vienna.

From Venice *to* Mestre *five miles by water.*

TRE-

The European *Itinerary.*

State of Venice.

VENICE
TREVISO	post & half
Conegliano	post & half
Sacil	post & half
St. Vogadro	post
Spilimbergo	post
Ospitaletto	post
Venzon	post
Chiusa	post
Pontieba	post

Here ends the state of Venice. *On this side there is a bridge that divides* Italy *from* Germany. *From* St. Vogadro *to* Pontieba *the posts are not regulated.*

Communication of the above-mentioned road from *Venice* to *Gorizia* and *Trieste.*

From Venice *to* Mestre *five miles.*

State of Venice.

VENICE
TREVISO	post & half
Conegliano	post & half

Here you pass the Piave.

Sacil	post & half
Pordenon	post & half
Codroipo	posts two

Here you pass the river Taglimento.

Palma Nova	posts two

This is a fortress of the state of Venice, *and here ends* Italy *on this side.*

GORIZIA	posts two
Trieste	posts three

It is much better to go by water to Trieste *from* Venice, *for the posts are not regulated all the way.*

JOURNEY *from* Venice *to* Trent, *thro'* Bassano.

From Venice *to* Mestre *five miles.*

State of Venice.

Castel Franco, *or* Treviso	post & half
Bassano	

Baſſano	poſt & half	State of Venice.
Primolano	poſts two	
Borgo di Valſugana	poſts two	Germany.
Pergine	poſt & half	
TRENT	poſt & half	

JORRNEY *from* Padua *to* Trent, *by* Verona.

PADUA		
Sleſega	poſt	State of Venice.
VICENZA	poſt	
Montebello	poſt	
Caldier	poſt & half	
VERONA	poſt	
Volarni	poſt & half	
Peri	poſt	
Hala	poſt	Biſhopric of Trent.
ROVEREDO	poſt	
TRENT	poſts two	

JOURNEY *from* Rimini *to* Venice.

RIMINI		
Ceſenatico	poſts two	Eccleſiaſtical State.
Savio	poſt	
RAVENNA	poſts two	
Primaro	poſt	
Magnavacca	poſt	
Volani	poſts two	
Goro	poſt	State of Venice.
Fornaci	poſt	
CHIOZZA	poſt	

From Chiozza *to* Venice *twenty-five miles by water.*

Communication from *Ravenna* to *Ferrara.*

RAVENNA		
Fuſignano	poſt & half	Eccleſiaſtical State.
St. Alberto	poſt & half	

Cade-

Cadeolpi	poft & half
Longaftrino	poft & half
Argenta	poft
St. Nicolo	poft
FERRARA	poft

JOURNEY *from* Ravenna *to* Ferrara.

Ecclefiaftical State.
RAVENNA	
St. Alberto	poft
Argenta	poft
St. Nicolo	poft
FERRARA	poft

JOURNEY *from* Turin *to* Genoa.

State of Piedmont.
TURIN	
Truffarello	poft
Poverino	poft
St. Michele	poft
Gabellane	poft
ASTI	poft
Annon	poft
Felizano	poft
ALEXANDRIA	poft & half
Novi	poft

State of Genoa.
Ottaggio	poft
Campo Maron	poft

Here you pafs the Bocchetta.

GENOA	poft

Communication from *Tortona* to *Genoa*, by Ottaggio.

State of Genoa.
TORTONA	
Bettola	poft
Seravale	poft
Ottaggio	poft

Campo

ITALY

Campo Maron   post
   Here you pass the Bocchetta.
GENOA   post

  Communication from *Alexandria* to *Final*.

ALEXANDRIA		State of *Genoa.*
Gui	post	
Spigno	post	
Carcere	post	
FINAL	post	
GENOA	post	

  JOURNEY *from* Leghorn *to* Genoa, *through* Lerice.

LEGHORN		*Tuscany.*
Toretta	posts two	
Viareggio	post	
Pietra Santo	post	
MASSA	post	State of
Lavenza	post	*Genoa.*
Lerice	post	

  Here you embark for Genoa.

Ricco	post & half
Levante	post
Moneglia	post
SESTRI	post
Chiavari	post
Rapallo	post
Recco	post
GENOA	post & half

Scarce any body goes farther by land from Leghorn *than* Lerice, *except couriers.*

    JOURNEY *from* Fornovo *to* Sestri.

FORNOVO
Borgo Val di Taro   post

                            Varese

	Varese	post
	Chiavari	post
	SESTRI	post

Communication from *Parma* to *Sarzana*, through *Fornovo*.

State of Parma.	PARMA	
	Fornovo	post
	St. Terenzio	post
	Bercetto	post
	Pontremoli	post
	Villafranca	post
	Ola	post
	SARZANA	post

JOURNEY *from* Genoa *to* Monaco *and* Nizza.

State of Genoa.	GENOA	
	Utri	post
	Arezzano	post
	Varaggio	post
	SAVONA	post
	Noli	post
	Final	post
Montferrat.	Albenga	post
	Alas	post
	ONEGLIA	post
	Porto Maurizio	post
	ST. REMO	post
	Ventimiglia	post
	Mentone	post
State of Monaco.	MONACO	post
	Villafranca	post
County of Nice.	Nizza	*Here ends* Italy *on this side*.

JOURNEY *from* Turin *to* Nizza.

State of Piedmont.	TURIN	
	La Loggia	post royal

Carig-

Carignano	post
Raconigi	post
Savigliano	post
Villa Faletto	post
Borgo	post
Limon	post
Tenda	post
Suspello	post
NIZZA	post & half

JOURNEY *from* Milan *to* Genoa.

MILAN		
Binasco	post	State of
PAVIA	post	Milan.
Pancarana	post	
Voghera	post	
TORTONA	post	
Bettola	post	
Seravalle	post	State of
Ottagio	post	Genoa.
Campo Maron	post	

Here you pass the Bochetta.

GENOA   post

JOURNEY *from* Venice *to* Genoa, *by* Este *and* Brescia.

From Venice *to* Fusina *five miles.*

Dolo	post & half	State of
PADUA	post & half	Venice.
Moncelese	post & half	
Este	post	
Bevilacqua	post & half	
Isola Pancarana	posts two	
Castel Novo	posts two	
Defenzano	post & half	
Ponte di S. Marco	post	
	Brescia	

State of Venice.	BRESCIA	post & half
	Orzi Novi	post & half
State of Milan.	CREMA	posts two
	LODI	post
	PAVIA	post
	Voghera	post
	TORTONA	post
	Novi	post
	Ottagio	post
State of Genoa.	Campo Maron	post

Here you pass the Bochetta.

	GENOA	post

JOURNEY *from* Milan *to the Mountain of* Sempione *and* Geneva.

State of Milan.	MILAN	
	Castelanza	posts two
	Sesto	posts two
	Lago	three & half
	Dumodossola	posts two
	Duveder	post

Here end the posts of Italy. *You must now dismount from your chaise, and hire mules to carry the chaise and baggage to* Briga, *the first town in the* Valese, *paying at the rate of post, with drink-money to the postilion, until you come to* Briga. *From* Duveder *you come to* Sempione. *Here ends* Italy.

	SEMPIONE	posts three
The Valois.	Briga	post
	Veipia	post
	Tortomagna	post
	Ciera	post
	SION	post
	St. Pietro	post
	Martiniz	post & half
	St. Maurizio	post

Eghel

Eghel	post & half	*Swisserland.*
Vivé	post	
LAUSANNE	post	
Margia	post	
Evian	post	
Thenon	post	
GENEVA	post	

JOURNEY *from* Milan *to* Turin, *by* Casal *and* Montferrat.

MILAN		
Rusa	post	State of
Vigevano	post & half	*Milan.*
Mortara	post	
CASALE	posts three	
Trino	post & half	
Crescentino	post & half	
Chivasco	post & half	*Piedmont.*
Settimo	post	
TURIN	post	

JOURNEY *from* Turin *to* Mount Cinis, Chamberry, *and* Pont Beauvoisin.

TURIN		
Rivoli	post royal & half	
St. Ambrogio	post	
Giaconera	post	*Piedmont.*
Foresto	post	
SUSA	post	
Novalesa	post	

Here you must dismount from your chaise, and hire mules to carry both chaise and baggage over the mountain.

Gran Croce	post
Tavernette	post

Here ends Italy *on this side.*

Lane-

Savoy. Laneburg — post
Here you enter Savoy.

Braman	post & half
Villarardin	post
St. Michele	post
St. Giovanni di Morienne	post & half
La Chambre	post
Erpierre	post
Aiguebelle	post
Maltaverne	post
Montemigliano	post
CHAMBERRY	post
St. Giovanni de Cupao	post
Echelles	post
Pont Beauvoisin	post

Here you enter the territories of France.

Communication from *Alexandria* to *Final.*

ALEXANDRIA	
Gui	post
Spigno	post
Carcere	post
FINAL	post

Communication from *Tortona* to *Genoa.*

TORTONA	post
Bettola	post
Seravale	post
Ottagio	post
Campo Maron	post

Here you pass the Bocchetta.

GENOA — post

Another communication from *Tortona* to *Genoa,* by *Novi.*

TORTONA	
Novi	posts two

Otta-

ITALY.

Ottagio	post
Campo Maron	post
Here you pass the Bocchetta.	
GENOA	post

Another communication from *Tortona* to
    Genoa, through *Alexandria.*

TORTONA	
ALEXANDRIA	posts two
Pastorana	post
Ottagio	post
Campo Maron	post
Here you pass the Bocchetta.	
GENOA	post

Another communication from *Alexandria*
    to *Genoa,* through *Novi.*

ALEXANDRIA	
Novi	post
Ottagio	post
Campo Maron	post
Here you pass the Bocchetta.	
GENOA	post

THE EUROPEAN ITINERARY.

PART the SECOND.

The Posts through the Kingdom of France.

THE general directions for travelling post through this kingdom, you will find in the beginning of this volume, p. 17. The post routes in each journey, throughout this whole volume, have been taken from the last general list of the posts of *France*, published by order of the count *D'Argenson*; so that we have now only to refer to the respective pages where they are set down at full length, and to supply a few that have been omitted, with their different communications.

Route from Paris *to* Lyons, *through* Dijon, 59 posts, *vide* p. 146.

Another route from Paris *to* Lyons, *through* Moulins, 65 posts, *vide* p. 145.

Distances from Choisy le Roy *to the* Environs.
From Paris *to* Choisy le Roy, *through the* Plain, post royal, & half *simple*.

ITALY.

From Choify le Roi *to* La Croix de Berny poft,
 and taking horfes to
Villejuif   poft & half
From La Croix de Berny *to*
 Verfailles   pofts two
From Choify *to* Fromentau   pofts two
And taking horfes to Villejuif   pofts two & half
From Fromentau *to* La Croix
 de Berny   pofts two

Route from Paris *to* Melun *and* Fontainebleau,
 pofts feven & half.

PARIS
Charenton   poft royal
Villeneuve St. George   poft
Lieurfain   pofts two
Melun   poft & half
FONTAINEBLEAU   pofts two
     Crofs-roads near Melun.
From Melun *to* Brie Comte
 Robert   pofts two
From Lieurfain *to* Grofbois   pofts two

Route from Lyons *to* Aix *and* Marfeilles, *thro'*
 Valence *and* Pont St. Efprit, pofts thirty-
 nine & half, *vide p.* 148.

Route from Marfeilles *to* Toulon, pofts feven &
 half, *vide p.* 149.

Route from Aix *to* Toulon, pofts eight & half.
AIX
Roquevaire   pofts three
Cuges   poft & half
Bauffet   pofts two
TOULON   pofts two

Route from Aix *to* Antibes *and* Nice, pofts eighteen & half, *vide p.* 149.

Communication from Luc *to* Toulon.

Luc	
Pignan	post & half
Cuers	post & half
Toulon	post & half

Route from Lyons *to* Geneva, posts sixteen, *vide p.* 149.

Route from Lyons *to* Pont de Beauvoisin, posts nine, *vide p.* 150.

Route from Lyons *to* Grenoble, posts thirteen, *vide p.* 150.

Route from Grenoble *to* Chambery. *This route is not followed but in war-time.*

Grenoble	
Crolle	post & half
Touvet	post
Chaparillan	post
Chambery	post

Route from Grenoble *to* Valence, *through* Tullins *and* Romans, posts eleven.

Grenoble	
Voreppe	post & half
Tullins	post & half
Legrerie	post & half
St. Marcelin	post & half
Fories	post & half
Romans	post & half
Valence	posts two

Route from Lyons *to* Montpellier *and* Narbonne, *through* Pont St. Esprit *and* Nismes, posts forty-six, *vide p.* 236.

FRANCE.

Route from Narbonne *to* Perpignan *and* Mont Louis, posts fourteen, *vide p.* 234, 235.

Communication from Perpignan *to* La Jonquierre, *on the frontiers of* Spain, posts four.

PERPIGNAN
Boulu	posts two & half
La Jonquierre	post & half

Route from Lyons *to* Clermont *and* Limoges, posts thirty & half.

LYONS
Gresieu, post royal, & half *simple*	
Croisieu	post
Bordeliere	post
St. Martin de Lestra	post
Feurs	post & half
Boen	post
L'Hopital	post
La Pau	post & half
Peubru	post
Thiers	post
Lezoux	post & half
Pont du Chateau	post
CLERMONT	post

The remainder to Limoges, *vide p.* 235.

Route from Limoges *to* Bourdeaux, posts twenty-three & half.

LIMOGES
Aixe	post
Creusenet	post
Chalus	post & half
La Coquille	post & half
Thiviers	post & half
Corivaux	post
Tavernes	post

[*In a chaise* post & half.]

PERIGUEX	post
Maraval	post
[*In a chaise* post & half]	
Grignols	post
[*In a chaise* post & half]	
Mussidan	posts two
Montpont	posts two
Cousseaux	posts two
St. Meard	post
Chapelles	post
Libourne	post
Martinat	post & half
Carbon blanc	post
BOURDEAUX	post & half

Route from Paris *to* Bourges, posts thirty-seven, *vide p.* 254.

Route from Paris *to* Clermont *in* Auvergne, posts fifty-three, *vide p.* 235.

Route from Clermont *to* St. Flour, posts ten & half.

CLERMONT	
Vaire	post & half
Coude	post
Issoire	post
St. Germain Lambron	post
Pont de Lemps	post
Messiac	posts two
Vieillespece	post & half
ST. FLOUR	post & half

Communication of the same route with Puy en Velay.

From Pont de Lemps *to* Brioude post & half.
From Brioude *to* Puy en Velay

FRANCE.

Route from Paris *to* Orleans, Limoges, *and* Touloufe, *thro'* Cahors *and* Montauban, pofts eighty, *vide p.* 234.

Route from Touloufe *to* Narbonne, *thro'* Carcaffonne, pofts fourteen, *vide p.* 234.

Route from Carcaffonne *to* Mont Louis, pofts eight, *vide p.* 234, 235.

Route from Limoges *to* Tulles *and* Aurillac, pofts fifteen & half.

LIMOGES	
Boiffeil	poft
Pierre Buffiere	poft
Magnac	poft
Fregefond	poft & half
Uzerches	pofts two
Groliere	poft
TULLES	poft & half
La Garde	poft
Argentac	poft & half
Foffas Laubage	poft
Montvert	poft
St. Paul des Landes	poft
AURILLAC	poft

Route from Paris *to* Poitiers *and* Bourdeaux, *thro'* Orleans *and* Blois, pofts eighty-one & half, *vide p.* 219.

Route from Bourdeaux *to* Bayonne, S. John de Luz, *and* Orogne, pofts thirty, *vide p.* 220, 221.

Communication of the above route with Orthez *and* Pau.

CASTETS	
Tallers	poft
Q 2	DAX

Dax	post & half
Orthez	posts three
Pau	

Route from Bourdeaux *to* Touloufe, *thro'* Agen *and* Montauban, posts twenty-eight.

BOURDEAUX	
Bouscaut	post & half
La Prade	post
Castres	post
Birlade	post
Barsac	post
St. Macaire	post
La Reole	post & half
La Motte	post
Marmande	post
Tonneins	posts two
Aiguillon	post & half
Port S. Marie	post
Lusignan	post
AGEN	post
Croquelardy	post
Magistere	post
Malause	post
Luc	post & half
La Pointe	post
[*In a chaise* post & half.]	
MONTAUBAN	post
La Bastide	post
Grisolles	post
St. Jorry	post
La Courtansoul	post
TOULOUSE	post

Route from Paris *to* Rochelle, posts sixty-five. *vide* p. 256.

Route

FRANCE.

Route from Paris *to* Tours *and* Nants, *thro'* Angers, poſts fifty-nine & half, *vide p.* 260.

Route from Nants *to* L'Orient, poſts ſeventeen & half, *vide p.* 269.

Route from Tours *to* Rennes, poſts twenty-four.

TOURS
Tremblay   poſt & half
Souvigné   poſts two
Lude   poſts two & half
LA FLECHE   poſts two & half
Sablé   poſts two & half
Meſlay   poſts two & half
Laval   poſts two & half
Gravelle   poſts two & half
Vitré   poſt & half
Chateaubourg   poſt & half
Noyal   poſt
RENNES   poſt & half

Route from Paris *to* Angers, *thro'* Chartres *and* Le Mans, poſts thirty-two & half, *vide p.* 261.

Communication from Chartres *to* Orleans.

CHARTRES
Bonneval   poſts three & half
ORLEANS   poſts ſix

Communication from Chartres *to* Dreux.

CHARTRES
Boulay Thierry   poſts two & half
DREUX   poſt & half

. *Croſs road.*

From Maintenon *to* Boulay
 Thierry   poſt & half

From Boulay Thierry *to* Chateauneuf   poſt & half

Route from Paris *to* Angers, *thro'* Dreux, Be-
  leſme, Le Mans, *and* La Fleche, thirty-
  three poſts.

PARIS
VERSAILLES poſts two, *the firſt* poſt royal

Neauphle	poſts two
La Queue	poſt
Houdan	poſt & half
DREUX	poſts two
Chateauneuf	poſts two
Digny	poſt
La Loùppe	poſt & half
Remalard	poſts two
Beleſme	poſts two
St. Coſme	poſt & half
Bonneſtable	poſt
Savigny L'Eveque	poſts two
MANS	poſt & half
Gueſſelard	poſts two
Fouilletourte	poſt
La Fleche	poſt & half
Bourgneuf	poſts two & half
Pelouaille	poſt & half
ANGERS	poſt

Route from Paris *to* Alençon *and* Rennes, *thro'*
Mortagne, thirty-nine poſts, *vide p.* 321.

    Croſs-roads from Alençon *to* Mans.
From Alençon *to* Beaumont   poſts two & half
From Beaumont *to* Mans   poſts two & half
          Other croſs-roads.
From Beaumont *to* St. Remy
  du Plain   poſts two

FRANCE.

From St. Remy du Plain *to*
  Mamers   post & half
From Mamers *to* Belesme   posts two
From Mamers *to* Mortagne   posts two & half
From Mamers *to* Mesle sur
  Sarthe   post & half

Route *from* Paris *to* Rennes, *thro'* Dreux, La Louppe, *and* Le Mans, forty-two posts. *You follow the route from* Paris *to* Angers *as far as* Mans, *which see p.* 261. *From* Paris *to* Mans posts twenty-three.

MANS	
Guesselard	posts two
Malicorne	posts two
Sablé	posts two
Meslay	posts two & half
Laval	posts two & half
Gravelle	posts two & half
Vitré	post & half
Chateaubourg	post & half
Noyal	post
RENNES	post & half

Route *from* Rennes *to* Brest, *thro'* St. Brieux *and* Morlaix, posts twenty-five, *vide p.* 261.

Route *from* Rennes *to* L'Orient *and* Quimperlay, posts twenty.

RENNES	
Pontreane	post & half
Plat d'Or	posts two
Guers	post & half
Monteneu	post
Malestroit	post & half
Eleven	posts two
VANNES	post & half

Auray

The European Itinerary.

Auray	posts two
Landevant	posts two
Henebon	post & half
L'Orient	post
Quimperlay	posts two & half

Route from Rennes *to* Nants, posts eleven, *vide* p. 261.

Route from Rennes *to* S. Malo, posts seven & half, *vide* p. 273.

Route from Paris *to* Caen, *thro'* Dreux, Nonancourt, Evreux, *and* Lisieux, posts twenty-seven.

PARIS
VERSAILLES posts two & half, the first royal

Neauphle	posts two
La Queue	post
Houdan	post & half
Dreux	posts two
Nonancourt	post & half
Damville	post & half
EVREUX	posts two
La Commanderie	posts two
La Riviere	posts two
Marchéneuf	post
Duranville	post
L'Hotellerie	post
LIZIEUX	post & half
St. Aubin	post
Moux	posts two
CAEN	posts two

Another route from Paris *to* Caen, *through* Mante, Evreux, *and* Lizieux, posts twenty-five.

PARIS
St. Germain posts two, *the first* post royal.
Trielle

FRANCE.

Trielle	post & half
Meulan	post
Mante	post & half
Bonnieres	post & half
Paſſy	posts two
EVREUX	posts two

The rest as in the preceding route.

Route from Caen *to* Pontorſon *and* S. Malo, *thro'* Avranches, ſeventeen poſts.

CAEN	
Mouen	post
Villers le Cocage	post & half
S. Martin de la Beſace	post & half
Pontfarcy	posts two
Ville Dieu	posts two
AVRANCHES	posts two
Pontorſon	posts two & half
Vivier	posts two & half
ST. MALO	posts two

Route from Caen *to* Cherbourg *and* La Hogue, *through* Valognes, poſts twelve and half.

CAEN	
Breteville	post & half
BAYEUX	post & half
Formigny	posts two
Iſſigny	post & half
Carentan	post
St. Mere Egliſe	post & half
Valognes	post & half
CHERBOURG	posts two
From Valognes *to* La Hogue	posts two

Communication from Bayeux *to*

Valbadon	post & half
From Valbadon *to* St. Lo	posts two

Another

Another from Carentan *to* Ville Dieu.

CARENTAN
Desert   post & half
St. Lo   post & half
Pontfarcy   posts two & half
VILLE DIEU   posts two

Route from Caen *to* Alençon, posts eleven.

CAEN
Hautmesnil   post & half
Falaise   post two
Argentan   posts two & half
SEEZ   posts two & half
ALENÇON   posts two & half

Communication from Argentan *to* Orbec.

From Argentan *to* Vimontier posts two & half
From Vimontier *to* Orbec   posts two

Route from Paris *to* Anet, posts eight & half.

PARIS
VERSAILLES post two, *the first* post royal
Neauphles   posts two
La Queque   post
Houdan   post & half
Anet   posts two

Communications.

From Anet *to* Dreux   post & half
From Anet *to* Passy   posts two
From PASSY *to* Evreux   posts two
From EVREUX *to* Louviers   posts two
From Louviers *to* Port St. Ouin posts two
From Port St. Ouin *to* ROUEN posts two
From EVREUX *to* Conches   posts two
From Conches *to* L'Aigle   posts three & half

Route

FRANCE.

Route from Versalles *to* Crecy, posts eight.

VERSAILLES	
Neauphle	posts two
La Queue	post
Houdan	post & half
Dreux	posts two
Crecy	post & half
Chateauneuf	post

Route from Paris *to* Rouen, *thro'* Mante *and* Vernon, posts fifteen, *vide p.* 280.

Route from Paris *to* Rouen *thro'* Pontoise *and* Magni, posts fourteen & half, *vide p.* 279.

Route from Rouen *to* L'Aigle, *thro'* Neufbourg, posts nine.

ROUEN	
Lissart	post royal
Hautes terres	post & half
Neufbourg	post
Beaumont le Roger	post & half
Lire	posts two
Rugles	post
L'AIGLE	post

Communication.

From St. Ouin *to* Montore	posts two
Neubourg	posts two

Route from Rouen *to* Alençon, fifteen posts.

ROUEN	
Moulineau	post royal & half *simple*
Bourgteroude	post
Bernay	posts three & half
Broglie	post

The European Itinerary.

Montreuil L'Argile	post
Noyers Menard	post & half
Melleraut	post & half
SEEZ	post & half
ALENÇON	posts two & half

Route from Rouen *to* Caen, posts thirteen & half, *vide p.* 279.

Route from Rouen *to* Honfleur, posts eight.

ROUEN	
Moulineaux	post royal & half *simple*
Bourgachart	post & half
Rougemontier	post
Ponteau de Mer	post & half
HONFLEUR	posts two & half

Communications.

From Honfleur *to* Dive	posts three & half
From Dive *to* CAEN	posts three
From Honfleur *to* Pont L'Eveque	post & half
From Ponteau de Mer *to* Cormeille	post & half
From Cormeille *to* Lizieux	posts two

Route from Rouen *to* Havre, posts nine, *vide p.* 292.

Route from Rouen *to* Dieppe, Abbeville, *and* Lisle, posts twenty-four & half.

ROUEN	
Cambres	post royal & half *simple*
Tostes	post & half
Osmonville	post & half
DIEPPE	post & half
Ville Dieu	posts three

Fres-

FRANCE.

Freſſenville	poſt & half
ABBEVILLE	poſt & half
Auxy le Chateau	poſts two & half
S. Pol	poſts two & half
Bethune	poſts three
Waquet	poſts two
LILLE	poſts two

Route from Rouen *to* Amiens, poſts twelve.

ROUEN	
Vergelant	poſt royal & half *ſimple*
La Boiſſiere	poſt & half
Neufchatel	poſt & half
Aumale	poſts two & half
Lignieres	poſt
Poix	poſt
Quevauviller	poſt
AMIENS	poſts two

Route from Paris *to* Forges, poſts fourteen.

PARIS	
St. Denis	poſt royal
Franconville	poſt
Pontoiſe	poſt & half
Bordeau de Vigny	poſts two
Magny	poſt & half
Giſors	poſt & half
Gournay	poſts three
Forges	poſts two & half

Route from Paris *to* Beauvais, *thro'* Beaumont ſur Oyſe, poſts eight.

PARIS	
St. Denis	poſt royal
St. Brice	poſt

Beau-

Beaumont	posts two
Puiseux	post
Blainville	post & half
BEAUVAIS	post & half

Route from Paris *to* Amiens, Abbeville *and* Calais, posts thirty-two, *vide p.* 23.

Communications.

From Marquise *to* Ardres	posts two
From Ardres *to* Gravelines	posts two

Other Communications.

From Calais *to* Gravelines	posts two
From Gravelines *to* Dunkirk	posts two
From Dunkirk *to* Bergues	post

Route from Montreuil sur mer *to* Arras, nine posts.

MONTREUIL	
Hesdin	posts two & half
St. Pol	posts two & half
Tinques	post & half
ARRAS	posts two & half

Route from Abbeville *to* Lille, *thro'* Arras, posts thirteen & half.

ABBEVILLE	
Auxy le Chateau	posts two & half
Dourlens	posts two
L'Arbret	posts two
ARRAS	posts two
Lens	posts two
Carvin	post
LILLE	posts two

Route

FRANCE.

Route from Amiens *to* Lille, *thro'* Arras, posts twelve & half.

AMIENS
Tallemart   posts two
Dourlens   post & half
The remainder as in the preceding route.

Another route from Amiens *to* Lille, *thro'* St. Pol, posts thirteen & half.

AMIENS
Tallemart   posts two
Dourlens   post & half
Frevent   post & half
St. Pol   post & half
Bethune   posts three
Waquet   posts two
LILLE   posts two

Communication from Arras *to* Doway.

ARRAS
Gavrelle   post
DOWAY   post & half

Route from Amiens *to* Cambray, posts eleven & half.

AMIENS
Tallemart   posts two
Dourlens   post & half
Sailly au bois   posts two
Hervillé   posts two
Marquion   posts two & half
CAMBRAY   post & half

Route from Amiens *to* S. Omer, posts eleven & half.

AMIENS
Tallemart   posts two
Dourlens   post & half
Frevent

Frevent	post & half
St. Pol	post & half
AIRE	posts three & half
ST. OMER	post & half

Communication near Amiens.

From Amiens *to* Villers	posts two
From Villiers *to* Faucaucourt	posts two
From Faucaucourt *to* Peronne	post & half
From Amiens *to* Ourges	posts two
From Ourges *to* S. Martz	post
From St. Martz *to* Roye	posts two

Another from Roye *to* Ham *and* St. Quintin.

From Roye *to* Ham	posts two & half
From Ham *to* Roupy	post & half
From Roupy *to* St. Quintin	post

Another from Amiens *to* Compeigne.

AMIENS	
Moreuil	posts two & half
Montdidier	posts two
Cuvilly	posts two
COMPEIGNE	posts two

Route from Paris *to* Lille, *thro'* Arras, twenty-six posts, *vide p.* 350.

Route from Arras *to* St. Omer *and* Calais, posts twelve.

ARRAS	
Souchet	post & half
Bethune	posts two
Lilliers	post & half
AIRE	post & half
ST. OMER	post & half

Ardres

FRANCE.

Ardres	posts two & half
CALAIS	post and half

Cross-roads.

From Aire to Cassel	posts two
From Cassel to Bergues	posts two & half
From Bergues to Dunkirk	post
From St. Omer to Bergues	posts three & half
From St. Omer to Cassel	posts two

Route from Lille to Dunkirk, posts nine.

LILLE	
Varneton	posts two
YPRES	posts two
Poperinge	post and half
Rosburgh	post
BERGUES	post and half
DUNKIRK	post

Route from Lille to Ostend, posts nine & half.

LILLE	
Varneton	posts two
YPRES	posts two
Dixmude	posts two & half
OSTEND	posts three

Route from Lille to Bruges.

LILLE	
MENIN	posts two
Rousselar	posts two
BRUGES	

Route from Lille to Gaunt, posts seven & half.

LILLE	
MENIN	posts two
COURTRAY	post
Vive St. Eloy	post & half

Peteg-

Peteghen	post & half
GAUNT	post & half

Route from Lille *to* Tournay *and* Gramont, posts seven & half.

LILLE	
Pont à Treffin	post
TOURNAY	post & half
Leufe	posts two
ATH	post & half
GRAMONT	post & half

Route from Lille *to* Maubeuge, *thro'* Valenciennes, posts nine & half.

LILLE	
Pont à Marque	post & half
Orchies	post & half
St. Amand	post & half
VALENCIENNES	post & half
St. Vast	posts two
MAUBEUGE	post & half

Route from Lille *to* Cambray *and* St. Quintin, posts ten.

LILLE	
Pont à Marque	post & half
DOWAY	posts two
Bac à Bencheux	post & half
CAMBRAY	post
Catelet	posts two
ST. QUINTIN	posts two

Route from St. Quintin *to* Rheims, *thro'* Laon, posts ten.

ST. QUINTIN	
La Ferre	posts two & half
LAON	posts two & half

Cor-

FRANCE.

Corbeny — posts two
Berry au bac — post
RHEIMS — posts two

Route from Paris *to* Peronne, Cambray, Valenciennes, Mons *and* Brussels, posts thirty-four.

PARIS
Bourget — post royal
Louvres — post & half
La Chapelle — post & half
SENLIS — post
Pont St. Maixence — post & half
Bois de Lihieu — post & half
Gournay — post
Cuvilly — post
Conchy les Pots — post
Roye — post & half
Fonches — post
Marché le Pot — post
PERONNE — post & half
Fins — post & half
Bon-Avis — post & half
CAMBRAY — post
BOUCHAIN — post & half
VALENCIENNES — posts two
Quievraing — post & half
Carignon — post & half
MONS — post
Casteau — post
Braine le Comte — post & half
Tubise — post & half
BRUSSELS — posts two & half

From Bouchain *to* Doway — posts two
From Valenciennes *to* Condé — post
From Valenciennes *to* Quesnoy — post & half

The European Itinerary.

Route from Paris *to* Compeigne, St. Quintin, Maubeuge, *and* Mons, *thro'* Senlis, Noyon, *and* Le Quesnoy, posts twenty-five & half.

PARIS	
Bourget	post royal
Louvres	post & half
La Chapelle	post & half
SENLIS	post
La Brasseuse	post
Verberie	post
La Croix	post
COMPEIGNE	post
Bac à belle rive	post & half
NOYON	post & half
Guiscard	post & half
Ham	post
Roupy	post & half
ST. QUINTIN	post
Sequart	post
Maraye	post & half
Forest	post & half
QUESNOY	post & half
St. Vast de Bavay	post & half
MAUBEUGE	post & half
From ST. VAST *to* MONS	posts two
From St. Vast *to* Douzies	post
From Douzies *to* Cousors	posts two

Communication from Compeigne *to* La Ferre.

COMPEIGNE	
Bac à belle rive	post & half
NOYON	post & half
Chauny	posts two
La Ferre	post & half
From Chauny *to* Ham	posts two

Com—

FRANCE.

Communication from Compeigne *to* Villers Cotterets.

COMPEIGNE
L'Essart Abesse   posts two
Villiers Cotterets   posts two

Another from Compeigne *to* Soissons.

COMPEIGNE
Jaulzy   posts two & half
SOISSONS   posts two & half

Another from Ham *to* Cambray.

HAM
Beauvoir   post & half
Chatelet   posts two & half
CAMBRAY   posts two

From Catelet *to* Maraye   posts two

Another from St. Quintin *to* Peronne.

ST. QUINTIN
Beauvoir   post & half
PERONNE   posts two

Another from St. Quintin *to* Landrecy.

ST. QUINTIN
Sequart   post
Maraye   post & half
Forest   post & half
LANDRECY   post

Another from St. Quintin *to* Guise *and* Avesnes.

ST. QUINTIN
Origny St. Benoist   post & half
Guise   post & half
AVESNES   posts four

From

From Origny *to* La Ferre   posts two & half
From Origny *to* Crecy   posts two

Route from Paris *to* Maubeuge, *through* Soissons *and* Laon, posts twenty-five, *vide p.* 344; *where you will find this route as far as* Soissons.

SOISSONS	
Chavignon	post & half
LAON	posts two
Crecy	post & half
Guise	posts two & half
LANDRECY	posts three
Bachant	posts two
MAUBEUGE	post

Communication from Soissons *to* Noyon.

SOISSONS	
Jaulzy	posts two & half
NOYON	posts two & half

Cross-road from Laon *to* Avesnes *and* Maubeuge.

LAON	
Marle	posts two & half
Vervins	post & half
La Capelle	post & half
Avesnes	post & half
Bachant	post & half
MAUBEUGE	post

Another from Laon *to* Rocroy.

LAON	
Moncornet	posts three & half
Aubenton	posts three & half
ROCROY	posts two & half

Another

FRANCE.

Another from Landrecy *to* Cambray.

LANDRECY	
Foreſt	poſt
Solemn	poſt & half
CAMBRAY	poſts two

Another from Cambray *to* Arras.

CAMBRAY	
Marquion	poſt & half
ARRAS	poſts three

Route from Landrecy *to* Meziers *thro'* Aubenton, poſts eleven & half.

LANDRECY	
Aveſnes	poſts two
La Capelle	poſt & half
Hirſon	poſt & half
Aubenton	poſt & half
Aubigny	poſts two
Launoy	poſt & half
MEZIERES	poſt & half

Route from Landrecy *to* Givet *and* Rocroy.

LANDRECY	
Aveſnes	poſts two
Terlon	poſt & half
Marienbourg	poſts three & half
GIVET	poſts two
From Marienbourg *to* Rocroy	poſts two

Another from Landrecy *to* Barbençon.

LANDRECY	
Aveſnes	poſts two
Sorre le Chateau	poſt & half
BARBENÇON	poſt & half

Route

Route from Maubeuge *to* Givet, seven posts.

MAUBEUGE
Cousors . .   post & half
And taking horse at Rouzies   posts two
Barbençon   post & half
Philippeville   posts two
GIVET   .   posts two

Route from Paris *to* Rheims *and* Sedan, *through* Soissons *and* Rethel, posts twenty-seven & half, *vide p.* 344.

Communication from Rheims *to* Chalons.

RHEIMS
Petites Loges   -   posts two
CHALONS   posts three

Another from Rethel *to* Mezieres.

RETHEL
Launoy   posts two & half
MEZIERES   posts two.

Route from Paris *to* Givet, *thro'* Soissons, Rheims, Rethel, *and* Rocroy, posts thirty-two. *You follow the route p.* 344, *as far as*

RETHEL
Launoy   posts two & half
Aubigny   post and half
Rocroy   posts two
Marienbourg   posts two.
GIVET   posts two

Route from Paris *to* Strasburg, *through* Meaux, Challons, Verdun, *and* Metz, posts fifty-five & half, *vide p.* 201.

Route

FRANCE.

Route from Metz *to* Thionville *and* Luxemburg.

METZ
Agondange	post & half
THIONVILLE	post
Rouſſy	post & half
LUXEMBURG	

Another from Agondange *to* Aumetz *and* Longwy.

AGONDANGE
Fontoy	post & half
Aumetz	post
LONGWY	posts two & half

Route from Metz *to* Sarrelouis, posts six.

METZ
Les Etangs	posts two
Boulay	post
Tromborne	post & half
SARRELOUIS	post & half

Communication from Metz *to* St. Avold.

METZ
Pont à Chauſſy	posts two
Fouligny	post
ST. AVOLD	post & half

Route from Metz *to* Nancy, posts five & half.

METZ
Corny	post & half
PONT à MOUSSON	post & half
Belleville	post
NANCY	post & half

Route from Verdun to Longwy and Luxemburg.

VERDUN
Morgemoulin	post & half
Spincourt	post & half
Longwy	posts two

LUXEMBURG

Route from Verdun to Sedan and Givet, posts fifteen & half.

VERDUN
Samoigneux	post
Sivry sur Meuse	post
Stenay	posts two
Mouzon	post & half
SEDAN	post & half
Mezieres	posts two
Lony	post
Rocroy	post & half
Marienbourg	posts two
GIVET	posts two

Cross road.

From Stenay to Montmedy	post & half
From Montmedy to Vezin	post & half
From Vezin to Longwy	posts two
From Vezin to Samoigneux	posts two & half

Route from Chalons to St. Dizier, posts seven.

CHALONS
Chepy	post
Chauffée	post
St. Amand	post
Vitry le François	post
Faremont	post
Pertes	post
ST. DIZIER	post

Route

FRANCE.

Route from St. Dizier *to* Langres, posts ten & half.

St. Dizier	
La Neuville	post & half
Joinville	post & half
Vignoris	posts two & half
Chaumont	posts two
Vesigne	post & half
Langres	post & half

Route from St. Dizier *to* Strasburg, *thro'* Bar, Toul, Nancy, *and* Saverne, posts twenty-eight.

St. Dizier	
Sauldrup	post & half
Bar	post & half
Ligny	post & half
St. Aubin	post
Void	post & half
Layes	post
Toul	post
Velaine	post
Nancy	post & half
Domballe	post & half
Luneville	post & half
Benaminy	post & half
Blamont	post & half
Heming	posts two
Sarrebourg	post
Hommartin	post
Phalsbourg	post
Saverne	post & half
Wiltem	post & half
Stiffen	post
Strasburg	post & half

Route from Saverne *to* Landau, *thro'* Wissemburg, posts ten.

Saverne

Hoch-

Hochfeld	post & half
HAGUENAU	posts two
Surbourg	post & half
Wissemburg	posts two
Nideroterback	post
LANDAU	posts two

Communications.

From Saverne *to* Boussevilliers post
From Hagenau *to* Souflemheim post & half
From Souflemheim *to* Fort Louis post
From Souflemheim *to* Bienheim post & half
From Bienheim *to* Lauterburg post & half
From Strasburg *to* Molsheim posts two & half

Others.

From Brumpt *to* Niderbron posts three
From Niderbron *to* Bitche posts three
From Bitche *to* Exveiller post & half
From Exveiller *to* Deux Ponts post & half
From Haguenau *to* Niderbron posts two

Route from Strasburg *to* Landau, posts nine & half.

STRASBURG	
Brumpt	post & half
HAGUENAU	post & half
Sturbourg	post & half
Wissemburg	posts two
Nideroterback	post
LANDAU	posts two

Communications.

From Nideroterback *to* Candel post & half
From Candel *to* Rhinzabern post

FRANCE.

Route from Strasburg *to* Fort Louis, posts four & half.

STRASBURG	
Gambs	posts two
Drusenheim	post
FORT LOUIS	post & half

Route from Fort Louis *to* Landau.

FORT LOUIS	
Bienheim	post
Lauterburg	post & half
Candel	post & half
LANDAU	post & half

Route from Strasburg *to* Spire.

STRASBURG	
Gambs	posts two
Drussenheim	post
Bienheim	posts two
Lauterburg	post & half
Rhinzabern	posts two
Gersmersheim	post & half
SPIRE	

Route from Strasburg *to* Hunningen *and* Basil, posts fourteen.

STRASBURG	
Krafft	posts two
Friemheim	post & half
Markelsheim	posts two
Briesheim	post & half
[*And* two posts *if you come by* New Brisac]	
Fessenheim	post & half
Otmarsheim	post & half
Groskempt	post & half
St. Louis	post & half
BASIL	post

Route from Paris *to* Troyes *and* Langres, poſts thirty-one, *vide p.* 210.

Route from Langres *to* Beffort, poſts fourteen & half, *vide p.* 210.

Route from Beffort *to* Straſburg, *thro'* Colmar *and* Scheleſtat, poſts fourteen, *vide p.* 211.

Route from Beffort *to* Huningen *and* Baſil.

BEFFORT
Chavanne	poſt & half
Alkirk	poſt & half
Trois Maiſons	poſt & half
St. Louis	poſt & half

BASIL

Route from Langres *to* Nancy, poſts twelve.

LANGRES
Montigny le Roy	poſts two
Cleſmont	poſt & half
S. Thibault	poſt & half
Harville	poſt
Neufchateau	poſt
Martigny	poſt
Colombey	poſt
Bainville	poſt & half
NANCY	poſt & half

Route from Langres *to* Beſançon, *thro'* Veſoul, poſts fourteen.

LANGRES
Griffonettes	poſt & half
Faybillot	poſt
Saintrey	poſt & half
Combeau Fontaine	poſt & half
Port ſur Saone	poſt & half

Veſoul

Vesoul	post & half
Maisonneuve	posts two
Veray	posts two
BESANÇON	post & half

Communication from Vesoul *to* Plombieres.

VESOUL
Saulx	post & half
St. Sauveur	post & half
Fougerolle	post
PLOMBIERES	post & half

Another from Fougerolle *to*
Remiremont	posts two & half
From Lure *to* St. Sauveur	post and half

Route from Langres *to* Dijon, posts six & half, *vide p.* 211.

Route from Paris *to* Dijon *and* Besançon, *through* Dole *and* St. Wit, posts forty-six & half, *vide p.* 211.

Route from Besançon *to* Pontarlier, posts seven & half.

BESANÇON
La Grange Seri	posts two
Ornaus	post and half
La Grange d'Aleine	posts two
Pontarlier	posts two

THE EUROPEAN ITINERARY.

PART the THIRD.

Regulation of the Posts thro' Germany.

SEE what has been said in regard to the manner of travelling in *Germany*, Vol. II. p. 66. Each post is about two German miles.

Rout from Schaffhausen *to* Tubingen.

Swisserland.	SCHAFFHAUSEN	
	Hohentwiel	leagues four
	Datlingen	leagues seven
	Alting	post
	Balingen	post & half
Suabia.	TUBINGEN	posts two

Rout from Schaffhausen *to* Inspruck.

Swisserland.	SCHAFFHAUSEN	
	Singen	post
	Zelle	post and half
	CONSTANCE	leagues four
Suabia.	Lindau	leagues twelve
	Wangen	post
	Holzleiten	post
	Kempten	

Kempten	post	*Suabia.*
Kemptenwald	post	
Weisbach	post	
FUSSEN	post	
Aiterwang	post	
Lermes	post	*Tyral.*
Nazareith	post	
Parwis	post	
Dorssenbach	post	
INSPRUCK	post	

Rout from Inspruck *to* Ulm.

INSPRUCK		*Tyral.*
Wölters	post	
Schwatz	post	
Gundel	post & half	
Elman	post & half	
Waidring	post & half	
Unken	post	
SALTSBURG	posts two	*Bavaria.*
Waging	posts two	
Stein	post	
Frabertsham	post	
Steinering	posts two	
MUNICH	posts two & half	
Bruck	posts two	
Degerbach	post & half	
AUGSBURG	post & half	*Suabia.*
Sommerhausen	post & half	
Guntzburg	post & half	
ULM	post & half	

From Ulm *to* Feldsetten   leagues two
From Feldsetten *to* Tubingen leagues fifteen
From Urach *to* Tubingen   leagues four
From Tubingen *to* Stutgard   leagues five

From Stutgard *to* Eſlingen   leagues two
From Eſlingen *to* Ludwigſburg leagues two

Rout from Ludwigſburg *to* Straſburg.

Suabia.	LUDWIGSBURG	
	Entweichingen	poſt & fourth
	Pforzheim	poſt & half
	DRULACH	poſt & half
	Karlſruh	half poſt
	Eſlingen	three fourths
	RASTADT	poſt & half
	Stollhoffen	poſt
	Biſchofsheim	poſt
	Kehl	poſt
Aſace.	STRASBURG	poſt & half

Rout from Straſburg *to* Geneva.

From Straſburg *to* Baſil *they reckon* twenty-five leagues. *For a carriage with four horſes you pay about* 38 florins *of* Straſburg, *which are about* 30 per Cent. *leſs than the* Rheniſh florins.

From Baſil *to* Solothurn *is* twelve leagues, *and from* Solothurn *to* Bern ſix leagues *further. For a carriage with four horſes from* Baſil *to* Bern *you pay* three piſtoles and half.

From Bern *it is* nineteen leagues *to* Lauſanne ; *from* Lauſanne *to* Role *it is* five leagues ; *from* Role *to* Geneva *it is* eight leagues.

Rout from Venice *to* Vienna, *by the way of* Trieſte.

At Venice *you embark for* Trieſte, *which is* ninety Italian miles.

From Trieſte *to* Fiume, *over the mountains, is above* forty-five Italian miles.

From

From Fiume *to* Porto Re *is* two leagues.
From Fiume *to* Scalitz *is* four leagues.
From Fiume *to* Adlſberg *is* ſeven German miles.
From Adlſberg *to* Planina *is* two leagues and a quarter.
From Planina *to* Cirkniziſchen-ſee two leagues.
From Planina *to* Ober Laubach three leagues.
From Ober Laubach *to* Ydria five leagues.
From Ober Laubach *to the city of* Laubach three leagues.

Laubach		
Popedſch	poſt	*Carniola.*
St. Oſwald	poſt	
Franz	poſt	
Cilley	poſt	*Carinthia.*
Ganowitz	poſt	
Weiſtritz	poſt	
Mahrbug	poſt	
Ehrnhauſen	poſt	*Stiria.*
Wildon	poſt	
Gratz	poſt	
Peggau	poſt	
Retelſtein	poſt	
Pruck	poſt	
Muerzhofen	poſt	
Kriegla	poſt	
Muerzuſchlag	poſt	
Schadwien	poſt	
Neunkirchen	poſt	*Auſtria.*
Neuſtadt	poſt	
Draſkirchen	poſt & half	
Vienna	poſt & half	

Route from Vienna *to* Prague.

Vienna	
Enzerſdorf	poſt
Stockerau	

The European *Itinerary.*

Auſtria.	Stockerau	poſt
	Malebern	poſt
	Hollabrunn	poſt
	Mondorf	poſt
	Pulkau	poſt
	Langau	poſt & half
———	Frating	poſt
Bohemia.	Pieſling	poſt
	Zlawings	poſt
	Konigſeck	poſt
	Neuhaus	poſt
	Somoſoll	poſt
	Koſchitz	poſt
	Tabor	poſt
	Sodomoſchitz	poſt
	Woiditz	poſt
	Biſtritz	poſt
	Noſsbeck	poſt
	Geſſnitz	poſt
	PRAGUE	poſt

Route from Prague *to* Halle *in* Saxony, *through* Dreſden *and* Leipſick.

Bohemia.	PRAGUE	
	Turſko	poſt
	Welwarn	poſt
	Budyn	poſt
	Lobeſchutz	poſt
	Auſſig	poſt & half
	Peterſwalda	poſt
———	Sehift	poſt
Upper Saxony	DRESDEN	poſt
	MEISSEN	poſt & half
	Stauchiz	five fourths
	Wermſdorf	poſt
	Wurtzen	poſt
	LEIPSICK	poſt & half
		Groſkugel

ˢ⁾ skuge	post & half	
HALLE	post & half	

Route from Halle *to* Ratisbon, *through* Gotha.

HALLE		Upp: Saxony
MERSEBURG	post	
NAUMBURG	post & half	
JENA	post & half	
WEIMAR	post	
ERFURT	post & half	
GOTHA	post & half	
Arnstadt	post & half	
Ilmenau	post	
Schleusingen	posts two	
Hilpershausen	three fourths	Franconia.
Rodach	three fourths	
COBURG	post	

From Coburg *to* Culmbach *it is* five German miles, *and from thence to* Bareith *it is* three German miles.

From Coburg *to* Bamberg *it is* six German miles.

From Bamberg *to* Pommersfeld *it is* three leagues.

From Pommersfeld *to* Erlangen, five leagues.

From Erlangen *to* Nurenberg *it is* three leagues.

From Nurenberg *to* Ratisbon *you have* six posts, *thro'* FEUCHT, Poschbaur, Teining, Parsberg, *and* Laber.

Route from Ratisbon *to* Heidelberg.

RATISBON		
Sahl	post & half	Bavaria.
Neustadt	post & half	
INGOLDSTADT	posts two	
NEUBURG	post & half	

DONA-

Suabia.	Donawerth	post & half
	Nordlingen	post & half
	Dinckelspiel	post & half
	Krailsheim	post
	Hall	post & half
	Oehringen	post & half
	Heilbrunn	post & half
Palatinate.	Sintzheim	posts two
	HEIDELBERG	

Post-stages in the Bergstrafs.

From Heidelberg *to* Weinheim	three leagues
MANHEIM	three leagues
Heppenheim	two leagues
	German miles
DARMSTADT	three & 1 fourth
FRANKFORT	three
Edersheim	two
MENTZ	two

Route from Manheim *to* Nancy *in* Lorrain.

	From MANHEIM *to* LANDAU	ten leagues
Alsace.	Otterbach	four leagues
	Weissenburg	two leagues
	Surburg	four leagues
	HAGENAU	three leagues
	SAVERNE	seven leagues
	PFALZBURG	three leagues
	Homerting	three leagues
	Sarburg	two leagues
	Hemin	two leagues
	Blamont	four leagues
Lorrain.	Benamini	three leagues
	LUNEVILLE	three leagues
	S. Nicholas	three leagues
	NANCY	two leagues

Route

GERMANY.

Route from Venice *to* Vienna, *thro'* Trent, Bolſano, Inſpruck, Saltzburg, *and* Lintz.

From Venice *you come to* Meſtre, *by water.*

Mestre		
Treviso	poſt & half	State of
Baſſano	poſt & half	*Venice.*
Primolano	poſts two	
Borgo Valſugana	poſts two	
Trent	poſts three	
S. Michel	poſt	*Tyrol.*
Egne	poſt	
Brondſol	poſt	
Bolsano *or* Botzen	poſt	
Teutſchen	poſt	
Colman	poſt	
Brixen	poſt	
Mittewald	poſt	
Stertzingen	poſt	

This is the foot of the famous mount Brenner.

Brenner   poſt

This is the top of the mountain.

Steinach	poſt	
Schoenberg	poſt	
Inspruck	poſt	
Wolters	poſt	
Schwatz	poſt	
Gundel	poſt & half	
Elman	poſt & half	
Waidring	poſt & half	*Bavaria.*
Unken	poſt	
Saltzburg	poſts two	
Neumarck	poſt & half	
Franckenmarck	poſt & half	
Volcklabruck	poſt	*Auſtria.*
Lambach	poſt & half	
Wels	poſt	

                              Lintz

	LINTZ	posts two
	Ens	post & half
	Stahrenberg	post
	Amstedten	post & half
	Kemmelbach	post
	Melck	post & half
	S. Polten	post & half
	Perstin	post
	Sigariskirch	post
	Burckersdorf	post
	VIENNA	post

Route from Vienna to Hamburgh, thro' Prague, Dresden, Leipsick, and Brunswick.

From Vienna to Prague, vide p. 371.
From Prague to Leipsick, vide p. 372.

Upper Saxony	LEIPSICK	
	Groskugel	post & half
	HALLE	post
	Konnern	posts two
	Aschersleben	posts two
	HALBERSTADT	posts two
Lower Saxony	Rickling	posts two
	WOLFEMBUTTLE	posts two
	BRUNSWICK	posts three
	ZELL	posts three
	LUNEBURG	posts three
	HAMBURG	posts three

Route from Vienna to Berlin, thro' Olmutz and Breslaw.

Austria.	VIENNA	
	Wolckersdorff	post
	Gauersdorff	post
	Katzeldorff	post
	Niclasburg	post

Porlitz

Porlitz	posts two	*Moravia.*
BRINN	post & half	
Wiskow	post	
Prostnitz	post	
OLMUTZ	post	
Sternberg	post	
Braunseiffen	post	
Engelsburg	post	
Zuckmantel	post	
Neustat	post	*Silesia.*
GROTKAU	post	
Olau	post & half	
BRESLAW	posts two	
Neumarck	posts two	
Parchwitz	post	
Luben	post & half	
Polchwitz	post	
Neustadtel	post & half	Marquisate
Grunberg	post & half	of *Branden-*
CROSSEN	post & half	*burg.*
Ziebingen	post & half	
FRANKFORT *on the* ODER	post	
Eggersdorff	post & half	
Jasdorff	post	
BERLIN	post	

Route *from* Vienna *to* Strasburg.

From Vienna *you go to* Lintz, *and from thence to*
  Lambach, *according to the rout,* p. 376.

LAMBACH		
Haag	post & half	*Bavaria.*
Riet	post	
Althaim	post	
Braunau	post	
Markl	post	

Oetting

	Oetting	post
	Ampfing	post and half
	Hag	post & half
	Anzing	post & half
	MUNICH	post & half
	Bruch	posts two
	Degenbach	post & half
	AUGSBURG	post & half
Suabia.	Somerhaufen	post & half
	Guntzburg	post
	Elchingen	post
	Weidenstatten	posts two
	Gretzingen	post
	Goppingen	post
	Blockingen	post
	CANSTADT	post & half
	Enzweing	post & half
	Pforzheim	post & half
	Etlingen	post & half
	RASTADT	post & half
	Stolhofen	post
	Bischoffsheim	post
	STRASBURG	posts two & half

Route from Vienna *to* Rotterdam, *thro'* Ratisbon, Nurenberg, Wurtzburg, Frankfort, *and* Wesel.

From Vienna *you go to* Lintz, *according to the rout, p.* 376.

	LINTZ	
Austria.	Efferdingen	post
	Peyerbach	post
	Eysembin	post
Bavaria.	PASSAU	post
	Vilshofen	post
	Pladling	post
	STRAUBINGEN	post

Pferter

Pferter	post	
RATISBON	post	
Laber	post	
Parsberg	post	
Teining	post	
Poschbaur	post	
Feucht	post	
NUREMBERG	post	*Franconia.*
Fahrensbach	post	
Embskirchen	half	
Neustadt	half	
Langenfeld	post	
Possenheim	post	
Kitzingen	post & half	
WURTZBURG	post & half	
Remlingen	post	
Esselbach	post	
Rohrbrunn	post & half	
Rosenheim	post & half	
Dettingen	post	
HANAU	post	
FRANKFORT	post	Circle of the Upper Rhine.
Konigstein	post	
Wirges	post	
Diekirch	post	
Walmroth	post	
Freiling	post	
Gulroth	post	
Weyerbusch	post	*Westphalia.*
Warth	post	
Brugg	post	
Ublaten	post	
Pempelfurt	post	
DUISBURG	post	

From

From Ublaten *is only one post to*

	DUSSELDORP	
	Wesel	post & half
	Rees	post
	EMERICK	post
United Provinces.	ARNHEIM	post & half
	UTRECHT	posts three
	ROTTERDAM	posts two

Another route from Wesel *to* Utrecht *is by* Cleves.
From Wesel *to* Santen
From Santen *to* Cleves
From Cleves *to* Nimeguen
From Nimeguen *to* Utrecht

Route from Vienna *to* Nurenberg, *thro'* Bohemia.

	VIENNA	
Austria.	Entzersdorff	post
	Stokerau	post
	Malabern	post
	Hollabrun	post
Moravia.	Pulkau	post & half
	Langau	post
	Frating	post
	Piesling	post
	Slabing	post
Bohemia.	Konigseck	post
	NEWHAUS	post & half
	Weseli	post & half
	Teyn	post & half
	Wodnian	post & half
	Strakonitz	post
	Horazovits	post
	Elishau	post & half
	CLATAU	post & half
	Neudighem	post & half
		Klintsch

GERMANY.

Klintfch	post	
Waldmunchen	post	
Retz	post	
Furn	post	Upper Palatinate.
Schwartzenfeld	post & half	
AMBERG	three fourths	
SULTZBACH	post	
Hartmanhoffen	post	
Sittenbach	post	
Rukerfdorff	post	Franconia.
NURENBERG	post	

Route from Lintz to Prague.

LINTZ		
Freyftadt	posts two	Auftria.
Koblitz	post	
Buchweis	post	
Wefle	post	Bohemia.
Kofchitz	post	

The remainder you will find in the route from Vienna to Prague, p. 372.

Route from Rotterdam to Prague and Breflaw, through Frankfort and Nuremberg.

From Rotterdam to Nuremberg, see p. 378.

NUREMBERG		
Erlang	post	Franconia.
Streitberg	post	
Truppach	post	
BAREITH	post	
Berneck	post	
Frankenheim	post	
EGER	post	
Santau	post	Bohemia.
Plan	post	

Sher-

	Scherlaschin	post
	Meiss	post
	Ullitz	post
	PILSEN	post
	Rockitzan	post
	Zerwitz	post
	Zitz	post
	Trappeschitz	post
	PRAGUE	posts two
	Radonitz	posts two
	Lissau	post
	Nymburg	post
	Koningstat	post
	Clumetz	post
	Konigs	post
	Tarowitz	post
	Nahod	post
	Reinetz	post
Silesia.	GLATZ	post
	Frankenstein	post
	Nimptsch	post
	Tordansmuhle	post
	Domsla	post
	BRESLAW	post

Route from Amsterdam *to* Hamburgh, *through* Benthem *and* Bremen.

United Pro-vinces.	AMSTERDAM	
	NARDEN	post
	AMERSFORT	post
	DEVENTER	posts three
	Oldenzell	posts three
	Benthem	post
Westphalia.	Lingen	posts three
	Hasselohn	posts two
	Loningen	post

Klop-

GERMANY.

Kloppenburg	post	
Wilshausen	post	
DELMENHORST	post	Lower
BREMEN	post	Saxony.
Otterſberg	post & half	
Cloſter ſeven	post & half	
Hornburg	post & half	
Crantz	post & half	
HAMBURG	post	

Communication from Bremen *to* Hanover, *paſſing through* Verden.

BREMEN	
VERDEN	posts two
Neinſdorff	posts two
HANOVER	posts four

Route from Amſterdam *to* Hamburg, *through* Oſnabrug.

From Amſterdam *you go to* Benthem, *as in the preceding route.*

BENTHEM		
Rhenen	post	Weſtphalia.
Iperbunen	post & half	
OSNABRUG	posts three	
MINDEN	posts two & half	
Nienburg	post	
Reten	post & half	
Fiſſelhoven	posts three	Lower
HARBURG	half	Saxony.
HAMBURG	half	

Route from Frankfort *to* Bruſſels *and* Rotterdam, *through* Mentz, Triers, *and* Liege.

FRANKFORT	
Ederſheim	post

MENTZ

Circle of the	MENTZ	post
Lower Rhine	Creutzenach	posts two
	Eckweiller	post
	Haag	post
	Budelich	post
	TRIERS	post
	Marche	post & half
	Bonchin	post & half
Westphalia.	Naudin	post & half
	LIEGE	post & half
Austrian Netherlands	Warem	post
	Lantferme	post
	LOVAIN	post
	Cabel	post
	BRUSSELS	post
	Trois Fontaines	post & half
	Willebrock	post & half
	ANTWERP	post & half
	Moerdyke	posts two
Holland.	DORT	post & half
	ROTTERDAM	post & half

Route from Amsterdam *to* Breslaw, *thro'* Hanover, Leipsick, *and* Dresden.

From Amsterdam *you go to* Osnabrug, *according to the route given in the preceding page.*

Westphalia.	OSNABRUG	
	Minden	post & half
Lower Saxony.	Rickemburg	post
	Stocken	posts three
	HANOVER	post
	Zehn	post
	Peina	post & half
	BRUNSWICK	post & half
	WOLFEMBUTTLE	posts two

Rocklen

GERMANY.

Rocklen	posts two	
HALBERSTAT	posts two	
Ascherfleben	posts two	
Kondern	posts two	Upper
HALL	posts two	Saxony.
Groskugel	posts two	
LEIPSICK	posts two	
Urtzen	posts two	
Colbitz	post	
Sehrhausen	post	
MEISSEN	post	
DRESDEN	posts two	
Harte	post	
Bischoffswerda	post	
BAUTZEN	post	Lusatia.
Rothkretschen	post	
Reichenbach	post	
GORLITZ	post	
Waldau	post	
Bunzlaw	post	Silesia.
Hainau	post	
LIGNITZ	post	
Neumarch	post & half	
BRESLAW	post & half	

Communication from Hanover *to* Halberstat *passing thro'* Hildesheim.

HANOVER		
HILDESHEIM	posts two	Lower
Steyerwald	post & half	Saxony.
Krasdorf	post	
Kniestat	post	
Hornburg	post	
Tilli	post	
HALBERSTAT	post	

VOL. IV.   S

Route from Frankfort to Berlin thro' Leipsick.

Circle of the Upper Rhine.	FRANKFORT	
	HANAU	post
	Gelnhausen	post & half
	Salmunster	post
	Schlichtern	post
	Neuhoff	post
	FULD	post
	Hunfeld	post
	Vach	post & half
———	EISENACH	post & half
Upper Saxony.	GOTHA	post & half
	ERFURT	post & half
	Buddelstat	post & half
	Auerstat	post
	NAUMBUR	post
	Rippach	post & half
	LEIPSICK	post & half
	Duben	post & half
	WITTENBERG	post & half
	Treuenbritzen	post & half
	Saarmund	post & half
	Coln	post
	BERLIN	post & half

Other route from Leipsick *to* Berlin, *through* Torgaw.

Upper Saxony.	LEIPSICK	
	Eulenburg	post
	TORGAW	post
	Hertzberg	post
	Hohenbuka	post
	Luckaw	post
	Luben	post
	Beseckow	post
	Storka	post

GERMANY.

Coln	posts three
BERLIN	post & half

Route from Frankfort *to* Berlin, *thro'* Halberstat *and* Magdeburg.

You follow the route from Frankfort *to* Leipsick, *p.* 386, *as far as* Eisenach.

EISENACH		
MULHAUSEN	post	
Duderstat	post & half	*Upper*
Elrich	post & half	*Saxony.*
Elbingeroda	posts two	
HALBERSTAT	post & half	
Hallersleben	post & half	
Wansleben	post	
MAGDEBURG	post	*Lower*
Neletis	post	*Saxony.*
Hochziatz	post & half.	
Niesar	post & half	
Golze	post & half	
Blicseudorff	post & half	
POTSDAM	post	
Coln	post	*Upper*
BERLIN	post	*Saxony.*

Route from Amsterdam *to* Leipsick, *thro'* Munster *and* Cassel.

NARDEN	post	
AMERSFORT	post	*United Pro-*
Achtevelt	post	*vinces.*
Lunteren	post & half	
ARNHEIM	posts two	
Dysburg	post & half	
Bockholt	post	*Westphalia.*
Berken	post	
Coesvelt	post	

S 2   MUN-

The European *Itinerary.*

	Munster	poſt
	Warndorff	poſt & half
	Hirſchbruck	poſt
	Neukirch	poſt
	Paderborn	poſt & half
	Litchtenau	poſt
	——— Warburg	poſt & half
Circle of the Upper Rhine.	Waſthuſel	poſt
	Cassel	poſt
	Lichtenau	poſt
	Biſchauſen	poſt
	Wanfried	poſt & half
	——— Mulhausen	poſt
Upper Saxony.	Langenſaltza	poſt
	Weiſſenſee	poſts two
	Gros Neuhaus	poſt
	Cloſter Eſlar	poſt
	Freyburg	poſt
	Merseburg	poſt & half
	Leipsick	poſt & half

Route from Hamburg *to* Venice, *thro'* Hanover, Gottingen, Caſſel, Frankfort, Augſburg *and* Inſpruck.

	Hamburg	
	Zarendorff	poſts two
	Witzendorff	poſts two
	Zell	poſts two
Lower Saxony.	Engſen	poſt & half
	Hanover	poſt & half
	Bruggen	poſts two
	Ammanſen	poſt
	Eimbeck	poſt
	Northeim	poſt
	Gottingen	poſt
	Munden	poſt

Cassel

GERMANY.

CASSEL	post	Circle of the Upper Rhine.
Werckel	post & half	
Jesberg	post	
Halsdorff	post	
MARBURG	post	
GIESSEN	post & half	
FRIEDBERG	post & half	
FRANKFORT	post & half	
Dettingen	post	
ASCHAFFENBURG	post	
Miltemburg	post	
Bischoffsheim	posts two	*Franconia.*
Mergentheim	post	
Blaufelden	post & half	
Kreilsheim	post	
Dinkelspiel	post & half	
NORDLINGEN	post	*Suabia.*
DONAWERT	posts two	
Meitigen	posts two	
AUGSBURG	posts two	
Degerbach	post & half	
Bruck	post & half	
Savinaister	post	
FUSSEN	post	

From Fussen *to* Inspruck, *vide p.* 369, *and from* Inspruck *to* Venice, *vide p.* 375.

Route *from* Hamburg *to* Stralsund, *thro'* Wismar *and* Rostock.

HAMBURG		
Trittau	post & half	*Lower Saxony.*
Smilau	post & half	
Gadebusch	post & half	
WISMAR	post & half	Duchy of Mecklenburg
Alten Carin	post & half	
ROSTOCK	post & half	

S. 3   Ribnitz

Swedish Pomerania.	Ribnitz	post & half
	STRALSUND	posts two

Route from Hamburg to Berlin.

Lower Saxony.	HAMBURG	
	Bocken	posts two
	Koltzin	post & half
	Hagenau	post & half
	Grabau	posts two
Marquisate of Brandenburg.	Perleberg	posts two
	Kletsche	post & half
	Kyritz	post & half
	Fehrbellin	post
	Butzau	post & half
	BERLIN	post & half

Communication on the above road from Perleberg to Hamburg.

From Perleberg to Lentzen	post
From Lentzen to Tripkou	post & half
From Tripkou to Boitzenburg	post & half
From Boitzenburg to LAWEMBURG	posts two
From Lawemburg to Escheburg	post & half
From Escheburg to Hamburg	posts two

Route from Berlin to Dantzick.

Marquisate of Brandenburg.	BERLIN	
	Bernau	post & half
	Neust Eberswald	post & half
	Angermund	post & half
	Koeningsburg	post & half
	Pyritz	posts two
	STARGARD	post & half
	Massou	posts two
	Neugardt	post

Pinnow

Pinnow	post & half	Prussian Pomerania.
Corlin	post & half	
Coslin	post & half	
Zahnou	post	
Schlawe	post & half	
STOLPE	post	
Luppow	post	
Wutskow	post	
Dunemorse	post & half	
DANTZICK	posts two	Polish Prussia.

Route from Berlin *to* Stettin.

BERLIN		
Orainienburg	posts two	
Zehdenick	post & half	Marquisate of *Brandenburg*.
Templin	post & half	
Prentzlau	post & half	
Lockenitz	post & half	
STETTIN	post & half	Prussian Pomerania.
And from Stettin *to* Stargard	post & half	

Route from Berlin *to* Konigsberg *in* Prussia.

BERLIN		
Tasdorff	post & half	Brandenburg
Muncheberg	post & half	
CUSTRIN	post & half	
Carzig	post & half	
Ruhr	posts two	
Ratzebour	posts two	
Schwetz	posts three	
Marienwerter	post & half	
Reisenbach	post & half	Prussia.
Preuss Marck	post	
Preussisch	posts two	
Heiligenheil	posts four	
Brandenburg	posts four	
KONIGSBERG	posts two	

Communication from Cuſtrin *to* Pyritz *and* Stargard.

From Cuſtrin *to* Solding	poſts three
From Solding *to* Pyritz	poſts two
From Pyritz *to* Stargard	poſt & half

Other Communications from Cuſtrin *to* Drieſſen.

From Cuſtrin *to* Landſberg	poſt & half
From Landſberg *to* Frideberg	poſt
From Frideberg *to* Drieſſen	poſts two

Route from Berlin *to* Brunſwick, *thro'* Stendel.

Marquiſate of Brandenburg.	BERLIN	
	Spawdaw	poſt
	Barnewitz	poſt
	Ratenau	poſt
	Tangermund	poſt
	STENDEL	poſt & half
Lower Saxony.	Gardeloben	poſt & half
	Diſdorff	poſts three
	BRUNSWICK	

Communication from Brunſwick *to* Magdeburg.

Lower Saxony.	BRUNSWICK	
	Konigſluter	poſt & half
	HELMSTAT	poſt & half
	Aſcherſleben	poſt & half
	MAGDEBURG	poſt & half

Other Communication from Magdeburg *to* Lentzen, *paſſing through* Stendel.

Upper Saxony.	MAGDEBURG	
	Colbitz	poſts two
	STENDEL	poſts two
	Arentzee	poſts two
	Lentzen	poſts two

GERMANY.

Route from Hamburg *to* Leipsick, *thro'* Magdeburg, Stenel, *and* Lentzen.

HAMBURG		
Escheburg	post & half	*Lower*
LAWENBURG	post & half	*Saxony*
Boitzenburg	post & half	
Triptau	post & half	
Lentzen	post	
Arentsee	post	
STENDEL	posts three	
Colbitz	posts two	
MAGDEBURG	posts two	
Kalbe	posts two	
Kothen	post & half	*Upper*
Lansberg	post	*Saxony.*
LEIPSICK	posts three	

Communication from Dessaw *to* Leipsick.

From Dessaw *to* Dolitz	posts two
From Dolitz *to* Leipsick	posts two

Communication from Kothen *to* Leipsick.

From Kothen *to* Halle	posts two
From Halle *to* Leipsick	posts two

Route from Nurenberg *to* Dresden, *through* Bareith.

NURENBERG		
Erlangen	posts two	*Franconia.*
Streitberg	posts two	
Truppach	posts two	
BAREITH	posts two	
Berneck	post	
Munchberg	post & half	
Hof	post	*Bohemia.*
Plauen		

	Plauen	poſt
——————	Reickenbach	poſt
Upper Saxony.	Zwickau	poſt
	Chemnitz	poſts two
	Freyburg	poſts two
	DRESDEN	poſts two

Communication from Dreſden *to* Groſſen, *thro'* Cotbus.

Upper Saxony.	DRESDEN	
	Koningſbruck	poſt
——————	Hoyerſwerda	poſt & half
Luſatia.	COTBUS	poſts two
——————	Guben	poſts two
Sileſia.	GROSSEN	poſt & half

Route from Inſpruck *to* Ratiſbon.

Bavaria.	RATISBON	
	Saal	poſt
	Neuſtat	poſt
	Geiſenfeld	poſt
	Hochinkamer	poſts two
	Wolferhauſen	poſts two
——————	Benedictbeueren	poſt & half
	Walerſee	poſt & half
Tyrol.	Mittewald	poſt & half
	Seefeld	poſt
	INSPRUCK	poſts two

Route from Ratiſbon *to* Prague, *thro'* Pilſen.

Bavaria.	RATISBON	
	Kirn	poſt
	Nittenau	poſt
	Neukirch	poſt
	Retz	poſt
	Waldmuncheon	poſt
		Klemiſch

GERMANY.

Klemisch	post	*Bohemia.*
Teinitz	post	
Stenkau	post	
Staab	post	
Pilsen	post	

The rest as in the route, p. 382.

Communication from Nittenau to Nurenberg, passing through Amberg.

NITTENAU		
Schwartzenfeld	post & half	*Upper Palatinate.*
AMBERG	post	
Pachtesfeld	post	
Sittenbach	post	*Franconia.*
Rychterdorsff	post	
NURENBERG	post	

Route from Ratisbon to Leipsick, thro' Eger.

RATISBON		
Kirn	post	*Upper Pala-*
Nittenau	post	*tinate.*
Schwartzenfeld	post	
Wernberg	post	
Weidhan	post	
Tuschenreut	post	
EGER	post	
Asch	post	*Bohemia.*
Adorf	post	
Plauen	post	
Reichenbach	post	
Zwickau	post	
Gosnitz	post	*Upper*
Altemburg	post	*Saxony.*
Rotha	post	
LEIPSICK	post	

The European *Itinerary*.

Communication from Eger *to* Dresden, *through* Zwickau.

Bohemia.	EGER	
	Asch	post
	Adorf	post
———	Plauen	post
	Reichenbach	post
Upper Saxony	Zwickau	post
	Lichtenstein	post
	Stilberg	post
	Chemnitz	post
	Oderan	post
	Freyburg	post
	Hertzogswalda	post
	DRESDEN	post

Another Communication from Zwickau *to* Leipsick, *passing through* Altemburg.

From Zwickau *to* Gosnitz	post & half
From Gosnitz *to* Altemburg	post
From Altemburg *to* Rotha	post
From Rotha *to* Leipsick	post

Route from Nurenberg *to* Leipsick, *thro'* Bareith. *You follow the route* p. 393, *from* Nurenberg *to* Dresden *as far as* Hof.

Upper Saxony	HOF	
	Gesell	posts two
	Schlaitz	posts two
	Gera	posts two
	Wirstauden	posts two
	LEIPSICK	posts two
	Or from Gera *to* Zeitz	post
	From Zeitz *to* Pegau	post
	From Pegau *to* Zwenka	post
	From Zwenka *to* Leipsick	post

Route

Route from Nurenberg *to* Leipsick, *passing thro'* Bamberg, Coburg, *and* Jena.

NURENBERG		*Franconia.*
Erlangen	post	
Altendorf	post	
BAMBERG	post	
Ratelsdorf	post	
Gleusse	post	
COBURG	post	
Judenbach	post	
Grafentahl	post	
Saalfeld	post	*Lower Saxony.*
Rudelstadt	post	
Uhlstadt	post	
Kahla	post	
JENA	post	
NAUMBURG	post	
Rippach	post	
LEIPSICK	post	

Or from Naumburg *to* Weisfenfels post.
From Weisenfels *to* Merseburg post
From Merseburg *to* Leipsick post

Communication from Zeitz *to* Eisenach, *passing through* Erfurt.

ZEITZ		
Eisemberg	post	*Upper Saxony*
JENA	post	
WEIMAR	post	
ERFURT	post	
GOTHA	post	
EISENACH	post	

Route from Hamburg *to* Nurenberg, *thro'* Coburg.
From Hamburg *to* Brunswick, *see the rout p.* 376.

Lower Saxony.	BRUNSWICK	
	WOLFEMBUTTLE	post & half
	Goslar	posts three
	Sessen	post & half
	Duderstat	posts three
Upper Saxony.	MULHAUSEN	posts two
	EISENACH	post & half
	Breitung	post & half
	Meinungen	post & half
	Multz	post & half
	Rothac	post & half
	COBURG	post & half

The remainder to Nurenburg *see in the route p.* 397.

Communication of the above route from Duderstat *to* Halderstat.

DUDERSTAT	
Elrich	post & half
Elbingeroda	posts two
HALBERSTAT	post & half

Route from Coburg *to* Leipsick, *through* Erfurt *and* Merseburg.

Franconia.	COBURG	
	Rodach	post
	Hilbergausen	post
	Schleusingen	post
	Ilmenau	post
	Arnstat	post
	ERFURT	post
Upper Saxony.	Colleda	post
	Betra	post
	Freyburg	post
	Mersburg	post
	LEIPSICK	post
	And from Arnstat *to* Gotha	post & half
	From Gotha *to* Eisenach	post & half

GERMANY.

Route from Hamburg *to* Venice, *thro'* Nurenberg.
From Hamburg *to* Nurenberg, *see the route p.* 397
From Nurenburg *you take the following route to* Augsburg.

NURENBURG
Hembach	post	*Franconia.*
Pleinfeld	post	
Dietfurt	post	
Monheim	post	
DONAWERTH	post	————
Meitingen	post & half	*Suabia.*
AUGSBURG	post & half	

From Augsburg *you take the route to* Inspruck, *which see p.* 369.
From Inspruck *you take the route to* Venice, *which see p.* 375.

Route from Lintz *to* Munich, *passing through* Braunau.

LINTZ
Wels	posts two	*Austria.*
Lambach	post	
Haag	post & half	
Riet	post	
Altheim	post	
BRAUNAU	post	
Marckl	post	
Oetting	post	
Ampfing	post & half	
Haag	post & half	
Anzing	post & half	
MUNICH	post	

Route from Ulm *to* Nurenberg, *passing thro'* Nordlingen.

ULM

Elchin-

Suabia.	Elchingen	post
	Gienge	post
	Dischingen	post
	NORDLINGEN	post
	Oetting	post
	Gunzenhausen	post
	Waffermumle	post
Franconia.	Schwobach	post
	NURENBERG	post

Rout from Stutgard *to* Nurenberg, *passing thro'* Dinckelspiel *and* Anspach.

Suabia.	STUTGARD	
	Canstat	posts two
	Schornedorf	post & half
	Gemund	post
	Ahlen	post
	Elwang	post
	DINCKELSPIEL	post
	Bechofen	post
Franconia.	Anspach	post
	Hailbrun	post
	NURENBERG	posts two & half

Communication from Stutgard *to* Kreilsheim, *passing thro'* Hailbron.

Suabia.	STUTGARD	
	Canstat	post
	Bitigheim	post
	Hailbrun	post
	Oringen	post
	Hall	post
Franconia.	KREILSHEIM	post

Route from Donawerth *to* Frankfort, *passing thro'* Dinckelspiel *and* Mergentheim.

DONAWERTH

GERMANY.

Nordlingen	post & half	Suabia.
Dinckelipiel	post & half	
Kreilsheim	post & half	
Blaufelden	post	
MERGENTHEIM	post & half	———
Bischoffsheim	post & half	Franconia.
Mittemburg	post & half	
ASCHAFFENBURG	post	———
Dettingen	post	
HANAU	post	Circle of the
FRANKFORT	post	Upper Rhine.

Route from Coblentz *to* Luxemburg, *passing through* Triers.

COBLENTZ		
Carden	post	
Alst	post & half	Circle of the Lower Rhine
Lifer	post	
TRIERS	post	———
Verquiers	post & half	Duchy of
LUXEMBURG	post & half	Luxemburg.

Route from Cologne *to* Brussels, *passing through* Mastricht *and* Lovain

COLOGNE		
Bergen	post	Westphalia.
JULIERS	post	
MASTRICHT	posts two	
Tongres	post	
St. Tron	post	———
Tirlemont	post	Brabant.
LOVAIN	post	
Cabel	post	
BRUSSELS	post	

Route from Cologne *to* Brussels, *passing thro'* Ruremond *and* Louvain.

COLOGNE

Stomel

Westphalia.	Stomel	post & half
	Elsen	post
	Ercklens	post
	RUREMOND	post & half
———	Boxen	post
Brabant.	Werth	post
	Hechten	post
	Diest	post
	LOVAIN	post
	Cabel	post
	BRUSSELS	post

Route from Dusseldorp *to* Antwerp, *passing thro'* Ruremond.

Westphalia.	DUSSELDORP	
	Furt	post
	Ercklens	post
	RUREMOND	post & half
———	Boxen	post
Brabant.	Werth	post
	Achelen	post
	Postel	post
	Turnhout	post
	Westmal	post
	ANTWERP	post
	From Antwerp *to* Breda	posts two
	From Breda *to* Bois le duc	posts two

Route from Saltzburg *to* Strasburg, *thro'* Inspruck, Ravenspurg, *and* Freyburg.

From Saltzburg *to* Inspruck, *see the route,* p. 369.
From Inspruck *to* Kempten, *see* ibid.

Suabia.	KEMPTEN	
	Kimmershofen	post
	Leutkirch	post
	Weingarten	post

Marck-

Marckdorf	post	
Difendorf	post	
Stokach	post	
Engen	post	
Handing	post	
Gnading	post	
Neustat	post	
Steig	post	
FREIBURG	post	
Kentzing	post	
Friffenheim	post	
Offenburg	post	*Alsace.*
STRASBURG	post	

Route from Augsburg *to* Kempten.

AUGSBURG		
Schwabmenchigen	post	
Mindelheim	post	*Suabia.*
Memmingen	post	
Leutkirch	post	
Schrottembach	post	
KEMPTEN	post	

Communication from Memingen *to* Lindau.

MEMINGEN		*Suabia.*
Leutkirch	post	
Wangen	post	
LINDAU	post	

Route from Lindau *to* Ulm, *passing thro'* Ravensburg.

LINDAU		
Tetnag	post	*Suabia.*
Ravenspurg	post	
Waldsee	post	
Biberach	post	
	Laubheim	

	Laubheim	post
	ULM	post

Route from Ulm *to* Schaffhausen, *passing thro'* Meskirch.

Suabia.	ULM	
	Ehingen	post
	Riedlingen	post
	Mengen	post
	Meskirch	post
	Stokach	post
————	Singen	post
Swisserland	SCHAFFHAUSEN	post

Communication from Schaffhausen *to* Stutgard, *passing thro'* Dutlingen.

Swisserland.	SCHAFFHAUSEN	
	Engen	post
————	Dutlingen	post
Suabia.	Alting	post
	Baling	post
	Tusling	post
	Waltembuch	post
	STUTGARD	post

THE

THE EUROPEAN ITINERARY.

PART *the* FOURTH.

Poland, Russia, Hungary, Spain, *and* Portugal.

Rout from Berlin *to* Warsaw.

From Berlin *to* Frankfort *on the* Oder, *see p.* 377.

FRANKFORT *on the* ODER		
Drossen	post	Marquisate
Konigswald	post	of *Branden-*
SWERIN	post	*burg.*
POSEN	posts four	
Kleskow	posts two	*Poland.*
Wurzesnick	posts two	
Lubionicky	posts two	
Katnow	post	
LOWITZ	posts two	
Ratzky	posts two	
WARSAW	posts three	

Rout from Grossen *to* Thorn *in Polish Prussia.*

GROSSEN		
Meseritz	posts two	*Lusatia.*
	Pnieff	

	Pnieff	posts two
	Samter	posts two
Polish Prussia.	Oberniki	post
	Wangrawitz	post
	Calixki	post
	Sultz	posts two
	Schinen	post
	Lebaschau	post
	THORN	posts two

Route from Breslaw *to* Warsaw.

Silesia.	BRESLAW	
	OELS	post
	WARTENBERG	post
	Werischow	post & half
	Radliza	post & half
Poland.	Wittawa	post
	Rosnotawitza	post
	Pietrekow	post
	Sabrowa	post & half
	Rawa	post & half
	Microwau	post & half
	WARSAW	posts two

Route from Breslaw *to* Cracow.

Lower Silesia	BRESLAW	
	BRIEG	posts two
	Schurgast	posts two
Upper Silesia.	OPPELEN	posts two
	Strelitz	posts two
	Tarnowitz	posts two
	Bentzhin	post
Poland.	Schlacka	post
	Schdelitz	post
	CRACOW	post

Route from Olmutz *to* Cracow.

OLMUT		
Sterenberg	post & half	*Moravia.*
Hoff	posts two	
TROPPAU	posts two	
RATIBOR	posts two	*UpperSilesia*
Rauden	post & half	
Gleibitz	post & half	
Tarnowitz	post & half	

The remainder as in the preceding route.

Route from Vienna *to* Cracow.

VIENNA	German Miles.	
Ulrichskirch	three	*Austria.*
Missellbach	three	
Niclasburg	three	
Auspitz	two	
Austerlitz	three	*Moravia.*
Wischa	two	
Kojeden	three	
Bowarelitsch	two	
Weiskerch	two	
Neuotschein	two	
Ostra	four	
Freystadtle	two	
Strummen	two	*UpperSilesia*
Pless	two	
Oswieczin	three	
Lipowitz	two	*Poland.*
CRACOW	five	

Route from Warsaw *to* Moscow.

WARSAW	
Poschin	two
Goura	posts two & half
Minischow	two & half

Here you pass the Bilza.

Ritziwol

The European *Itinerary.*

		German Miles.
P*oland.*	Ritziwol	three
	Rosticez	two
	Guewouchof	three

At Poulan *you pass the* Vistula.

Konskawolja	three
Pokuzin	three
LUBLIN	two
Piasky	three
Krosnoslaw	three
Woislewitz	four
Steffankowitz	three

Here you pass the Boug.

Ozillac	three
Wlosdimiers	two
Woiskize	three
Hulsnick	four
Millevisch	two

Here you pass the Sty.

Boroschof	one & half
Romanof	two
Olyka	two
Klewan	one

By Suska *you pass the* Horin.

Alexandria	four
Tuczin	two
Meseritz	three
Korez	three

Here you pass the Sluz.

Swial	five
Neslowan	three
Socolom	two
Iwany	three
Tzeracho	three
Choroſtoſſoff	four

Here you cross the Tetenof.

Brauſ-

MUSCOVY, &c.

	German Miles.	
Brauſſilow	ſix	
Molyſin	four	
Balogrodko	three	
An Inn	one	
Kyoff	two	

Here you croſs the Boryſthenes.

Browary	three	
Semypolcka	four	
Goſcliky	three	
Naſſoka	five	
Nyssin	five	
An Inn	three	———
Barſena	three	The
Batturin	four	Ukraine.

Here you paſs the Sem.

Croſlewitz	ſix	
A Hamlet	three	
Glouchow	three	
Dobrowna	three	———
A Hamlet	two	Muſcovy.
Siofska	two	
Nevary	ſix	
A Hamlet	four	
Brattioff	two	
Jazinus	five	
Milovaya	three	
Selichan	five	
Boulchow	five	
Dolce	five	
Terratuchyin	two	
Belloff	two	

You paſs the Occa *twice.*

Vol. IV.   T   A

	German Miles.
A Hamlet	five

You pass the Occa *the third time.*

| A Hamlet | one |

You pass the Occa *the fourth time.*

Calugga	five
A Hamlet	four
Reddiely	eight
Letefchova	five
A Hamlet	four
Paſtraza	ſeven
Moscow	ſeven

Route from Warſaw *to* Konigſberg.

WARSAW	
Prezewedowa	four
Zagrowowa	four
Leſlnow	four
Opolonice	four
Ortelſburg	four
Raſtenburg	ſeven
Schippenbeil	two
Aſchwanger	one
KONIGSBERG	one

Rout from Riga *to* Revel.

RIGA	
Neuermuhlen	one & half
Ab ſterohm	one & half

Here you paſs a river.

Bieringſhoff	three
Mattieſkirchen	one & half
Pangelkrug	three
Saliſbach	two

Here

HUNGARY, &c.

German Miles.

Here you cross a river.

Kablikrug	four
Woifte	three
Pernaw	three

Here you pass the river Pernaw.

Jacobfkirch	five
Fickelfkirch	two

Betwixt these two places you pass the rivers Conno *and* Reschbach.

Margenfchekirch	three
Schwartzen	two
Rugel	three
Goggis	one & half
Revel	three

Rout from Vienna *to* Constantinople.

Vienna		
Fiffamet	posts two	*Austria.*
Teiffaltemburg	posts two	
Tarendorff	post & half	
Wiffelburg	post & half	
Hochftrafen	post & half	
Raab	post	*Hungary.*
Geny	post	
Comora	posts two	
Nefmiilh	post	
Neudorf	post	
Dorack	post	
Werefwar	post & half	
Buda	post & half	
Amfabè	post & half	

T 2   Ertzin

	Ertzin	post
	Adon	post
	Pontelli	post
	Fuldwa	post & half
	Pax	posts two
	Tolna	posts two
	Sechzar	post
	Bataffech	post & half
	Suttfui	post
	Mohacz	post
	Iffiis	posts two
Scalvonia:	Kolluth	post
	Samber	posts two
	Labfcora	post & half
	Carabuhcora	post & half
	Glofens	posts two
	Patich	posts two
	PETERWARADIN	posts two
	Befchie	posts two
Servia.	Banochie	posts two
	BELGRADE	posts two

From Belgrade *to* Hiffargik *it is* six leagues *thro' a large plain. At* Hiffargik *you must hire* Janiffaries *to conduct you thro' this country as far as* Haffan, *being infested with robbers.*

Collar	six leagues
Haffan Bafcia	six leagues
Jagodna	twelve leagues
Rama	six leagues

Here you pass thro' a dangerous country.

NISSA	twelve leagues

HUNGARY, &c.

Here you pass thro' a very dangerous country, being all woods, and infested by robbers.

Schiarchioi	twelve leagues	

Here you have fine plains, and the rest woods.

Sopha	twelve leagues	*Bulgaria.*

Here you have plains inhabited chiefly by Greeks.

Jutiman	twelve leagues
Tartarpoſſagik	twelve leagues

Here you pass thro' Iſſargik *and* Senichoi. *With these horses you paſs thro' the iron gate, by the* Turks *called* Kapider Vent.

PHILIBE, *or* Philippoli	twelve leagues	*Thrace, or*
Ebepce	twelve leagues	*Romania.*
ADRIANOPOLE	ten leagues	
Apſa	six leagues	
Baba	six leagues	
Birgas	six leagues	
Ciorlu	ten leagues	
Ciliurea	ten leagues	
CNSTANTINOPLE	twelve leagues	

Route from Bayonne to Madrid.

This route you will find p. 222 of this Volume. In Spain *they reckon by* leagues, *and not by* posts; *for every two* leagues, *which is equivalent to an* Italian post, *you pay half a piece of eight each horse, and a real to the postilion.*

Route from Lisbon to Madrid.

At Lisbon *you take boat on the river* Tagus, *and you land at* Aldea, *a small town of* Portugal, *in four hours;*

hours; the distance being twenty miles; the freight is about a pistole. Three posts.

From Aldea *you travel post to* Elvas, *changing horse in six places, and you pay for nine posts.* Nine posts.

Elvas *is the first town on the frontiers of* Portugal, *and well fortified. From hence you go to* Badajox, *the last fortified town on the frontiers of* Spain, *and you travel four posts, which indeed are not regular, but you find horses and mules without difficulty.* Four posts.

From Badajox *you go to* Merida, *a city of* Estramadura, *on the river* Guadiana, *and you travel five posts in the same manner as above.* Five posts.

From Merida *you proceed to* Truxillo, *another city of* Estremadura, *and you travel seven posts in the same manner as above.* Seven posts.

Here at Truxillo *you pass the river* Tagus, *and you proceed to the village of* Talavera, *which is* Two posts.

From Talavera *to* Madrid *there are* five *regular* posts.

Route *from* Bayonne *to* Lisbon.

From Bayonne *you go to* Burgos, *according to the route given p.* 222. *From* Burgos *you may proceed to* Madrid, *according to the same route, and from thence to* Lisbon; *or you may take the following route, which is much the shortest.*

BURGOS

SPAIN and PORTUGAL.

leagues.

BURGOS		Spain.
Quintanilleja	two	
Cellada	two	
La Venta de Villa Marco	three	
Torquemada	three	
Turrecremata	two	
Duennas	four	
Cabeçon	four	
VALLADOLID	two	
La Puente de Duero	two	
Valdaſtillas	two	
La Venta della Ventoſa	two	
Rodillana	one	
MEDINA DEL CAMPO	one	
La Gloſa	one	
Carpio	three	
Freſno	one	
Las Villorias	two	
Alva de Tormes	four	
La Maya	three	
Alguyo	three	
Calcada	four	
Vannos	two	
Aldea Nuova	two	
La Venta de Caprara	three	
Carcavoſo	three	
Aldehueia	one	
Galiſteo	one	
La Venta las Barranca	one	
Holguera	one	
Cannaveral	two	
Las Barcas de Conneta	two	
La Venta del Camerero	two	
Arroyo el puerco	two	

		leagues
	La Lifeda	two & half
	La Venta del Tejarejo	one & half
	ALBUQUERQUE	two
	Ronges	four
Portugal.	Monforte	two
	Velros	two
	Eftremoz	two
	La Venta del Duque	three
	Royvelos	three
	Monteamor	three
	La Venta la Laia	two
	La Venta la Silvera	one
	La Venta la Reyna	one
	La Venta la Vica	three
	La Venta la Ydera	one
	Riofrio	two
	Aldea Gallega	three & half
	LISBON	three

Route from Sevil *to* Lifbon.

Spain.	SEVIL	
	Caftilleja de la quefta	one
	Apartines	two & half
	S. Lucar de Afpechin	two
	Caftillejo	two
	Mancanilla	one
	Villalva	one
	Villa Rofa	one
	La Palma	one
	NIEBLA	one
	Frigueros	three
	Ordalguiilo	five
	Adqueria	three

Pay-

SPAIN and PORTUGAL.

	leagues.
Paymongo	six
Cerpa	five
Cuba	five
Hortaran	five
Cacar d' Osar	three
Palma	two
Marteca	two
Palmella	four
Cuba	two
Almada	three
LISBON	one

Portugal.

Route from Perpignan *to* Barcellona, *and from thence to* Madrid.

There is no post-road from Perpignan *to* Barcellona. *It is customary therefore to hire horses at* Perpignan *for* Girona, *a city in the province of* Catalonia, *thirty-six miles from* Perpignan. *The road is very bad thro' the* Pyrenean *mountains, so that you pay* four *pistoles for two horses and a man.*

From Girona *to* Barcellona *they reckon about forty miles, and you pay* three *pistoles for two mules and a man.*

From Barcellona *there is a post-road to* Saragozza, *and from thence to* Madrid.

From Barcellona *to* Madrid *you may have very good mules for* twelve *or* fourteen *pieces of eight each mule. For a litter you pay about* three and twenty *pistoles.*

BAR-

		leagues.
Spain.	BARCELLONA	
	Molin de Reig	two
	Martorel	one
	Masquesa	two
	Piera	two
	Puebla	one
	Golada	one
	Porcarises	one
	Monmanca	one
	Los Mesconcillos	one
	Cervera	two
	Taraga	two
	Belpuig	one
	Mollarusa	two
	Belloch	one
	LERIDA	one
	Alcaraz	two
	Fraga	two
	Candasnos	two
	Burialaroz	three
	La Vinta de S. Lucia	three
	Ossera	two
	Alfajarin	two
	Puebla	one
	SARAGOZZA	two
	Muela	two
	Romera	two
	Almunia	two
	Fresno	two
	CALATAYUD	two
	Bavera	two
	Hariza	two
	Arcos	two
	Moncallette	two

Torre

SPAIN, and PORTUGAL.

	leagues.
Torre Moza	two
Mondroneso	two
Canalajeos	two
Jorigas	two
Guadalaxara	two
Alcala	four
Madrid	six

THE

THE INDEX.

A

	Page		Page
Abbeville	25	Beffort	215
Aiguesperse	247	Besançon	217
Aix	186	Beziers	253
Alençon	274	Blaye	232
Amboise	205	Blois	221
Amiens	26	Boulogne	24
Ancenis	264	Bourdeaux	229
Angers	263	Bourges	254
Antibes	194	Brest	268
Argenton	237	Briançon	199
Arles	195	Briare	152
Arney le duc	177	Brie Count Robert	212
Auxerre	168	Brignole	193
Auxonne	216	Brives	238
Avignon	184		
Auray	266		
Avranches	291		

B

	Page		
		C	
		Caen	284
		Cahors	238
		Carcassone	243
		Carentan	287
Bagnols	284	Castelnaudary	243
Bagnolet	143	Caudebec	292
Bapaume	304	Challons	172
Barbesieux	229	Challons	203
Barfleur	291	Chambord	225
Bar-sur-aube	214	Chantilly	28
Bayeux	286	Charenton	175
Bayonne	230	Charité	153
Beaumont	33	Chartres	270
Beaune	171	Chateau-Thierry	203
Beauvais	32	Chateau-roux	237

Cha-

The INDEX.

	Page		Page
Chatelherant	227	Gannat	246
Chaumont	214	Grenoble	197
Cherbourg	287	**H**	
Choisy	142	Harfleur	293
Citeaux	172	Haver de Grace	293
Clagny	143	Hennebon	266
Clairvaux	214	La Hogue	295
Clermont	28	**I**	
Clermont	204	Ingrande	227
Clermont	247	Joigny	168
Clery	224	Issigny	287
Conflans	144	Issy	143
Cosne	152	**L**	
Coutances	290	Lamballe	269
D		Langon	232
Dammartin	295	Langres	214
Dax	232	Laval	276
Dieppe	294	Limoges	237
Dijon	169	Lisieux	290
Dole	216	Louvres	302
Domfront	275	Luines	262
Dreux	374	Luneuille	209
E		Lusarche	29
Ecouen	29	Lusignan	256
Etampes	223	Lyons	157
Evreux	289	**M**	
F		Macon	173
La Ferté	203	Magny	281
La Ferté	236	Maisons	144
La Fleche	271	Maintenon	270
Fontainbleau	137	Mans	271
Fismes	297	Mante	288
Frejus	193	Morly	131
G		Marseilles	189
Gaillon	288	Mayenne	275
		Meaux	

The INDEX.

	Page		Page
Meaux	202	Pecquigny	26
Melun	175	Peronne	303
Metz	204	Perpignan	245
Meudon	134	Pezenas	253
Montargis	152	Phaltzburg	206
Montauban	239	Pignerol	200
Montheliard	218	Poitiers	227
Montmorency	144	Pont a Mouffon	205
Montelimart	183	Pont-audemer	284
Mont-Louis	246	Pont de Beauvoifin	151
Montpellier	251	Pont du Guard	250
Montreuil	25	Pont S. Efprit	183
Mont S. Michel	275	PontSainteMaxence	303
Moret	167	Pontoife	281
Morlaix	269	Port Louis	266
Mortagne	274	Pougues	153
Morrain	275	Prades	246
Moulins	175	Provins	212

N

Nancy	208
Nanteuil	295
Nants	264
Narbonne	244
Nemours	151
Nevers	153
Niort	257
Nifmes	249
Nogent de Rotrou	271
Nogent fur Seine	212
Nuys	171

O

Orange	184
Orient	267
Orleans	223

P

Paris	39

Q

Quimpercorentin	267
Quimperlay	267

R

Rambouillet	269
Rennes	276
Rheims	297
Rethel	299
Riom	247
Roane	156
Rochfort	259
Rochelle	257
Romorentim	236
Rouen	281
Roye	303

S. Baume

The INDEX.

	Page		Page
S		Toulon	192
S. Baume	197	Toul	208
S. Brieux	269	Toulouse	240
S. Cloud	140	Tours	226
S. Denis	29	Tournon	181
S. Germains	135	Tournus	173
S. John de Luz	131	La Trappe	274
S. Maixent	257	Trevoux	174
S. Malo	277	Trianon	120
S. Maur	143	Tryes	213
S. Maximin	196		
S. Memin	224	**U**	
S. Menehoud	204	Userches	238
S. Pierre le Montier	154		
S. Purçain	246	**V**	
S. Saphorin	179	Valence	182
Saintes	232	Valogne	287
Salon	195	Vannes	265
Sarrebourg	205	Vesul	215
Saverne	206	Verdun	204
Saulieu	177	Vernon	288
Saumur	262	Versailles	112
Sceaux	143	Vienne	179
Sedan	300	Villers Cotterets	295
Senlis	302	Villefranche	174
Sens	167	Villeneuve le Roy	168
Strasburg	206	Vincennes	133
T		Vivonne	229
Tarare	156		

The End *of the* Fourth Volume.

www.ingramcontent.com/pod-product-compliance
Lightning Source LLC
Chambersburg PA
CBHW022106290426
44112CB00008B/568